Flashpoints
in Environmental Policymaking

SUNY Series in International Environmental Policy and Theory
Sheldon Kamieniecki, Editor

Flashpoints in Environmental Policymaking

Controversies in Achieving Sustainability

EDITED BY

Sheldon Kamieniecki,
George A. Gonzalez,
and
Robert O. Vos

State University of New York Press

Published by
State University of New York Press, Albany

Printed in the United States of America

For information, address State University of New York Press, State University Plaza, Albany, N.Y. 12246

Production by Diane Ganeles
Marketing by Bernadette LaManna

Library of Congress Cataloging-in-Publication Data

Flashpoints in environmental policymaking : controversies in achieving sustainability / edited by Sheldon Kamieniecki, George A. Gonzalez and Robert O. Vos.
p. cm. — (SUNY series in international environmental policy and theory)
Includes bibliographical references and index.
ISBN 0-7914-3329-3 (alk. paper). — ISBN 0-7914-3330-7 (pbk. alk. paper)
1. Sustainable development. 2. Environmental policy. I. Kamieniecki, Sheldon. II. Gonzalez, George A., 1969– III. Vos, Robert O., 1970– . IV. Series.
HC79.E5F557 1997
333.7—dc20

96-17898
CIP

10 9 8 7 6 5 4 3 2 1

CONTENTS

Introduction: Competing Approaches to Sustainability: Dimensions of Controversy*

ROBERT O. VOS

Following the report by the "World Commission on Environment and Development" (the Brundtland Commission) in 1987, ideas of sustainable development, sustainable societies, and "sustainability" have gained increasing prominence in political and scholarly discourse about environmental policy.[1] The struggles of various actors in the policy arena now often appear to involve active attempts to co-opt the ideas and language of "sustainability" for particular ends (Ophuls and Boyan 1992; O'Connor 1994). Thus this volume, in extensively updating and expanding earlier work (Kamieniecki et al. 1986), is unified in its attempt to think through longstanding controversies (i.e., "flashpoints") about environmental policy that, if not resolved, will present serious obstacles to achieving sustainable societies.

To accomplish this, the book presents a blend of normative and empirical policy discussions. The underlying purpose is to explore the relationship between policymaking and the past, present, and future exercise of political power. While this discussion is carried on within each chapter, it also forms the "bookends" of the volume. On the one hand, scholars have the luxury to articulate more fully normative visions of "sustainability," and this introductory chapter explores the controversies that have arisen around these visions. On the other hand, political actors operate under empirical constraints that lead to the

*I would like to thank Professor Sheldon Kamieniecki and George A. Gonzalez for insightful comments on earlier drafts of the chapter. I would also like to thank Professor Judith Grant for helpful formative discussions on matters of political theory.

fragmentation of issues and interfere with attempts to reach any normative vision. The concluding chapter assesses major flashpoints in light of the mechanics of political constraint.

The six major flashpoints in environmental policymaking selected for review in this volume have been chosen to offer insight into the widening conflicts over achieving sustainability as we enter the twenty-first century. Debates previously contained to national arenas must now consider global implications if sustainability is to be achieved (see Deudney in this volume). Thus, the last two sections in the book deal with two key flashpoints: trade and national security. Depending on the approach one adopts for achieving sustainability, global free trade may be seen as more or less desirable, and one may advocate different types of regimes for achieving sustainability within a rubric of increasing trade among nations. Closely tied to this debate is growing concern with national sovereignty and self-determination for indigenous peoples, concerns that are encapsulated in the debate about links between environmental protection and national security (see Scully Granzeier's chapter, for example).

The middle portion of the book details two flashpoints that have emerged more recently in debates about environmental protection generally. Equity issues revolving around who pays the costs of clean up and who bears the burden of pollution became a lightning rod for debate in the late 1980s. The "environmental justice" movement has already done a particularly effective job of focusing attention on the latter concern (see Bowman's chapter in this regard).

The second section of the volume is concerned with longstanding but quickly evolving debates about the role of the state in achieving sustainability. The issue of the appropriate mix of public versus private control of common resources goes right to the heart of varying approaches to achieving sustainability. With states constrained by concerns of maintaining legitimacy in the immediate present and private interests lashed to current consumer choices, whom can we trust to ensure the sustainability of common ecological resources for the future? The varying regulatory approaches that states may adopt forms another important flashpoint in debates about achieving sustainability. How directly should states regulate private production processes to best ensure sustainability for the future?

Varying conceptions of risk within the scientific community and among the public have also already led to important debates about hazardous and toxic materials policy in the U.S. The flashpoint surrounding "comparative risk assessment" may well expand in the near future to compare risks outside of chemical contamination (see Rosenbaum in this volume). Further, the means of measuring risk says a lot about a society's orientation toward new technologies and the future (see Linder in this volume). Thus, debates about risk are likely to become increasingly germane in evaluating and choosing among different approaches to achieving sustainability.

This introductory chapter takes a detailed and critical look at three predominant approaches to sustainability that are found in the literature and the political arena. Authors throughout the volume can be seen drawing from these approaches as they grapple with defining sustainability in the context of particular flashpoints. The chapter concludes with a brief introduction to the other chapters in the volume.

SUSTAINABILITY: EMPTY PHRASE OR PROMISING DEVELOPMENT?

It is important to remember the influence of politics even at the outset of an analysis of sustainability. The concept of "sustainability" has become a hotly contested domain within public discourse. One critic has even written that "Sustainable development is in real danger of becoming a cliche like 'appropriate technology'—a fashionable phrase that everyone pays homage to but nobody cares to define" (Lele 1991, p. 607). Indeed, the very word "sustainable" can be found in many phrases with starkly different implications: "sustainable growth", "sustainable yield", "sustainable societies", and "sustainable development". The idea of sustainability functions as what Baudrillard (1993) calls a "floating-signifier" in that it masks underlying disagreement, can function differently in varying contexts, and may finally lose relevance to concrete policy choices.[2]

But it would be a mistake to dismiss the idea of sustainability prematurely. There are at least two reasons why the idea of sustainability has proven such a powerful force in shaping discourse about the environment. First, the role of sustainability as a "floating-signifier" provides common ground for parties with deeply opposed interests to search for agreement. Any agreement forged about the content of "sustainability" would offer a powerful benchmark for evaluating difficult policy choices. Second, the notion of sustainability raises crucial issues of intergenerational justice that place environmentalists in a stronger position in relation to the American (Lockean) Liberal tradition (e.g., Gore 1992). At its best, therefore, an expanding discourse of sustainability may lead to a more integrated (in the sense of ecological systems) and long-term view of the environmental problematic.

APPROACHES TO SUSTAINABILITY

The power potentially inherent in the discourse of sustainability is revealed by the number of scholars, politicians, and policymakers who would like to coopt the term for their own use. When leaders as divergent as Albert Gore, Margaret Thatcher, and Alan Greenspan make use of the term "sustainability", different positions are clearly being implied (Matthews 1991). Even within this volume, we can find scholars on opposing sides of an issue committed to a discourse of sustainability. Activists, politicians, and scholars have found, and continue to search for, ways to bring previously held positions under the umbrella of sustainability.

To simplify the dimensions of these conflicts, I propose and review three positions on the issue of sustainability in this chapter (see Table I.1). Of course, such a simplification is necessarily reductive of the complex mixtures of ideas proposed by some scholars in a growing literature on the idea of sustainability (e.g., Daly and Cobb 1989; Milbrath 1989). Yet, the enterprise of simplification points out divisions that exist among many scholars and policymakers who must make key choices across a range of dimensions. It also allows us to consider how divisions that exist in the political arena, which often emerge as fragments of the three positions identified here, are linked to larger choices because of their conceptual interrelationships.

Each of the three approaches demonstrates the adaptation of some system of thought to the idea of sustainability. Each has roots that go back long before the emergence of "sustainability" as a central organizing principle of economic, political, or scientific study of the environment. Indeed, it quickly becomes evident that the different disciplinary roots involved in each concept often result in a situation where scholars "talk past one another" or simply ignore the implications of work outside their disciplinary boundary.

The first approach reviewed here is the most recent school of thought to adapt itself, at least tentatively, to the idea of sustainability. Neoclassical economists have traditionally been reluctant to theorize about the environment at all. Yet, recently an entire school of thought, sometimes called "free-market" environmentalism, has begun to emerge (Anderson and Leal 1991). In fact, neoclassical economists have a long tradition with the terms "sustainable" and "steady-state" as it relates

Table I.1. Dimensions of Controversy over Sustainability

Competing Approaches / **Dimensions**	*Free-Market Advocates/ Economists' View*	*Ecological-Science Advocates/ Biologists' View*	*Deep-Ecologists/ Philosophers' View*
Human Ontology	Possessive-Materialist	Human as Evolved	Bio-centric Human Subject
Ontology of Nature	Object of Use (Resource), Benevolent Forms of Adaptation	Object of Study; Emphasis on Dynamic Equilibrium of Ecosystems	Granted Status as a "Subject," Viewed as Fragile
Limits? Rate/Scale	None/None	Yes/Yes, hard to define	Yes/Yes
Role of Technology	Technological Rationality	Cautiously Skeptical	Highly Skeptical
Equity/Distributive Questions	Choices Left to the Market	Consider Equity as it Relates to Population	Must Include Nature
Leading Causal Factor in Environmental Degradation	Externalization of Costs (Leads to Inefficiency in Growth)	Overpopulation and Overconsumption	Ethical Crisis Following the Enlightenment
Mode of Transition	Privatization/ Deregulation	"Objective" Scientific Management	Social Learning/ New Values
Intergenerational Ethic?	Current Accumlation Can "Compensate" Future Costs	Concern for Human Survival/ Wellbeing in the Near Future	Strong Concern for Futures of all Species

to the capacity of the economy for continual growth (Dore 1995). Traditional economists, therefore, look to inefficiencies caused by rising "external" environmental costs as a potential drain on the capacity of the economy to grow (any costs external to an individual producer but borne by others).

The concept of sustainability originated with the second approach. In this context, the term "sustainable" comes from biologists and ecologists who use it to describe the rates at which renewable resources (e.g., fish, trees, etc.) can be extracted (or damaged by pollution) without threatening the underlying integrity of an ecosystem (Lele 1991; see Davis in this volume). A major and controversial concept in the ecological-science approach is called "carrying-capacity". It originated with population biologists who use it to describe the number of a particular species that can be supported in a given ecosystem without degrading the resource base and ending in a population crash (Hardin 1993; Myers 1993).

The third locus of controversy is that presented by deep-ecologists. Here the term refers to the appropriate ethical and moral framework for the relationship of humankind with nature. This ethical framework is often seen as directly linked to a social structure or normative political theory (Milbrath 1989). The issue of intergenerational justice is directly implicated in providing the opportunity for future generations to experience well-being through a spiritually satisfying relationship to the natural world.

Although each approach presents some strength as a guide for policymaking, each is also undermined by a key weakness: the lack of an ethical or normative underpinning that can provide for human freedom and liberation into the future. The deep-ecology approach offers an explicit ethical framework. But the radical rejection of the canon of enlightenment thought posited in deep-ecology leads to questions about its intelligibility as a framework for guiding moral and political choices, its capacity to provide a theory for liberty, and its far-flung departure from traditional political culture (Stark 1995).

In the free-market and ecological science dimensions, normative and ethical frameworks are only implicit. Advocates of the free-market framework masquerade as defenders of "free consumer choice" while actually positing a rough utilitarian ethical calculus rooted in the concerns of the present (Alier 1994). For ecological scientists, sustainability functions as a materially determined theory that compels concurrence with its operational conclusions regardless of "one's fundamental ethical persuasions and priorities" (Lele 1991, p.608). What is particularly troubling about this approach is the essentialist view of the human subject rooted in sociobiology, a view that free-market advocates have always been quick to criticize, in a narrow sense, as lacking an appreciation of human technological ingenuity (e.g., Simon 1981).

FREE-MARKET ADVOCATES OF SUSTAINABILITY

Free-market advocates are somewhat hostile to the idea of sustainability as it has developed among scholars less enamored with market approaches. Anderson and Leal (1991) protest that often, pervasive externalities identified as "market failures" are not really market failures when evolving regimes of property rights and liability claims are taken into account. However, they also argue that the idea of "maximizing-subject-to-constraints" provides for sustainability and is not inconsistent with neoclassical economics (p.167). If policies change to allow external costs into the market, including taxes and fees when absolutely necessary, consumer choice will signal the most efficient, and thus sustainable, growth (see Baden and O'Brien as well as Bryner in this volume; Anderson and Leal 1991).

Many of the ideas contained in the free-market approach are quite commonly held by policymakers, particularly at the international level. A major element in the discourse of sustainable development is that it is a "meta-fix" for contradictions between economic expansion and environmental protection (Lele 1991). Thus, it is meant as a catchall to describe "win-win" situations where economic expansion and environmental protection are successfully reconciled and "win-win" anecdotes are common in the literature.

In light of its vague definition of sustainable development, the call by the Brundtland report for substantial economic growth in developing countries as a fix for poverty and thus environmental degradation is hardly out of step with a free-market approach (see Goodman and Howarth's chapter; Goodland et al. 1992).[3] And the quick incorporation of sustainable development in "Agenda 21" at the Rio conference and by large international lending agencies leaves little doubt that a free-market approach has taken top priority.

Within Agenda 21 the concept has become part of a program to redistribute investment to the developing world in order to encourage economic growth that is "essential for sustainable development and cannot be overly restrained" (Sitarz 1993 p.234). The idea is to challenge barriers to free trade in order to increase the flow of capital to developing countries, and subsequently to build "growth" industries in pollution control technologies by accounting for externalities (see Allison in this book; Sitarz 1993).

Major international lending agencies including the World Bank, the Asian Development Bank, and the Organization for Economic Cooperation and Development (OECD) have also adopted the idea of sustainable development following Brundtland, signalling a free-market approach. Lending agencies explicitly depend on further economic expansion to recoup their loans (Rich 1994). For example, at World Bank workshops on "sustainable agriculture" participants interpret sustainable development in agriculture as simply maintaining growth in agricultural production (Lele 1991).

The focus on economic growth as a primary objective is what distinguishes the free-market advocates most directly from the other approaches (see Table I.1). Free-market advocates believe that if environmental costs are appropriately priced in the market, there needs be no limit to the rate of expansion or the ultimate scale of the human use of environmental sources and sinks.[4] It is around this contention that other dimensions are organized in the free-market approach. Humans are conceptualized as "possessive-materialists" who desire consumption above all else and can only be trusted to defend their property interests. Nature is conceptualized as a resource that can be manipulated to achieve human interest. Technology is considered the ultimate and proper application of human reason ("technological rationality"), allowing complete domination and infinite exploitation of nature (see Linder in this volume).

These basic assumptions in turn drive the key policy recommendations. Anderson and Leal (1991) argue that environmental protection is always accomplished with more efficiency and effectiveness, at least in the case of common resources, in an unfettered free market than with state management. Rooted in the possessive-materialist view of humanity, private ownership is seen as the only effective incentive to use resources efficiently: abuse will directly harm the material interest of the owner. Also, while downplaying the existence of negative and pervasive externalities, they argue that privatizing common resources will create incentives for private actors to hold each other liable through lawsuits for degradation.

Free-market advocates argue that enforcing private property rights creates an incentive for developing knowledge about the environment and technologies to protect it. The system of property rights provides an incentive for the property owner to "know" his or her own business. Free-market advocates argue that the knowledge of individual property owners will take better account of ecological variations than central regulatory management (Anderson and Leal 1991, p.4). Private ownership will lead to thousands of "individual experiments" in managing ecosystems, and the most successful experiments may be emulated (see Baden and O'Brien in this volume).

But knowledge of the environment is not as straightforward as this analysis implies. Many functions of ecosystems fluctuate randomly across a particular range (i.e., stochastic effects) and across geographical scales (McCay and Acheson 1987). Systems theory indicates that critical points of ecosystem degradation can cause nonlinear effects. Lele (1991) argues that frameworks guiding sustainable development must go beyond the notion of an annual increment to take into consideration "the dynamic behavior of resources, stochastic properties of and uncertainties of environmental conditions" (p.615). When an additive or linear approach is wrongly assumed for externalities, "information costs" may appear too large for particular producers to gather information on pollution accumulation until after sudden perturbations have already occurred (i.e., the information comes too late to take proper care of the resources).

Free-market advocates also hope technology may solve the often intractable difficulties of ownership in ecosystems. Anderson and Leal (1991) report that it is easier to create private property rights for land disposal than air, ground water, or surface water disposal because it is a relatively simple matter to fence off and create legal title to land. They hope that fencing technologies will soon develop to make other parts of ecosystems easy to commodify or at least to allow for tracing of liability through the ecosystem.

In the immediate term, free-market advocates have a variety of proposals for making a transition to sustainability, including rejuvenation of liability and privatization of public lands. However, it is less clear what these schemes might mean in the longer term for complete market accounting of externalities. In a competitive economy, we should expect major political struggles against establishing property rights (and thus full cost inclusion) in traditionally common (and thus subsidized) benefit streams. Also, the free market contains important incentives to implement technologies that externalize the costs of production to the maximum extent feasible. Individual companies become more profitable by lowering their own microeconomic costs even at the expense of other producers and society at large.

Economists recognize that consumers are generally unable to respond to the externalization of cost because they face much higher "information and opportunity costs" for political action relative to lower costs faced by narrow producing interests. As a result, government subsidizes environmental degradation in both direct and indirect ways, even by creating distortions in the liability market (e.g., the Price-Anderson Act that limits the liability of nuclear power producers). Full pricing of externalities is a political conundrum that free-market advocates have hardly begun to address (see Bryner in this volume). Myers (1993) estimates, for example, that if the price of gasoline actually reflected all of its external costs, including urban smog, acid rain, global warming, and the costs of securing oil in the Persian Gulf, the "true" price would be roughly four times the present U.S. price.

Holding aside the political problems faced by a transition to the free-market approach, there are important practical problems to recognize as well. Even with optimistic advances in "fencing technologies", it is practically difficult to divide ecosystems that are inherently connected in complex ways, especially when considering time frames as short as even a few decades. Disposal on land leads to unknown external costs in ground water pollution from leachate, and the use of "in-flow" water resources may eventually deplete the processes that recharge ground water aquifers: How can the value (the true external costs) of clean ground water to future generations be calculated in the present? These problems exist in the Superfund program which must confront the practical and legal difficulties of tracing complex liability schemes through to actions from decades past (as Kamieniecki's and Steckenrider's chapter shows).

Given changing information, complex interactions among pollutants in ecosystems, and disputes about impacts, pervasive externalities cannot be calculated within politically acceptable levels of accuracy. At the least, a fairly sizeable and active governmental role is implied to meet the information costs involved in monitoring ecosystems and gathering data on externalities. But while some free-market advocates have suggested that the provision of information to the public can be an important incentive in shaping market forces (see Cohen in this volume), funding for development and dissemination of information is not a common prescription by strict advocates of the free-market approach.

FREE-MARKET ADVOCACY: AN APPROACH FOR THE FUTURE?

By rooting itself in consumer choices of the present, the free-market approach seems to ignore the future. But on the surface, at least, a simple intergenerational ethic is proposed (see Table I.1). Anderson and Leal (1991) argue that by devoting itself to the lot of the living ("accumulation") a society will transmit a more productive world to the future and thus compensate future generations for any problems that might emerge (p.172). Also, private property rights are viewed as encouraging good "stewardship" of resources. As Baden and O'Brien argue in this book, firms looking to self interest may think in terms of both present and future demand.

The key to understanding the potential weakness of the stewardship argument lies in recognizing that the time frame in which the prices and values upon which economic calculations are made diverges sharply from the time frame in which resources and wastes flow within the geo-chemical processes of the planet (Altvater 1994). Thus, what may appear to be good stewardship in a five-year or ten-year range may eventually be unsustainable given rates of ground water recharge or soil replacement. Phaelke (1989) points out that future demand is always uncertain, and therefore an incentive exists to draw down too heavily on renewable resources in the present. Furthermore, there is a long history in the U.S. of shifting investment following abuse of a resource for short-term gain (Cahn 1995). Unless resource substitution is infinite, this will eventually be unsustainable (Goodland et al. 1992).

There are good ethical grounds upon which to question the claim that economic accumulation in the present will allow for the compensation of liabilities incurred by future generations through "basic transfers" of money and technology.[5] Spash (1993) distinguishes between "basic" and "compensatory" transfers between individuals (in the present or intergenerationally). Basic transfers involve money, technology, and investments in capital that provide for individual welfare. He suggests a hypothetical parable whereby an individual who has received such basic transfers is later found to have been injured by long-term impacts of a radioactive leak in the environment. Society would find it difficult to say to this individual that he had already been compensated for his injury by basic transfers. Instead, a "compensatory" transfer that attempted to remedy the injury directly would be viewed as the just outcome.

Spash's creative parable applies with particular force to future generations because they would be compelled to accept any substitute "basic" transfer with no economic choice in the matter. Even with perfect technology and substitution, for example, future generations might be forced to accept "ex situ" conservation of a species and technological imitations of wilderness if present consumer demand was inadequate to preserve species in their original habitat into the future. The free-market model of "consumer choice" breaks down here, and its ethical roots in maximizing individual utility in the present become evident in the rupture. The approach undermines its own claims to provide freedom: Future generations will accept "freely" the degradation past onto them.

FREE-MARKET APPROACH: ECONOMIC GROWTH AS ENVIRONMENTAL PROTECTION?

An important contention of the free-market approach, particularly as it has been adopted in the international discourse of sustainable development, is that environmental protection must be linked to economic growth (see Goodman and Howarth in this volume). The Brundtland Commission and Agenda 21 reflect the idea that economic growth provides the technological, financial, and political impetus to handle pollution. Further, high rates of population growth are linked to poverty, especially to poor health care for infants and the marginalization of women.

Lonergan (1993) has done an extensive conceptual analysis of the very roughly understood link between poverty and environmental degradation. Identifying a dearth of empirical work on the topic, he proposes to utilize the concept of "equity" as embodied in the unequal distribution of production between nations and resulting unequal treatment of citizens through human rights abuses, marginalization of women, and the corruption and power exercised by ruling elites in developing nations. Also, information is often distributed unequally among corporations, governments, and nongovernmental organizations. Thus, he argues that a nation may be less able to protect its environment, not precisely because it or its citizens are poor, but rather because of its unequal position in relation to the global political-economy.

Absolute measures of poverty like income reveal little about people around the world who meet their needs from common resource pools. Lonergan (1993) proposes conceptualizing equity in terms of "sustainable livelihood security". The point is that it is not poverty that leads to environmental degradation, but rather a combination of economic, spatial, and cultural dislocation that occurs when common resources are expropriated or destroyed during development (a manifestation of underlying inequities) (see Scully Granzeier's chapter, for example). When resources are undermined, migration of large groups of people to cities leads to unsanitary conditions and agricultural foraging ("slash and burn") leads to degradation of forests and species-extinction (Wilson 1992).

Comparative studies of debt have not yet shown statistical associations between levels of indebtedness and rapid resource depletion or environmental degradation (Sanderson 1993; Pearce et al. 1995). But the process of going into debt and subsequent structural adjustment policies can be linked to the loss of sustainable livelihood security

(Rich 1994). Debt is a manifestation of inequity that has historically deprived countries of control over resources and ecosystems. Long-range (time series) studies of the effect of debt are needed to understand what role debt forgiveness may play in giving nations the control needed to achieve sustainability.

A more detailed analysis of the role of poverty sheds light on a central contention of the free-market approach: if poverty is not the problem, is economic growth the answer? To answer this question it is important to view the problem in distributive terms. If the assumption is that economic growth will eliminate poverty especially in the developing world, then most empirical and theoretical evidence suggests this is at best a risky proposition. Growth is not in itself any guarantee of distribution, while some incomes rise, sustainable livelihood security may be compromised. But if economic growth is shaped such that it also means greater equity, and this results in secure land tenure, population control, and honest administration of environmental laws in developing countries, then it might contribute to sustainability (see Goodman and Howarth in this volume).

ECOLOGICAL-SCIENCE ADVOCATES OF SUSTAINABILITY

The major controversy between free-market advocates and the advocates of an ecological-science approach turns on the issue of limits to economic growth (i.e., expansion of environmental sources and sinks).[6] A range of authors hold that the first and second laws of thermodynamics define an ultimate limit to the rate at which energy can be appropriated for useful work on earth (Ophuls and Boyan 1992; Meadows et al. 1992; Hardin 1993; Ehrlich and Ehrlich 1993).[7] Since no energy can be created or destroyed and all closed systems tend toward greater entropy, there is a limit to stocks of energy. Fortunately, the earth is not precisely a closed system. It receives constant inputs of solar energy, but this implies that energy use is in the long run restricted to the rate at which solar energy reaches the earth.[8] There is a "speed limit" for energy use defined by solar renewable resources (Meadows et al. 1992). Therefore, even with full internalization of costs, economic growth will eventually be unsustainable since increasing energy inputs are required to expand sources and sinks (i.e., to repair environmental degradation) (Daly and Cobb 1989; Goodland et al. 1992).

This position is fundamentally at odds, on technical grounds, with the free-market approach. It means that for the free-market approach to succeed we must not only: (1) define and enforce exclusive property rights in ecosystems and their functions, and (2) correctly estimate and incorporate the cost of externalities. We must also never run into limits blocking expansion in the magnitudes of sources and sinks. To avoid limits, technology (i.e., human capital) must provide infinite "substitutability" of resources. As ecological-scientists argue, however, the laws of thermodynamics specify that the magnitude of energy available at any point in time is limited. Energy can be "neither created nor destroyed". Substitution is not possible (i.e., no amount of human ingenuity can create energy).[9]

The often cited formula in the ecological-science approach, "Environmental Impact = Affluence * Technology * Population" (I=A*T*P) perhaps implies an exactitude that is unwarranted. Meadows et al. (1992) take a systems approach, using computer models to trace complex interactions between sources and sinks, and point out that the formula must be expressed as a multiplication because of interactive potentials between each component. Hardin (1993) writes that although the supply is strictly limited, we are unable to state the limits with precision. This is because there are simply too many unknowns about the future (including a range of choices yet to be made by human societies). Yet this need not undermine the claim by ecological-science advocates of the need to search for structured limits to growth. The consequences of even approaching limits will likely mean a lower material standard of living and less economic freedom as more capital resources must be diverted to repair and maintain the environment (Ophuls and Boyan 1992; Meadows et al. 1992).

Limits as theorized by the application of the first and second laws of thermodynamics are the core of the ecological-science approach, driving the views of these scholars on the issues of technology and population (see Table I.1). Myers (1993) writes that, " . . . human population—both present numbers and rates of growth—is a prominent factor, often a predominant factor, in problems of environmental decline and unsustainable development" (p. 205). Ehrlich and Ehrlich (1993) have long raised concerns about the results of exponential population growth. Population growth functions as a sort of first among equals in the "I=A*T*P" formula. Several scholars argue that the planet is already overpopulated, and thus changes in technology and lifestyle will be compelled in the future (Ehrlich and Ehrlich 1993; Hardin 1993).

The position of ecological-scientists on the role of technology is a cautiously skeptical critique of technological rationality. Hardin (1993) argues that on balance predictions of technological optimists (e.g., nuclear power "too cheap to meter") have been at least as bad as those of pessimists, criticizing the notion that social problems can be solved by expanding resources from technological development. Ophuls and Boyan (1992) question the generous assumption that human society will be able to organize itself to implement technological fixes even if they are invented in a timely matter. E.O. Wilson (1992) makes a similar point, arguing that solely technological solutions will be unable to store or conserve species "ex situ" because the rate and magnitude of species extinction is so much larger than either resources for conservation or knowledge about the species.

This approach argues that while technological development is essential, it cannot produce sustainability by itself. A narrow technological rationality eventually falls back upon itself because technology requires human will, capital, and organization to be implemented. Also, it is dangerous to imagine that the only new technical knowledge will show means to expand sources and sinks instead of revealing that certain limits really are binding (Daly and Cobb 1989). The critique of technological rationality reveals that we need not give neoclassical economists a monopoly on the quality of human ingenuity. Human ingenuity as confined to technological rationality is a highly truncated version of the real potential for human rationality. A broader understanding would encompass social organization, cultural goods, and creative adaptation of lifestyles.

GROWTH VERSUS DEVELOPMENT: A PATH TO SUSTAINABILITY?

An increasingly conventional distinction shared in the literature on sustainability is that between "growth" and "development" (e.g., Milbrath 1989; Daly and Cobb 1989; Hardin 1993; see Goodman and Howarth in this volume). This distinction seeks to reconcile the conflict between human freedom expressed as a desire for continual change or improvement and the realization of limits to economic growth. Scholars argue that in ceasing to expand sources and sinks of the economy (i.e., "to grow") we need not cease to improve the quality of life in terms of aesthetic production, better relationships among human beings, and human comfort through specialized services (i.e., "to develop"). Thus, while there are limits to quantitative growth, there are no limits to qualitative development.

As Milbrath recognizes (1989), such a change would require a major transformation in the desires, goals, and ambitions of many human beings. Humans would have to move beyond "possessive-materialism," a key component within Milbrath's (1989) "Dominant

Social Paradigm". Yet neither Milbrath (1989) nor Daly and Cobb (1989) seem to recognize the implications of this position in terms of the capitalist economy. An ongoing process of accumulation of capital resources is at the foundation of a free-market economy. Accumulation directly undergirds the money-commodity-money exchange. As such, accumulation forms a sharp contradiction with the limits to growth recognized in the ecological-science approach (O'Connor 1994).

Daly and Cobb (1989) hint at this when they offer that it is important to understand "savings" as a "lien against future production" (p. 38). Without careful modifications to a growth-oriented economy, savings could be employed to expand the use of sources and sinks in the future, and the capacity to honor the lien will at some point become an issue. Also, expanding service sectors may well require larger transportation and information sectors. "Development" as understood by these scholars is possible only if it involves the elaboration of human potentials *outside* of traditional market activity. To provide for this will eventually require deeper modifications in the market economy than have thus far been recognized.

DEEP-ECOLOGY AS AN APPROACH TO SUSTAINABILITY

The extensive critique of economic theory and practice proffered by ecological-scientists has often led to the conflation of their view with deep-ecology. However, there are several key elements of deep-ecology that distinguish it from the approach identified above (see Table I.1). In general, deep-ecologists focus on the spiritual or cultural aspect of the environmental problematic, and see the solution in terms of a shift in both human and natural ontologies (Eckersley 1992). Deep-ecologists see technological rationality as irretrievably embedded in a relationship of human domination of the natural world, and are thus highly skeptical of claims that technology can offer a solution to the environmental problematic. Instead, they argue that a better solution is for humans to relearn their ethics and values in a more eco-centric fashion (Milbrath 1989).

As used here, the term "deep-ecology" describes a radical critique of the canon of enlightenment political thought that finds the roots of the environmental crisis in the dominating position of the human subject over nature (conceived as an object) (e.g., Stone 1974 and 1987; Devall and Sessions 1985; Milbrath 1989; Naess 1989). As a solution, deep-ecologists would like to locate subjectivity in the natural world. In the standard enlightenment ontological arrangement, the subject/

object dichotomy grants free will and consciousness to humans but not to nonhuman nature (an "I" to "it" relationship). Deep-ecologists argue that it is important to conceive both humans and other forms of life as subjects (an "I" to "thou" relationship) (Michael and Grove-White 1993). Thus, sustainability for deep-ecologists is as much about considering the role of the natural world in future human well-being as it is about " . . . protecting, maintaining, and developing nature for its own sake (sustainability of nature)" (Achterberg 1993, p. 82).

Some deep-ecologists view history as an expanding circle of "rights" predicated on subjectivity and hope that the next expansion of rights will encompass the nonhuman world (Nash 1989). In this vein, nature is seen to be oppressed by the same hierarchical values and exploitative institutions that have in various times and places denied rights to particular human groups (e.g., women, racial minorities, etc.) (Merchant 1980). In *Should Trees Have Standing?*, Christopher Stone urges that the common law tradition should include rights of property "in-self" for nonhuman nature (Stone 1974). Why, he suggestively asks, if corporations have fictional individual legal identities should a river not share in such standing to sue? Guardians could be appointed for natural entities after which they could sue in national courts. The advantage or right assigned to natural entities would be one of "intactness" or making the entity whole. The subjectivity of the natural entity is derived from its identity—for example the "riverhood" of a river.

Deep-ecologists have advocated subjectivity for nature in other ways. Milbrath (1989) theorizes sustainability from the premise that all natural entities are equal, and refuses to engage thinkers who will not accept his formulation. In this volume, Scully Granzeier advocates a concept of security that includes, in part, nonhuman forms of life. Devall (1988) argues that the defense of nature, even in violent protest actions, amounts to "self-defense". The justification for such action then rests upon a Lockean formulation of the right to revolution. Finally, for Arne Naess, "self"-realization is the realization of the potentialities of life for each organism. Maximum realization is the ultimate good and means realization for the entire biotic community. Nature is here considered as a subject in even a self-conscious fashion—it knows and strives towards its ultimate teleological unfolding.

In relearning ontology, the human subject is viewed as malleable, and in need of change in order to embrace a bio-centric approach (see Table I.1). Devall (1988) describes an "ecological self" that values relations with plants and animals in a home bio-region equally with social relations, and therefore implies a kind of intersubjectivity with the natural world. Devall and Sessions (1985) assert that "there are no boundaries and everything is related" (p. 52). Indeed, the person "dissolves" into the natural world. The identity of the self is no longer a transcendental subject, but rather finds itself with reference to its location in nature or a home bio-region.

WEAKNESSES IN THE DEEP-ECOLOGY APPROACH

While I am sympathetic to the claim that the Enlightenment was principally about the domination of nature, several important questions remain. First, is the domination of nature within our ethical system the leading cause of environmental degradation? Second, do deep-ecologists propose a replacement ethic that is intelligible for guiding difficult choices and preserving freedom? Third, does positing a radical rejection of our political tradition by granting subjectivity to nature work to advance pragmatically the interests of sustainability?

For deep-ecologists, the ultimate cause of environmental degradation is located in the historically-specific European ideological transformation of nature into an object to be dominated by humans. In contrast, the deep-ecologists assert that most often indigenous cultures are "rooted" in the land, and possess ontologies that lack the subject/object dichotomy. Therefore, these cultures often live in harmony with nature (Devall and Sessions 1985; see, in part, Scully Granzeier in this volume). If such assertions were true, it would provide the beginnings of an analysis that might conclude the subject/object dichotomy needs to be transformed. However, the archaeological record and contemporary research indicate that a wide variety of indigenous cultures have wrought great changes upon the land without the aid of Enlightenment thinking. There are a substantial number of examples where environmental degradation has taken place, even to the point of cultural extinction, despite a cultural framework that granted divinity or some type of subjectivity to nature (Stone 1993).

Stark (1995) has questioned the intelligibility of deep-ecology as an approach for guiding choices about the relationship between humans and nature. He points out the paradox between the reliance in deep-ecology on intuition and the reliance among advocates of environmental protection on scientific evidence to understand and respond to crises in ecosystems. Stark (1995) also notes the inherent difficulty in founding an ethical system upon subjects who are unable to reflect upon and take control of their own agency. How can trees or birds be expected to evaluate and participate in an ethical or political discourse?

Arne Naess's (1989) self-realization standard allows for consideration of this difficulty. In Naess, nature would pursue its own path of realization as an equal with humanity. Any conflict that would arise between humans and nature would be relegated to an anthropocentric category. Human unwillingness to share realization with all beings is normatively bad while equal realization for all beings is good. What this would mean in practice is unclear: Whose standard would determine what constituted equal self-realization? How can theorists conceive of self-realization for entities that lack consciousness? The assumption that we can know the appropriate teleological endpoint for the unfolding of the natural world is an element of hubris in a philosophy which claims to be humble.

As an important ecological principle, nature is constantly evolving. It is not within the present capacity of humans to know the final destination of nature. Indeed, there may not be a final destination to know. Naess's conceptualization of subjectivity in nature undermines this ecological principle by implying an endpoint: How else to judge self-realization? In a similar manner, Stone's (1974 and 1987) standard of "intactness" undermines the evolutionary principle as well. Intactness seems by its very definition to imply a static situation.

An important problem for deep-ecology is that the thinkers want to talk about freedom and liberation while also undermining the very basis that has guided the discussion of these ideas since the Enlightenment. Deep-ecology privileges the categories of "intuition" and "instinct" over "rationality" and "science" (Stark 1995). In very general terms, however, the Enlightenment canon posits that freedom is possible precisely because humans have the capacity to put aside instinct and desire in order to choose: The act of choosing is what makes humans free. We should hold deep-ecology to the traditional standard of moral agency because it relies on so many important Enlightenment ideas, including notions of "rights", "freedom", and "equality". Also, we should hold deep-ecologists to the traditional standard because it undergirds theories of egalitarian and democratic politics, which many deep-ecologists also support.

PRAGMATIC PROBLEMS IN THE DEEP-ECOLOGY APPROACH

Both Naess (1989) and Stone (1974) see an immediate advantage to granting subjectivity to nature in that it helps to discredit rationale for policies built strictly on present consumer choices (i.e., the free-market approach) (also see Allison's chapter in this book). Entities invested with "person-hood" are placed beyond the reach of the free market in advanced capitalist societies. The notion of using cost-benefit analysis, for example, in a case involving human life is viewed as repugnant. As appealing as these results may be in the abstract, ontological status has not always served securely in practice—even human life has at times been put to the test of economic analysis. Furthermore, often a rigorous economic analysis will suggest additional measures to protect ecosystems. At the least, an economic analysis can serve as a starting point for policy discussions.

What about the cases, however, where economic analyses undervalue nature because of human ignorance, greed, or discounting practices? In such cases, humans may still choose either to add specific values to nature—or, reasoning that a particular value is infinite or unknowable, remove a given decision from the realm of economics. The normative need not necessarily follow the ontological as many deep-ecologists imply. There is no reason that a particular metaphysical conception of nature must be deterministically linked to a normative one: humans can value nature intrinsically without logically or scientifically reconstructing metaphysics (Fieser 1993; see Scully Granzeier in this volume).

Other practical problems with the deep-ecological approach deserve exploration as well. The early attempts to formulate rights for nature may undermine the ecological principle of interconnection. The problem is that formulations such as Stone's *Should Trees Have Standing?* read a Liberal individualism into natural processes. Consider a food chain: For example, could a tree sue a deer for chewing off its leaves or bark? In practice, the theory of individuated rights could potentially set the entire ecological web against itself. Furthermore, in Stone's conceptualization, nature could find itself in a position of legal disadvantage. People seeking retribution against the whims of nature could conceivably sue natural entities, and therefore appropriate particular natural values whatever the cost to the ecosystem as whole.

Lewis (1992) sees the normative idea of "getting into nature" that emerges from deep-ecology as impracticable and potentially destructive of the environment. After all, what would be the effect on ecosystems of millions of humans suddenly trying to get back into nature? On similar grounds, he criticizes proposals for decentralization that are common in portions of the deep-ecology literature. The consequences of human settlement, even in a "light" fashion, across uninhabited terrains could be severe. In contrast, urban settlement that is well designed and implemented may offer greater efficiency and thus less overall environmental degradation. The magnitude of human population growth means that it is no longer pragmatic to make the complete turn away from technology that deep-ecologists would prefer; such a move would undermine their own chief desideratum, the preservation of wilderness.

SUSTAINABILITY AS A UNIFYING THEME: SKETCH OF THE BOOK

The three approaches to sustainability presented in this chapter are useful as a basic guide to the dimensions of the controversy presented in various sections of the book. Each conceptual and policy approach may be linked to the definitions and positions that various authors assume.

The consideration of risk as a scientific and cultural phenomenon by Rosenbaum and Linder relates broadly to making choices among the three approaches. In the face of uncertainty about the impacts of present choices on the future, the public and policymakers must debate ways to measure and conceptualize the risks involved in adopting one approach over another. How much consumer choice ought to be given up in the present to ensure a sustainable future? As Linder points out, the way we conceptualize risk, particularly the risks inherent in new technologies, in many respects shapes our answers to this question.

Kamieniecki and Steckenrider take a two-sided view of equity questions in the Superfund program. On the one hand, they explore the problems inherent in intergenerational equity in toxic waste disposal. They point out that liabilities are often unknown until decades after pollution is disposed in the environment, thus raising important questions about the practicality of a strictly free-market approach to sustainable societies. On the other hand, they explore the still evolving literature on equity as it relates to the distribution of pollution within one generation and society.

Bowman picks up the second equity concern in her review of the contribution of the environmental-justice movement to debates about sustainability. As is evident in the disputes noted in this chapter, distributive questions at both the national and global levels are becoming increasingly crucial to garnering the consensus necessary to support sustainable environmental policies. The environmental justice movement brings a new perspective to longstanding environmental controversies, raising important questions about equity and fairness in decision-making.

Cohen presents a deliberate consideration of the strengths and weaknesses of a range of regulatory approaches as public policy. He argues that the environmental policies needed to achieve sustainability will require flexibility to allow for a mixture of various economic incentives, direct regulatory structures, and public education. Bryner presents a similar consideration of the strengths and weaknesses of free-market regulatory approaches, paying particular attention to the political context. Bryner notes the interaction between policy and politics, wondering what mixture of policies will be required to sustain the political impetus behind environmental protection.

Baden and O'Brien are the most direct advocates for the free-market approach to sustainability in the volume. They argue that privatizing public lands is the most efficient way to provide for economic growth since it allows for effective communication of consumer choice to those who make decisions about land uses. Charles Davis takes issue with this position by arguing that a range of values (including sustainability for future generations) may be inadequately expressed through the mechanism of consumer choice.

A section on trade and development policy focuses attention on the increasing importance of controversies at the international level to debates about environmental protection. Allison takes a free-market approach, arguing that the benefits of free-trade outweigh the risks. She argues that public pressure and regional trade organizations may force nations to account for externalities increased by trade. One result might be an "upward harmonization" of environmental standards, and more competition and technology transfer among nations in creating and implementing technologies to meet those standards. However, Goodman and Howarth worry that political forces involved in expanding global trade may leave the developing world out of the free-trade equation. In addition, they question one central rationale of the free-market approach: that economic growth for the developing world—through increases in trade—is the primary means for achieving sustainability.

The expansion of the environmental problematic to encompass ever broader policy concerns has been an important outcome of the debate over sustainability. Daniel Deudney criticizes the expansion of environmental concerns into the arena of national security, arguing that conflation of the environment with national security will inflame nationalist passions and thus threaten hopes for achieving a global coalition for sustainability. In contrast, Margaret Scully Granzeier argues from a developing world perspective. Taking into account the direct reliance of many people around the world on various common resources, Scully Granzeier argues that many would find it important to embrace a linkage of the environment and security in order to protect access to the resources necessary for sustaining their cultures.

In relating the wide range of controversies selected for inclusion in this book to varying ideas of sustainability, the viability of the concept for shaping environmental policymaking becomes readily apparent. Each of the flashpoints detailed here represents a critical obstacle in the attempt to achieve sustainable societies. Resolving these controversies will require the public to develop a broad and deep understanding of the intricacies and interconnections of opposing positions across the different debates. It is hoped that this book will be a step in that direction.

NOTES

1. The earliest references to the idea of sustainability as a "social" or policy-making concept generally date from the mid-1970s, particularly in work done under Lester R. Brown at the Worldwatch Institute (e.g., Hayes 1978). From limited use in this context, the concept has gained increasing prominence. In 1992, 172 nations including the U.S. adopted Agenda 21 at the United Nations Conference on the Environment (the "Earth Summit"), agreeing to develop and implement a strategy for "sustainable development" (Sitarz 1993).

2. Problems with relying on sustainability are becoming increasingly apparent. Already at the Rio summit, the Bush administration was a reluctant participant, refusing to join other developed nations in support of fundamental changes to induce a transition toward sustainability (e.g., a lack of American funds, a refusal to embrace the Bio-diversity convention). The large partisan transition in the American Congress in 1994 also leaves open the question of whether the discourse of sustainability will simply be drowned out for the time being by a chorus calling for deregulation. Even free-market advocates are somewhat uneasy, wondering if the political strength can be garnered for real reform or whether we should simply anticipate the wholesale dismantlement of U.S. environmental laws (e.g., see Baden and O'Brien in this volume).

3. Brundtland's well-worn definition, "Sustainable development is development that meets the needs of the present without compromising the ability of future generations to meet their own needs" is inherently vague in its definition of "need" (WCED 1987, p. 41).

4. Environmental "sinks" are those elements of ecosystems that have the incredibly important and often invisible role of filtering pollution. A good example of this is the role of the aquatic life in the oceans and forests in acting as a "sink" or filter for carbon dioxide, processing it chiefly into oxygen. In

practice, "sources" and "sinks" often interact and the destruction of one results in the destruction of the other. For example, clear-cutting not only degrades a "source" (i.e., timber) but also affects several "sinks" (i.e., the control of erosion, the filtering of carbon dioxide, etc.).

5. Although the selection of a "discount" (or interest) rate is claimed to rest on "free" consumer choice to use money in the present, it actually implies an ethical position regarding future generations: that consumption (expansion in the use of sources and sinks) is more valuable in the present than in the future (Spash 1993).

6. Some may object to my application of the often highly privileged term "science" to this approach. Of course, there are some natural scientists who disagree with aspects of this approach. However, 104 Nobel Laureates signed the 1992 report of the Union of Concerned Scientists acknowledging that the "Earth's ability to provide for growing numbers of people is finite" and that, "we are fast approaching many of the Earth's limits" (quoted in Myers 1993, p. 205).

7. Eckersley (1992) has adopted a similar grouping of many of these authors, setting them apart from deep-ecologists who see sustainability in terms of a "crisis of culture" (p. 17). She argues convincingly that the group of authors I call "ecological scientists" see the environmental problematic in terms of a "crisis of human survival" (p. 11).

8. Wilson (1992) points out that humans are already an ecologically anomalous species because we are estimated to use between twenty and forty percent of "net primary production", the energy captured by plants in photosynthesis. This reveals a major reason why other species are being pushed out of ecological niches and rendered extinct. Humans are literally taking away the energy of the other species.

9. Although large gains have already been made in energy efficiency, and even larger gains will hopefully be made in the near future, this is not substitution in the strict sense of "material balance". Human and natural capitals are not substitutes but rather complements, they need each other for production.

REFERENCES

Achterberg, Wouter. 1993. "Can Liberal Democracy Survive the Environmental Crisis? Sustainability, liberal neutrality, and overlapping consensus". In *The Politics of Nature*, eds. A. Dobson and P. Lucardie, 81–101. New York: Routledge.

Alier, Juan Martinez. 1994. "Ecological Economics and Ecosocialism". In *Is Capitalism Sustainable? Political Economy and the Politics of Ecology*, ed. M. O'Connor, 253–274. New York: Guilford Press.

Ophuls, William, and A. Stephen Boyan, Jr. 1992. *Ecology and the Politics of Scarcity Revisited: the Unraveling of the American Dream*. New York: W.H. Freeman and Company.

Pearce, David, Neil Adger, David Maddison, and Dominic Moran. 1995. "Debt and the Environment". *Scientific American* June: 52–56.

Phaelke, Robert C. 1989. *Environmentalism and the Future of Progressive Politics*. New Haven: Yale University Press.

Rich, Bruce. 1994. *Mortgaging the Earth: The World Bank, Environmental Impoverishment, and the Crisis of Development*. Boston: Beacon Press.

Sanderson, Steven E. 1993. "Environmental Politics in Latin America". In *Environmental Politics in the International Arena: Movements, Parties, Organizations, and Policy*, ed. S. Kamieniecki. Albany: State University of New York Press.

Simon, Julian. 1981. *The Ultimate Resource*. Princeton, N.J.: Princeton University Press.

Sitarz, Daniel, ed. 1993. *Agenda 21: The Earth Summit Strategy to Save Our Planet*. Boulder, Colorado: Earth Press.

Spash, Clive L. 1993. "Economics, Ethics, and Long-Term Environmental Damages". *Environmental Ethics* 15: 117–132.

Stark, Jerry A. 1995. "Postmodern Environmentalism: a Critique of Deep Ecology". In *Ecowarriors and the Ecological Apocalypse: The Global Emergence of Popular Environmental Resistance*, ed. B. Taylor, 259–281. Albany: State University of New York Press.

Stone, Christopher D. 1974. *Should Trees Have Standing? Toward Legal Rights for Natural Objects*. Los Altos, California: Kaufman.

Stone, Christopher D. 1987. *Earth and Other Ethics: the Case for Moral Pluralism*. New York: Harper and Row.

Stone, Christopher D. 1993. *The Gnat is Older than Man: Global Environment and Human Agenda*. Princeton, N.J.: Princeton University Press.

Wilson, Edward O. 1992. *The Diversity of Life*. Cambridge, Massachusetts: Harvard University Press.

World Commission on Environment and Development. 1987. *Our Common Future*. New York: Oxford University Press.

SECTION ONE

Risk Assessment

1 Regulation at Risk: The Controversial Politics and Science of Comparative Risk Assessment

WALTER A. ROSENBAUM

> Risk assessment means never having to say you're certain.
>
> —Joke among professional risk assessors.

Less than two decades ago, quantitative risk assessment (QRA) in any form was rare among governmental regulatory procedures. The President's Council on Environmental Quality committed a whole chapter of its 1976 *Report* to an exhaustive study of environmental carcinogens with scant attention to QRA, and none to comparative assessment, in governmental regulation (U. S. Council on Environmental Quality 1977). Between 1976 and 1980, federal agencies performed quantitative risk assessments (QRAs) for only eight chemicals proposed for regulation. During the 1980s, however, QRAs rapidly proliferated throughout federal environmental and health agencies, impelled by the passage of Toxic Substances Control Act (1976), the Resource Conservation and Recovery Act (1976), and the Comprehensive Environmental Response, Compensation, and Liability Act (1980) better known as "Superfund." Between 1980–1990 more than one hundred QRAs were prepared by federal agencies (Andrews 1994). By the early 1990s, quantitative risk assessment was so widely institutionalized in federal law that it had become the most common and fundamental procedure for integrating regulatory science and policymaking in federal health and environmental protection.

In the 1990s, QRA could assume even greater significance through its use for *comparative* risk assessment. Numerous public and private environmental leaders, together with influential activists in environmental and health regulation, now advocate comparative assessment as a principal means to set priorities in health and environmental regulation and, in the process, to achieve greater efficiency and rationality in environmental regulation. The debate over comparative risk assessment—often called "risk-based regulation"—has become a defining, and ferociously contentious environmental issue of the 1990s whose resolution will have major implications for the future of environmental regulation.

An understanding of the controversy and its implications begins, as does this chapter, with an explanation of the growing interest in QRA aroused by rising concern over the cost, efficiency, and complexity of environmental regulation, with particular attention to why QRA's advocates prefer it to the more traditional cost-benefit analysis as a solution to regulatory problems. The discussion then illuminates why proponents believe QRA can make an especially significant contribution to ecological sustainability by encouraging among governmental regulators a much stronger sensitivity to environmental risks when determining whether specific hazards should be regulated. Next, three major controversies about QRA methodology are examined: Is QRA sufficiently scientific? Does it give administrators too much discretion in policymaking? And does it ignore other considerations that should be included in risk assessment? Finally, several significant proposals for implementing QRA in current governmental policymaking are examined. It is helpful to begin with a brief description of how QRA is usually designed in governmental policymaking.

THE POLICY ANATOMY OF QRA

The Carnegie Commission provides a very simple and serviceable definition of risk assessment. It is "essentially the process of deciding how dangerous a substance is. The first step...is to identify and qualitatively describe the hazard to be assessed. Next, the level of exposure to the hazardous entity is estimated, along with the response of the organisms in question..to different dose levels. Finally, the above information is combined to characterize the risk quantitatively" (Carnegie Commission 1993: 76). The "risk" assessed in QRA can be any harm created to humans or the environment by a "hazard" which, in turn, is the substance or action creating the risk. Most often, risk is defined in terms of the *probability* of harm to human health or safety from a specific hazard—for example, the likelihood of one new case of a specified illness for every thousand individuals exposed to a particular chemical. Cancer is the human health risk most often emphasized in QRA and in environmental regulation. In contrast, "environmental risk"—far less often the major goal of QRA—may involve many kinds of damage such as threats to survival of a species, or destruction of specific ecological systems or animal habitat.

To the extent risk assessment rests upon empirical testing and validation of its theories and conforms to rigorous scientific standards in its use of evidence, risk assessment can be called 'scientific.' Quantitative risk assessment borrows as much of its protocols as possible from science and thus claims to be more scientifically rigorous, and thereby more accurate and reliable, than 'qualitative' risk assessment using less empirical methods. Numerous experts, including many risk specialists, believe this distinction exaggerates the precision of QRA. Nonetheless, QRA has become the standard for most governmental risk assessment and, thus, the major focus of the risk assessment debate.

Most risk assessment performed by governmental agencies is required by federal regulations concerning the environment, public health, and public safety. Generally, congressional guidelines in health and environmental laws passed since 1970 have encouraged the responsible regulatory agencies to be "risk averse"—to adopt QRA methodologies that are more likely to overestimate than to underestimate the danger from a suspected hazard when uncertainties exist. Nonetheless, these laws usually define the criteria to be used in performing the risk assessments very broadly, leaving agencies with great latitude in determining how to interpret and to apply these guidelines in actual QRA.

In health and environmental regulation, risk assessment is usually the beginning of a three-step process leading to the regulation of a hazardous or toxic substance. Assuming that a risk assessment reveals a hazard that apparently requires management, regulatory decision-making proceeds to *risk management* and risk communication. (If QRA reveals no hazard meeting regulatory criteria, of course, no further regulatory action is taken). The entire process is illustrated in Figure 1.1, which is essentially a paradigm of risk-based regulatory decision-making (National Research Council, 1983: 21).

In practice, these phases are not so easily separable, nor are all the relevant factors bearing on a risk-based regulatory decision captured by attention to the formal processes prescribed by law. Also, many important controversies about QRA arise directly, or indirectly, from

Figure 1.1. Regulatory Risk Decision-Making within Governmental Agencies

Risk Assessment ⟶	Risk Management ⟶	Risk Communication
Laboratory and field observation of adverse health effects and exposure to particular agents.	Deciding upon a regulatory strategy to deal with the risk or group of risks. A variety of legal, economic, political and social factors are considered.	Discussion of risk between relevant agencies and the public. Interaction between agencies and public about the nature of risks and their remedy.
Extrapolation from high to low dose and animals to humans.		
Field measurements, estimated exposures, characterization of populations.		

the existence of a risk assessment *politics* as well as a risk assessment *science*, and from the existence of *informal* as well as *formal* QRA procedures. Regulatory agencies could not carry out their missions without accepting, and sometimes initiating, informal arrangements and without responding to the political forces permeating risk assessment. Nonetheless, such situations provoke controversy, for critics often perceive these informal and political elements to involve bureaucratic "trafficking with the Devil" because they create decision-making arrangements outside those explicitly sanctioned by law or administrative codes.

THE QRA CONTROVERSY

QRA in all its forms has never been more controversial. Its growing use exacerbates an abiding debate over QRA's reliability into an increasingly public conflict between partisans and critics of regulation and among risk scientists themselves. When an eminent risk practitioner, for instance, asserts before a congressional committee—as one did not long ago—that an emerging consensus exists within his profession that "risk numbers generally are not credible," profound questions clearly exist even among practitioners about the appropriateness of QRA as a fundamental regulatory strategy (Finkel 1989b: 11). Conflict over QRA has intensified with growing numbers of influential regulatory officials, economists, environmental leaders and other experts proposing that QRA should be used by public agencies to compare environmental risks, thus setting priorities for regulation among health and environmental hazards. In effect, proponents of comparative risk assessment argue that it should be the primary means for deciding which environmental or health problems have the greatest claim to governmental regulation. Proponents of comparative QRA predict that it will promote greater regulatory efficiency and effectiveness—an appeal that even many critics of current regulation could embrace. However, a legion of critics regard QRA as a specious science. Citing its many data deficiencies and problematic assumptions, they believe that using it to set environmental priorities would be a clumsy misalliance of means and ends that will yield neither scientifically defensible choices nor more efficient regulation.

Apprehension about the relentlessly rising cost of environmental regulation, and waste cleanup especially, also resonates through all discussions of risk-based regulation. Critics blame QRA for much of this cost escalation and assert that comparative risk assessment will only worsen matters. Proponents of comparative risk assessment, however, believe it will inhibit cost increases. The critics attribute bloating regulatory costs to risk assessment's flawed methodology which, they assert, exaggerates the health risks posed by pollutants and thereby unnecessarily increases the scope of cleanup. The President's Office of Management and Budget (OMB) under the Reagan and Bush administrations was particularly outspoken in its criticism of current risk assessment methodology which, it complained, "distorts the regulatory priorities of the Federal Government, directing societal resources to reduce what are often trivial carcinogenic risks while failing to address more substantial threats to risk and health" (OMB 1992: 33).

To the critics, the very incarnation of this problem is the "Superfund" program. Begun in 1980 as a $1.6 billion enterprise to clean up the nation's abandoned hazardous waste sites, Superfund has swelled to an estimated completion price of $27.2 billion; the average site cleanup, once costing about $2.1 million, is calculated in the future to exceed $25 million (U.S. GAO 1993: 47). Proponents believe that comparative QRA would be a major step toward containing Superfund's cost. Comparative assessment, they suggest, could be used to distinguish between facilities on the basis of relative risk and thus arm regulatory officials with a scientifically defensible, non-politicized metric for setting priorities among sites. Moreover, the argument continues, risk-based regulation would also improve Superfund by establishing a common metric for establishing priorities for waste containment at each site, thereby facilitating the presently protracted, highly expensive business of negotiating cleanups on a site-by-site basis. "In the absence of specific statutory cleanup goals and levels," notes the recent report of a congressional investigating committee, "EPA must determine "how clean is clean" at each Superfund site, a process requiring lengthy investigation and decision-making. At the same time, the Superfund statute and EPA's regulation that interprets this law specify multiple and conflicting criteria . . . " (House Committee on Public Works 1993: 79–80). Moreover, as Daniel Mazmanian and David Morell observe, "risk" currently has no common meaning to the many different factions customarily involved in Superfund siting controversies. "Project proponents and opponents," they observe, "in using the same words—'risk,' 'risk assessment,' 'acceptable risk,' and the like—were usually talking past one another. That they could never come to agreement should not be surprising" (Mazmanian and Morell 1992: 183).

Although less frequently admitted publicly, risk-based regulation often appeals to environmentalists and environmental regulators because it is more ideologically acceptable as a calculus for setting regulatory priorities than the frequently proposed alternative, cost-benefit analysis. C/b analysis strongly appeals to critics of current environmental regulation—and especially to traditional economists and political conservatives—because they believe its wider use would compel administrators to develop a sensitivity to cost and economic efficiency in creating environmental regulations that is presently lacking in most environmental regulatory programs (Freeman 1994). So strongly identified is cost-benefit analysis with the idea of regulatory cost containment and reduced regulation, that the new Republican majority in the House of Representatives proposed in 1995 as a centerpiece to its regulatory reduction program a measure requiring all federal regulatory agencies to perform c/b analysis for all new regulatory proposals and to certify that the compliance costs were justified by the anticipated benefits.[1]

In effect, c/b analysis is presumed to be a sort of policy damper that smothers many excessively costly and economically inefficient regulatory proposals. President Ronald Reagan assumed as much when he initiated Executive Order 12291 in February 1981, requiring environmental agencies and all other federal regulatory authorities to produce a "Regulatory Impact Analysis" [RIA]—in effect, a cost/benefit analysis—for all major regulatory proposals. The Order did impede agencies in proposing new regulations but it never had the massive impact anticipated because many environmental laws, such as the Clean Air Act, explicitly prohibited the use of c/b analysis in their implementation and, in many other instances, agencies were reluctant to defend their c/b analyses when challenged in the courts. Nonetheless, c/b proponents assert that Congress itself, or the White House, if so disposed could write new requirements for c/b analysis with a much sharper bite, reaching more broadly and deeply into agency regulation writing. Apparently taking the cue, the new Republican majority in the House of Representatives proposed in 1995 that laws, like the Clean Air Act, requiring only health-based criteria for regulatory decisions be amended to replace these criteria with c/b and risk assessment procedures.

Opponents of c/b approaches to environmental regulation, including most environmentalists, believe that c/b analysis is biased against regulation because of the manner in which it assigns costs and benefits when evaluating regulatory proposals. Nonetheless, its aura of economic precision and rationality entails considerable public credibility and political appeal. Comparative QRA creates a different standard based on risk, but has a scientific *cachet* that can also imply credibility.[2] Moreover, environmentalists are convinced that QRA is much more congenial to aggressive environmental and health regulation. Thus, risk-based regulation has been a weapon of choice in the battle to neutralize the appeal of c/b analysis. In turn, proponents of c/b analysis have often launched their fiercest attack upon the scientific credibility of risk assessment, in good measure to restore the appearance of methodological superiority for c/b approaches.

The debate over risk-based regulation inevitably leads into a labyrinth of scientific, technical, and political issues, which must be recognized before judgments are made about its usefulness and impact. It is not a journey for those who like their epistemologies neat or their science plain. There are no simple explanations, or remedies, for QRA's deficiencies, and no certainties about its presumed virtues. Nor are the alternatives to QRA, such as "risk versus cost" comparisons, necessarily superior. The stakes, in any case, are profoundly important. The attack on risk assessment drives at the scientific foundation of governmental health and environmental regulation, the fundamental grounding upon which the current structure of regulatory policy is erected. The debate over risk assessment is, in effect, a controversy over the continuation, and possibly the enhancement of the primary calculus now used by government to assess risks to public health and the environment. These current controversies about QRA can be understood by focusing upon the generic issues that continually arise across regulatory programs.

FROM COMPARATIVE RISK ASSESSMENT TO "RISK-BASED REGULATION"

The concept of comparative risk assessment is beguiling, its appeal seductive to administrators struggling to manage continually multiplying and competing regulatory goals. "Comparative risk projects," explains former EPA Deputy Administrator Al Alm, "are simply a formal way of gathering together available information and professional judgments to produce estimates of relative seriousness" among environmental hazards (Alm 1991: 15). Assuming these estimates are based upon comparable units of analysis (e.g., increased risk of cancer over a normal lifetime), it is theoretically possible to rank numerically health or environmental hazards in terms of relative risk and to use these rankings to set regulatory priorities. Even if risks cannot be compared according to a common parameter, such as fatalities per million of population, experts can rank them less precisely according to how serious they are thought to be—"high risk," "medium risk," or "low risk", for example. Either way, the methodologies could result in a ranking among regulated hazards and thus create "risk-based regulation." So closely linked is "comparative risk assessment" to "risk-based regulation" that the terms are often used interchangeably although they are not identical procedures.

In advocating that federal health and environmental agencies adopt risk-based regulation, The Carnegie Commission on Science, Technology, and Government illustrates how the process might work administratively:

> No federal agency currently enjoys this latitude to compare and rank its regulated risks or to set its priorities by such a ranking, but the imperative for some arrangement to facilitate the setting of priorities grows with time. It was already obvious in the late 1970s that most federal health and environmental agencies were overwhelmed by the avalanche of new health and regulatory responsibilities created by Congress, even as the pile-on continued. In the mid-1980s, the Council on Environmental Quality was warning that the EPA "cannot possibly do all the things its various mandates tell it to do" and EPA

> Administrators were among the earliest and most aggressively outspoken advocates of comparative QRA and risk-based regulation (U.S. Council on Environmental Quality 1986: 14). By 1993, the National Commission on the Environment, a private sector policy panel including four former EPA Administrators, articulated a widely shared opinion among environmental advocates that the U.S. environmental regulatory system was "woefully inadequate" and "cumbersome" and concluded darkly: "Comprehensive reform is imperative to refocus the regulatory system on coherent policies" (National Commission on the Environment 1993: iv, 8).

By the early 1990s, EPA Administrator William K. Reilly had become a leading public advocate of risk-based regulation as one of these imperative reforms. Risk-based regulation seemed to him a way out of what had become intractable morass of multiplying health and environmental laws that piled regulatory burdens on public and private sectors without priorities or coherence. "For twenty years we have established goals on a pollutant-by-pollutant and medium-by-medium basis," he observed. "Rarely have we evaluated the relative importance of pollutants or environmental media—air, land, and water...We have seldom if ever been directed by law to seek out the best opportunities to reduce environmental risks, *in toto*, or to employ the most efficient, cost-effective procedures" (Reilly 1991: 3). Using comparative risk assessment, assert Reilly and other proponents, would for the first time permit regulatory officials to rank environmental hazards according to their relative risk. "Using risk as a common denominator creates a measurement that lets us distinguish the environmental equivalents of heart attacks and indigestion, the broken bones from bruises," he asserted, thus "targeting our limited resources, and . . . mobilizing and deploying experience in an efficient and rational way" (Reilly 1991: 2).

Many environmental advocates believe risk-based regulation might also insulate agencies against what many experts believe to be excessive and uninformed public pressure in setting regulatory goals. "Public policy in the United States reflects public perceptions," remarked Jonathan Lash, a member of EPA's Science Advisory Board. "Public perceptions about the environment are based on a haphazard combination of good and bad information, well learned fear, outrage, and skepticism about official assurances minimizing risks"—in short, not a proper mindset for setting a rational regulatory agenda (1991: 19). In contrast, risk-based regulation would presumably establish policy priorities by a more enlightened standard grounded in scientific rigor and objectivity rather than public passion. By 1995, some administrative form of comparative risk assessment and risk-based regulation was advocated by many important scientific and administrative panels, including the Carnegie Commission on Science, Technology and Government, the EPA's Science Advisory Board, and the National Academy of Science's National Research Council (Carnegie Commission 1993; EPA Science Advisory Board 1990; National Research Council 1983).

COMPARATIVE RISK, ECOLOGICAL RISK, AND SUSTAINABILITY

One of the most potentially attractive features of risk-based regulation, especially to environmental scientists and activists with a global perspective, is that it could encourage the explicit comparison of ecological risks to human health risks in setting priorities for regulation. Presently, regulatory laws and public attitudes strongly bias regulation toward human health risks because these are more easily understood and defended, politically as well as scientifically. Most current environmental statutes, such as the Food and Drug Act and the Toxic Substances Control Act, explicitly encourage, or require, administrators to consider primarily human health risks—often confined largely to cancer—in identifying environmental and health hazards. However, many environmental scientists, risk experts, and public health professionals believe that some hazards posing serious risks of ecological disruption will be more evident in a risk-based approach to regulation and, additionally, some ecological risks may appear more significant than many human health risks when put in a comparative risk context.

In contrast to hazards that threaten the health and safety of humans, "ecological risks" may involve the direct physical destruction or major alteration of ecosystems, changes in ecological communities, the reduction of species richness or diversity, or other transformations in the natural order presumed to create long-term, adverse consequences for the human population. Experts on the EPA's Science Advisory Board, for example, estimated that stratospheric ozone depletion, global climate change (the "greenhouse effect") and the loss of biological diversity were "high-risk" problems of greater human significance than the danger from chemical pesticides and herbicides, or from chemical toxics generally. In contrast, the public normally considers the chemical dangers far more significant than the ecological ones (Loehr 1991). Studies of the media also suggest that television, newspapers, and news magazines generally attribute far more importance to cancer-causing environmental hazards than to any other kind, thereby reinforcing the public preoccupation with human health risks and carcinogens especially (Lichter 1993: 1). Many risk experts and environmental advocates were particularly pleased when the state of California recently released a 600-page report in which a panel of 100 scientists ranked risks according to their estimated effect upon human health, ecosystem vitality, and social welfare. On the basis of this comparative approach, for instance, airborne particulates were rated a high risk to human health, while wetlands loss and introduction of exotic species were rated high risks to ecosystems. Thus, carcinogenic and non-carcinogenic risks were compared and ecosystem issues were introduced alongside human health concerns (Stone 1994: 215).

A risk assessment methodology sensitive to ecological dangers is especially relevant for those concerned with promoting policies of ecological sustainability. Sustainability addresses primarily questions of ecological vitality and threat, and thereby attributes special importance to those forces which threaten ecosystems and biospheres with all their complex supporting chemical and biological infrastructures. Risk assessment methodologies focusing on human health problems, to the virtual exclusion of the larger ecosystem context in which they evolve, are likely to breed a policy myopia in addressing environmental issues which directly affect the sustainability of whole ecosystems.

Comparative risk assessment, by definition, creates a certain intrinsic parity between ecological and human health risks in evaluation methodologies that facilitates greater sensitivity to the ecological implications of human health risks. The chemical dioxin, for example, has been known for more than three decades to be a significant cancer risk to humans when they are exposed to unusually high levels of the chemical. In the early 1990s, however, researchers discovered that even minute amounts of dioxin could wreak biological havoc among fish, birds, and other wild animals. Thus, exposure to small amounts of dioxin, which might appear tolerable from a human health standpoint, seemingly poses serious danger of persisting ecological damage which may, in the long run, adversely affect large human populations as well. Regulatory decisions regarding human exposure to dioxin, as a consequence, can now be made with much greater appreciation of the "trade-offs" between human and ecological risks involved (Rosenbaum 1995: 172).

SHOULD COMPARATIVE RISK ASSESSMENT BE PUBLIC POLICY?

The debate over comparative risk assessment has resolved none of the salient issues but has clarified the major ones and politicized much of the controversy. Generally, the debate over comparative risk assessment focuses upon two broad aspects of risk-based regulation: the methodology's reliability for estimating risk and the appropriateness of QRA for selecting priorities among different environmental risks. Viewpoints on these issues often seem to be influenced as much by political attitudes—especially by convictions concerning the proper scope and form of governmental regulation—as by technical or scientific opinions.

Methodology: Too Little Science, Too Much Conservatism?

The most frequent criticism of comparative QRA is that it purports to be scientific but, in reality, entails a specious precision because it relies on a multitude of assumptions and subjective judgments as much as it depends upon empirical observation or testing. Scientific critics have asserted, for instance, that at least twenty variables essential to QRA largely involve subjective human judgment, including decisions whether to include benign tumors in reporting toxicological studies of animals, what cancer latency periods to use, and which (if any) sensitive subpopulations to include or omit in the study[3] (Karstadt 1988; Thornton 1991: 67). The U.S. General Accounting Office illuminated these judgmental elements in the setting of federal radiation exposure standards. "The science that supports the limits is complex, difficult, and multidisciplinary. It involves conceptual modeling of the interactions of low-level radiation with the surrounding environment and human body. The limits often rely less on actual measurement of such interactions than on judgements and assumptions . . . " (GAO 1994a: 28). Many estimates affect fundamental components in risk analysis, such as the "exposure pathways" and "levels of exposure" associated with human risks from hazards.

Many procedures used to create quantitative risk assessments are criticized as unscientific. Proponents of QRA acknowledge that many of the components used in estimating risk, such as statistical modelling, theoretical assumptions, and incomplete empirical data, involve assumptions and hypotheses. But they defend such assumptions as inevitable when little scientifically sound risk data about many hazards are yet available. Many risk experts concede that the risk numbers they generate are often crude approximations. Proponents believe the primary goal of QRA should be not to produce precisely correct risk estimates (which may be impossible within the time available), but rather to err in a direction most protective of human health—in short, to be excessively "conservative" in their estimations (Finkel 1989a; Formaini 1990: chapter 1). Two procedures common to standard risk assessment are especially important in creating this "conservative" bias. First, a "worst case" assumption is made when estimating human exposure and response to a suspected hazard. Second, estimates of safe exposure to a hazard include an extra "margin of safety" which, in effect, increases the range of exposure that must be controlled. Many experts consider this conservatism to be unavoidable when the experimental or observational data necessary to reduce significantly the risk estimation errors for many hazards will be available, if at all, only many years or decades after statutory regulatory standards are required.

Unfortunately for QRA's proponents, the tentativeness of many risk estimates assures that the risk science supporting governmental health and environmental regulations is continually vulnerable to challenge and repudiation by new research, creating chronic instability to the regulatory science base. The highly publicized experience of tiny Times Beach, Missouri, is one example of the consequences. In 1974, federal studies revealed that waste oil sprayed on dirt roads and horse arenas throughout the community had been illegally laced with the chemical 2,3,7,8-tetracholrodibenzo-*p*-dioxin—commonly known as "TCDD" or "dioxin"—and described by the U.S. Environmental Protection Agency at the time as perhaps the most potent chemical carcinogen known. Further study revealed concentrations of dioxin in soil and water far exceeding EPA standards throughout the city. Moreover, TCDD appeared responsible for sickness and death among horses in the community and for the illness of several local children. Confronted by the possibility of an imminent public disaster and thrown into the public spotlight by growing media attention, the government officials responsible ordered all residents to evacuate the city. At a cost exceeding $139 million, state and federal agencies later purchased the abandoned property from its owners. Less than a decade later, the federal official responsible for the initial 1974 decision, Vernon N. Houk (later, the Assistant Surgeon General), testified before a congressional committee that the evacuation had been a mistake. Citing toxicological studies of dioxin since the Times Beach evacuation, he concluded: "Given what we know now about the chemical's toxicity, it looks as if the evacuation was unnecessary" (*New York Times*, August 15, 1991).

This testimony, however, did not put the dioxin controversy to rest. A later EPA report, based on a three-year study by more than 100 scientists, concluded that while there was "currently no clear indication of a disease burden in the general population attributable to dioxin-like compounds," the human health threat from dioxin was still "worrisome." To environmentalists, dioxin was equivalent to a "health emergency," but not in the view of EPA officials (*New York Times*, September 14, 1994). Thus, the regulatory risk status of dioxin remains problematic and experts will continue disputing the import of the latest, but by no means the last, risk analysis (Moore 1993).

A second major criticism of QRA procedures, and a principal provocation of the dioxin debate, is that federal agencies and risk assessment experts follow no consistent, or consistently tested, "inference guidelines" when using animal studies to estimate human risks from exposure to suspected hazards. In general, an "inference guideline" is any rule, or set of rules, that risk assessors use when estimating (or "extrapolating") some unknown value in QRA on the basis of known values. An inference guideline, for example, is necessary when deciding how to estimate the incidence of cancer among humans exposed to low levels of pesticide on the basis of dose-response rates obtained from animals exposed to the same chemical. Different inference guidelines can create very different estimates of human cancer risk and, thus, may strongly influence decisions about regulation. It is common for the QRA of a single chemical to require as many as fifty or more inference guidelines. It is also common for federal agencies to use different inference guidelines in dealing with similar problems. For example, animal experiments often involve exposing animal populations to very high doses of a suspected hazard and then estimating the animal response to low doses from the high-dose data. The statistical formulae used to make this extrapolation varies widely among federal agencies. EPA's guidelines for extrapolating from high-dose to low-dose responses in animal exposure experiments assumes a greater transfer of risk than those advocated by the White House Office of Science and Technology Policy (OSTP), thus creating a subtle but important bias toward findings of significant risk from low-level exposures that might not be true of the OSTP guidelines. Inference guidelines in animal studies may vary so much between agencies and governments that enormous differences in risk assessments may result for the same hazard. "It is not uncommon," observed one nationally respected risk expert, "when you look at risk assessments done by this government and compare it with what is done in governments . . . in Western Europe . . . to have differences of a hundred to a thousandfold in the quantitative estimates of risk between the two . . . " (Moore 1993: 171).

Generally, federal health and environmental regulatory agencies have a strong institutional bias toward conservatism in risk assessment. This tilt toward conservatism has been, in good measure, a response to the congressional mood which, in the past, favored a similar conservatism when writing regulatory guidelines in environmental legislation. But such conservatism also means that federal regulators are sometimes slow to revise their risk estimates in the light of new research, even when their original estimates are clearly based upon insufficient information, because the earlier estimates are likely to err, as earlier noted, on the side of protectiveness toward human populations. This agency bias toward protectiveness is, in part, a defensive political posture against accusations that the agency is insensitive to human health risks. It may also make agency critics appear to be indifferent to human life or welfare and perhaps secure the agency a measure of congressional sympathy.

From an agency viewpoint, then, human protectiveness is probably the good news about QRA's "conservative" bias. The bad news is that such bias exposes the agency to accusations that its methodology is deliberately congenial to regulation—the most common criticism of QRA and an especially grievous flaw in the opinion of regulatory critics. Among QRA's many technical assumptions attacked by critics as biased toward regulation, the most commonly cited include assumptions that:

1. Dose-response functions are linear, so that the high-level and low-level slopes are equal.
2. Responses of the most sensitive animals tested resemble human responses.
3. All rodent tumors are indicative of human cancer risks (Finkel 1989a).

Another commonly cited example of the scientifically conservative slant in standard QRA protocols is the procedure for characterizing the "maximally exposed individual" (MEI) to air, water, or soil pollutants—an essential concept in risk measurement. A common approach is to assume that this hypothetical person lives at the boundary of the facility releasing the pollutant and has an "uptake" of the pollutant at the upper-level of human parameters. Additionally, any concentrations of the pollutant not actually detected in soil, water, or air samples are assumed to be just below the limit of detection (Finkel 1989a). This hypothetical MEI must often substitute for missing information about actual human exposures at a specific pollution site. The MEI is often troublesome because it may postulate—perhaps with good technical reason—the existence of a weirdly improbable individual who can provoke public misunderstanding and skepticism about the whole QRA process. Even QRA's partisans recognize this problem. "I cannot emphasize enough the need to have adequate information on actual human exposures," observes Dr. Paul J. Lioy, a leading risk health scientist. "These must be based on fundamental research within a sound and defensible framework. . . . It will also reduce the public's misconception about who is exposed to what, where, when, why, and how (1991: 71).[4]

DOES COMPARATIVE QRA GIVE OFFICIALS TOO MUCH DISCRETION?

Another major concern about risk-based regulation is whether it allows too much opportunity for administrators and risk-assessment professionals to introduce non-scientific, subjective, and political considerations into the risk assessment process. In reality, all governmental risk assessment procedures create opportunities for the intrusion of non-scientific values and discretionary judgements into many aspects of the process. Moreover, it is impossible to create an impermeable wall institutionally or behaviorially to insulate the scientific and technical elements of risk characterization, which are supposed to constitute the foundation of risk assessment, from the social, economic, and political considerations that assume importance in the risk management phase of regulation.

Nonetheless, the discretion issue assumes unusual importance when risk-based regulation is proposed because the strategy might accomplish a *de facto* displacement of power to agency risk assessors in determining national environmental and health priorities. Critics of risk-based regulation perceive this to be one of the most insidiously dangerous aspects of comparative risk assessment because such a transfer of power, and its subsequent exercise, could be veiled in the scientific and technical language of risk assessment methodologies. Such power might then be exercised, so the argument runs, without public recognition or public accountability. Critics point to California's recent report on risk-based regulation, earlier discussed, to illustrate their concern. In addition to human health and ecological risks, the report recommends a third category of comparative risk called "social welfare" relating, among other things, to a society's economic health and even its "peace of mind." Using this "social welfare" criterion, the report writers determined that growing global concentrations of "greenhouse gases" created only a moderate health and ecological risk but constituted a major threat to social welfare because climate warming could impair "mental health, trust of governmental institutions, access to reliable information, personal security, and personal relationships" (Stone 1994: 214). The determination of such a "social welfare" risk would seem to require a multitude of highly controversial political and economic judgements amounting to the formulation of major social policies more appropriate for elective institutions such as Congress or the presidency.

Opportunities for the insinuation of non-scientific values into comparative QRA are well documented. The National Research Council has estimated conservatively that at least fifty such opportunities exist during technical risk assessment because of uncertainties inherent to the process, including missing or ambiguous information and inadequate scientific theories (National Research Council 1983: 29–33). "Policy considerations inevitably effect, and perhaps determine, some of the choices . . . " the report noted (National Research Council 1983: 33). Other studies suggest that a risk expert's professional judgments can be influenced by beliefs concerning how government should regulate the economy and by their institutional affiliations (Dietz and Rycroft 1987). Risk experts associated with private corporations or trade associations, for instance, appeared to differ in their judgments about how risk should be managed from those working for government or academic institutions (Lynn 1986). Often, however, the judgmental elements in risk assessment remain unrecognized, even by the experts themselves. "Expert judgments, in large part, influence analytical results in more fundamental, but less visible ways . . . judgments about defining the problem, choosing models and analytic forms, and interpreting and using the results for policy purposes," comment risk experts Harry Otway and Detlof von Winterfeldt. "Most expert judgments . . . are informal and quite often seem so intuitively obvious . . . that they are not consciously recognized as judgments" (Otway and von Winterfeldt 1992: 85). Moreover, better science or "more research" will never eliminate many of these judgmental problems.

It is unrealistic to suppose, additionally, that a political quarantine could be imposed upon risk assessment. Risk assessment and risk-based regulation will be affected by political forces both external and internal to the agencies using the procedures. Consider, for instance, what may happen when an agency has prescribed a certain control technology for a hazard (perhaps hydrostatic "scrubbers" to control sulfur oxide emissions from coal-burning electric utilities) and the technology comes under attack. If the subsequent conflict over the merits of the technology is highly public and political, it is not uncommon for an agency and its client industry to divide experts into "friends" or "foes" according to their verdict on the technology and to evaluate the expert's scientific data with that bias.

Sometimes, risk assessments *depend* upon essentially political determinations. In attempting to set priorities for cleaning up hazardous nuclear and chemical wastes at the nation's nuclear weapons facilities, for instance, the Department of Energy is considering which, among more than 100 facilities, pose the greatest human health hazards. Estimates of human exposure to on-site and off-site waste frequently depend upon decisions concerning the future status of the sites and the surrounding property—essentially, upon political determinations about future land use (U.S. GAO 1994b: 2).

Administrators also inherit a large measure of discretion in defining the meaning of "risk" because the statutory standards they are expected to observe are frequently vague, often bewilderingly complex and inconsistent from one law to another. Thus, agencies follow no common criteria in defining such important terms as "significant risk," or "unreasonable risk" or other crucial statutory phrases that characterize the kinds of hazard they must regulate or, perhaps, compare. Moreover, agencies do not promulgate uniform standards for controlling known hazards. These problems could be greatly diminished if Congress created consistent guidelines in statutory risk definition, *if* it made its understanding of critical risk terms statutorily clear, *if* it kept risk criteria within reasonable limits, if . . .

However, Congress seems incapable of such statutory coherence. There is no reasonably consistent statutory language for defining risk or for enumerating the criteria that agencies must consider when determining whether a risk exists under laws they must implement. Instead, each health or environmental regulatory program seems to produce yet another set of statutory formulae for defining risks and characterizing their magnitude, the unique distillation of each law's peculiar political compromises and coalitions. Consider, for example, the divergent definitions of an environmental hazard which EPA is mandated to control under different environmental statutes:

> *Air Pollution*: Substances which cause an "increase in mortality or serious, irreversible, or incapacitating, reversible illness." [Clean Air Act 42 USC 7412(a)(1)]
>
> *Water Pollution*: Substances which create "imminent and substantial danger to the public health or welfare, including but not limited to fish, shellfish, wildlife, shorelines, and beaches." [Clean Water Act 33 USC 1321(b)(2)(A)]
>
> *Hazardous Waste*: Substances that cause an "increase in mortality or an increase in serious irreversible, or incapacitating reversible, illness or . . . pose a substantial hazard to health or the environment." [Resource Conservation and Recovery Act 42 USC 6903(5)]

In this illustration, the EPA is required by law to evaluate the same substance—sulfur oxides, for example—by three different criteria, depending on whether it is found in ambient air, surface water, or solid waste, before determining that it is a hazard meriting regulation.

Congress can provide agency risk assessors with extremely valuable guidance by writing into regulatory statutes a clear and ordered set of criteria for officials to follow in determining whether a hazard should be regulated. Unfortunately, the "statutory criteria" commonly found in federal environmental laws are rarely clear or orderly. Here are the criteria, for instance, that EPA is expected to observe in deciding whether the risks from exposure to a chemical substance are "unreasonable:"

> The type of effect (chronic or acute, reversible or irreversible); degree of risk; characteristics and number of humans, plants and animals, or ecosystems, at risk; amount of knowledge about the effects; available or alternative substances and their expected effects; magnitude of the social and economic costs and benefits of possible control actions; and appropriateness and effectiveness of TSCA as the legal instrument for controlling the risk [Toxic Substances Control Act 15 USC 2603 (a) (ii)]

This kind of statutory stockpiling leaves agency risk assessors with little more than a shopping list of criteria they must somehow render into a coherent risk assessment methodology. Nor does it necessarily clarify the meaning of any single criterion. Often, agencies are left to make their own informal definitions according to their own best judgment—or to ignore definitions. In the case of TSCA, for instance, the EPA decided in 1990 not to enforce the law against three chemicals because the agency had determined that the chemicals did not constitute a "significant risk to human health or the environment" as required by TSCA. When challenged, the EPA explained that it had not developed any criteria or methodology for determining whether a risk was "significant" or "unreasonable" according to TSCA but, nonetheless, it set "an informally high standard for making such a determination and . . . the chemical testing program has never found an existing chemical to present such risks" (U.S. GAO 1991: 14) Such cavalier rulemaking is to critics of risk-based regulation the essence of administrative discretion at its worst.

IS RISK-BASED REGULATION INSENSITIVE TO OTHER IMPORTANT VALUES?

A major criticism of risk-based regulation, especially among environmentalists, is that it focuses upon a very limited range of risks, which excludes other important social values that ought to be considered when setting regulatory priorities. As presently practiced, for example, comparative QRA attends almost exclusively to death risk while largely ignoring risks of chronic or debilitating disease, treats all human populations equally without regard for age, special vulnerability or other social conditions, fails to distinguish between voluntary and involuntary risks to which populations are exposed, disregards the difference between risks to present and future populations, and makes no determination of how much risk is too much. In short, it does not address crucial social and political questions inherent to environmental management, especially *what risks* to consider, *how much risk* is acceptable, and *what values* to protect in management decisions.

Moreover, many environmental critics believe that risk-based regulation will inevitably end in environmental *triage*. "The top three or five or even ten issues will receive attention, resources and perhaps some progress will be made in these areas," argues Lawrie Mott, a senior scientist for the Natural Resources Defense Council. "Other risks not on the short list will languish, or worse, be ignored . . . environmental protection cannot become management through triage. If current resources are inadequate for addressing problems, we should seek additional funds" (1991: 21).

Finally, many critics believe that risk-based regulation gives too little attention to risk prevention and, instead, focuses almost entirely upon pollution management. In the long run, they assert, it is less costly and far more environmentally beneficial to invest resources in preventing risk rather than in managing it, but comparative QRA does not focus attention upon either prevention or the comparative advantage of prevention over pollution management.

TOWARD A POLICY FIX: MAKING RISK-BASED REGULATION WORK

The nation's environmental regulation is severely impaired by a relentless accretion of laws, by a continual distention of their scope and substance—the Clean Air Act of 1970 required 60 pages; the Clean Air Act Amendments of 1990 required 788 pages—and by increasingly constrained policy resources. Some policy fix that imposes priorities and rationalizes resource allocation seems essential, and probably inevitable. Although a reduction in the number or scope of existing environmental laws is not unthinkable, the political carnage would be considerable (the Reagan administration's failed attack on the Clean Air Act has been a lesson for both parties), and neither Congress nor the White House is likely to have incentive for such a frontal assault. A more politically appealing and administratively feasible solution would involve a policy calculus for setting regulatory priorities and for discriminating between management strategies, a "regulatory feasibility standard" that could be administratively implemented across many different health and environmental programs. From this perspective, cost-benefit analysis (c/b) is the logical substitute or supplement to risk-based regulation as a means of reforming environmental and health risk assessment. Thus, the issue facing Congress and administrative agencies is not likely to be whether risk-based regulation should be adopted, but whether it should be adopted in preference to, or perhaps in combination with, c/b analysis.

C/b analysis has some initial advantage over risk assessment. In the guise of "Regulatory Impact Analysis" (RIA) it has been used, in limited ways, by health and environmental agencies to evaluate risk management strategies since 1981 when RIAs were mandated by President Reagan in Executive Order 12291 (Cooper and West 1988; Grubb, Whittington, and Humphries 1984). Many agencies have experience with cost-benefit analysis, its administrative implementation is widely studied and understood, and its strong ideological appeal to many political and economic conservatives will make it attractive to an increasingly conservative Congress. It has an articulate and influential constituency among economists, and it enjoys a significant measure of public support. Moreover, environmentalists may correctly believe that c/b analysis is tainted by an "anti-regulatory" image after its strong association with the Reagan administration's anti-environmental administrative reforms, but this identification may work in its favor. C/b analysis will attract support from many political and economic critics of existing regulation, such as large segments of the Republican majority in both houses of Congress, whose program of "regulatory reform" often includes an effort to diminish drastically the scope of governmental regulation at all levels. Moreover, even critics concede that c/b analysis has a legitimate role to play in evaluating many proposed environmental regulations, provided that its bias and limitations are recognized.

IMPROVING METHODS AND MODELS

Advocates of comparative risk assessment who expect it to be competitive with c/b analysis—or any other approach—for setting regulatory priorities, need to advertise its virtues better and to attack more aggressively its deficiencies. Perhaps the most fundamental reform required is one that explicitly addresses the most conspicuous flaws in current risk assessment methodology: the scientifically "conservative" tendency to tolerate, and sometimes to encourage, error on the side of overestimating risk and the frequent reliance upon unrealistic models of human behavior in risk assessment. Risk assessment expert Adam Finkel has proposed several reforms of QRA's basic protocols, which many other risk professionals would endorse, whose purpose is to reduce QRA's conservative bias and to promote more realistic models in human risk estimation (Finkel 1989a):

1. In dose-response chemical testing using experimental animals, the way in which low-dose animal responses are estimated from high-dose results should be revised by assuming there is an exposure threshold below which adverse risks do not exist. This 'sublinear' dose-response curve would reduce the likelihood that significant risks would be estimated from extremely low concentrations of a suspect substance.

2. Pool findings from all rodent groups used in a dose-response experiment, thereby increasing its statistical accuracy.

3. Omit data in animal dose-response studies that involve tumor sites or tumor development not found in humans.

4. Obtain data about the "maximally exposed individual" (MEI) at a hazard site from actual cases.
5. Estimate human "uptake" of a hazardous substance by using average human values and not the maximum ones.
6. Assume that when a hazardous substance cannot be detected, the substance is not present in any amount.

A related reform would be to use reasonable, rather than "worst case" scenarios, as the standard model in estimating human exposure to hazards. This would probably expose regulatory agencies to severe criticism from many segments of the environmental movement, and perhaps from some congressional sources, because less stringent risk models allegedly fail to protect adequately the public health. Nonetheless, the alternative is to invite increasing public and political criticism of risk assessment categorically and to diminish its appeal as an alternative to c/b analysis.

FACING DOWN PUBLIC OPINION

Any expansive use of comparative risk assessment in environmental and health regulation is an implicit attack on past congressional deference to public opinion in setting environmental priorities. The frequent collision between the public's perception of environmental risk and priorities and those of risk professionals and many environmental administrators has already been noted. Any ambitious promotion of comparative risk assessment as a major regulatory strategy will inevitably politicize the issue. Congressional proponents of mandatory risk assessment who extol its virtues for reducing the frequency and cost of environmental regulation may not be prepared for a possibly nasty public backlash if these assessments demonstrate the need to attack vigorously environmental problems whose importance the public neither understands nor accepts. Altering the public's risk perceptions—often reinforced by environmentalist activism—would seem to require, at a minimum, an aggressive public education campaign and considerable time. The results, in any case, would be problematic. A more realistic approach to institutionalizing comparative risk assessment in governmental regulation would be to treat the tension between public and expert perceptions of risk as inevitable and to ameliorate the problem as much as possible by promoting comparative risk assessment on the basis of its economic, scientific, and administrative appeal, particularly in Congress and among scientific professionals.

In this perspective, risk assessment needs better public relations, some "spin control" on its image. Risk experts, for instance, have not been as forceful or artful as they could be in counteracting the image among public officials of QRA as inherently "conservative." Not all of its models are biased toward regulation. Some of the air dispersion models used to describe the movement of pollutants in ambient air will underestimate their concentrations when terrain is complex. Most QRA models, moreover, tend to reduce estimates of risk by ignoring the adverse effects from indirect exposure to a pollutant (as, for example, when estimates of human risk from exposure to carcinogens do not take account of the effect on succeeding generations). Given the highly technical and esoteric nature of risk assessment, its capacity for public misunderstanding is enormous and, consequently, the need for better public and political explanation is imperative.

AN ADMINISTRATIVE AGENDA

A number of practical initiatives could be undertaken to promote wider experimentation with comparative risk assessment among federal regulatory agencies. These initiatives would require collaboration between Congress, administrative agencies, and the White House in revising administrative rules and regulations but probably would not require a significant rewriting of important existing environmental statutes. A comparative risk assessment initiative could plausibly develop as a series of limited reforms involving at first a few major environmental programs where reform seems most imperative. These reforms ought to require periodic review and assessment by expert panels. Such an initiative might involve some combination of the following elements:

1. The institutionalization of a comparative risk assessment approach initially limited to setting the National Priority List for abandoned waste site cleanup in "Superfund" and for regulating air pollutants under the Clean Air Act and its 1977 and 1990 amendments.

2. The requirement that comparative risk assessments be performed and reviewed in concurrence with any required cost/benefit analysis for a proposed environmental or health regulation.

3. The development of a Model QRA Protocol to be used by administrators implementing comparative risk assessments. The Protocol would define "reasonable" standards for models and inference guidelines to be used in risk assessment.
4. A requirement that agencies implementing laws to which comparative risk will be applied must define by administrative regulation the significant risk terms in these laws if such terms are not satisfactorily defined in the laws themselves.

Administrative restructuring alone is unlikely to facilitate greater use of risk-based regulation without a concurrent reform in governmental research support for risk assessment. Presently, the same confusion of priorities epidemic to federal environmental laws also afflicts federal governmental research support for risk assessment—indeed, for all federal research and development spending. A persuasive case can be made that the science base for risk-based regulation needs to be restructured to reflect, in some significant manner, the environmental priorities suggested by comparative risk assessment in regulatory agencies. For example, if EPA comparative assessments confirm the opinion of many risk experts that radon or other indoor air pollutants are a more serious health threat than municipal or industrial waste, EPA's research and development budget should provide much more money than it presently does to indoor air pollution research and much less than it currently does to risk from municipal waste sites. In a similar vein, research which clarifies the relative risk from the wastes most commonly found at Superfund sites could improve the presently expensive and time-consuming process of determining site-specific cleanup priorities.

CONCLUSION: THE EMERGING POLITICS OF RISK ASSESSMENT

The controversy over risk-based regulation in the latter 1990s has assumed a character quite different from its earlier manifestations. During the 1980s and early 1990s, the controversy was primarily a collision between partisans of aggressive federal health and environmental regulation and critics of these new regulatory programs emerging in such abundance from Washington. Proponents of the new regulation saw in comparative risk assessment a sophisticated, scientifically credible administrative strategy that could create a more rational and economically efficient regulatory regime, thereby enhancing its political appeal and rebutting the critics of regulation's high cost and glacial pace. Opponents of the new federal regulatory programs tended to view comparative risk assessment darkly, essentially as the same old costly and scientifically discredited risk assessment in a different guise. In their view, risk assessment was specious science in the service of the enemy.

As the 1990s have progressed, however, the terms of the conflict appear to have shifted. The debate over risk-based regulation no longer appears to be largely a conflict aligning mostly environmentalist proponents of QRA against QRA opponents heavily recruited from critics of current environmental laws. Instead, the QRA controversy has propagated a curious new politics in which former critics often embrace QRA, expecting it will somehow impede the pace, scope, and cost of environmental regulation. Thus, critics of the environmental regulatory laws passed during 1970s and 1980s, such as most congressional Republicans, now often find themselves aligned with many of their former environmentalist opponents in promoting QRA—but for very different reasons: environmentalists believe QRA will encourage better regulation, their opponents believe it will create less of it. In turn, some environmental leaders—suspecting that the opposition's enthusiasm for QRA is inspired by hope that it will further delay and complicate environmental regulations—now *oppose* mandatory QRA in environmental laws. One pattern, at least, emerges from this political tangle: political cleavages over QRA in the latter 1990s seem increasingly to be shaped primarily by very different, even contradictory, expectations about its regulatory impact.

In effect, a subtle but important transformation in the political setting of the risk debate seems to be emerging in which both sides of the dispute over federal regulation appear to expect—in fact, to welcome—much greater reliance upon comparative risk assessment in health and environmental management but for very different reasons. In this perspective, the future debate about risk-based regulation may well focus less upon whether it will be practiced in some measure by governmental regulators and more upon what assumptions and guidelines will be used in its application. The politicization of risk-based regulation is already a reality and future struggles between friends and foes of current regulation are likely to be fought in the arcane and publicly mystifying language of legislative or administrative guidelines for technical risk assessment. Inevitably, risk assessment experts and other risk scientists will be drawn into the controversy, often in spite of themselves, as the struggle over the scope of regulation is translated into conflicts over how comparative risk assessment will be implemented within government.

NOTES

1. This proposal did not *require* that agencies base their decisions on c/b analysis—a tacit recognition of the inherent limitations to c/b analysis. In fact, the House proposals only required that regulatory agencies show that the benefits were likely to justify, and be reasonably related, to costs.

2. Strictly speaking, c/b and QRA are not mutually exclusive procedures. Some federal laws, such as the Toxic Substances Control Act, permit regulators to consider both c/b and QRA when deciding whether to regulate a suspected hazard. Moreover, some hybrid forms of risk analysis, such as those which compare monetary benefits to risks, or costs to risks, or even risks of regulation against risks of nonregulation, blend the two approaches. These latter approaches are not commonly used in policymaking, however. Many QRA proponents do not object to c/b analysis in combination with QRA during regulatory decision-making. They do reject arguments favoring the *exclusive* reliance on c/b analysis, or asserting c/b's alleged superiority to risk assessment during regulatory policymaking.

3. Including benign (noncancerous) tumors in risk assessments from animal experiments may significantly increase the likelihood that a suspected hazard will be considered a health risk. An increase in the latency period permitted for the development of cancerous tumors in experimental animals may have a similar effect. Moreover, animals vary greatly in their sensitivity to chemicals. Dioxin, for instance, is five thousand times more toxic to guinea pigs than to hamsters, thus making the choice of experimental animals crucial in determining the exposure risks from that chemical.

4. Of course, exploring risks itself brings costs, raising the question of who should pay.

REFERENCES

Alm, Al. 1991. "Why We Didn't Use 'Risk' Before." *EPA Journal* 17: 13–16.

Andrews, Richard N. L. 1994. "Risk-Based Decisionmaking." In *Environmental Policy in the 1990s*, 2nd ed., ed. Norman J. Vig and Michael E. Kraft, 209–232. Washington, D.C.: CQ Press.

Burke, Thomas A., Nga L. Tran, Jane S. Roemer, and Carol J. Henry, eds. 1993. *Regulating Risk: The Science and Politics of Risk*. Washington, D.C.: International Life Sciences Institute.

Carnegie Commission on Science, Technology and Government. 1993. *Risk And The Environment: Improving Regulatory Decision Making.* New York: The Carnegie Corporation.

Center for Risk Analysis, Harvard School of Public Health. 1991. *OMB vs. The Agencies: The Future of Cancer Risk Assessment.* Boston, Mass.: Center for Risk Analysis.

Cohrssen, John J., and Vincent T. Covello. 1989. *Risk Analysis: A Guide to Principles and Methods for Analyzing Health and Environmental Risks.* Washington, D.C.: Council on Environmental Quality.

Cooper, Joseph, and William F. West. 1988. "Presidential Power and Presidential Government: The Theory and Practice of OMB Review." *Journal of Politics* 50: 864–895.

Dietz, Thomas M., and Robert W. Rycroft. 1987. *The Risk Professionals.* New York: Russell Sage Foundation.

Edgerton, Sylvia A., et al. 1990. Priority Topics in the Study of Environmental Risk in Developing Countries: Report on a Workshop Held at the East-West Center, August 1988. *Risk Analysis* 10: 273–283.

Finkel, Adam M. 1989a. "Is Risk Assessment Really Too Conservative? Revising the Revisionists." *Columbia Journal of Environmental Law* 14: 427–467.

———. 1989b. "Has Risk Assessment Become Too 'Conservative?' " *Resources* xx: 11–13.

Formaini, Robert. 1990. *The Myth of Scientific Public Policy.* New Brunswick, N.J.: Transaction Publishers.

Freeman, A. Myrick III. 1994. "Economics, Incentives, and Environmental Regulation." In *Environmental Policy in the 1990s*, 2nd ed., eds. Norman J. Vig and Michael E. Kraft, 189–208. Washington, D.C.: CQ Press.

Graham, John D., Laura C. Green, and Marc J. Roberts. 1988. *In Search of Safety: Chemicals and Cancer Risk.* Cambridge, Mass.: Harvard University Press.

Grubb, W. Norton, Dale Whittington, and Michael Humphries. 1984. "The Ambiguities of Cost-Benefit Analysis: An Evaluation of Regulatory Impact Analysis under Executive Order 12,291." In *Environmental Policy Under Reagan's Executive Order*, ed. V. Kerry Smith, 121–166. Chapel Hill, N.C.: University of North Carolina Press.

Karstadt, M. 1988. "Quantitative Risk Assessment: Qualms and Questions." *Teratonegesis, Carcinogenesis, and Mutagenesis* 8: 137–152.

Lash, Johnathan. 1991. "Should We Set Priorites Based on Risk Analysis?" *EPA Journal* 17: 19.

Lave, Lester B. 1991. "Testimony on Standardization of Risk Analysis Methods." *Risk Assessment: Strengths and Limitations of Utilization for Policy Decisions.* Hearing before the Subcommittee on the Environment, Committee on Science, Space, and Technology, House of Representatives, May 21, 1991. Washington, D.C.: Government Printing Office.

Lichter, S. Robert. 1993. *Scientific Opinion vs. Media Coverage of Environmental Cancer: A Report of Research in Progress.* Washington, D.C.: Center for Media and Public Affairs.

Lioy, Paul L. 1991. Testimony before the House of Representatives, Committee on Science, Space, and Technology, Subcommittee on the Environment. In *Risk Assessment: Strengths and Limitations of Utilization for Policy Decisions.* Hearings before the Subcommittee on Environment of the Committee on Science, Space, and Technology, 77–116. Washington, D.C.: Government Printing Office.

Loehr, Raymond. 1991. "What Raised the Issue?" *EPA Journal* 17: 6–12.

Lynn, Frances M. 1986. "The Interplay of Science and Values in Assessing and Regulating Environmental Risks." *Science, Technology and Human Values* 11: 40–50.

Main, Jeremy. 1991. "The Big Cleanup Gets It Wrong." *Fortune* xx: 95–100.

Mazmanian, Daniel, and David Morell. 1992. *Beyond Superfailure: America's Toxics Policy for the 1990s.* Boulder, Colo.: Westview Press.

Moore, John A. 1993. Testimony of John. A. Moore, President, Institute for Evaluating Health Risks, before the Subcommittee on Science, Space, and Technology, U.S. House of Representatives. In *How Safe Is Safe Enough? Risk Assessment and the Regulatory Process.* Hearing before the Subcommittee on Investigations and Oversight, Committee on Science, Space, and Technology, U.S. House of Representatives. July 27, 1993.

Mott, Lawrie. 1991. "Risk Analysis: The Policy." *EPA Journal* 17: 21.

National Commission on the Environment. 1993. *Choosing A Sustainable Future.* Washington, D.C.: Island Press.

National Research Council, Commission on Life Sciences. 1983. *Risk Assessment in the Federal Government: Managing the Process.* Washington, D.C.: National Academy Press.

Otway, Harry, and Detlof von Winterfeldt. 1992. "Expert Judgment in Risk Analysis and Management: Process, Context and Pitfalls." *Risk Analysis* 12: 83–93.

Reilly, William K. 1991. "Why I Propose a National Debate on Risk." *EPA Journal* 17: 2–5.

Rosenbaum, Walter A. 1995. *Environmental Politics and Policy*, 3rd ed. Washington, D.C.: CQ Press.

Stone, Richard. 1994. "California Report Sets Standard for Comparing Risk." *Science* 266: 214.

Thornton, Joe. 1991. Written Testimony for the U.S. House of Representatives Committee on Science, Space, and Technology, Subcommittee on the Environment. In *Risk Assessment: Strengths and Limitations of Utilization for Policy Decisions.* Hearing before the Subcommittee on Environment of the Committee on Science, Space, and Technology, 55–76. Washington, D.C.: Government Printing Office.

Travis, Curtis C. 1991. Risk Assessment: Strengths and Limitations of Utilization for Policy Decisions. Testimony before the U.S. House of Representatives, Committee on Science, Space, and Technology, Subcommittee on the Environment, 18–29. In U.S. House of Representatives, Commmittee on Science, Space, and Technology, Subcommittee on the Environment, *Risk Assessment: Strengths and Limitations . . .*, op. cit.

Uman, Myron E., ed. 1993. *Keeping Pace with Science and Engineering: Case Studies in Environmental Regulation*. Washington, D.C.: National Academy Press.

U.S. Congress, House, Committee on Public Works and Transportation, Subcommittee on Investigations and Oversight. 1993. *Administration of the Federal Superfund Program: Report*, November 1993. Washington, D.C.: Government Printing Office.

U.S. Congress, House, Committee on Science, Space and Technology, Subcommittee on Investigations and Oversight. 1993. *How Safe Is Safe Enough? Risk Assessment and the Regulatory Process.* Hearings before the Subcommittee on Investigations and Oversight, Committee on Science, Space, and Technology, July 27. Washington, D.C.: Government Printing Office.

———. 1993. *Technology Development and Transfer in the Superfund Program.* Hearings before the Subcommittee on Investigations and Oversight, Committee on Science, Space, and Technology, April 28–29, 1993. Washington, D.C.: Government Printing Office.

U.S. Environmental Protection Agency, Science Advisory Board. 1990. *Reducing Risk: Setting Priorities and Strategies for Environmental Protection.* Washington, D.C.: Environmental Protection Agency.

U.S. Executive Office of the President, Council on Environmental Quality [CEQ]. 1977. *Environmental Quality, 1976*. Washington D.C.: Government Printing Office.

———. 1986. *Environmental Quality, 1985*. Washington, D.C.: Government Printing Office.

———. 1993. *Environmental Quality, 1993.* Washington, D.C.: Government Printing Office.

U.S. Executive Office of the President, Office of Management and Budget. 1992. *Regulatory Program of the United States Government: April 1, 1990–March 31, 1991.* Washington, D.C.: Government Printing Office.

U.S. General Accounting Office. [GAO]. 1991. *EPA's Chemical Testing Program Has Not Resolved Safety Concerns.* Report No. GAO/RCED 91–136.

———. 1993. *Superfund: Cleanups Nearing Completion Indicate Future Challenges.* Report No. GAO/RCED 93–188. Washington, D.C.: General Accounting Office.

———.1994a. *Consensus on Acceptable Radiation Risk to the Public Is Lacking.* Report No. RCED 94–90. Washington, D.C.: General Accounting Office.

———. 1994b. *Nuclear Cleanup: Completion of Standards and Effectiveness of Land Use Planning Are Uncertain.* Report No. GAO/RCED 94–144. Washington, D.C.: General Accounting Office.

2 The Social and Political (Re)Construction of Risk

STEPHEN H. LINDER

"Risk" is a protean concept, much like "power" and "rationality," whose changing image seems to track ongoing disputes over social and political values. Its mutability, in this instance, comes not so much from any inherent weakness in the concept as from its volatile position, straddling the ideological divide between industrial production and government action, a major fault line in our political landscape. Distinctive images of risk accompany challenges to technology and environmental injustice, as well as defenses of private property and regulatory relief. Changes in the meaning of risk also mark the ebb and flow of scientific authority and shifting claims of professional expertise. Here, the images emerge from different risk paradigms. From its early link to gambles and imperfect information, "risk" has been defined variously as a measure of possible harm, as a tradeoff, as a gauge of credibility, and as a stand-in for technology. Risk has also appeared as a register for politicized dangers, as a reflection of moral defect, and as the inevitable idiom of the next stage of modernity.

These images, in turn, are tied to more fundamental disagreements over knowledge and truth. Some experts contend, for example, that risk exists as an objective property of physical systems. Others find only the harm it implies to be "real" in this sense, while "risk" itself is bound up with assumptions about consequences and accountability. Hence, it is socially constructed and culturally mediated, rather than brute fact. Still others find that, while risk may be real, what matters is how it is perceived and the way these perceptions are formed and changed. A conceptual history of "risk," then, would likely reveal as much about our professional disputes over method and premises as about our environmental and regulatory politics. My attempt here is to offer a stylized version of this history.

As a preliminary step, however, it is important to put some distance between understanding "risk" as the officially sanctioned metric for environmental problems (National Research Council 1994) and "risk" as a contestable concept (Connolly 1993). The former notion serves as the axis for a host of technical issues and filters down into the vernacular of environmental politics as generic threats to health and safety. While the appeal is cognitive, the apprehension is ultimately viceral: risk counts as death and disability. As a result, this notion is easily reified as a noxious attribute present in varying amounts in different locales and environmental media. Dramatic increases in risk amounts, signal deteriorating environmental quality. As they accumulate, sustainability of the environment itself comes into question, further escalating the threat. This is the basic narrative that rationalizes clean air and clean water statutes as risk reduction strategies. It is not, however, the only narrative, even if it appears to be, nor is it one that brooks heterodoxy.

In contrast, if risk is viewed as a contestable concept, the presuppositions of risk claims move into focus, and with them, a variety of narratives linking sentiments of safety and danger to broader conceptions of sustainability and collective action. Risks, even when conveyed by environmental media, may relate more to the sustainability of a way of life or of trusted institutions than to ecological integrity (Clarke and Short 1993). Under these circumstances, the rationales for government activity and the strategies for protection may be quite different. In their exclusion from the dominant narrative on environmental policy, these alternative images of risk may help to expose its weaknesses and blind spots.

The narrative to follow advances an interpretation of certain central ideas about risk, organized around three themes—science, modernity, and liberalism—and arrayed in a developmental sequence that unfolds over the last three decades. This approach steers clear of chronologies and lengthy expositions of sentinel works; the movement of ideas about risk appears neither linear nor cumulative. Instead, ideas are found to coalesce in phases devoted principally to working a single theme. Because of the overlap among themes, however, none is ignored altogether. Nevertheless, the backgrounded themes in a given phase tend to be treated naively, with conventional wisdom standing in for careful scrutiny. The ideas in each successive phase, then, either reconstruct those dominant in a preceding phase, or shift emphasis to relatively neglected ones.

The first phase attempts to rectify an earlier, liberal construction of individual interests and expertise, and the second phase to reconstruct them, in a more fundamental way. The third phase attends to the rectification of science and its image, thought to have been mistreated in earlier phases. The fourth phase introduces elements from late modernity. Rather than taking arguments in the risk literature at face value, this thematic approach permits us to track the movement of ideas about risk, closer to their roots. The apparent complexity of this scheme yields simple patterns that highlight shifting assumptions and contradictions. Moreover, ideas from the most recent, fourth phase support new insights into current trends in both risk politics and regulatory science. The final section will speculate on their significance.

THE POST-WAR BENCHMARKS

The extensive developments in risk research in the '70s and '80s are part of an extended narrative on science and government that emerged after the Second World War. There was a rare consensus of sorts on the burgeoning relationship between technology and industrial growth, on the image and authority of science backing this relationship and on the contours and demands of social progress. Although this consensus would change fairly dramatically over the next decades, it represented a set of benchmarks against which future changes can be measured. In the case of risk research, new developments were largely framed relative to these benchmarks, even when committed to discarding them.

The logical reconstruction of science, under the aegis of positivism, for example, provided a unified view of scientific method and a justification for the privileged status of scientific knowledge. While resistance to positivism from pragmatists was unrelenting, the image of science it presented was remarkably consonant with the prevailing views of social progress and liberal politics. Although several of the subsequent phases in risk research offer challenges to scientific knowledge and its preeminence, none can avoid contending with the positivist image of science long after philosophers have abandoned it. Subsequent views about science must invariably pay homage to the positivist image, even in its rejection; no rectification of the elements of scientific practices can escape positivism as a benchmark for risk studies.

The essential elements at play in the risk literature's treatment of science are typically not exclusive to positivism but legacies of British empiricism and Cartesian anxieties about observer detachment and access to a neutral observational language (Bernstein, 1983). Still, the central position of positivism in the Post-War image of science, as well as its reputation for intellectual arrogance and professional superiority, make it the perfect foil. The key concepts are (1) the separation of facts from values and, (2) a procedural concept of objectivity that rests on the maintenance of undistorted observation and strict control over sources of bias, including one's own predispositions. Fact-value separation and objectivity not only had a firm hold on Americans' image of science, it insured that the 'factual' would be a defining feature of scientific reasoning, valorizing science's jurisdiction. The factual side of the separation established a territorial claim for the definitive authority of science relative to other nonscientific claimants. The valuative was largely left to liberalism to dictate.

Although the post-war foundation of liberalism represented a complex mixture of Lockean individualism and New Deal Progressivism, the elements most involved in the risk literature typically drew from one side of a pair of binary oppositions, not coincidentally, the same side favored by benchmark views of science and modernity. The central opposition of relevance to our discussion separates expertise from interest. The individual, consistent with liberal premises, "self-contained and self-sustaining" is an autonomous actor whose actions are based on knowledge of two kinds: of the self and of external objects (Arblaster 1984). Self-knowledge reflects desires and wants and clarifies the motives to satisfy them in the form of preferences. Knowledge of the external world provides the means for satisfying these self-defined interests. The efficient choice of means to advance one's interests serves as a universal standard for behavior, defined as rational. Since knowledge of material objects falls within the domain of science, there is institutional support for this kind of knowledge. Its extension to means and their proper ordering also finds support in the form of technical expertise. Knowledge of one's interests, however, remains idiosyncratic and intuitive; it is thought to admit neither scientific nor rational treatment. In other words, interests, wants and motives serve as the raw materials of rationality but not their proper object. Similarly in liberal moral theory, interests are the givens upon which moral calculations operate. Values encompass the interests themselves and are regarded as personal, subjective and reflected in emotional rather than cognitive attachments, a matter of private choice.

This conception of the self and its interests support a market-like model of politics, with competitive pursuit of interest as its motive force. Although accommodations may occur, they are generally intended to mediate existing interests rather than alter them. Outcomes are expressed as allocations of valued things to the most able competitors. The only normative challenges admitted are over distributional issues—unfair exclusion of certain interests from the process of its rewards. Generalizing this model from individuals to groups and adding a central arena for contesting interests yields the familiar profile of interest-group pluralism.

Governance in a liberal state must augment this notion of interest-based politics in ways that not only maintain public support but also mitigate social and economic conflict. The chosen route reflects a commitment in the U.S. to economic expansion and macro-economic stabilization. The bureaucratic burden of actualizing this commitment, together with maintaining an arms race, gave new life to the scientific management doctrines built around efficiency, and pioneered decades earlier. Technical expertise in administration would displace politics; it would be neutral with respect to interests, highly specialized in its functioning, and formally rational in its decision making. Although this separation between politics and administration was difficult to maintain in practice and was occasionally disavowed, it provided a powerful ideal that continues to exert its influence on ideas about governance outside of its original focus. Esteem for expertise and the deprecation of politics is not an uncommon subtext in the contemporary risk literature, four decades later.

The third theme supporting a post-war benchmark for risk studies is a conception of modernity that complements and reinforces the binary oppositions advanced in the images of science and liberal government. Social progress and improvements in well-being, material and otherwise, are linked to economic growth, and the driving force behind this growth is thought to be science and technology. Some critical commentary from this era find technology and its instrumental forms of rationality to represent a new form of modern consciousness that has replaced the class consciousness of nineteenth century industrialization.

An attachment to modernity as progress based on technology has several implications. First, technological development embodies aspirations for the future; our decisions, investments, and support, then tends to be anticipatory. When developments are not salutary or present unanticipated problems, these are largely side-effects, remediable either through more development, a technical fix, or through better anticipation. Risk has a negative connotation not only as a side effect detracting from further development, but also as a failure in anticipation due to a lack of proper knowledge. Risk, then, becomes a problem to be solved through better prediction and control, that is, through better science and more technology. With unquestioned commitment to progress as the backdrop, matters of prediction and control fell within the domain of science, to be accommodated free of values and implemented by experts insulated from the pressures of political interests. Side effects that are political must either be depoliticized for treatment as technical problems or sequestered for consideration by nonexperts on extra-scientific grounds. This conception of modernity cedes a rather large jurisdiction over to scientific authority and technical modes of reasoning, and to modern illusions of choice and control.

While much of the writing on risk throughout the 1960s involves one or another of these three themes and builds on the post-war consensus surrounding it, several benchmark pieces by Starr, Whipple, Otway and others build on all three (Shrader-Freckette 1985). The conception of modernity they employ hinges on technology-based social progress that is linked to the economic prosperity of advanced industrial societies. Here, the prevailing economic order and its trajectory are taken to reflect the adaptive and self-correcting character of technology, along with an implicit consensus that inhibits dissent and value-based challenges. Risk itself appears as a calculable side effect of progress amenable to objective modeling and estimation; its proper control follows the efficiency-based logic of technical rationality. The intrusion of nonexperts is successfully resisted by deprecating their motives as opportunistic, or assailing their fears as irrational and unfounded. The binary oppositions are given full play in establishing and policing large areas of professional authority at the occasionally jagged interface between government and industry. Each successive round of risk studies will question the character or the import of these oppositions and finally will contest this view of modernity itself. None, however, will be able to define its own position without clear reference to the benchmark pieces as responsible for first consolidating the binary oppositions and an ethos of modernity into a professional ideology.

PHASE I—RECTIFYING INTERESTS

The benchmark claims that distinguished the risk profession in the 1960s not only embraced binary oppositions but typically took sides.

Objective access to the facts was not only distinct from subjective construction of values, it was deemed superior. In the case of expertise and interests, the privileging of expertise was accompanied by arguments to extend its reach. Technical rationality, in other words, was not only an enlightened basis for directing industry, it suited government as well; messy conflicts over interests could be reframed in technical terms and treated systematically. The result would be more "rational" social choices (Fischer 1990). In terms of risk, this meant joining quantitative assessment to determinations of acceptability. To the extent that public views had some bearing on acceptability, these could be inferred from prevailing patterns of behavior and treated as a constraint on technical judgment regarding acceptability.

The first phase of reconstruction began in the early 1970s, initiated by a group of empirical researchers intent on renegotiating the boundary between expertise and interest in the face of public distrust (see Fischhoff et al. 1981). The task was twofold. First, the nonexpert public's view of risk had to be characterized in terms that made it appear less irrational and capricious. To be credible to the profession, this had to be done in a scientific idiom that sought predictability and ultimately, mitigation. Secondly, this systematized view would be promoted as a complement to, rather than a substitute for, the technical depiction of risk. What emerged was a model of public judgment that incorporated cognitive and noncognitive factors as internal psychological constraints impinging upon risk determinations. Most judgment was still considered inaccurate relative to technical renderings, but it could at least be predicted based on certain external features of the risk's source (Slovic et al. 1979). While the public was thought to be far from objective in its view of risk, there were grounds for its judgment that could be identified in ways that would make public involvement in determinations of risk acceptability more reasonable and less inappropriate.

Much of the literature in this phase of reconstruction has its roots in one of two families of preference models developed principally at the University of Michigan in the 1950s. One family is based on the efforts of a few behavioralists, most notably, Ward Edwards and Jacob Marschak, to subject the postulates of normative decision theory to empirical test. These early studies led to empirically based notions of probability encoding and to the characterization of biases in judging uncertain prospects. The second family sprang from psychophysical studies of preference structure. The emphasis in this research was upon understanding properties, such as consistency and dimensionality, and in perfecting measurement tools. This experience supported studies of information integration, on the one hand, and survey methods for quantifying social judgment, on the other. While softening the condescending treatment of public judgments about risk at the hands of technical experts, these studies did not exactly build a case for parity either.

They did demonstrate, however, that idiosyncratic interests could be redefined as "facts" and subjected to scientific scrutiny. From this, a set of universalizing statements could be drawn, making these interests more consistent with the technical framing of risk problems. The price for this redefinition, in terms of the integrity of the public's contribution, was rather high. The emphasis on universal claims about "psychological factors" to support predictability treated variability around these claims as error. Consistent with the reductionist roots of these studies, and their reliance on instrumental calculations as the defining feature of judgment, the role of context and any deliberative features of preference formation were excluded. In other words, the liberal conception of the atomistic, self-regarding individual making tradeoffs was preserved intact and along with it, the pluralist notion of competing aggregates of like-minded interests. Although public skepticism over technical depictions and assessments of risk could now be accommodated and afforded some regard by the professional community, the political and moral dynamics of public opposition to expert authority over risk matters was no better understood. Public acceptability was a professionally legitimate, subjective factor to be reckoned with, but needed to be kept clearly separate from the technical details of objective assessment. In short, the binary oppositions of facts against values and expertise against interests were reinforced rather than revoked, leaving mostly conceptual and empirical refinements in the public's image. In so doing, however, the matter of acceptability—framed now as public perception—fell under the public's purview and earned them a role in risk analysis.

PHASE II—THE RECONSTRUCTION OF BINARY OPPOSITIONS

The next round of work represents a fundamental rejection of the benchmark studies and their reliance on binary oppositions. The focus remains on developing a plausible account of public sentiments regarding risk. Yet, the tidy separation of facts from values and expertise from interests was claimed to be not only untenable in practice, but conceptually flawed, surviving largely by virtue of its support for prevailing patterns of professional authority (Wynne 1987).

Accordingly, the challenge posed in this phase operated on two levels. First, the components of the binary oppositions were carefully merged. Facts appear as value-laden, not in the sense of being contaminated or distorted by values brought in from the outside, but in a constitutive sense. Facts are redefined as socially and historically contingent and thus culturally mediated (Jasanoff 1991). Given this, there can be no fully detached, neutral observation, no universal and context-free forms of reasoning, and no privileged access to brute facts. Similarly, expertise becomes suffused with interests; technical knowledge is not so much biased by extra-scientific factors, such as loyalty and greed, as it represents a given bias in itself (Schwarz and Thompson 1990). On a second level, there was a reflexive focus on the standing and status of the analysts and professionals themselves. What disadvantages would accrue from rejections of the binary opposition and how would this affect professional authority (Mayo 1991)?

In contrast to the psychological flavor of the first phase, this second phase is predominantly sociological. Further, depending upon the tradition this work draws upon, it can appear in weak or strong forms. The weak form begins with a basic tenet of Schutzian phenomology, that there are multiple realities rather than objective and subjective ones, and that each is constituted and reproduced through social practices and institutional arrangements. The strong form adds the converse of this relationship; multiple realities and their associated symbolic systems of meaning also shape social practices and institutional forms (Douglas and Wildavsky 1982). Although both forms have been identified as "social constructionism", the weak form tends to generate more conventional structuralist explanations, while the strong form attends more closely to cultural norms, values and forms of discourse.

Weak-form explanations for public concern rely heavily on social factors in a particular context. In contrast to the psychological models in the first phase, these accounts attribute variation in individual responses to the workings of institutional settings, economic conditions and social relations (see Johnson and Covello 1987). With the suspension of the fact-value dichotomy, however, the weak-form approach can easily be extended to account for elite responses to risk by contextualizing them as well. Interpretations of risk evidence, for example, can be influenced by the dynamics of the regulatory process and its institutional setting (Jasanoff 1991). Much of the third phase of work described in the next section is intended to revise this account of disagreements among scientific claims by rectifying the fact-value dichotomy rather than suspending it. Contextual factors will once again be reduced to the cognitive and noncognitive attributes of individuals. The principal legacy of the weak form will be the admission in the third phase that extra-scientific factors often intrude upon scientific judgment and that disagreements are not exclusively a function of incomplete information. More information, then, is not a panacea for controversies over risk (Hollander 1991).

Despite its departures from Phase I work, the weak form of constructionism retains the benchmark depiction of modernity and the liberal view of interest-based politics. Interests could well be grounded in a particular social and economic setting and rationalized as the product of social forces operating therein. They stand as a proxy for the valued features of one's setting. Politics is about the protection and, perhaps extension, of these features. Clearly, political stances differ according to predispositions formed in a given context. Here, the interpretation of scientific evidence can easily be used strategically to bolster one's advantage. The result is an alignment of political positions around the familiar dichotomy of "for or against", with winners and losers determined by a division of benefits and burdens. The association of risk with the economic processes of large-scale production units, reflecting the benchmark view of modernity, brings most of the disputes over risk that are cast along these political lines, down to conflicts over material advantage. The prospects of peremptory moral claims, other than property rights, or of an active search for a general interest, other than through aggregation, are largely precluded.

The strong form of constructionism recasts the exogenous role of context, portrayed by the weak form as social setting and institutional arrangements, as an interactive one. Context not only sustains but is shaped by the symbolic and cognitive elements of culture, including shared values, beliefs and social practices (Douglas 1990). Together, these constitute self-sustaining ways of life, each with its own distinctive forms of rationality and selective certainties. Responses to risk and views about the technologies that generate it are contingent upon how a given technology and its risks relate to a particular way of life. Acceptability of risk, from this perspective, is neither a psychological phenomenon, nor determined by contextual factors surrounding the source. Rather, it is conditioned by compatibility; how well does this risk contribute to rationalizing, justifying or promoting one's preferred way of life (Schwarz and Thompson 1990)? Accordingly, worries about risks relate only incidentally to incomplete knowledge or to the quality of risk assessment. The issue of whether the formal assessment of risk can or should be separated from its acceptability simply dissolves.

The strong-form owes a great deal to the cultural theorying of Douglas, who in turn is heavily indebted to Durkheim. For Douglas, culture embodies a pattern of mutual accountability, along with collective agreement on the means of its enforcement. Accountability is maintained, and the solidarity of the community assured, by designating certain beliefs and practices as permissible and others as sanctioned (Marcus and Fischer 1986). These moral prescriptions, with their attendant notions of blame and attribution, are inculcated in the patterns of social organization best adapted to enforcing them. In these terms, knowledge and risk are not so much socially constructed as culturally and morally redefined in ways that protect the solidarity and authenticity of the group (Thompson et al. 1990). The physical dangers posed by a given risk are not ignored or dismissed as fiction; they are linked morally to some disapproved behavior and viewed culturally in terms of their threat to valued institutions (Douglas 1991).

The binary oppositions of fact-value and expert-interests may possibly endure within the strong form, but only relative to a particular scheme of accountability, not across them. Both the credibility of facts and the authority of expertise will vary widely from one type of culture to another. For example, hierarchical cultures will demand specialized knowledge, privilege claims of objectivity and rely on centralized direction; egalitarian cultures will do just the opposite (Thompson et al. 1990).

In contrast to the cultural relativist, only four cultural schemes are viewed by Douglas as socially viable. Later writers expand the number of viable schemes to five or more and abandon the label, 'cultural types', for socio-cognitive orientations, in part, to deflect charges of cultural relativism (Schwarz and Thompson 1990). Consistent with the boundary preserving function of cultural biases, each orientation reinforces its identity and justifications in large measure through shared criticism of what goes on outside. Rival orientations effectively sustain one another. Politics in this milieu of bounded pluralism takes the form of relatively stable tensions among contradictory certainties. Rather than reverting to the benchmark model of competitive opportunism, the strong form involves the Deweyan notion that all five schemes have complementary roles to play in societal development. In lieu of arbitrarily sanctioning one scheme over the others, there is a structured opportunity for interplay among the schemes along the lines of the Dutch concept of 'sociale kaart' (Schwarz and Thompson 1990). Here, politics begins with a social map of contending claims and certainties regarding technology, intended to promote insight as well as accommodation.

PHASE III—RECTIFYING FACTS AND EXPERTISE

The work in this phase invariably begins with an indictment of the strong form of constructionism. Changes of relativism, social reductionism, and misapprehension of science serve as a starting point for a return to benchmark claims in order to rectify them properly (Mayo 1991). Although much of this work is compatible with the weak form of constructionism, there is a sense that the weak form went too far in emphasizing the part played by extra-scientific considerations in scientific disagreements over risk. Further, the weak form's grounding of risk acceptability in a given context extends too easily to the fashioning of formal risk assessments (Shrader-Frechette 1991). The answer can be found in rectifying the binary opposition posed by the benchmark view of science to reflect post-positivist understandings of how facts relate to values. Similarly, to preempt the intimation of politically-biased assessment, these accounts pay special attention to the matter of resolving scientific disputes over evidence in ways that preserve the authority of technical expertise (Hollander 1991).

The origins of the key ideas behind the rectification offered in this phase can be found in Popper's critical rationalism and the pre-constructionist, social studies of science, exemplified by Merton. For the Popperian, facts exist in the external world but cannot be known except in partial and approximate ways. While scientists may strive toward accurate observations, they are flawed observers, whose accounts are both enabled and distorted by values. Objectivity, from this vantage point, is not achieved by being value-free, an impossibility, but by subjecting one's views to refutations by others (see Popper 1972). Note the appeal of this view for the recovery of objectivity from the skepticism of the constructionists. Scientific disagreement is transformed from vice to virtue. Disagreement need no longer imply predisposing biases or partisanship; it is instead a central feature of the proper validation of scientific knowledge. Further, the intensity of the disagreement need not vary with the level of uncertainty or the tentativeness of the observations. There is no impetus for substituting value-based certainties for factual uncertainty, since the scientific process will eventually sort these out. The contribution from Merton is to specify a limited role for extra-scientific factors; they are permitted to account exclusively for errors and lapses in scientific judgment (Merton 1973).

By this point, the need to separate quantitative risk assessment from determinations of acceptability, loses its urgency and rationale. Science need not be isolated to protect its integrity. Public views on acceptability should have little influence on scientific judgment. And yet, scientific judgment should influence public views. Separation should be avoided, not because it is a rouse as the constructionists would have it, but because technical expertise is critical to collective judgment. The preoccupation of the prior two phases with explaining public reactions to risk comes from them having ignored the contribution of credible, authoritative evidence to securing agreements. Hence, the problem that remains is how to assure acceptable evidence in the face of probative disagreement. Liberalism provides the necessary guidance.

Technical disputes can be resolved in a juridical process, whose outcome then serves as a basis for adjudicating among competing views of acceptability (Jasanoff 1990). The public is several steps removed from these processes and is left to pressure elective officials. These officials determine acceptability assisted by scientific determinations of risk magnitude and consequences. This recapitulates the benchmark view of science free of the dichotomies that forced an artificial separation between assessment and acceptability. Nonetheless, the partisan implications of separating assessment and acceptability are not so easily overcome. Anti-regulatory sentiment within EPA following Ronald Reagan's election led to the conflation, at least by political appointees, of risk assessment with risk management. Formal separation was then called for by the NRC (National Academy of Sciences 1983). By the late 1980s scientific evidence appeared to some in the risk research community to be playing less and less of a role. The case in this phase for bringing such evidence to bear systematically on management issues can be viewed, in part, as an effort to regain lost ground for expertise in risk matters.

PHASE IV—RECONSTRUCTING MODERNITY

In contrast to the compatibility between Phase III work and some elements of weak-form constructionism, the work in this phase finds some parallels with the strong form of Phase II, but rejects most of the Phase III effort to rectify benchmark positions. The pattern of development, across these phases of risk studies if one can be imputed, is not cumulative so much as dialectical. Phase IV work not only finds little use in the prior phases, it culminates in a fundamental reconstruction of the three themes common to them. Modernity, typically backgrounded in earlier phases, becomes the primary focus; the recapitulation of science and liberalism, then, is derived from presuppositions about late modernity rather than from the binary oppositions posited as the benchmark of risk studies.

Conceptions of modernity that link technological development to economic growth and social progress rely on a mid-twentieth century view of industrial society. Production and distribution are accomplished through local and regional markets, and macroeconomic intervention by a central government is capable of stabilizing and perhaps enhancing growth. As mentioned earlier, this scenario typically depicts risk as a cost of doing business, or, at worst, as a side effect of progress in need of mitigation. Once we acknowledge the transition of the last few decades to a globalized economy of multinational production units, risk escalates from occasional side effect to potential ecological disaster. At the same time, the capacity for mitigation by any particular government action diminishes. Nonetheless, centralized efforts may be redoubled along lines that jeopardize the legitimacy of government action. Rulemaking proliferates and becomes more formalized. The administrative apparatus depends increasingly on highly specialized expertise and its deliberations become less accessible or accountable to the public. Meanwhile, risks are being produced and distributed throughout the society the way wealth used to be, threatening the credibility of the institutions that generate them. As a result, many of the bonds between individuals and social structures are weakened and broken, clearing the way for local opposition and new forms of social organization on the left and right.

This, in brief, is the scenario for Beck's risk society (1992), the successor to the industrial society with its normative attachment to progress. For Beck, the normative element behind social development is not progress itself, but reflexivity. Reflexivity entails fundamental questioning of the forms of power and social control implicated in contemporary conflicts over risks. Such questioning serves as a basis for the formation of less oppressive social and economic relationships and as a means of repairing credibility and trust. The binary oppositions of fact-value and expertise-interests are antithetical to reflexivity, since their core function is to privilege instrumental and reductionist forms of knowledge and establish the premises for legitimating their dominance. Experts not only deal in facts, they are able to frame issues in ways that make nonexperts dependent upon them. As the burden of risk increases, however, loss of security and mistrust grows, and along with it, resistance to remote technical idioms and their inflexibility. One paradox of the fact-value dichotomy in this context is that having been responsible for the creation of many of the manmade sources of risk, experts managed to shift responsibility for risk mitigation away from their industrial origins to the government and indirectly to the public; once values become a corrective for the untoward outcomes of technology, the boundary between them and facts—upon which sciences' authority depended—could no longer be maintained or accorded societal deference.

The opposition between expertise and interests is treated much the same as in the strong form of constructionism. Deliberation over risk, in this instance, should support reflexive learning by experts and regulators through the admission of different discourses and recognition of contending certainties and fundamental biases. This is not a plea, however, for a symbolic form of politically inclusive multiculturalism applied to risk disputes; rather, it aspires to dislodge technical rationality in favor of communicative rationality, consistent with Habermas' criteria for uncoerced and undistorted public argument (Habermas 1979). While formal methods of risk assessment will continue to have a role to play, their premises and concepts will no longer frame the conversation. Once the authority of science in risk matters is shaken and the larger social consensus on growth and progress dissipates, instrumental values, such as efficiency, lose their rationale. Deliberation, then, will need to reestablish a rationale, perhaps on post-material grounds.

CONCLUSION

Our conception of risk has changed as the parameters of risk studies have shifted of the last decades. A summary of the shifts arranged in the phases described above appears in Table 2.1. Perhaps the most striking aspect of this display is the ongoing level of contention within the field as conveyed by successive efforts to undo the work of an earlier phase. While the relative strengths and weaknesses have been touched upon in analytical and normative terms, the question remains, "which construction is the more adequate or appropriate?" Since all but the last phase have marshalled cases that may be used to judge their adequacy, it might be useful to speculate on the implications of the last phase for our understanding of recent trends in risk disputes.

Consider first, how the dynamic of reflexivity might be altering the political landscape of risk disputes. The dichotomous view of pro and anti-regulatory stakeholders and decision makers no longer captives oppositional sentiment. The political struggle to control risk in the U.S. has until recently been waged on two fronts—in the courts and through regulatory rulemaking. The legal formalism of judicial

Table 2.1. Thematic Changes in the Study and Understanding of Social Risk

Phases	*Science*	*Liberalism*	*Modernity*
		Reference Themes	
Benchmark Studies [1960s–1990s] [e.g., Starr '69]	Fact-Value Opposition	Expertise-Interests Opposition	Tech. Dev. Economic Growth-Social Progress
Phase I Psychometric Studies [1970s] [e.g., Fischhoff '81]	Benchmark Assumed	Rectify Interests	Benchmark Assumed
Phase II A. Weak 'Social' Constructionism [e.g., Johnson & Covello '87]	Rectify Values	Relativize Interests	Benchmark Assumed
B. Strong 'Cultural' Constructionism [e.g., Schwarz & Thompson '90]	Relativize Facts	Relativize Expertise	Benchmark Assumed
Phase III Social Reconstruction of Risk Science [late 1980s] [e.g., Mayo & Hollander '91]	Rectify Facts	Rectify Expertise	Benchmark Assumed
Phase IV Post-Industrial Development Studies [1980s–1990s] [e.g., Beck '93]	Benchmark Rejected	Relativize Expertise	Benchmark Replaced

proceedings and the increasingly technocratic character of regulatory decisions not only raise their costs to society but make them inaccessible and unresponsive to the public in the face of greater threats to safety. Accordingly, opposition has emerged on both the left and right to the process itself rather than to a given policy. Reflexivity, in this instance, generates challenges to the authority of technical expertise, the credibility of the evidence it produces, and the legitimacy of the modes of social control that it deploys. Consistent with the emancipatory potential of reflexivity, new social forms result.

The most intriguing forms to emerge in risk disputes might best be categorized as micro-corporatist (Cawson 1986; Williamson 1989). A limited number of groups are franchised by a responsible agency to participate in deliberations that extend from formulation issues to implementation. The most familiar incipient form is multiple stakeholder negotiation (Leiss and Chociolko 1994). While clearly distant from Beck's notions of reflexive learning, these forms represent serious inroads into the technocratic control of risk policies. For the right, they promise bargaining-based flexibility and locally adapted solutions. For the left, there is the prospect of enhancing participation and local control while building accountability.

In either case, the dominance of regulatory matters by centralized hierarchies, federal or corporate, is likely to give way to a proliferation of locally controlled forms intent on renewing trust and credibility. In this context, claims of efficiency and rationality, perhaps the idiom of choice in large-scale organizations, will no longer be decisive. Instead, there will be several idioms, some framed by the language of sustainability, and others by environmental justice, and perhaps personal security. Clearly, risks will continue to be controlled by money and by a central administration apparatus, but questions of risk acceptability will extend beyond their current focus on scientific assessments to encompass the acceptability of the risk-controlling institution themselves. While the image of risk advanced in Phase III reinforces the dominant narrative of risk reduction and Federal environmental regulation, the Phase IV image offers a counter-narrative of local construction and plural forms of sustainability, rather than a replacement.

The irony for environmental risk studies is that the phases signalling the greatest departures from the benchmark position of the '60s, also seem to pose the greatest threat to whatever mode of risk inquiry happens to be dominant at the time. Dominance may well be conferred through proper deference to the benchmark position. As we saw with the rectification undertaken in Phase III, the strong constructionists provoked a backlash of sorts, drawing fire from defensive efforts to protect the authority of risk science against possible competitors, equally certain of their knowledge. We can expect the Phase IV work to be ignored by those entrenched in the third Phase; that is, until events can no longer be accounted for exclusively as disputes over the acceptability of risk evidence or its technical parameters.

REFERENCES

Arblaster, Anthony. 1984. *The Rise and Decline of Western Liberalism*. New York, NY: B. Blackwell Inc.

Beck, Ulrich. 1993. *Risk Society*, translated by Mark Ritter. Newbury Park, CA: Sage Publications, Inc.

Bernstein, Richard. 1983. *Beyond Objectivism and Relativism*. Philadelphia, PA: University of Pennsylvania Press.

Cawson, Alan. 1986. *Corporatism and Political Theory*. New York, NY: B. Blackwell Inc.

Clarke, Lee, and James Short. 1993. "Social Organization and Risk: Some Current Controversies." *Annual Review of Sociology* 19: 375–99.

Connolly, William. 1994. *The Terms of Political Discourse*. 3rd edition. Princeton, NJ: Princeton University Press.

Douglas, Mary. 1970. *Natural Symbols*. New York, NY: Pantheon Books.

Douglas, Mary, and Aaron Wildavsky. 1982. *Risk and Culture*. Berkeley, CA: University of California Press.

Douglas, Mary. 1990. "Risk As A Forensic Resource." *Daedalus* 119: 1–16.

Fischer, Frank. 1990. *Technocracy and the Politics of Expertise*. Newbury Park, CA: Sage Publications, Inc.

Fischhoff, B., S. Lichtenstein, P. Slovic, S. Derby, and R. Keeney. 1981. *Acceptable Risk*. New York, NY: Cambridge University Press.

Habermas, Jurgen. 1979. *Communication and the Evolution of Society*, translated by Thomas McCarthy. Boston, MA: Beacon Press.

Hollander, Rachelle. 1991. "Expert Claims and Social Decisions." In *Acceptable Evidence*, eds. Deborah Mayo and Rachelle Hollander. New York, NY: Oxford University Press.

Jasanoff, Shelia. 1990. *The Fifth Branch: Science Advisors As Policymakers*. Cambridge, MA: Harvard University Press.

Jasanoff, Sheila. 1991. "Acceptable Evidence in a Pluralist Society." In *Acceptable Evidence*, eds. Deborah Mayo and Rachelle Hollander. New York, NY: Oxford University Press.

Johnson, B., and V. Covello, eds. 1987. *The Social and Cultural Construction of Risk*. Norwell, MA: Kluwer Academic Publishers.

Leiss, William, and Christina Chociolko. 1994. *Risk and Responsibility*. Montreal: McGill-Queen's University Press.

Marcus, George, and Michael Fischer. 1986. *Anthropology As Cultural Critique*. Chicago, IL: University of Chicago Press.

Mayo, Deborah, and Rachelle Hollander, eds. 1991. *Acceptable Evidence*. New York, NY: Oxford University Press.

Mayo, Deborah. 1991. "Sociological Versus Metascientific Views of Risk Assessment." In *Acceptable Evidence*, eds. Deborah Mayo and Rachelle Hollander. New York, NY: Oxford University Press.

Merton, Robert. 1973. *The Sociology of Science*. Chicago, IL: University of Chicago Press.

National Research Council. 1983. *Risk Assessment and the Federal Government*. Washington, DC: National Academy Press.

National Research Council. 1994. *Science and Judgment in Risk Assessment*. Washington, DC: National Academy Press.

Popper, Karl. 1992. *Objective Knowledge*. New York, NY: Oxford University Press.

Schwarz, Michael, and Michael Thompson. 1990. *Divided We Stand: Redefining Politics, Technology and Social Choice*. Philadelphia, PA: University of Pennsylvania Press.

Shrader-Frechette, Kristin. 1985. *Risk Analysis and Scientific Method*. Hingham, MA: Kluwer Academic Publishers.

Shrader-Frechette, Kristin. 1991. "Reductionist Approaches to Risk." In *Acceptable Evidence*, eds. Deborah Mayo and Rachelle Hollander. New York, NY: Oxford University Press.

Slovic, Paul, Sarah Lichtenstein and Banch Fischhoff. 1979. "Images of Disaster: Perception and Acceptance of Risks from Nuclear Power." In *Energy Risk Management*, eds. G. Goodman and W. Rowe. New York, NY: Academy Press.

Starr, Chauncy. 1969. "Social Benefit Versus Technical Risk." *Science* 165: 1232–1238

Thompson, Michael, Richard Ellis, and Aaron Wildavsky. 1990. *Cultural Theory*. Boulder, CO: Westview Press.

Williamson, Peter. 1989. *Corporatism in Perspective*. Newbury Park, CA: Sage Publications, Inc.

Wynne, B. 1987. *Risk Management and Hazardous Waste: Implementation and the Dialectics of Credibility*. London: Springer.

SECTION TWO

Alternative Regulatory Approaches

3 Market Incentives in Air Pollution Control

GARY BRYNER

Market-based approaches to environmental regulation are an indispensable part of the effort to move to more environmentally sustainable societies. Economic instruments in regulation offer a number of important potential advantages, particularly in helping to streamline bureaucratic structures and procedures and reduce the cost of achieving environmental goals. However, there are significant limitations in moving towards market-based regulatory instruments. Their interaction with other kinds of regulatory approaches, as required by current laws, raises a myriad of questions about how they can work. These pragmatic issues challenge many of the benefits they appear to bring to environmental regulation. This chapter examines the advantages of market-based approaches in environmental regulation as well as some of their limitations. Illustrations are drawn from efforts to control air pollution, but the assessment is relevant to other environmental protection policies as well.

Economic instruments are increasingly heralded as the most efficient and effective mechanism for accomplishing environmental and other regulatory goals of government. While they only address some of the criticisms leveled at environmental regulation, their advantages are compelling. The costs of pollution control are reduced if sources are permitted to find the most cost efficient way of reducing emissions. Economic incentives are essential in harnessing self-interest to promote the common good. They are also preferable to more traditional approaches because they promote flexibility and freedom of choice, minimize the need for coercion, and reduce overreliance on centralized bureaucratic procedures that sometimes defy common sense. Putting a price on pollution can require firms to pay the full or true costs of what they produce, including the costs imposed on the public of damage to health or property resulting from pollution.

However, there are a number of concerns with market-like approaches to regulation. The emphasis on buying and selling permits to pollute reduces the powerful moral and symbolic appeal of pollution control. Environmental regulation is no longer seen as a moral imperative in protecting human health, and, in particular, protecting innocent third parties who suffer few of the benefits of pollution-producing activity and most of the burdens, but simply another cost of doing business. One of the most serious problems is distributive: environmental quality will improve for some people, since some sources are cheaper to clean up than others. For those who reside near facilities that are more expensive to clean up, however, emissions might increase.

Perhaps most serious, from the perspective of realizing sustainable economic and social activity, is the challenge of ensuring that economic instruments lead to internalizing more of the costs of producing the goods and services we consume. Emissions trading programs, the most prominent form of market incentives applied to environmental regulation, fall short in ensuring that true costs are reflected in prices charged. However, they can help prepare the way for emissions taxes and fees, by providing a framework on which fundamental reforms can be built, as well as by reshaping expectations towards more effective means of regulating pollution.

This chapter begins with a review of some of the general criticisms aimed at environmental regulation, reviews the arguments made for expanding the use of market instruments in environmental regulation, and concludes with an examination of some of the problems that have been encountered in making this policy shift and the challenges market instruments pose in environmental policy making.

CRITICISMS OF ENVIRONMENTAL REGULATION AND THE PROMISE OF MARKET INSTRUMENTS

While environmental statutes have evolved significantly over the past two decades, several criticisms have recurred about the administrative and bureaucratic shortcomings in the implementation of environmental laws, the means or regulatory approaches used to achieve environmental goals, the goals themselves, regulation in general, and the way environmental regulation impacts other policy efforts.[1] For decades, economists have criticized the means by which the EPA and other agencies pursue environmental goals, particularly the inefficiency that results from national standards imposed on all sources, regardless of local conditions and environmental needs. The Office of Management and Budget (OMB) and other executive branch agencies, beginning with the Nixon administration, have focused on the costs of compliance with regulations and their impact on economic activity. Tension between the EPA and the White House continues in both Democratic and Republican administrations. By the early 1980s, the OMB began a concerted effort to push the EPA and other agencies to demonstrate that the benefits of proposed regulations outweighed their costs. All of these concerns have ultimately been fueled by the fear that regulation is too expensive, given the benefits it produces, and that the EPA and other agencies must find more cost-effective means to achieve the goals delegated to them. These concerns culminated in the House Republican "Contract with America" promise to roll back government regulation and bills passed in the first days of the 104th Congress to overhaul the regulatory process.[2] In contrast, environmentalists have urged the EPA to emphasize pollution prevention, rather than treatment, as well as encourage and even force fundamental changes in industrial processes and individual behavior in order to reduce damage from pollution (Commoner 1990).

INEFFICIENCY OF CONVENTIONAL ENVIRONMENTAL REGULATION

The debate begins with criticisms of the conventional approach to regulation—creating national standards applicable to major sources of pollution. Under this approach, the EPA issues national standards that usually take one of three forms: ambient standards that place limits on total concentrations of pollutants permitted; emission standards that limit what individual sources can emit; and design standards that require the use of particular pollution control equipment or production processes. These standards are then usually enforced by state regulatory officials.

This centralized approach to environmental regulation is inefficient, some argue, because it imposes nationwide standards on sources and problems that differ according to local conditions. It requires all relevant sources to comply even though the costs of compliance vary considerably across sources, and the benefits to be gained differ greatly.

It mandates control technologies that lock industries into existing equipment and processes, and fails to create incentives for new, cleaner, more efficient technologies. As a result, the cost-effectiveness of regulations varies considerably, raising concerns that some regulations are too expensive when compared with others. The EPA and states have been slow to find alternatives to this conventional (often called command-and-control) approach to regulation. In order to reduce discretion and insure that agencies are not blamed for doing any harm, elaborate, detailed regulations are issued that try to anticipate every possible problem. Instead, they only produce delay and increase costs, frustration, and hostility to government (Howard 1994). But Congress has also been reticent to mandate market instruments in the regulatory programs they create, and the prescriptiveness of environmental statutes places limits on the mechanisms by which the EPA is to pursue the environmental objectives.

Economists have long lamented the inefficiency of environmental and other regulations. Traditional complaints about the burdens regulations impose on industry have been joined by other criticisms that environmental regulation is simply too inefficient and expensive, and that more "efficient" regulatory strategies can replace current command-and-control approaches (Kneese and Schultze 1975). A study of the 1977 Clean Air Act charged that imposing technological controls on all new stationary sources was making policy "in an ecological vacuum—without a sober effort to define the costs and benefits of designing one or another technology into the plants of the future" (Ackerman and Hassler 1981, 12). Crandall argued that standards imposed on stationary sources "do not generate pollution reduction at the lowest possible cost" (1983, 3). Portney reviewed studies assessing the costs and benefits of the clean air regulation and concluded that while there was great uncertainty and tremendous range in the estimates of costs and benefits, there was little disagreement that it is possible to "substantially reduce the costs of meeting the nation's current air quality goals" (1990, 87).

THE ADVANTAGES OF MARKET INSTRUMENTS IN REGULATION

Economic incentives are increasingly heralded as the most efficient and effective mechanism for accomplishing environmental goals. If sources of pollution are permitted to find the cheapest way of reducing emissions, the costs of pollution control will be minimized. Incentives are championed as being essential to "harnessing the 'base' motive of material self-interest to promote the common good" (Schultze 1977, 18). It is simply not effective to condemn polluters as being immoral or selfish, their advocates argue; what is needed is clear incentives to encourage them to change their behavior, to ensure that they take actions that are consonant with the public good. Incentives are also preferable to traditional regulatory interventions, because they promote flexibility and freedom of choice and minimize the need for coercion. Putting a price on pollution encourages pollution control efforts up to the point where further controls would cost more than the value of the damage prevented. Revenue is generated that can be used to reimburse or prevent the adverse effects of pollution (Schelling 1983).

Both those who support and decry regulation may embrace the idea of making regulation more cost-effective. While there is little agreement over what environmental goals should be, once they are established, there is wide support for approaches to regulation that create market-based incentives. Changes in regulatory instruments will do little to alter the overall context in which environmental regulation takes place, or to redress concerns that environmental goals are misdirected. But, they can make some important contributions to environmental decisionmaking and the increased integration of economic and environmental considerations. Regulatory approaches that emphasize dissemination of information and enhance consumer choices, for example, can increase awareness and understanding of the environmental choices we face and engage a broader segment of the public in explicitly making those choices. Disclosure of information about pollution is one of the most powerful means available to reduce pollution.

Economic instruments may also foster support for environmental regulation. Advocates of increased regulation can find common ground with those who champion industry autonomy and flexibility. The debate over environmental goals is extremely contentious; some of that contentiousness can be softened by reducing the cost of achieving those goals. If economic instruments can be devised to achieve environmental goals at lower cost than conventional command and control regulation, they will become one of the most important developments in public policy and will play a major role in the move toward more sustainable societies.

There are several categories of market-like mechanisms that might be employed in environmental regulation: monetary incentives, including taxes, fees, subsidies, and tax incentives; government-created markets for trading emissions; deposit/refund systems that discourage disposal and encourage collection or recycle of pollution-producing materials; disclosure of information to consumers; environmental auditing and release to the public data on kinds and levels of emissions; and government procurement policies (National Commission on the Environment 1993, 21–44). The two most controversial instruments are pollution charges and emissions trading.

Pollution Charges

When using pollution charges, taxes are levied on emissions of pollutants or on input to activities producing pollutants. Polluters are charged a fee for each unit of pollution they emit.[3] In theory, the tax should be high enough to generate resources that could compensate for the environmental damage resulting from the emissions. Such taxes, sometimes called "Pigouvian" after their earliest proponent, Nicholas Pigou (1928), ensure that marginal private costs, plus the added tax, equals marginal social costs. Revenue could be used to pay for the medical costs of treating victims of air pollution, the damage to crops and buildings, the cost of monitoring and regulating air pollution, or other relevant efforts. A pollution tax or fee, if it is high enough, can provide a strong incentive for companies to reduce their emissions in whatever way is most efficient for them—closing down some operations, using cleaner fuels, investing in control technologies, changing work practices, and so on. It also provides a clear incentive for reducing emissions below permitted levels. Under the traditional approach to regulation, companies gain no economic advantage in emitting less pollution than is legally permitted them; under a pollution tax, they save money every time they reduce emissions. Pollution taxes operate like other cost factors in production and can be dealt with in a way that preserves the flexibility and autonomous decision making that are important to businesses. Agency officials are also given important incentives to enforce the law if pollution tax revenues remain with the agency. Companies that are complying with the law support strong enforcement efforts aimed at ensuring that their competitors also pay the required taxes (Stewart 1988).

In some cases, administration of the program can be simplified by imposing a tax on inputs or materials rather than effluents or emissions, since there may be fewer firms subject to the tax and monitoring may be simpler. A charge on final products might be used in areas where input or emission charges are not effective, or where environmental problems are primarily a function of consumer demand. This approach might create a more direct incentive for reduced consumption or a switch to less damaging products (Government of Canada 1992, 9). Emissions charges can also create significant incentives to reduce waste and save money. Such an approach requires careful monitoring and vigorous enforcement of requirements, but the revenues from the charges can finance these efforts.

It is difficult to make the calculations required to ensure that taxes added to marginal private costs equal marginal social costs, so that, as Pigou argued, all the costs of production are accounted for in the prices charged. An alternative approach is to tax the consumption of resources directly by shifting taxes away from labor and income and levy them on the resources that are consumed during production (Daly 1994, 6). In this way, the total costs of these resources can include at least a rough accounting for the costs of depleted resources and pollution produced. But even more difficult than making the economic calculations may be mobilizing sufficient political power to overcome industry opposition to pollution charges. Increased costs, industry warns, will make it difficult for domestic producers to compete with foreign firms not subject to emissions fees.

Emissions Trading

In emissions trading, polluters are allocated a limited number of allowances or units of emissions for release into the environment. These allowances, usually specified in operating permits, require a reduction in pollution. Companies can either make the changes necessary to stay within their limits, or they can buy allowances from others. Tradable emission permits can be traded, banked (i.e., saved for future use), or sold by polluting companies as long as limits on total emissions are not exceeded. The process is relatively straightforward: establish the ambient environmental quality goal—what maximum level of concentration of pollution is acceptable; determine the total number of units of emissions required to meet the ambient goal, usually expressed in pounds or tons of pollutant during a specified time period; allocate permits to polluters to emit specified units of pollutants by selling or auctioning them, or by simply distributing them freely; and enforce these limits by monitoring emissions from the regulated sources. Over time, total emissions can be reduced further by decreasing the number of allowances distributed to polluters (Hahn 1988, 174). Polluters have an incentive to reduce their emissions beyond the allowances given to them so that they can generate revenues through the sale of excess allowances.[4]

An important advantage of marketable permits is that less information about the production process is needed by regulatory agencies. Efforts are aimed at achieving environmental goals, not complying with procedures. The burden is redirected toward industry engineers to devise ways to reduce emissions efficiently. Companies cannot use the legal system to delay development and imposition of technology-based standards as usually happens. The key question becomes much simpler: did the company's emissions exceed levels provided in its permit? The regulatory agency tasks are still considerable: estimating how much pollution exists in an airshed, auctioning rights to pollute, permitting rights to be transferred, and monitoring and penalizing polluters who exceed limits. These are, overall, less demanding tasks than under the command and control approach to regulation.[5]

MARKET-BASED INITIATIVES IN AIR POLLUTION REGULATION

A number of market-based approaches to regulation are in place or are being discussed.[6] One important market-oriented innovation developed by the U.S. EPA and begun in 1974 was an emissions trading program that allowed companies to receive credit for emissions reductions in some areas for higher emissions elsewhere. Total emissions from each industry plant could be viewed as encapsulated within a large "bubble," rather than from individual smokestacks. Regulatory officials established maximum total allowable emissions and then left managers free to determine optimal emissions from individual sources.[7]

One of the most important innovations in the Clean Air Act of 1990 was the market-based incentive system to reduce acid rain-producing emissions from coal-fired power plants. The heart of the acid rain emissions trading system is the idea of a cap on total emissions that will, by the year 2010, result in a reduction of sulfur dioxide emissions of ten million tons from 1980 levels. The plan proceeds in two phases. In phase I, 110 plants in 21 midwestern and eastern states are given allowances in the law; an allowance is a permit to emit one ton of sulfur dioxide. In phase II, the number of sources included in the program is greatly expanded; the allowances for these sources are allocated by a formula that is based on the amount of fuel used during a base year period. The number of allowances will be capped at 8.95 million tons per year by 2010. Power plants are required to obtain permits indicating the number of allowances they possess. Plants that are able to control emissions below the levels allocated to them can save them for future use, or trade or sell their excess emission permits to others who exceed their allowance.[8]

A number of states have begun to develop plans for emissions trading programs designed to combat photochemical smog (Georgia Institute of Technology 1994). The Illinois Environmental Protection Agency (1993a), for example, concluded in a September 1993 report that market-based approaches to reducing ozone levels would be less expensive than conventional command and control regulation. Illinois also instituted a pilot program of buying and scrapping pre-1980 automobiles (Illinois EPA 1993b). The state purchases vehicles for between $600 and $1,000 and measures the tailpipe emissions and fuel evaporation before destroying them (*Clean Air Report* 1992a, T-9). The Northeast States for Coordinated Air Use Management, an air quality planning organization comprised of the eight northeastern states, has proposed a regional trading program that promises to reduce the cost of achieving ozone standards (Palmer Bellevue Corporation 1992). Maryland is the first state to institute a "gas guzzler" law that imposes a surcharge on the sale of cars that consume high levels of fuel and a rebate to buyers of fuel-efficient automobiles (Jensen 1992). A consortium of New England industries has outlined plans for an emissions bank that would permit firms to save surplus credits and trade them in or sell them as new facilities are constructed (*Clean Air Report* 8 October 1992b, T-10, T-9). The Texas Air Control Board considered a range of programs, including emission reduction credit banking, community banking, early vehicle retirement, conversion of motor vehicles to alternative fuels, and Nox trading (Texas Air Control Board 1993).

The most ambitious emissions trading scheme has been developed in southern California. The South Coast Air Quality Management District (1992a), the agency responsible for addressing the Los Angeles area's air pollution problems, proposed an emissions trading program called the Regional Clean Air Incentives Market or RECLAIM. The new program is designed to reduce hydrocarbon or reactive organic compound (ROC) emissions by 85% and nitrogen oxide emissions by 95%. Controlling these two major precursors of ozone would help bring the area into compliance with the national ambient air quality standard for ozone. (The South Coast Air Basin is classified under the 1990 Clean Air Act as a severe nonattainment area for ozone.) Under the plan, oil refineries and other large industrial polluters are to reduce their emissions by a fixed percentage each year for different pollutants. Companies that reduce pollution by more than the required amount can sell pollution credits to other companies that exceed their limits. The plan was approved in January 1994.

CHALLENGES IN USING MARKET INSTRUMENTS

The EPA's Economic Incentive Program (EIP) Rule, issued in April 1994, outlines some of the challenges involved in employing market instruments in clean air and other environmental regulatory programs. The rule provides that state EIP programs must include clearly defined goals and incentive mechanisms to achieve them; clearly defined scope of coverage, including the sources affected; a program baseline from which quantifiable emissions reductions can be determined and replicable procedures for quantifying emissions; procedures to certify that reductions are surplus, quantifiable, permanent, and enforceable; and an implementation schedule and enforcement provisions that will ensure enforcement of the program.[9]

Satisfying these standards is a challenging task in formulating and implementing regulatory programs that use market instruments. While the theory of market instruments in regulation seems compelling, their implementation and use raise a host of questions and concerns.

Proposals for market instruments, while based on the virtue of the simplicity of the market, are nevertheless often complex. Discussion over the details of trading plans may obscure broader questions about how much reduction in emissions are required, and how much should be spent to improve environmental quality. Regulatory goals that are poorly designed or misdirected are not salvaged because the cost of complying with them is reduced through trading programs. Trading schemes may become the focus of attention themselves, as interests jockey over the specific provisions and mechanisms to be used. The environmental goals may be slighted or ignored, and discussions and analyses center on *how* the trading will work, rather than on whether or not it *will* work to reduce emissions.

One of the most important contributions economic instruments can make is to help internalize the cost of the environmental consequences of producing goods and services, so that costs of production, and, eventually, the prices charged, reflect true costs. As indicated above, in a political economy fundamentally committed to market exchanges, regulatory strategies that help ensure the real costs of production are included in the prices charged can make a critical contribution to achieving environmental protection goals and a sustainable economy. Economic goals of efficient use of resources are similarly fostered as prices are adjusted to reflect more accurately the real costs of production. Despite the significant advantages emissions charges represent in environmental regulation, however, they have rarely been adopted at levels sufficient to internalize costs. One problem is that it is difficult to calculate what levels of charges are required to reduce emissions by the amount required to meet air quality goals. More importantly, as noted above, it is usually exceedingly difficult to overcome the opposition of regulated industries to new fees or charges (Smil 1993, 215).

However, economic incentive innovations that stop with trading schemes fail to encourage the internalization of true costs. While, in the aggregate, trading schemes may help internalize some of the costs for an entire sector of the economy, they do not require every source to do so. Companies that find it more expensive to clean up than to purchase emission reduction credits from others may do little to reduce their pollution. Community members who insist that major sources of pollution do all they can (while remaining economically viable) to reduce their emissions, may be dissatisfied when those sources can escape that obligation. Trading schemes are also, in one sense, inconsistent with the "polluter pays" principle that is one of the key values underlying environmental regulation. Trading tends to distribute equally the cost of pollution controls across all sources, rather than imposing the greatest control costs on the sources that produce the greatest emissions. Some firms are still able to externalize some of their costs of production to other sources, rather than ensuring they account for all of those costs (Seligman 1994, 8–10).

One of the underpinnings of environmental policy has been to encourage or force the development of cleaner, less polluting technologies. Despite the flaws in the conventional approach to regulation, it has often served to expand the use of cleaner technologies and to encourage the development of new technologies. This momentum can be lost if firms find emission credits available at a lower price than investing in newer, cleaner technologies. In contrast, emissions taxes provide a continuous incentive to devise new processes and technologies, since every time reductions are made, lower taxes result. Emissions trading programs, unless aggressively structured, may reduce the pressure for developments in technology.

Challenges in Emissions Trading Programs

Since emissions trading programs have become the most commonly utilized market instrument for environmental regulation, the challenges they pose deserve particular attention. The process usually begins with a decision concerning the amount of emissions to be allowed. This is done by calculating the volume of emissions that will ensure that the ambient standards are not exceeded. The calculation requires an accurate inventory of existing emissions and the selection of the baseline to be used in allocating emission allowances. The selection of the baseline year is difficult since emissions from sources of pollution vary considerably over time as a result of fluctuations in levels of economic activity, problems with maintenance and operations, investments in pollution control equipment, and a host of other factors. The initial allocation of emission credits is similarly critical: If it is too low or based on recession year output, then companies may not be able to comply when production increases. If the allocation is too high, real reductions may not occur for years.[10]

Allocation based on existing levels of emissions is much less threatening to operating sources, but the selection of the base year is also complicated by the competitive economic environment. The host of factors identified above impact different firms disparately, and selection of one baseline year will advantage some firms and disadvantage others. Firms that have already reduced their emissions may believe they are being punished for doing well when other sources that have done nothing are required to make the same level of reductions.[11]

A further complication in calculating baseline emissions is that many areas lack the kind of inventory that is required to make the trading system work efficiently. Emissions reductions that are to be traded should not be considered as "surplus" until it is clear what levels of reductions are required to attain environmental goals. Similarly, it is not clear whether regulatory officials can accurately measure emissions to ensure that sources comply with the limits outlined in their permits. This is a challenge in almost any kind of scheme, but is particularly important here since the program assumes detailed monitoring of all sources, including fugitive ones. (Under the traditional, technology-based regulatory scheme, enforcement focuses on whether the equipment has been installed and is operating.) The South Coast Air Quality District has recognized that the "largest obstacle facing the design of any market incentive program is enforcement," and that "enhanced compliance programs" are necessary to permit the increased flexibility given to sources under the trading program (South Coast Air Quality District 1992b, EX-4,7). Different requirements are imposed on each of the three pollutants regulated, making implementation even more complicated.

The next step in implementing a trading program is to distribute pollution allowances. Allowances can be sold, auctioned, or simply distributed to sources without charge. There are important benefits in charging for permits. An auction can be a useful means of determining the value of the permit because market forces ensure the lowest expenditures for the required cleanup. Control efforts that cost less than the price of the allowances will be undertaken. Some have even argued that markets should be extended to the number of allowances so that polluters and the community negotiate what levels of pollution they want (Anderson and Leal 1991). Areas desiring to achieve more environmental protection than provided through the minimum national standards could ratchet down over time the number of allowances, or they can permit environmental and other groups to buy allowances and reduce emissions even further. These innovations would reinforce the economic incentives that polluters have to reduce emissions beyond permitted levels.

New and existing sources are both required to obtain allowances, thus ending the traditional approach of imposing more stringent standards on new sources than on existing ones. This may encourage the construction of new, less polluting sources, in contrast to the traditional approach that created an incentive for companies to continue to operate old sources and avoid the costs of complying with more stringent new source standards.

If allowances are sold or auctioned, the revenues can be used to finance monitoring and enforcement efforts, research on pollution prevention, and mitigate the effects of pollution. State regulators could also continue to rely on EPA issuance of technology-based standards, but permit sources to develop alternative technologies that meet or exceed the EPA mandates. This, in turn, reduces the burden on the EPA to update standards continually as new technologies are developed.

Some of the simplicity of market instruments is lost as they are folded into current complicated regulatory schemes. These include: new source and operating permits, technology-based standards, and, in the case of air pollution, State Implementation Plans that outline how states will achieve the national ambient air quality standards. Trading programs can be combined with minimum technological controls that balance the flexibility from trading with the internalization of costs that come from technology controls. Indeed, most emission trading programs under clean air and other environmental laws require that they operate alongside technology control requirements, reasonable further progress requirements, measurable milestones, and other specific requirements.

The Clean Air Act's "expeditious attainment" requirement does not permit all reductions in emissions beyond the minimum, statutorily-mandated requirements to be classified as surplus. Trading programs must first identify what is the most expeditiously attainable reductions that are possible, independent of any trading. Only true surpluses that represent more rapid or greater reductions than would occur under a nonconventional or nontrading regulatory scheme can be traded. As long as the regulated sources have different marginal costs, there will be an incentive to trade. The savings from trading must (1) be large enough to provide an incentive for trading; and (2) must also be used to reduce emissions in ways that are consistent with the statutory requirement that reductions be as expeditious as possible.[12]

Opportunities for regulated sources to gain emissions credits may inhibit the achievement of environmental goals. One of the most attractive features of trading schemes is a declining cap that requires lower total emissions each year as a way to improve air quality. However, loopholes can provide opportunities to circumvent the shrinking cap. If, as is the case in the RECLAIM program, stationary sources can purchase mobile source credits through vehicle scrappage and other programs, these sources may have virtually an open-ended supply of credits.[13] Emissions trading programs alone often do not necessarily contribute to improved environmental conditions, and must be combined with a cap on emissions that is ratcheted down over time, or emissions reduction credits that are discounted over time so that there is a real reduction in pollution.

Another challenge confronting the development of market instruments in environmental regulation relates to the impact on plant shutdowns. Credits earned by plant shutdowns may create incentives for regulated industries to close existing facilities and move to new, less regulated areas. Accurate past emissions from these sources may be difficult to obtain. In response, emission credits from shutdown facilities can be heavily discounted in response to these kinds of problems (Seligman 1994, 30).

A significant factor in an emissions trading scheme is determining the scope of trading: the broader the geographic scope of trading, the greater the likelihood that permits will be traded, that "each zone contains a sufficient number of emission sources to create an active permit market. Ideally, from an environmental and economic standpoint, all *sources of pollution* would be included in a given trading program" (Government of Canada 1992: 4; Emission Trading Working Group, Canadian Council of Ministers of the Environment 1992). But there are some constraints, such as the inefficiencies in trying to enforce permits for many small sources. More serious is the problem of interpollutant trading, since not all pollutants pose the same kinds of risks. Even more troubling is the distribution of pollution levels that result from trading. Areas near sources that buy emission credits rather than clean up will have higher levels of pollutants than areas where investments in pollution control equipment permit sources to sell their excess allowances.

Differences among pollutants make interpollutant trading particularly challenging. Fugitive emissions generally pose a greater health threat to workers and the community than stack emissions because they are released closer to the ground and disperse more slowly. Since some controls on fugitive emissions, such as replacing leaking valves, flanges, and seals, can be expensive, trading between fugitive and stack emissions may create an incentive to make reductions in stack emissions or purchase credits. Fugitive emissions are notoriously difficult to measure and control because they are often so diverse and small. Under the traditional regulatory approach, estimates of emissions are less critical, because control technologies are applied regardless of the actual emissions. Under a trading scheme, if emissions are poorly estimated, they may actually increase (Citizens for a Better Environment 1992, 16–21).

Differences between the traditional air pollutants and toxic air pollutants pose additional challenges. Pollutants regulated to control ozone are also defined as toxic air pollutants. Some toxic "hot spots," areas of concentrated levels of air pollutants, may be created if sources choose to purchase emission reduction credits from other sources rather than reduce their own emissions (South Coast Air Quality Management District 1992a, 3–8). Toxic air pollutants are affected by meteorological conditions differently than are ozone-forming substances. Ozone pollution usually peaks in the summer months because photochemical reactions increase in warmer air, while air toxics tend to peak in the winter months. If trading occurs across seasons, increased exposure to toxic air pollutants during the winter months may result.

Finally, monitoring and enforcement are critical elements of the emissions trading scheme, and, in some ways, are more important than in traditional regulatory schemes. Precise monitoring is essential. If compliance with permitted levels is not vigorously enforced, the incentive to clean up is lost. Standards that require sources to install pollution control equipment or change procedures are, in general, easier to monitor and enforce than emissions standards, since they require less sophisticated monitoring and inspections. State officials may permit sources to monitor themselves, or may themselves assume that responsibility. This is particularly difficult in trading programs that take place across state boundaries. The Northeast States for Coordinated Air Use Management is exploring the possibility of an interstate emission trading program for nitrogen oxides. It is not clear how enforcement of such a program would be integrated with state operating permit and implementation plans (Amar, Bradley, and Boysen 1993, 1–7).

THE FUTURE OF MARKET INCENTIVES

Environmental laws, policies, and institutions have created tremendous expectations for environmental protection that many people believe have largely gone unsatisfied. While some progress has been made in reducing pollution, few problems have been eliminated. Treatment or removal of toxic substances in one environmental medium, for example, often only moves them to another medium. Environmental regulation is permeated by conflict between the legislative and executive branches, legal challenges to virtually every major regulation issued, other delays in issuing regulations, charges of minimal enforcement and compliance with laws and regulations, and complaints of rigid and unreasonable bureaucratic mandates. Environmental regulation is highly politicized, blamed for plant shutdowns and layoffs. Protests by governors and other state and local officials over federal regulations that impose requirements without funding compliance costs ("unfunded mandates"), claims that regulation amounts to a "taking" of private property, and efforts by members of Congress in 1995 who sought to impose new cost-benefit and risk assessment requirements on agencies are only the latest in a long line of criticisms of environmental policy.

Regulatory red tape has provided fertile fodder for decades as politicians see advantages in running against Washington. But it is important to recognize that while there are many policies that need to be adjusted, environmental regulation can and has worked. We have made considerable progress in cleaning our air and water (U.S. Council on Environmental Quality 1993: 7–16; 223–34). There is great potential for improving public health through even more aggressive and effective environmental controls. A growing body of research, for example, points toward major savings in terms of longer lives and lower health care costs through reduced emissions of fine particulate pollution (Lipfert 1994). Effective regulation is consistent with a strong, sustainable economy (Hawken 1994).

Emissions trading and other market incentives in regulation will become increasingly important in our overall regulatory efforts. Their limitations and shortcomings need to be well understood. It is critical that the ground rules surrounding their creation, regulation, and eventual elimination be clearly understood. Emissions trading seems most promising when the same emissions have the same effect throughout the area in which they occur; emissions are relatively easy to measure; and a limited number of major sources that can afford the transaction costs are involved. Conversely, trading schemes do not work well when there are a large number of small sources, such as residential woodburning stoves, because the transaction costs will be too high. Monitoring and accounting become critical; emissions are evaluated not just to determine compliance or noncompliance, but must be measured accurately for accounting purposes (Pedersen 1994). Aggressive penalties for excess emissions, including fines and reduction in the allowances for subsequent years, are essential to make trading work effectively. Perhaps most importantly, emissions permits are only temporary permits to pollute: they should not be seen as permanent rights that can never be taken away by governments. They are temporary licenses to do what could always be prohibited by governments in order to protect commonly held resources, protect private property rights, and achieve environmental goals (Breger et al. 1991, 480).

The idea of buying permits to pollute may threaten the moral, symbolic, power, and appeal of pollution control; environmental regulation is no longer seen as a moral imperative in protecting human health, and, in particular, protecting innocent third parties who suffer few of the benefits of pollution-producing activity and most of the burdens, but simply another cost of doing business. The efficiency promised by emissions trading may unwittingly produce equity problems. For instance, trading may result in increased pollution levels in areas where residents are poor or lack the political clout to demand pollution reductions instead of purchases of more pollution allowances. Some EPA officials are skeptical of emission trading policies, warning that they have been oriented more toward "regulatory relief than regulatory reform," and that these policies often lack "equivalency in accountability, enforceability, and environmental progress" (*Environment Reporter*, 29 May 1992, 437). Reliance on pollution taxes and fees may serve to weaken public commitment to a shared environmental ethic. As decisions are left to the marketplace, there is less need for educational and other collective efforts to foster public awareness of and concern for the environment.

If trading systems are used to create property rights in pollution emissions, communities may have less opportunity to make decisions about what level of air pollution they want to accept. The kind of regulatory instrument selected may have an impact on the political system and the policy-making process as well as on environmental quality (Gartner 1992, 26). Market-like incentives may send the wrong signal that pollution is acceptable if the polluter is wealthy enough to pay for it. Proponents of environmental regulation have long rested their arguments on the belief that individuals have the right to breathe clean, healthy air, and that public health and natural resource goals should be pursued independent of cost calculations. Clean air, clean water, national parks, and the environment in general are all part of a shared common endowment. Placing all of these values in a market may ultimately result in their unequal distribution and eventual devaluation (Kelman 1981). The creation of a free market in pollution simply allows companies to buy permits when they choose not to install control measures or otherwise prevent pollution (Commoner 1990, 188).

In assessing proposals and possibilities for the use of market incentives in air pollution regulation, several questions might be asked: Will environmental standards be met? Is there an accurate emissions inventory in place? How are allowances allocated? What is the geographic scope of trading? What pollutants are involved, and will interpollutant trading be permitted? What will be done to ensure effective enforcement and monitoring? Can the proposal eventually lead to a system of emissions fees or taxes? Answers to these questions are critical in deciding where and when to employ market instruments to achieve air quality and other environmental goals. Different communities may answer them differently, but answering them is an essential part of weighing the advantages and disadvantages of market-based regulatory programs. They have great potential, if carefully crafted, to help make environmental law more efficient, effective, and reasonable.

NOTES

1. This discussion is a revision and abridgement of Bryner (1994).

2. For some of the arguments underlying the pledge to roll back regulations, see Eckerly and Ferrara (1994); for a review of the major legislative action in early 1995, see Kriz (1995) and Benenson (1995).

3. Many countries have had some experience with emissions fees for pollutants released into lakes and streams. Germany and France were among the earliest to develop pollution charges. (International Environmental Reporter 1986; Repetto et al. 1992; and Organization for Economic Co-operation and Development 1994).

4. For a discussion of tradeable permits, see Hahn and Hester (1989ab), Dudek and Palmisano (1988), and Russell (1981).

5. See Stewart (1988). An even more ambitious use of market-like mechanisms like emissions trading in environmental regulation has been proposed by Anderson and Leal (1991) who argue that markets should be created to determine the number of emission credits to be bought and sold. Persons who pollute and those who are affected by the pollution can come together and bargain for acceptable pollution levels. "Only when rights are well-defined, enforced, and transferable," Anderson and Leal write, "will self-interested individuals confront the trade-offs inherent in a world of scarcity" (1991, 22).

6. See, generally, U.S. EPA (1992a), Wirth and Heinz (1988), and U.S. EPA (1994).

7. In *Chevron, U.S.A., Inc. v. Natural Resources Defense Council* the Supreme Court upheld the EPA regulations providing for a plant-wide definition of stationary sources as a permissible, reasonable policy decision within the discretion of the agency. 467 U.S. 837 (1984). In 1986 the EPA issued an "Emissions Trading Policy Statement" that outlined requirements states must meet in creating, using, and banking emission reduction credits 51 *Fed. Reg.* 43,814 (1986).

8. The EPA is also required to establish emissions limits for nitrogen oxides from utility boilers and to issue revised New Source Performance Standards for fossil fuel-fired steam generating facilities. Standards are to require the "best system of continuous emission reduction, taking into account available technology, costs and energy and environmental impacts." The EPA was to report to Congress by 1994 on the economic and environmental consequences of permitting the trading of SO2 and NOx allowances. Section 406, 403(c). The acid rain provisions are the most prominent example of the use of economic incentives but the approach is taken elsewhere in the 1990 Clean Air Act. Marketable permits will be used to phase out the manufacturing of chemicals that deplete the ozone layer. Emission fees for severe ozone nonattainment areas that fail to meet the deadline for coming into attainment are provided for and states are authorized to employ emission fees, auctions of emission rights, and other innovations in their regulatory programs. For discussion of proposals for market-based instruments that have resulted from the Clean Air Act, see Environmental Defense Fund and General Motors (n.d.) and U.S. EPA (1992b).

9. 59 FR 16690 (April 7, 1994), at 16991.

10. In October 1992, district officials and industry representatives agreed on a plan for establishing the baseline inventory and the rates of reduction for stationary sources. Industry representatives insisted that sources be permitted to select their peak emissions year from 1987 to 1991 to account for recession-caused downturns in output (*Clean Air Report* 1992c).

11. Using the highest figures, as in California's RECLAIM program, for example, might fail to account for shifts in production between companies in the industry over time, and permit emissions that are higher than have ever actually occurred. In general, using an average production figure from recent years is a better base for determining the original allocation than using one year. See Feuer and Kun (1994).

12. Sections 110(a)(2), 172(a)(2), 181(a), 186(a), 188(c), and 192(a) of the Clean Air Act, 42 U.S.C. 7401 et seq. See Natural Resource Defense Council (1993).

13. California Air Resources Board, rule 2015(c)(1) only provides that the Executive Officer must propose to the Governing Board that increased allocations be offset from non-RECLAIM sources that are identified in California's Air Quality Management Plan. See Feuer and Kun (1994).

REFERENCES

Ackerman, Bruce, and William Hassler. 1981. *Clean Coal/Dirty Air*. New Haven, CT: Yale University Press.

Amar, Praveen K., Michael J. Bradley, and Donna M. Boysen. 1993. "A Market-Based Nox Emissions Cap System in the NESCAUM Region." *Regulatory Analyst* 1:3 (March):1–7.

Anderson, Terry, and D. Leal. 1991. *Free Market Environmentalism*. Boulder, CO: Westview.

Benenson, Bob. 1995. "Complaints Don't Delay Action On Regulatory Overhaul Bills," *Congressional Quarterly Weekly Report* (18 February, 1995): 520–21.

Breger, Marshall J., Richard B. Stewart, E. Donald Elliott, and David Hawkins. 1991. "Providing Economic Incentives in Environmental Regulation." *Yale Journal on Regulation* 8: 463–95.

Bryner, Gary C. 1994. "Rethinking Environmental Regulation: Review of Critiques of EPA and Environmental Regulation." Paper prepared for the U.S. Congress, Office of Technology Assessment (August).

Citizens for a Better Environment. 1992. "Comments on the Draft Environmental Impact Report for Proposed Amendments to the 1991 Air Quality Management Plan To Implement a Marketable Permits Program and Replace Source Control Measures" (25 June): 16–21.

Claiborne, William. 1994. "Unfunded Mandates Occupy Center Stage." *Washington Post* (May 18):A21.

Clean Air Report. 1992a. "Illinois Begins Pilot Project to Scrap Old, Polluting Cars in Chicago" (8 October):T–9.

Clean Air Report. 1992b. "Northeast Proposes to Cut Compliance Costs, Shield Region's Economy," and "Businesses Offer Plan for Banking, Trading to Cut Costs, Allow Growth" (8 October):T-9—T-10.

Clean Air Report. 1992c. "California Regulators, Industry Close to Accord on 'RECLAIM' Baseline" (8 October):6.

Commoner, Barry. 1990. *Making Peace with the Planet*. New York: Pantheon.

Crandall, Robert W. 1983. *Controlling Industrial Pollution: The Economics and Politics of Clean Air*. Washington, D.C.: Brookings Institution.

Daly, Herman E. 1994. "Farewell Lecture to World Bank" (January 14, 1994).

Dudek, Daniel J., and John Palmisano. 1988. "Emissions Trading: Why is this Thoroughbred Hobbled?" *Columbia Journal of Environmental Law* 13:217–256.

Eckerly, Susan, and Peter J. Ferrara. 1994. "Regulation" in *Issues '94: The Candidate's Briefing Book*. Washington, D.C.: The Heritage Foundation, 71–88.

Emission Trading Working Group. 1992. Canadian Council of Ministers of the Environment. "Emission Trading: A Discussion Paper" (May).

Environment Reporter. 1992. "California: Problems Seen Setting Baseline Levels in South Coast Emissions-Trading Program" (29 May):437.

Environmental Defense Fund and General Motors. (n.d.) "Mobile Emissions Reduction Crediting."

Feuer, Gail Ruderman, and Veronica Kun. 1994. Natural Resources Defense Council, letter to California Air Resource Board (March 8).

Gartner, Michael. 1992. "A Skeptic Speaks." *EPA Journal* 18:2 (May/June):26.

Georgia Institute of Technology. 1994. "Emissions Banking and Trading: A Survey of U.S. Programs" (April).

Government of Canada. 1992. "Economic Instruments for Environmental Protection: Discussion Paper."

Hahn, Robert W. 1988. "Innovative Approaches for Revising the Clean Air Act." *Natural Resources Journal* 28 (winter):171–84.

Hahn, Robert W., and Gordon L. Hester. 1989a. "Marketable Permits: Lessons for Theory and Practice." *Ecology Law Quarterly* 16: 361–406.

Hahn, Robert W., and Gordon L. Hester. 1989b. "Where Did All the Markets Go? An Analysis of EPA's Emissions Trading Program." *Yale Journal on Regulation* 6:109–153.

Hawken, Paul. 1994. *The Ecology of Commerce*. New York: Harper Business.

Howard, Philip K. 1994. *The Death of Common Sense*. New York: Random House.

Illinois EPA. 1993a. "Feasibility Study for Market-Based Approaches to Clean Air" (September).

Illinois EPA. 1993b. "Draft Proposal: Design for Nox Trading System" (September 22).

Inside EPA. 1994. (August 5):6–7.

International Environmental Reporter. 1986. February 2:53–55.

Jensen, Peter. 1992. " 'Gas guzzler' law's value as tax source questioned." *The Baltimore Sun* (22 April):1A.

Kelman, Steven. 1981. *What Price Incentives?* Boston: Auburn House.

Kneese, Allen V. and Charles L. Schultze. 1975. *Pollution, Prices, and Public Policy*. Washington, D.C.: Brookings Institution.

Kriz, Margaret. 1995. "Risky Business." *National Journal* (18 February, 1995): 417–21.

Lipfert, Frederick W. 1994. *Air Pollution and Community Health: A Critical Review and Data Sourcebook*. New York: Van Nostrand Reinhold.

National Commission on the Environment. 1993. *Choosing a Sustainable Future*. Washington, D.C.: Island Press.

Natural Resource Defense Council. 1993. "Comments Before the U.S. EPA on Economic Incentive Program Rules and Related Guidance" (June 13).

Organization for Economic Co-operation and Development. 1994. Environment and Taxation: the Cases of The Netherlands, Sweden and the United States. Paris: OECD.

Palmer Bellevue Corporation. 1992. "Emissions Reduction Trading in the Chicago Metropolitan Area: A Pre-Feasibility Analysis of the Effectiveness of Market Measures to Control Ground-Level Ozone." Chicago, Illinois (May).

Pedersen, William F. Jr. 1994. "The Limits of Market-Based Approaches to Environmental Protection." *Environmental Law Review* (April): 10173–76.

Pigou, Nicholas. 1928. *A Study in Public Finance*. London: Macmillan & Co.

Portney, Paul R. 1990. "Air Pollution Policy" in *Public Policies for Environmental Protection*, ed. Paul Portney, 27–96. Washington, D.C.: Resources for the Future.

Repetto, Robert, Roger C. Dower, Robin Jenkins, and Jacqueline Geoghegan. 1992. *Green Fees: How a Tax Shift Can Work for the Environment and the Economy*. Washington, D.C.: World Resources Institute.

Russell, Clifford S. 1981. "Controlled Trading of Pollution Permits." *Environmental Science & Technology* 15, 1 (January):24-28.

Schelling, Thomas. 1983. *Incentives for Environmental Protection*. Cambridge, MA: MIT Press.

Schultze, Charles L. 1977. *The Public Use of Private Interest*. Washington, D.C.: Brookings Institution.

Seligman, Daniel A. 1994. "Air Pollution Emissions Trading: Opportunity or Scam?" Washington, D.C.: The Sierra Club, unpublished paper, April.

Smil, Vaclav. 1993. *Global Ecology: Environmental Change and Social Flexibility*. London: Routledge.

South Coast Air Quality Management District. 1992a. "Regional Clean Air Incentives Market, Summary Recommendations" (spring).

South Coast Air Quality Management District. 1992b. "Draft Environmental Impact Report for Proposed 1991 AQMP Amendments" (13 May).

Stewart, Richard B. 1988. "Controlling Environmental Risks Through Economic Incentives." *Columbia Journal of Environmental Law* 14:153–69.

Texas Air Control Board. 1993. "Marketable Permits Feasibility Study" (June).

U.S. Council on Environmental Quality. 1993. *Environmental Quality: 23rd Annual Report, the Council on Environmental Quality*. Washington D.C.: U.S. Government Printing Office.

U.S. Environmental Protection Agency. 1992a. *The United States Experience with Economic Incentives to Control Environmental Pollution*. Washington, D.C.: U.S. EPA.

U.S. Environmental Protection Agency. 1992b. "Market-Based Incentives and Other Innovations for Air Pollution Control." Research Triangle Park, N.C.: U.S. EPA, June.

U.S. Environmental Protection Agency. 1994. "The New Generation of Environmental Protection," working draft (April 15).

Wirth, Timothy, and John Heinz. 1991. *Project 88-Round II, Incentives for Action: Designing Market-Based Environmental Strategies*. Washington, D.C.: Office of (former) Senators Timothy E. Wirth and John Heinz.

4 Employing Strategic Planning in Environmental Regulation*

STEVEN COHEN

In the past decade we have heard a good deal of political, popular, and scholarly discussion of the concept of regulation. Regulation is criticized for harming the economy, stifling entrepreneurial initiative, discouraging technological advances and for being insufficiently cost effective. Economists criticize lawyers for being overly formalistic and not understanding how firms behave. Policymakers criticize economists for proposing policies that seem sensible but are not politically feasible. In my view, however, the most competitive economies of the twenty-first century are likely to be those that protect the environment at the least possible cost. This will require the development of patterns of institutional interaction that are far more cooperative than those of industry and environmental agencies in the United States. If an ecologically sustainable economy is to be achieved in the United States, industry must become convinced of the economic advantages of pollution prevention and resource conservation.

This chapter addresses the issues surrounding effective regulation. Understanding the procedures involved in the development and implementation of regulation is the first step. I then describe the tools of strategic regulation. Next, criticisms of different modes of regulation are discussed. The chapter concludes with a summary of the strategic approach to regulation.

*I gratefully acknowledge the research assistance of Pamela Caird (Columbia MPA '96), Bonnie Mackey (MPA '96), and Dorena Rodriguez (Columbia MPA '96).

DEFINING REGULATION

Kenneth Meir has defined regulation as "any attempt by the government to control the behavior of citizens, corporations, or subgovernments" (Meir 1985, p.1). Regulation is a set of rules or directives intended to cause specific behaviors in target populations. Modifying his definition slightly, I would substitute the word "influence" for "control." Regulated behaviors in my view represent tendencies and incremental actions rather than goal-seeking, rationally controlled behaviors. Control is simply too strong a term. Organizations for the most part do not truly control their own actions; instead, these actions are the result of a variety of internal exchange relationships and influence evidenced by explicit and implicit bargains and the deployment of potential and actual incentives.

The goal of regulation is to influence individual or organizational behavior. To provide a graphic example, consider the case of automobiles converging at a corner traffic light. The behavior of the driver is hopefully influenced by the color of the traffic light. The signal is relatively clear, although when the light turns amber the driver is faced with the need to make a quick decision (slow down or speed up?). What factors affect the driver's decision to slow down, speed up, or stop? Certainly, the following factors come into play:

1. Is the signal working?
2. Does the driver see and understand the signal?
3. Is the driver willing to adhere to the signal?
4. Is the car mechanically capable of stopping and/or accelerating?

Are the regulated parties, in this case the drivers, capable of changing behavior in the desired direction and are they willing to do so? The goal of regulation is to influence the variables that enter into a regulated party's calculus of the costs and benefits of compliance. What are the incentives and disincentives to stopping at a red light?

1. An incentive to stop might be the presence of a fully loaded trailer truck that will hit the driver if he/she does not stop.
2. A second incentive to stop might be the ticket the highway patrol officer could give the driver if he/she goes through the light.

3. A third incentive to stop might be the driver's belief in the rule of law.
4. Another incentive to stop may be a pre-patterned behavior which causes the driver to see a red light and move his/her foot toward the brake.
5. A disincentive to stop might arise if the driver has a severely ill child sitting in the back seat, and the driver is on the way to a hospital.
6. A second disincentive to stop might arise if there were no traffic visible and the driver was in a hurry.

The goal of traffic regulation is to reinforce the incentives to comply so that they outweigh the potential motivation to pass the red light. The goal of regulation is to influence the perceptions and behaviors of regulated parties. Therefore, each regulatory program must be based on a strategy that seeks to understand the motivations of regulated parties and to influence their behavior.

HOW TO DEVELOP AND IMPLEMENT A REGULATORY STRATEGY

Strategic regulatory planning is an effort by government to develop a comprehensive strategy or tactic for influencing behavior. There are two components to this plan. The first is the formal regulation itself. The second part is the manner in which the regulatory plan is implemented. Extra-regulatory elements that can be manipulated to encourage compliance include funding, technical assistance, exhortation, and publicity. The goal of this type of regulation is not to alter the behavior of the implementing agencies, as with many government programs, but to modify the behavior of private parties. Therefore, a carefully considered strategy and tactical thinking are important in accomplishing compliance.

In earlier work on regulation, Cohen and Kamieniecki (1991) developed a seven-step model for strategic regulatory planning. The model built on the work of those in the field of business strategy formulation and included the following steps:

1. Problem recognition: What is at issue?
2. Identification of parties: Who is involved?

3. Historical analysis: What is the current level of performance?
4. Situational analysis:
    - Mission: What outcomes are desired?
    - Party analysis: What are the capabilities and attitudes of the regulated community?
5. Strategic regulation formulation: Design of specific strategies to influence compliant behavior of regulated parties.
6. Ex Ante review: Projecting the fit and feasibility of the regulatory plan before implementation and modification of the plan.
7. Ex Post review and revision: Review of the success of the regulatory strategy in changing the behavior of regulated parties and subsequent mid-course corrections.

Since willingness and capacity to comply with regulation can vary widely within a given regulated community, it is critical to have an array of regulatory mechanisms available. It is also important to approach the task of influencing behavior objectively and without preconceptions. An empirical and pragmatic approach is most beneficial.

The concept of strategic regulatory planning was applied in a National Academy of Public Administration study of the federal program to regulate leaking underground storage tanks (National Academy of Public Administration 1986).[1] In that project, and during subsequent activity undertaken by EPA's Office of Underground Storage Tanks, each of the steps of the strategic planning model was completed. One result was the creation of a unique, lean, and effective regulatory program: a program with less paperwork, less federal second guessing of state and local governments, and more environmental improvement than typical EPA programs.

It is true that the tank program was in some ways easier to implement than most EPA programs since the pollutant it sought to control was in most cases a product (gasoline) rather than a waste. Industry has a clear economic incentive to keep its product from leaking into the environment. Waste, however, is more difficult to regulate because a firm has every incentive to hope the material just disappears. Nevertheless, the federal tank program resulted in a dramatic increase in the number of new tanks installed with protection against corrosion. In 1984, prior to enactment of federal tank rules, 74 percent of the underground tanks sold in the United States were unprotected bare steel tanks. By 1988 less than half of the tanks installed (43 percent) were unprotected (Cohen and Kamieniecki 1991).

One might argue that it is not administratively or legally feasible to target regulation to maximize influence on the behavior of regulated parties. The administrative argument is easy to counter. First, regulations are now individually tailored to specific companies through the permit process. Second, it is possible to deal with groups of regulated parties and tailor approaches to classes of regulatory situations rather than to individual organizations. Finally, an approach focused on changing the behavior of regulated parties will tend to be less process oriented and, therefore, less administratively complex. It will also encourage the formation of strategic alliances between different parties who share a similar interest in the successful implementation of the regulatory program. For example, in the underground tank program an effort was made to include such nongovernmental actors as insurance companies, tank manufacturers, and tank installers in the regulatory process.

The issue of legal feasibility concerns whether the law can be adjusted to account for an organization's willingness and capacity to conform to the law's requirements. Regulatory enforcement through the courts, one should note, typically results in bargains that take into account what an organization is capable of and willing to do to move toward compliance. We might as well acknowledge that the application of environmental rules involves these negotiations, and the notion that the law is applied without consideration of feasibility is simply not true. In fact, Cass Sunstein (1990, p. 416) argues that when regulators are compelled to implement rules that do not allow them to consider issues of feasibility, they frequently fail to act. A more typical response than inaction is to negotiate a deal. Frequently, this involves a compliance schedule and other government concessions.

A strategic approach to regulation would acknowledge the reality of the bargaining situation up front and develop compliance strategies with input from the regulated community. Under these circumstances, enforcement and the threat of enforcement is reserved for recalcitrant organizations that willfully violate agreements, engage in deception, or are unwilling to change their practices.

THE TOOLS OF STRATEGIC REGULATION

The term command and control has been used to describe a process where government commands a regulated party to act in a certain way and then uses the legal system to control behaviors that are not in compliance with the rules. As Cohen and Kamieniecki (1991) write, the traditional notion of command and control is a very simplistic view of regulation. In their view, regulation involves all government policies and programs deployed to influence the behavior of regulated parties. Their definition of regulation includes command and control regulation, the use of market mechanisms, and a wide variety of other techniques of influence.

There is no need to choose between command and control and market mechanisms. Neither is necessarily better than the other. Rather, each target of regulation must be assessed to determine what mix of incentives and disincentives will result in the desired change in behavior. Alternative regulatory strategies include both coercive and relatively noncoercive actions. All things being equal, policymakers will prefer to use the least coercive methods that obtain the desired results at the least cost. The regulatory actions discussed below should be seen as a partial listing of activities typically available to regulators to influence the behavior of regulated parties. Some of the key regulatory techniques available to policymakers include:

- **Market solutions and economic incentives:** Government, for example, sells permits to pollute to firms who may only pollute to the level allowed in the permit and may sell these permits to other private parties. This encourages permit holders to reduce their own level of pollution and maximize the cost effectiveness of pollution control. The deposit/refund system is another example of market incentives. A surcharge or deposit is assessed on products that may cause environmental damage when they are disposed of incorrectly. The buyer returns the product to the seller for proper action and the deposit. Similar incentive programs include financial rewards, elimination of resource extraction subsidies, and post-consumer waste content requirements.
- **Insurance programs:** Government requires private parties to carry insurance in order to clean up unanticipated releases of pollution and compensate victims of negative

environmental impacts. For example, the owner of a gasoline station might be required to carry insurance to pay for the cost of cleaning up any gasoline leaks, and to pay third party liability claims arising from these leaks.

- **Self-regulation:** Government permits an industry to regulate itself. The use of industry codes and professional ethics are examples of such self-regulation.
- **Taxes and fees:** Government charges regulated parties for each unit of pollution or waste created. Alternatively, a tax is placed on the raw material that eventually causes the pollution, as in Superfund's tax on petroleum and chemical feedstocks.
- **Education, information disclosure, and the use of the media:** Government informs the public about regulatory violations or about dangers, causing negative public relations for a company. An example is the warning label requirement on cigarettes. Government may also use the media to educate regulated parties about regulatory requirements and their purpose.
- **Reporting and formal compliance tracking:** Government requires regulated parties to report on their compliance with rules. This is less expensive than inspections and can begin the process of creating the institutional capacity in regulated firms to comply with a rule. Whoever fills out the form must at least pay some attention to the regulation.
- **Licensing:** Government certifies competent professionals who can assist with compliance. A good example of this method is the regulation of Certified Public Accountants, who assure compliance with tax regulations. In the environmental area it might be possible to certify environmental auditors and other professionals who could help a firm reduce and prevent pollution.
- **Permitting:** Government requires firms to obtain a permit in order to pollute legally. A permit can call for gradual reductions in pollution. The absence of a permit can result in a judicial order to close a factory.
- **Standard setting:** This is the traditional command part of command and control regulation. There are two basic types

of standards. The first type is the performance standard, which requires the accomplishment of specific goals but does not specify how one achieves those goals. A second type of standard specifies a process, technology, or practice that a regulated party must deploy to be in compliance with a rule. This simplifies compliance and oversight of regulatory compliance by requiring a specific, easily measurable activity. However, it also reduces the discretion a firm has to determine the most cost-effective mode of compliance.

- **Grants, training, and compliance assistance:** Many of the targets of regulation are individuals and small businesses that are willing to comply but lack the capability or resources to do so. Sometimes grants, loans, or even loan guarantees can help a small business obtain the capital needed to comply with a regulation. Training and consulting services can also have a large impact, especially in areas where regulation and technologies are new.
- **Assessing penalties:** Penalties are typically fines charged against violators. Penalties are particularly complex disincentives that must be used with great care. A penalty that is too low is simply absorbed into the cost of doing business. A penalty that is too high can result in extensive litigation and high transaction costs for the agency. It can also lead to illicit avoidance behavior and/or political opposition to the legitimacy of the regulation and even the regulator. Nevertheless, as the Internal Revenue Service (IRS) has learned, a well-targeted penalty with sufficient publicity can result in widespread compliance to an agency's rules.
- **Inspections:** Visits by regulators to regulated parties to determine compliance is an important part of the traditional command and control model. Inspections provide evidence that regulated parties are following the rules. A more important use of inspections, especially if they are random and unannounced, is to stimulate compliant behavior due to fear of an impending inspection. Many people keep careful tax records out of fear that one day they will be examined by an IRS tax auditor.
- **Adjudication:** Formal adjudication is an administrative or judicial trial to determine if a regulated party has violated

a rule. The threat of adjudication can often promote compliant behavior.

This list of regulatory activities is by no means exhaustive, but it provides a behavioral-based operational definition of regulation. Each of these techniques has benefits and limitations and is most effective when deployed as part of a carefully considered strategy for influencing regulated parties. While the attacks on *both* command and control *and* market-oriented regulation are misguided, and the result of a narrow view of regulation, a review of the debate can help illuminate the strengths and weaknesses of these forms of regulation. It may suggest the type of situations and the phases in program implementation where command and control and market mechanisms are most useful.

CRITICISMS OF COMMAND AND CONTROL REGULATION

The fundamental criticism of command and control regulation is that it is a wasteful way to produce a social good. While it has worked effectively in some situations, its successes often come at a high price. According to Maury Weidenbaum (1992), the start of the 1990s marked a shift of the pendulum back toward regulation. Weidenbaum believes that regulation is a burden on the American economy, and he cites the example of the 1990 Clean Air Act Amendments, which in his view created an administrative nightmare for business and government alike. A decade earlier, writing in a similar vein, Robert Litan and William Nordhaus noted that "a dispassionate observer may fairly conclude that the rise of increasingly stringent command-and-control techniques as a method of regulation has poorly served the American economy" (Litan and Nordhaus 1983, p. 98). While the 1994 mid-term elections may have indicated new widespread public support for this sentiment, there is in fact a longstanding, recurrent critique of government regulation as unwarranted interference in the private economy. Marshall Breger et al. (1991) observe that the experience of the 1970s and 1980s has caused a recognition of the limits of traditional command and control regulation. Command and control has inhibited technological progress when it has commanded the use of specific control technologies such as catalytic convertors and scrubbers. Such requirements tend to freeze technological progress in place, making it difficult for more effective technologies to gain acceptance in the market place. Command and control has also tended to discourage cost-benefit analysis of regulatory programs.

While Cass Sunstein notes that command and control regulation has worked in the areas of air and water pollution as well as highway and occupational safety, he also observes that:

> . . . regulation has frequently failed. Sometimes it has imposed enormously high costs for speculative benefits; sometimes it has accomplished little or nothing; and sometimes it has aggravated the very problem it was designed to solve (Sunstein 1990, p.411).

Richard Stroup and Jane Shaw (1989) attack the concept of government regulation itself. They do not accept the argument that a clean environment is a public good that requires collective action to be maintained. They argue that the command and control system of regulation is "beset with difficulties" (Stroup and Shaw 1989, p.30). They maintain that environmental policies are determined by special interest politics, and are "often driven by groundless accusations [and] supported by public fear." In their view, "populist sentiment and pork-barrel politics, rather than actual environmental dangers, currently determine priorities" (Stroup and Shaw 1989, p. 31). Stroup and Shaw contend that the free market is capable of protecting the environment:

> Over the long run, private ownership is the most effective protector of the environment-provided ownership is transferable and backed by courts that make people liable when their pollutants invade the person or property of others. This system of private ownership would protect the environment for the same reason that it protects other kinds of property: because it encourages good stewardship (Stroup and Shaw 1989, p.31).

A principal argument against command and control regulation is that it places too much burden on administrative agencies to deal with an increasingly complicated economy. The effort to classify and regulate hazardous waste, toxics, and pesticides are examples of technological developments in the economy outstripping the capacity of administrative agencies to regulate them. Citing the complexity of regulating the vast number and types of solid wastes, William Pedersen (1991) argues that without a tax or other market oriented mechanism, it will be impossible to provide adequate regulation of these wastes.

Another argument against command and control is that, at times, overly stringent regulatory standards can be difficult to implement. Cass Sunstein maintains that:

> A stringent standard—one that forbids balancing or calls for regulation beyond the point of "feasibility"—makes regulators reluctant to act . . . Their inaction is not caused by venality or confusion. Instead, it reflects their quite plausible belief that the statute often requires them to regulate to an absurd point . . . a stringent standard will mobilize opposition to regulation . . . it will require agencies to obtain greater supporting information to survive political and judicial scrutiny, while at the same time making it less likely that such information will be forthcoming from regulated class members (Sunstein 1990, p. 416).

Richard B. Stewart notes that command-and-control regulation was "an understandable, first generation response to environmental problems . . . When the Earth Day explosion of interest in environmental problems came along, there was a perception that urgent things needed to be done . . . and that the most effective and appropriate way was to require specific controls on emissions and later, specific practices for disposal of toxic wastes" (Stewart in Breger et al. 1991, p. 467). While it may have worked at first, ". . . it is often, from industry's viewpoint cheaper to invest in litigation and delay than to find innovative ways to comply" (Stewart in Breger et al. 1991, p. 468).

In summary, command and control regulation can impede innovation, slow down the economy, cost too much, and be administratively cumbersome. In addition, it often relies too much on politics to set environmental goals. Given these drawbacks, it seems that using the market to protect the environment ought to be a viable alternative. While the theory behind market mechanisms seems sound, unfortunately, political reality sometimes intervenes, making the elegant theory difficult to apply.

CRITICISMS OF MARKET MECHANISMS OF REGULATION

Without question, a relatively free economic market tends to be a powerful and reasonably predictable influence on corporate and individual behavior. When harnessed toward a social goal, the market can result in remarkable accomplishments. This is especially the case when an effort is made to regulate complex technical or production processes. As Stephen Breyer observes, ". . . the true virtue of a tax, fee or similar system lies in its power to provide incentives to direct behavior in a socially desirable direction, without freezing current technology and while preserving a degree of individual choice" (Breyer 1982, p. 270).

There is widespread support among economists and policy analysts for utilizing market-based regulatory approaches (e.g., Ackerman and Stewart 1988; Stroup and Shaw 1989; Levenson and Gordon 1990; Breger et al. 1991; Weidenbaum 1992). However, a number of scholars have noted that markets are difficult to establish and that market-oriented regulatory regimes must be developed with great care. Others have argued that market-oriented approaches may not be necessary and that the economic impact of regulation on the American economy is overstated (Daneke 1985).

Eugene Bardach and Robert Kagan (1982) distinguish between protective or social regulation and industry-inspired regulation to control or at least influence market conditions. Companies often advocate regulation to control entry into a market or constrain unfettered competition. Typically, the case for such nonprotective regulation is the advancement of a public goal, such as establishing an industry or stimulating private investment in capital-intensive infrastructure. Environmental regulation is a form of protective regulation, and Bardach and Kagan are skeptical about the possibility of creating markets for protective regulation:

> It is easy to believe that beneficent market forces will rush in spontaneously to perform *price-setting* functions that government regulators had hitherto performed, but it is a very different matter to believe that they will provide incentives for politically acceptable levels of pollution abatement, nondiscrimination, and control of waste disposal sites. After all, most protective regulation originally came into being because society's first line of defense—market pressures and privately activated lawsuits for damages—had not been effective in deterring certain harms (Bardach and Kagan 1982, p.7).

Even those supporting market approaches have noted that some market mechanisms, such as emission trading programs, have had a mixed record of success (Hahn and Hester 1989). Active markets were slower to begin than some economists predicted. In part this is because political considerations resulted in trading policies that were significantly different than those advocated by analysts. Under the 1990 Clean Air Act, emission allowances can be traded, but EPA has explicitly stated that these allowances are not permanent property rights and that government can reduce or eliminate these allowances (Johnston 1991). While this is not a criticism of the concept of market-oriented regulatory mechanisms, it does indicate that the ideal conceptual frameworks proposed by scholars may not survive the less than ideal political process intact. Therefore, one attack on market mechanisms is their political feasibility. Other criticisms of market approaches include:

- The difficulty of pricing permits or of deciding how much pollution should be allowed.
- The information requirements placed on government to monitor whether firms are exceeding their emission allowances.
- The argument that tradeable pollution rights are a license to pollute.

A STRATEGIC APPROACH TO REGULATION

If it seems that proponents and opponents are talking past each other, it is probably because they are. In most cases, the scholars working in this field are working out of different paradigms. More likely, I suspect, we are seeing an ideological debate between advocates of the market and advocates of government intervention. Instead, the real challenge is to learn how and when to use market mechanisms and how and when to use direct regulation.

We have evidence that sometimes market approaches work and sometimes they do not. We need to ask why this is the case. One team of scholars asked that question and concluded that a carefully designed trading system could be implemented. James Tripp and Daniel Dudek (1989) developed the following guidelines for successful trading programs: (1) clear legal authority, (2) technical capability, (3) evasion-proof program, (4) clearly specified objectives, (5) problems of regional significance, (6) measurable economic value of tradeable rights, (7) equitable and administratively simple method for allocating rights, and (8) minimal transaction costs for buying and selling the use rights.

To develop these principles, Tripp and Dudek examined four programs, two successful ones—New Jersey's Pinelands Plan and EPA's CFC program, and two unsuccessful ones—the Los Angeles air pollution bubble program of the 1980s and a local water pollution control program in Fox River, Wisconsin. Trading programs that followed the principles listed above produced workable markets and achieved sufficient political support to be implemented. The unsuccessful programs were not able to incorporate the guiding principles effectively.

The choice between command and control and market-based regulation is a false one. All regulation involves gradual, strategic calculation and bargaining. Command and control results in regulations that adjust the law to reality, permits that interpret regulations in the light of real-world constraints, and judicial and administrative bargains on how permits should actually be implemented. Donald Elliot, former EPA General Counsel, notes that:

> It is important to recognize that we don't have to have—and we don't have—an all or nothing system in which we have either an incentive-based system or a health-based system of command and control regulations. Many of our environmental problems, like many of our other legal problems, involve a complex coming together of different goals and different moral norms. The system cannot simply optimize any single value-like controlling the total amount of pollution at the least cost—but must be responsive to multiple values . . . . Thus a combination of health-based standards and market-based incentives may be preferable to either standing alone (Elliot in Breger et al. 1991, p. 479).

A broader framework is needed that provides policymakers with a menu of devices depending on what and who is being regulated. Some substances are so toxic that command and control is needed. Some regulated parties are so weak that they will need to be paid to comply or driven out of business. In other cases a market can be created and environmental improvement can be accomplished through this mechanism.

Where possible, market mechanisms can be used to encourage compliant behavior and avoid the legal and administrative costs of direct regulation. Where necessary, government should provide subsidies and training and consulting services for organizations that do not have the capacity to comply with regulation. On occasion, government may decide that the costs of subsidizing regulation are so high and the benefits of regulation so important that a business should be allowed to die in order to protect the environment. These instances should be as infrequent as possible or the political support for protecting the environment will erode.

There is no reason to look for a magic bullet, a conceptual framework appropriate to all environmental problems. The proper policy tool should be determined by the situation. Sometimes a market device will work, sometimes command and control is required, and sometimes a blend of the two is needed.

Policy analysts often lament the fact that environmental goals are sold to the public with fear and inadequate risk assessment, and to politicians for their value as "pork." They argue that the goals of legislation and regulation should be based on careful scientific consideration of risks. Similarly, economists frequently argue that policy designs should reflect a careful assessment of costs and benefits, and should seek to achieve the maximum possible bang for the minimum possible buck. These ideas seem rational and attractive, but unfortunately they are not always feasible in the messy, pluralistic, federal political system in which we operate. Sometimes cost-benefit analysis is difficult to conduct. One problem is that the distribution of costs and benefits can be unpredictable and distribution effects can be more politically salient than overall costs and benefits. Another problem is that some costs and benefits cannot be compared without questionable assumptions about the relative weights assigned to specific cost and benefit factors.

There are no short cuts. Each regulatory program must be based on a strategy that seeks to understand the motivations of regulated parties and seeks to influence their behavior. Whether we decide to employ direct regulation, indirect market mechanisms, or direct subsidies, none of these approaches will work without a profound understanding of the parties and technologies being regulated. Developing the administrative capacity in government to make these assessments is far more important than making decisions on which regulatory mechanism is superior. With this knowledge in hand, environmental regulators can then develop flexible, dynamic strategies to reduce and prevent pollution in the real world. In turn, development of sustainable societies will become more feasible. More attention needs to be paid to the firms that create pollution and less attention to elegant but unworkable economic models and cumbersome legalistic formulations.

I am not suggesting that strategic planning is always easy or problem free. Some argue that it can only work in a politically calm climate. Admittedly, in times of turmoil and upheaval, implementing strategic planning will become more challenging. I believe that the potential results from successful strategic planning are worth the struggle.

NOTE

1. I served as staff director on that project and Sheldon Kamieniecki was the project's senior research fellow.

REFERENCES

Ackerman, Bruce A., and Richard B. Stewart. 1988. "Reforming Environmental Law: The Democratic Case for Market Incentives." *Columbia Journal of Environmental Law*, vol. 13, no. 2, pp. 171–200.

Bardach, Eugene, and Robert A. Kagan. 1982. "Introduction" in *Social Regulation: Strategies for Reform*, eds. Eugene Bardach and Robert A. Kagan. San Francisco: Institute for Contemporary Studies.

Breger, Marshall J., Richard B. Stewart, E. Donald Elliot, and David Hawkins. 1991. "Providing Economic Incentives in Environmental Regulation." *Yale Journal on Regulation*, vol. 8, pp. 463–495.

Breyer, Stephen. 1982. *Regulation and Reform*. Cambridge, MA.: Harvard University Press.

Cohen, Steven, and Sheldon Kamieniecki. 1991. *Environmental Regulation Through Strategic Planning*. Boulder, Colorado: Westview Press.

Daneke, Gregory. 1985. "Reassessing Attempts to Reform Environmental Regulation" in *Regulatory Reform Reconsidered*, eds. Gregory A. Daneke and David J. Lemak. Boulder, Colorado: Westview Press.

Hahn, Robert W., and Gordon L. Hester. 1989. "Where Did All the Markets Go? An Analysis of EPA's Emissions Trading Program." *Yale Journal on Regulation*, vol. 6, pp. 109–153.

Johnston, James L. 1991. "A Market Without Rights: Sulfur Dioxide Emissions Trading." *Regulation*, fall 1991, pp. 24–29.

Levenson, Leo, and Deborah Gordon. 1990. "Drive+: Promoting Cleaner And More Fuel Efficient Motor Vehicles Through A Self-Financing System of State Sales Tax Incentives." *Journal of Policy Analysis and Management*, vol. 9, no. 3, pp. 409–415.

Litan, Robert E., and William D. Nordhaus. 1983. *Reforming Federal Regulation*. New Haven: Yale University Press.

Meir, Kenneth J. 1985. *Regulation: Politics, Bureaucracy and Economics*. New York: St. Martin's Press.

National Academy of Public Administration. 1986. *A Strategy for Implementing Federal Regulation of Underground Storage Tanks*. Washington, D.C.: National Academy of Public Administration.

Pedersen, William F., Jr. 1991. "Future of Federal Solid Waste Regulation." *Columbia Journal of Environmental Law*, vol. 16, no. 1, pp. 109–142.

Stroup, Richard L., and Jane S. Shaw. 1989. "The Free Market and the Environment." *The Public Interest*, fall, no. 97.

Sunstein, Cass R. 1990. "Paradoxes of the Regulatory State." *The University of Chicago Law Review*, vol. 57, no. 2, pp. 407–441.

Tripp, James T.B., and Daniel J. Dudek. 1989. "Institutional Guidelines for Designing Successful Transferable Rights Programs." *Yale Journal on Regulation*, vol. 6, pp. 369–390.

Weidenbaum, Murray. 1992. "Return of the 'R' Word: The Regulatory Assault on the Economy." *Policy Review*, winter, pp. 40–43.

SECTION THREE

Environmental Equity and Environmental Justice

5 Two Faces of Equity in Superfund Implementation*

SHELDON KAMIENIECKI
JANIE STECKENRIDER

Policymakers argue that controlling and cleaning up toxic waste is essential to achieving a sustainable society (National Commission on the Environment 1993). Without instituting effective safeguards, toxic wastes tend to move through the air, water, and soil, threatening the survival of plants, animals, and the entire ecosystem. In addition to harming the environment, hazardous chemicals can enter underground aquifers, contaminate drinking water, and affect public health. Society must adopt recycling, recovery, resource conservation, and proper disposal techniques if the environment and public health are to be protected and sustained.

The problem of treating abandoned toxic waste sites is especially challenging. Many of these sites are huge and contain an unknown brew of extremely dangerous metals and chemicals. Even if hazardous waste specialists know the type and quantity of each chemical deposited at a site, they still remain in the dark about the combined effect of the chemicals, particularly after exposure to varying climatic conditions over long periods of time. Most environmental policymakers estimate that there are tens of thousands of such sites on both nonfederal and federal land (e.g., on military bases), and that it will cost hundreds of billions of dollars to clean up these sites (Church and Nakamura 1993).

*The authors would like to thank Robert O. Vos for sharing his ideas, thoughts, and materials on environmental justice with them, and George A. Gonzalez for his comments on this chapter.

The Superfund program, which is overseen by the federal Environmental Protection Agency (EPA), was originally created to clean up toxic waste sites that are decades old and, in most cases, long forgotten. The program has been much maligned by environmentalists, politicians, and the media for performing inefficiently and not meeting its goals. Among the chief criticisms of the Superfund program is that it has failed to abate chemical waste sites located in predominantly minority communities and that it unfairly requires certain companies to pay for cleanup at sites they never used for disposal. This chapter presents an in-depth examination of these two faces of equity in the Superfund program. More specifically, the study evaluates previous research on "environmental justice" and on financial liability. Although these two equity questions appear distinct on the surface, an argument is made at the end of the chapter that they share common ground on central issues related to risk assessment, the incentives of capitalism, and ideology. As will become evident, future revisions of Superfund must address serious environmental justice and financial liability controversies if the program is to achieve credibility. How these controversies are resolved, in turn, will provide important lessons for dealing with intergenerational environmental harm in other realms and for achieving a sustainable society. The study begins with a discussion of the evolution of the program.

THE SUPERFUND ODYSSEY

In 1977 an unusually wet spring thaw caused highly toxic chemical wastes to escape from a disposal site built in an abandoned canal in Niagara Falls, New York. Toxic chemicals contaminated private homes and an elementary school and eventually led to the evacuation of hundreds of Love Canal residents. The Love Canal incident, accompanied by scenes of frightened families and media reports of falling property values, caused many Americans to become deeply concerned about the possibility of "ticking time bombs" in their own neighborhoods (Hird 1994). EPA and health officials added to the panic by reporting that there actually might be thousands of similar toxic waste sites buried throughout the United States. As a consequence, Americans demanded immediate action, and Congress responded with legislation.

The Comprehensive Environmental Response, Compensation, and Liability Act (CERCLA) (Public Law 96–510), passed at the end of the Carter administration in 1980, represents an extremely bold and ambitious effort to clean up old and abandoned toxic waste sites across the country. The legislation established a $1.6 billion fund (a "Superfund"), financed by taxes on petroleum products and chemicals, for the purpose of abating land-based sites pending cost recovery actions against responsible parties. CERCLA also included liability provisions to force responsible parties to finance abatement costs. In cases where no party could be held liable or if the responsible party could not afford restitution, the fund, administered by EPA, would be used to cover cleanup costs.

O'Leary (1993) explains how the liability parameters of CERCLA have not been set by Congress or the EPA but by the courts (also see Grunbaum 1988). Specifically, the courts have interpreted liability under CERCLA as strict, joint and several for responsible parties. Strict liability, a term not included in the original bill, means that even if a company was dumping toxic wastes legally in the past, it can be found liable if it was dumping wastes that are now considered dangerous (e.g., see United States v. Tyson 1986). Hence, CERCLA's provisions are retroactive. Joint and several liability, a term deleted from earlier drafts of CERCLA, means that a company may be held legally responsible for the cleanup costs even if it disposed only a small portion of the waste (e.g., see United States v. Chem-Dyne Corp. 1983; United States v. Mirabile 1985). When this occurs, the burden remains with the responsible party to collect from the other negligent party(ies) (Hird 1994). Many responsible parties have turned around and sued their insurance company in an effort to recover cleanup costs assessed by the EPA.

The slow pace of cleanup at Superfund sites is directly attributable to the tangled web of litigation involving the federal government, corporate polluters, insurance companies, and occasionally unsuspecting small businesses and individuals. At a Superfund site in Long Island, New York, for instance, a toxic waste site occupying four acres leaked hazardous chemicals into groundwater and seawater. The EPA identified 257 responsible parties and determined they should pay for the $7.7 million cleanup. Over 135 law firms handled the original litigation. Four of the 257 responsible parties sued 442 insurance companies, which then hired 72 more law firms. The owner of the toxic waste site sued another 101 parties that he believed contributed to the pollution, prompting the hiring of many more attorneys (Healy 1994b).

At another Superfund site in Kalamazoo, Michigan, the Upjohn Company, a major pharmaceutical concern, was billed $20 million to clean up a toxic landfill. In an attempt to spread the cost among other polluters, Upjohn wrote letters threatening to sue to 741 parties that had dumped trash in the landfill. Among the parties that received letters were a flower shop and a little league. Even the mother of Upjohn's president at the time received a letter from Upjohn threatening to sue her (Healy 1994b).

Following the enactment of CERCLA, EPA officials spoke earnestly of a "shovels first, lawyers later" policy (Cohen 1984; Bowman 1988). The new law, however, met strong resistance from the Reagan administration, which was more interested in cutting federal regulation than in protecting the environment. EPA Administrator Anne Gorsuch-Burford withheld cleanup funds and delayed the program's implementation. The little Superfund money she did allocate was used to help Republican congressional candidates in 1982, most notably Republican Pete Wilson in his campaign against Democrat Jerry Brown for the U.S. Senate in California. Rita Lavelle, a deputy EPA administrator in charge of the Resource Conservation and Recovery Act (RCRA) and Superfund, was fired by President Reagan and later went to jail for lying to Congress about secret preferential treatment of certain chemical companies. Gorsuch-Burford was cited for contempt of Congress, and the resulting public scandal involving the RCRA and Superfund programs eventually forced her out of office.

Within four short years analysts began to characterize Superfund's implementation as "lunch now, lawyers maybe, but shovels never" (Bowman 1988). During this time morale among EPA officials sunk to its lowest level since the creation of the Agency in 1970. Most critics of the Superfund program (e.g., Rabe 1994) tend to overlook the damaging negative impact of the Reagan administration's four-year effort to politicize the program, nearly destroying it in the process. As a result, they generally reach misleading conclusions about the program's overall performance.

The Reauthorization of Superfund

William Ruckelshaus, the EPA's first administrator, replaced Gorsuch-Burford and immediately began working on improving agency morale as well as restoring outside confidence in the agency (Hird 1994). The Superfund program, in particular, had been poorly managed and was the subject of numerous complaints about its performance from Congress, environmentalists, and others. In four years, the EPA had successfully remediated only six sites.

Many in Congress believed that the problem of old, abandoned toxic waste sites was far more pervasive than earlier thought and that additional funds were needed as a result (Hird 1994). Unfortunately, members of Congress could not agree on Superfund's reauthorization and beginning in 1985 the program's taxing authority was suspended for a little over a year. This forced the EPA to scale back significantly the program's efforts and delayed cleanups even further. Finally, due to public pressure and effective lobbying by increasingly powerful environmental groups, Congress passed and President Reagan signed the Superfund Amendments and Reauthorization Act (SARA) (Public Law 99–499) into law in October 1986.

SARA represented a major expansion of the original Superfund program. The legislation established an $8.5 billion trust fund to be accumulated over five years, and it included strict cleanup goals for EPA. The trust fund was to be financed by a $2.75 billion tax on petroleum, a $2.5 billion broad-based tax on corporations with annual profits of more than $2 million, and a $1.4 billion tax on 42 basic organic and inorganic chemicals.[1] Another $1.25 billion was to come from general revenues, $300 million from interest on unused money in the fund, and $300 million from cost recoveries from responsible parties. As Table 5.1 shows, a large portion of the trust fund revenues between 1980 and 1993 (under CERCLA and SARA) has come from taxes on the petroleum and chemical industry and profitable corporations. Cost recoveries, in comparison, have contributed only a small fraction of revenues to the trust fund.

Table 5.1. Cumulative Trust Fund Revenues, Fiscal Years 1981–1993

Source	Dollar Amount[a]	Percent
Petroleum Tax	3,936	28
Environmental Income Tax	3,119	22
Chemical Tax	2,701	19
General Revenues	1,904	13
Interest	1,133	8
Advances	734	5
Cost Recoveries	732	5
Totals	14,259	100

[a]In millions of dollars.

Source: The data are derived from Katherine N. Probst, Don Fullerton, Robert E. Litan, and Paul R. Portney. 1995. *Footing the Bill for Superfund Cleanups: Who Pays and How?* Washington, D.C.: The Brookings Institution and Resources for the Future, p.15.

SARA included a number of other important provisions as well. The legislation directed EPA to use permanent cleanup remedies where feasible. An additional $500 million was appropriated for the abatement of leaking underground storage tanks (Cohen and Kamieniecki 1991).[2] SARA also included a Title III "right-to-know" provision requiring companies to provide local residents with information about which chemicals they use and dispose of, and a small grant program to finance technical studies for local interest groups to evaluate and possibly challenge EPA's recommended cleanup strategies (Hird 1994). In an effort to prevent the creation of future Superfund sites, the governor of each state was required to submit to EPA a capacity assurance plan (CAP) certifying that the state has a twenty-year capacity for hazardous waste treatment and disposal (Feldman, Peretz, and Jendrucko 1994; also see Peretz 1992; Rabe 1994). Failure to submit an approved CAP would result in a loss of Superfund money (except for emergency cleanups). Finally, the legislation affirmed the use of strict, joint and several liability.[3]

Superfund was granted a four-year extension in the 1991 budget reconciliation act (Public Law 101–508). The legislation extended the various tax provisions of SARA through December 31, 1995 or until $11.97 billion was credited to the trust fund, whichever came first. The Republican controlled Congress threatened to overhaul the entire Superfund program in 1995, particularly the program's liability provisions. President Clinton, who called the program "a disaster," responded with his own package of significant reforms (Healy 1994b).

SUPERFUND'S FAILURES AND SUCCESSES

The federal Superfund program has been the object of a number of criticisms, some involving the specific provisions of the law and others concerning the EPA's administration of the program. Potential responsible parties (PRPs), in particular, take issue with Superfund's retroactive, joint and several liability system which frequently implicates companies and individuals associated with a site regardless of whether they directly contributed to the contamination. Many old, abandoned toxic waste sites exist because of the actions, legal at the time, of either former company executives or firms that are no longer in business. Moreover, any liable party can be forced to pay for the total cost of abatement even if that party contributed only a fraction of the waste. In order to lessen the unfairness of the latter policy, the EPA has entered into early *de minimis* settlements with innocent landowners or firms that contributed minimally to a site (Glickman 1994). Similarly, "mixed funding" agreements, in which PRPs and the federal trust fund share costs of site abatement, expedite cleanup and allow EPA to pursue recalcitrant polluters for their share of remedial costs, including expenses borne by the fund.[4]

The projected total cost of abating all sites on the Superfund National Priority List (NPL) also is a major concern. The estimated average cost of cleaning up each site on the NPL varies widely, anywhere from $25 million (Congressional Budget Office 1994) to $50 million per site (Colglazier, Cox, and Davis 1991). The Congressional Budget Office (1994) estimates that the total cost of cleaning up all current and future Superfund sites will range between $106 billion to nearly $463 billion (adjusted for inflation). Such astronomical figures scare budget conscious lawmakers and companies that are paying for site cleanups now and who may have to pay for site cleanups in the future.

Still, Superfund is not the most costly federal environmental program as many critics imply. Overall, Superfund compliance expenditures account for less than five percent of the total amount spent each year on all federal environmental regulations (Probst et al. 1995). Hird's review of relative risks posed by radon, lead, and asbestos, however, "suggests that Superfund gains a disproportionate share of funding compared with the observed environmental and health risks of hazardous waste sites" and that "ozone depletion, habitat destruction, wetlands preservation, biodiversity, and others are more important environmental issues" based on scientific data (1994, p.114). Other criticisms of the Superfund program concern huge transaction costs due to extensive litigation (Acton and Dixon 1992), remedy selection (i.e., how clean should a site be?), the EPA's low rate of cost recovery (U.S. GAO 1994), the program's negative impact on property values and property transactions, and environmental justice issues.

Despite the chorus of negative assessments, Superfund has been successful in several ways. According to a report by the U.S. General Accounting Office (GAO), the "EPA has been successful in its efforts to compel responsible parties to clean up hazardous waste sites" (U.S. GAO 1994, p.3). As Table 5.2 shows, the EPA has reached over 2,000 settlements for Superfund cleanups. The estimated value of settlements with responsible parties rose from $2.1 million in 1980 to over $1.5 billion in 1992. (The decline in the value of cleanup agreements in fiscal year 1993, to $910 million, resulted primarily from a decrease in the average abatement costs for sites for which settlements were reached) (U.S. GAO 1994). Although most criticism has centered on the fact that few cleanups have been completed (only 237 of the 1,344 Superfund sites have been declared clean and safe) (Healy 1994b), the removal actions enumerated in Table 5.2 represent concrete measures that have been taken to protect public health and the environment. Unfortunately, as of the end of fiscal year 1993, the EPA had reached agreements with responsible parties or won court orders to recover only $1.2 billion (or 14 percent) of the $8.7 billion (recoverable costs) the agency spent in the Superfund program (U.S. GAO 1994). Nevertheless, the prospect of environmental audits and the looming threat of Superfund liability have clearly compelled industry to take more care in disposing their hazardous chemical waste (Glickman 1994; U.S. GAO 1994). Finally, the fact that private parties (and not government) are paying for site abatement encourages cost savings as well as managerial and technological innovation (Glickman 1994; Lindsey and Kelly 1994). Probst et al. (1995) report that responsible parties spend 15 to 20 percent less than the federal government when they implement site cleanup.

TWO FACES OF EQUITY IN ENVIRONMENTAL PROGRAMS

Researchers studying the implementation of Superfund and other environmental programs approach the question of equity from two seemingly different perspectives. From one side, a number of researchers, representing various disciplines in the social sciences, view equity strictly in terms of the disproportionate effects of pollution on minorities (e.g., United Church of Christ 1987; Bryant and Mohai 1992; Bullard 1983, 1993, 1994a, 1994b). These scholars, often affiliated with the "environmental justice" movement, seek to show how private industry exposes people of color (i.e., African-Americans, Hispanics, ethnic groups, etc.) to dangerous pollutants more than whites. At the same time they argue that government tends to delay pollution control and cleanup actions in minority areas.

Bullard (1994a), a sociologist, leading scholar, and advocate of the environmental justice movement, divides "equity" into three broad categories: procedural, geographic, and social. Briefly, "procedural equity" concerns "the extent to which governing rules and regulations, evaluation criteria, and enforcement are applied in a nondiscriminatory manner" (1994a, p.116). "Geographic equity" concerns the location, spatial configuration, and general proximity of minority communities to environmental threats, such as landfills, incinerators, Superfund sites, and other locally unwanted land uses (LULUs). "Social

Table 5.2. Settlements Made for Superfund Cleanups, Fiscal Years 1980–1993

	Cleanup Phases[a]				
Fiscal Year	**Removal No.**	**RI/FS No.**	**RD/RA No.**	**Totals**[b] **No.**	**Dollars**
1980	1	1	3	5	$ 2.1
1981	4	0	5	10	60.1
1982	8	4	8	21	22.8
1983	12	7	9	33	107.3
1984	54	20	11	98	147.6
1985	68	43	21	132	204.4
1986	51	59	18	132	743.2
1987	39	69	17	126	207.5
1988	97	79	43	221	578.6
1989	98	60	90	248	939.7
1990	127	73	112	312	1,461.9
1991	115	37	111	263	1,401.6
1992	102	42	102	246	1,530.4
1993	86	13	92	191	910.4
Totals	862	507	642	2,038	$8,317.6

[a]Superfund cleanups include three main phases: the removal phase, which typically consists of short-term cleanup actions; the remedial investigation and feasibility study (RI/FS) phase, in which a site's wastes and cleanup options are evaluated; and the remedial design and remedial action (RD/RA) phase, which involves long-term cleanup actions.

[b]Dollars in millions. Totals may include cases that are not listed by remedy or settlement type because the EPA categorizes them as unspecified.

Source: U.S. General Accounting Office, "Superfund: EPA Has Opportunities to Increase Recoveries of Costs." September 1994, p. 18.

equity" addresses the impact of social, political, and demographic factors on environmental policymaking. Bullard's (1994a) category designations reflect the view that equity narrowly means racial justice and equality. He pays almost no attention to how the burden of environmental risks should be distributed throughout the population and who should pay for pollution abatement. In Boerner and Lambert's (1994) view, most environmental justice advocates go beyond the familiar "NIMBY" ("not in my backyard") and instead call for "BANANA," or "build absolutely nothing anywhere near anything."

From a second side, a number of researchers, consisting mostly of economists and policy analysts, are mainly interested in financial equity, i.e., who should bear the cost of pollution control and who is liable for cleanups (e.g., Acton and Dixon 1992; Probst and Portney 1992; Probst et al. 1995). These researchers show little interest in environmental justice issues and are more concerned about matters related to cost-benefit analysis and the cost-effectiveness of Superfund and other environmental programs. The questions raised by environmental justice researchers on the one side, and economists and policy analysts on the other side are central to the successful implementation of Superfund. Yet, no one has analyzed and compared the assumptions and dynamics underlying the two different faces of equity.[5] Instead, the two groups of researchers overlook critical issues relevant to the varying conceptualizations of equity. An examination of the literature representing the different perspectives on equity in environmental programs, with particular attention paid to Superfund, follows.[6]

Environmental Justice

Bowman's chapter in this volume presents a comprehensive review of the environmental justice literature, and there is no reason to repeat what she already says in her study (also see Cutter 1995). Several investigations focus specifically on the Superfund program, however, and are worth exploring in this chapter.

Addressing issues in Bullard's (1994a) "procedural equity" category, Lavelle and Coyle (1992) analyze census data, the civil court case docket of the EPA, and the Agency's own record of enforcement and remediation at 1,177 Superfund sites between 1985 and 1991. They find that penalties for violating the law at Superfund sites with the highest number of whites are approximately 500 percent higher than penalties at sites with the highest number of minorities. In contrast, however, fines against polluters who have failed to abate toxic waste dumps tend to be higher in minority locations than in white locations. In addition, toxic waste sites in minority areas take 20 percent longer to be placed on the NPL than sites in predominantly white areas. Nevertheless, once a site is placed on the NPL, the pace of action quickens at minority sites compared to white sites. According to Lavelle and Coyle (1992), the EPA chooses "containment" over "permanent treatment" of sites more often in minority areas than in white areas.

Zimmerman's (1993) study, which covers issues related to "geographic equity," examines about 800 Superfund sites in the process of being abated to determine whether there is a statistical association between site location and percentage of minority residents. Her data show that racial and ethnic minorities are overrepresented in communities with sites in large urban locations, but are underrepresented with respect to the national average. In her analysis of cleanup decisions, she finds that predominantly African-American communities have fewer remediation plans than other communities.

Greenberg (1994) analyzes 113 NPL sites in 90 communities in New Jersey to determine whether priority ratings, based on the federal Hazard Ranking System (HRS), are related to race and ethnicity. The EPA uses the HRS to quantify the relative health hazard posed by a given site. Sites that exceed an HRS score of 28.5 on a one hundred-point scale are proposed publicly for placement on the NPL in the Federal Register.[7] Once on the NPL, sites become eligible for federal funding under Superfund, allowing cleanup to begin (Hird 1994). Greenberg (1994) finds higher rankings are not related to percentage of minority residents in municipalities and that the opposite might, in fact, be true. This is probably because minority communities are more reliant on surface water drinking sources than on potable ground water sources, which are more susceptible to contamination by nearby toxic waste sites. His study suggests that factors other than race and ethnicity can explain comparative risk assessments of toxic waste sites and whether such sites are included on the NPL.

Similarly, a study by Clean Sites, Incorporated (1990) finds no relationship between poverty and the location of hazardous waste sites. According to this study, only a small number of sites are situated in rural poor communities. Although fifteen percent of all counties are classified as rural and poor, these counties contain only four percent of Superfund sites and only two percent of RCRA facilities. The investigations by Clean Sites, Incorporated (1990) and Greenberg (1994) address elements central to Bullard's (1994a) three categories of equity.

Most studies find mixed results or no relationship between variables that measure procedural equity, geographic equity, social equity, and the designation and location of Superfund sites. In perhaps the most rigorous and sophisticated analysis of these relationships, Hird (1994) examines the distribution of NPL sites by counties in the U.S. and attempts to test competing hypotheses for site location by controlling for the overlapping influence of theoretically important variables. As Table 5.3 reveals, greater manufacturing presence is directly related to more county NPL sites, not a surprising finding. The data also

Table 5.3. Distribution of NPL Sites by County: Unweighted and Weighted Tobit Estimation Results[a]

Independent Variable	Unweighted Coefficient (t-statistic)	Weighted[b] Coefficient (t-statistic)
Quantity hazardous waste	–0.00 (1.17)	0.00 (1.60)
Manufacturing (%)	0.05*** (7.23)	0.04*** (4.72)
College educated (%)	0.07*** (2.72)	–0.01 (0.37)
Owner-occupied housing (%)	–0.07*** (4.18)	–0.09*** (5.14)
New housing units, 1970–80 (%)	–0.02*** (3.72)	–0.04*** (7.67)
Median housing value (/10,000)	0.55*** (5.15)	0.95*** (12.7)
Below poverty level (%)	–0.18*** (6.97)	–0.30*** (8.18)
Unemployed (%)	0.05 (1.58)	–0.05 (1.11)
Nonwhite (%)	0.02** (2.09)	0.05*** (4.57)
Population density (/10,000)	–0.58 (1.09)	–3.45*** (8.30)
Intercept	0.11 (0.07)	5.12*** (2.98)
Observations (N)	3138	3138
Log likelihood	–2202.39	–5992.58
Chi-square (10)	475.53	980.01
Prob ≥ chi-square	0.0000	0.0000

[a]Dependent variable = Number of final NPL sites per county.

[b]Weighted by county population.

Level of significance/two-tailed test:

* Significant at the .10 level.
** Significant at the .05 level.
*** Significant at the .01 level.

Source: John A. Hird, *Superfund: The Political Economy of Environmental Risk* (Baltimore: The Johns Hopkins University Press, 1994), p. 133.

indicate that a higher percentage of owner-occupancy housing and new housing units are associated with fewer NPL sites. Although Hird (1994) does not say this, these results may simply suggest that homeowners choose to live in the kinds of neighborhoods that are least likely to have toxic waste sites. In terms of an area's economic profile, the findings suggest that more affluent counties (determined by wealth and the absence of poverty) tend to have more sites.

A major debate in the literature is whether race or social class is more closely associated with polluted areas. In an effort to shed additional light on this question, Hird (1994) analyzes subsets of counties that contain high percentages of people living below the poverty level, the unemployed, nonwhites, and individuals residing in lower-valued housing. His findings appear in Table 5.4. As the data show, the number of Superfund sites in counties highly populated by the poor and unemployed is significantly below the national average. Moreover, a significantly larger number of sites are located where median housing values are higher than the national average for counties. Hird's (1994) further examination of the characteristics of counties with large numbers of Superfund sites reveal the same results and lead him to conclude that "NPL sites are located predominantly in more affluent counties and generally irrespective of race" (1994, p. 135). Other studies by Lester, Allen, and Lauer (1994) at the state level and by Allen, Lester, and Hill (1995) at the county level also demonstrate that race is not a factor in determining NPL designation and location.

Hird's (1994) results concerning race and wealth are open to varying interpretations. Ringquist (1995), who finds that race is a prominent factor in the siting of hazardous waste facilities, believes Hird's findings may indicate that, since inclusion on the NPL brings federal

Table 5.4. Average Number of NPL Sites per County

Poverty above 15.78 percent (N = 1292)	0.106* NPL sites
Unemployment above 8.7 percent (N = 1274)	0.230* NPL sites
Nonwhite population above 11.89 percent (N = 1195)	0.332 NPL sites
Median housing value above $35,296 (N = 1254)	0.738* NPL sites

*Statistically different from the average of 0.37 sites per county at the 99+ percent confidence level.

Source: John A. Hird, *Superfund: The Political Economy of Environmental Risk* (Baltimore: The Johns Hopkins University Press, 1994), p. 135.

funds and abatement, Superfund site designation will generally go first to those communities with the most political clout. Alternatively, as Greenberg's (1994) analysis suggests, other logical factors (e.g., proximity to sources of drinking water or to sensitive ecological areas) may explain why certain sites are included on the NPL. Of course, if Hird had in fact found more Superfund sites in predominantly minority areas, members of the environmental justice movement could have used the data to argue that industry and government have engaged in discriminatory practices for years by placing toxic waste sites in minority communities. It appears that the environmental justice literature is rich in data and poor in theory.

Most studies on environmental justice contain serious methodological flaws. Early analyses (e.g., Bullard 1983) tended to rely on isolated case studies to convey anecdotal accounts of environmental racism, and they failed to present solid empirical evidence to demonstrate the existence of an intentional policy to expose minorities disproportionately at the state or national level. More recent analyses, as Boerner and Lambert (1994) point out, define minority communities as those areas where the percentage of nonwhite residents exceeds the percentage of nonwhites in the entire population. Thus, a community may be coded "minority" even if a majority of its residents are white. Lavelle and Coyle's (1992) investigation, discussed earlier, suffers from this problem.[8] In some cases researchers fail to consider and correct for varying population densities (e.g., Bullard 1994a). Merely conveying the percentage of minority residents in a particular community does not provide information about how many citizens are actually exposed to environmental threats (Been 1994; Boerner and Lambert 1994). In addition, many studies define affected areas in geographic terms that are too broad. Previous research based on state (e.g., Lester, Allen, and Lauer 1994), county (e.g., Hird 1994; Allen, Lester, and Hill 1995), municipal (e.g., Greenberg 1994), or zip code areas (e.g., United Church of Christ 1987; Ringquist 1995) are likely to contain "aggregation errors" which can mask exposure patterns. Using census-tracts is better since they provide more precision in determining location of people and sites.

Other shortcomings of studies on environmental justice concern the actual risk of pollution sources and the failure to account for the changing dynamics of the area in which a site is located (Been 1994). Nearly all environmental justice investigations imply rather than explicitly state the actual risk presented by Superfund sites and other sources of pollution. Actual damage to the natural environment, including air and water quality and the soil, is rarely documented in research on environmental justice. Furthermore, most analyses simply match the location of industrial and waste facilities or toxic waste dumps with the present racial characteristics of the surrounding neighborhoods and do not consider community conditions when the facilities or dumps were located (Boerner and Lambert 1994). Given that neighborhoods can change drastically over time, there may be alternative explanations for high concentrations of minority residents near pollution sources. Been's (1994) reanalysis of Bullard's (1983) early study of environmental racism in the Houston area, for example, demonstrates that the dynamics of the housing market play a major role in creating environmental inequities. Future researchers, therefore, should consider historic patterns in employment opportunities, the housing market, zoning and land values, lending practices by banks, and other variables before reaching conclusions about environmental racism in a given locality.

While there has been a great deal of unsophisticated research on geographic equity, there has been little research of any kind on procedural equity. Lavelle and Coyle's (1992) work is a first step in this direction, however, more rigorous analysis on procedural equity is needed. How government responds to serious pollution problems, like Superfund sites, lies at the heart of equity, accountability, and the public trust.

Perhaps the most serious criticism of environmental justice studies is that they rely only on aggregate data to draw conclusions about individual behavior. Researchers who incorrectly generalize from one unit of analysis (e.g., state, county, zip code area, or census tract) to another (the individual) are said by statisticians to have committed an "ecological fallacy." Surveys based on scientific random sampling techniques and employing proper measurement procedures, although not without their problems, are a valuable source of information and should be used to supplement aggregate data analysis. Personal interviews with past and present decision makers and a randomly selected sample of residents can provide analysts important additional information about environmental racism in their communities. Future investigators in this field must develop theories and employ methodologies that take into account the dynamic and fluid changes which occur in industry, government, neighborhoods, and individuals over time. Only in this way will researchers arrive at a full and accurate understanding of whether and to what extent environmental racism exists in this country.[9]

Financial Equity: Who Should Pay for Site Cleanups?

A major obstacle to discussing who pays for cleaning up Superfund sites, as well as who should pay for site abatement, is a general lack of information. Unfortunately, very little is known about who pays for site cleanup under the current liability framework, much less how the distribution of cleanup costs would change under other liability schemes. As Probst et al. observe, "There is little publicly available information on how much is being spent to clean up the NPL sites . . . .Terms of settlement agreements are often confidential, making it impossible to estimate the distribution of costs among multiple parties at an individual site" (1995, p.25). These data are of critical importance to any assessment of financial equity in the Superfund program and to discussions of how best to correct present financial inequities (if they exist). Until such data becomes available, researchers will have to rely on estimates of the distribution of cleanup costs among different sectors of the population.

The literature presents three principles of financial equity. Most environmental laws, including CERCLA, are designed to follow "the polluter-pays" principle (Mazmanian and Morell 1992; Hird 1994; Probst et al. 1995). In following this principle, Superfund seeks to make those who generated the waste pay for damages caused by the pollution and its cleanup (at least ideally). In the same vein, those who have been harmed by pollution from a site, whether it be physically or economically, should be compensated.

"The polluter-pays" principle, as Hird maintains, "is potentially an effective and procedurally equitable policy instrument in regulating *prospective* pollution [author's emphasis]. By forcing polluters to pay the external costs imposed on others, using taxes or some other means, private decisions can be made to reflect social values" (1994, p.120). Thus, if a steel plant is faced with appropriate emissions penalties, it will not only factor in the costs of purchasing coal, raw materials, hiring employees, and other elements, but it will also consider the costs associated with emitting sulfur dioxide, particulates, and other air pollutants in doing business. If the level of the tax or financial penalty is set properly, the operators of the steel plant will limit the plant's pollution emissions to the point where the marginal costs of pollution reduction equal the marginal benefits (Hird 1994). In addition, the operators of the steel plant will be more likely to install advanced pollution control equipment in an effort to reduce long-term costs.

Several researchers, however, question whether Superfund truly satisfies "the polluter-pays" principle (e.g., Hird 1994; Probst et al.

1995). Since Superfund is intended to clean up abandoned toxic waste sites, it is extremely difficult to identify past beneficiaries (i.e., site owners, corporate executives, stockholders, and workers) of improper waste dumping and to recover their share of the ill-gained profits. Site owners, if they exist, are likely to be different, and most of the companies responsible for the disposal of waste at old sites are not likely to still be in business. Firms still in business will probably have different executives, shareholders, and workers. Under Superfund, however, current owners of businesses are considered responsible parties and must pay for cleanup costs. Furthermore, petroleum and chemical companies and large, profit-making corporations are taxed in order to raise money for the general trust fund which is used to finance the abatement of sites that are decades old. As one can see, therefore, retroactive liability and the tax scheme under Superfund runs counter to the standard of equity called for by "the polluter-pays" philosophy. This explains why insurance companies frequently go to court to block payment of cleanup costs of present policyholders who, in most cases, are not directly responsible for the pollution.

Equity in pollution control programs can also be achieved by adopting "the beneficiary-pays" principle (Fullerton and Tsang 1993; Probst et al. 1995). Under this principle the cost of cleanup is paid for by a tax on consumers who, when given a choice, buy products produced by polluting industries at a low cost. Similar to the problem with "the polluter-pays" principle under Superfund, however, those who presently purchase products sold by polluting industries are likely not the same ones who enjoyed the benefit of low prices through earlier consumption of the products. Incorporating "the beneficiary-pays" principle in Superfund would therefore be unfair.

A third way to achieve equity in environmental (and other) regulatory programs is by invoking "the ability-to-pay" principle (Probst et al. 1995). Following this principle, corporations and individuals are taxed on the basis of income, wealth, or some other measure of ability to pay taxes. State and federal personal income tax is based on this principle, with higher tax rates applied to those with higher incomes. "The ability-to-pay" principle could be applied under CERCLA by requiring polluting firms to pay annual Superfund taxes on the basis of the profits they earned during the previous year.[10] Tax revenues would then be deposited (as they are now) in a trust fund that would be used to pay for the cleanup of *all* Superfund sites which ceased operation prior to 1981 (when CERCLA became law). This would substantially decrease the number of liability suits and transaction costs. After 1981 PRPs should have exercised appropriate care in disposing their chemical wastes and would be held liable for site abatement.[11]

DISCUSSION AND CONCLUSION

This chapter has focused on the implementation of the Superfund program, with special attention paid to equity questions raised by advocates of the environmental justice movement and by economists and policy analysts concerning financial liability. As the review of the environmental justice literature showed, early research tended to rely on case studies and anecdotal evidence to support observations of environmental racism. While these investigations make for interesting reading, they tell us little about whether and, if so, to what extent environmental racism exists at the thousands of sites on and off Superfund's NPL.

Recent analyses tend to be more rigorous and sophisticated, allowing researchers to control for the overlapping associations between race, class, and other variables and permitting them to generalize their findings to the state or national level. The majority of these studies yield no correlation or mixed results concerning the association between race, class, and Superfund site designation, location, and abatement. Even these findings are questionable, however, since nearly all of the investigations rely solely on aggregate data and fail to track the dynamic social, economic, and political changes that have taken place since the Superfund sites were created many years ago. Although researchers may never be able to address the claims of the environmental justice movement in a definitive manner, there appears to be enough circumstantial evidence to indicate that, at some Superfund sites, the poor and people of color have been disproportionately exposed to chemical waste. This should be enough to warrant concern and government action to correct these kinds of inequities when they are found to exist.

This chapter has also analyzed whether the present tax and liability system under CERCLA is equitable. Based on this study's findings, and contrary to what environmentalists contend, Superfund does not follow "the polluter-pays" principle. Both the tax and liability scheme seeks to recover cleanup costs from parties and individuals who, in most cases, are not directly responsible for the contamination. Of course, one could argue (and many do) that, since these parties are members of industries that produce toxic waste, they should be held accountable for the cleanup of Superfund sites even if many of those sites were created over one hundred years ago. This argument has been a hard pill for responsible parties to swallow, and it has resulted in billions of dollars of litigation and associated transaction costs, producing long delays in the cleanup process. To be sure, Congress did not envision this kind of Superfund program. Future reauthorization of the program must address the equity problems concerning who should pay for site cleanups and how much.

While the debate over environmental justice and financial responsibility for abatement appears on the surface to touch upon different issues, there are major threads which tie the two faces of equity together. First, both environmental justice and liability must be addressed in the broader framework of risk assessment. Researchers and advocates of the environmental justice movement must first consider scientific information regarding level of exposure and risk before jumping to conclusions about environmental racism. Of course, as Rosenbaum's chapter in this volume demonstrates, how one defines and measures risk is controversial and deserves careful thought and consideration. Assuming a consensus can be reached on the definition and measurement of risk, future researchers and policymakers should integrate comparative risk assessment into analyses of environmental effects and the possible disproportionate exposure to pollution of low-income and minority residents living near Superfund sites. Risk should also be included in discussions concerning the designation of Superfund sites, the determination of responsible parties, the degree to which sites must be abated, and how much responsible parties should pay for cleanups. Although the HRS is flawed and probably needs to be revised or replaced by another measure, it is a fact that Superfund sites tend to differ substantially in terms of the threats they pose to the natural environment and public health. If good data on exposure and risk could be collected, the information could be used to determine the most cost-effective and environmentally protective, long-term abatement strategies. At present, political pressures rather than accurate scientific information often dictate the extent to which a site is abated.

The second connection between environmental justice and financial liability for site cleanup involves the incentives of the American capitalist system. As already mentioned, most NPL sites were created decades ago, long before CERCLA became law. Corporations, responding to the incentives of the market place, chose to dump their wastes at these sites for reasons of convenience and cost containment. The dynamic changes in employment patterns, land use, housing prices, and other related factors probably best explain the location and demographic composition of the neighborhoods in which most old toxic waste sites are located. No one has conducted a national study of these phenomena, casting further doubt on the race-based claims of the environmental justice movement. A competing theory, and one that deserves rigorous testing, might focus on the push-pull of market forces and the economic system on the least affluent in society over time. Such a theory might best explain why minority and disadvantaged groups live near certain Superfund sites.

Capitalism also sheds light on the current debate between corporations, insurance companies, and the federal government over liability under Superfund. The profit motive explains why Superfund sites were created in the first place as well as why corporations and insurance companies wish to avoid paying for site cleanups at the present time. The fact remains, however, that the contamination must be abated and someone has to pay for the cleanup. Since certain industries as a whole greatly benefitted financially from the inexpensive but harmful disposal of toxic waste, it is not unreasonable to require those industries to bear most if not all of the cleanup costs. Following "the ability-to-pay" principle, it would be fair to expect those companies with the highest profits to pay for site cleanups in cases where the parties cannot be identified or are no longer in business. In addition, moving toward a system of proportional liability in cases where there is a clear indication of which parties contributed to the pollution and how much would be more equitable than the present system. Under this framework, polluters at multiparty sites would be apportioned a "fair share" of the cleanup costs (Church and Nakamura 1993). Transaction costs, particularly those associated with protracted litigation, would be reduced substantially because polluters would only be held liable for their share of the contamination at a site rather than for the contamination of the entire site. The same economic incentives that were responsible for the existence of present Superfund sites (i.e., the drive to keep costs down and profits high) should be used to clean up current sites and prevent future hazardous waste sites from emerging.

Ultimately, ideology pervades the many controversies and opposing positions taken with respect to environmental justice and financial liability. Assessing costs and the distribution of costs, as well as whether the public or private sector pays for pollution control and cleanup and how much depends upon one's definition of fairness and justice. Unless economic self-interest is directly involved, one's deeply held liberal or conservative values will generally determine one's perspective and position on environmental justice and liability questions. This is probably why policymakers have found it difficult to reach agreements on the various equity issues in Superfund and other environmental programs.

From the standpoint of developing sustainable societies, the issue of equity in assessing costs for "unforeseen" environmental problems is an essential one. The determination of guilt and ability to pay must be carefully considered by legislators and policymakers in cases where the environmental damage took place at an earlier point in time. We will likely face this intergenerational question of liability many times in the future. Whether the legal system and the increasingly popular free-market approaches to pollution control can be adapted to deal more successfully with intergenerational environmental damage is uncertain at this juncture.

NOTES

1. As Hird correctly points out, "SARA's tax base was broadened due to fears that a tax only on chemical products would harm the international competitiveness of an industry where U.S. companies historically have thrived" (1994, p.13).

2. Kamieniecki, serving as a Senior Research Scholar, advised EPA on the development of an implementation strategy for this provision of SARA (see Cohen and Kamieniecki 1991). While he was in Washington, D.C., EPA circulated an unintentionally amusing memorandum informing those working on the implementation plan that the acronym for the leaking underground storage tank program, LUST, was to be changed to UST.

3. See Hird (1994) for a discussion of other provisions that were enacted under SARA.

4. As of 1994, the EPA had entered into only one hundred and one *de minimis* settlements and sixteen mixed funding agreements (Glickman 1994). Hird (1994) believes that the EPA has been hesitant to enter into mixed funding agreements because of fear that it will be accused of favoritism.

5. Hird (1994) might be considered an exception since his book empirically analyzes issues that are relevant to the environmental justice movement and the question of who pays for cleanups. His suggestions for reform at the end of his study, however, focus mostly on economic and process questions and very little on correcting future discriminatory practices in cleaning up Superfund sites.

6. For an excellent discussion of the definitions of environmental justice, environmental racism, and environmental equity see Kraft and Scheberle (1995).

7. See Mazmanian and Morell (1992) for an extensive discussion of the different factors used to compute HRS scores. Several investigations question the precision and equity of the HRS (Office of Technology Assessment 1988; Hird 1994; Cutter 1995). There is considerable debate, for example, over whether the HRS weighs ecological dangers too heavily over health threats. Nevertheless, it seems clear that EPA officials must employ some measure of risk in determining which sites should be included on the NPL and their priority for cleanup.

8. Boerner and Lambert (1994) requested the data on which Lavelle and Coyle (1992) based their findings. They were informed that the data would not be released because the results were "too controversial." It will therefore be impossible for future researchers to conduct tests of statistical significance on Lavelle and Coyle's data and verify their conclusions.

9. The federal government has only recently acknowledged the disproportionate exposure to pollution of disadvantaged and minority groups in some areas of the country. In 1992 the EPA released a report that found a strong relationship between the location of commercial hazardous waste facilities in communities and the percentage of minorities living in those communities (US EPA 1992). On the basis of this report the EPA created the Office of Environmental Equity. In February 1994 President Clinton signed Executive Order 12898 requiring federal agencies to "make environmental justice a part of all they do" (Healy 1994a, p. A21). Under the Executive Order, fair treatment of minority communities must be a factor in decisions ranging from the regulation of pesticides to the prosecution of polluters.

10. Insurance companies might also be included in this tax scheme. Many of these companies profited over the years through the low-cost, improper disposal of chemical wastes by their clients. Insurance companies were not held liable for the actions by their clients until after CERCLA was passed and many of the cases went to court. It would therefore be reasonable to impose a modest tax on these lucrative businesses.

11. Probst et al. (1995) recommend using federal revenues collected from personal income taxes to pay for site cleanups. Since the Internal Revenue Service is already collecting personal income tax, there would be less transaction costs than setting up an entirely new tax collection system or maintaining the existing one. Their suggestion is probably not politically feasible.

REFERENCES

Acton, Jan Paul, and Lloyd S. Dixon. 1992. *Superfund and Transaction Costs: The Experiences of Insurers and Very Very Large Industrial Firms*. Santa Monica, CA: RAND Institute for Civil Justice.

Allen, David W., James P. Lester, and Kelly M. Hill. 1995. "Prejudice, Profits, and Power: Assessing the Eco-Racism Thesis at the County Level." Paper presented at the Annual Meeting of the Western Political Science Association, Portland, Oregon, March 16–18.

Been, Vicki. 1994. "Locally Undesirable Land Uses in Minority Neighborhoods: Disproportionate Siting or Market Dynamics?" *Yale Law Journal* 103 (6):1383–1422.

Boerner, Christopher, and Thomas Lambert. 1994. "Environmental Justice?" Policy Study Number 121, Center for the Study of American Business, Washington University, St. Louis, Missouri.

Bowman, Ann O'M. 1988. "Superfund Implementation: Five Years and How Many Cleanups?" In *Dimensions of Hazardous Waste Politics and Policy*, eds. Charles E. Davis and James P. Lester, 129–46. Westport, CT: Greenwood Press.

Bryant, Bunyan, and Paul Mohai, eds. 1992. *Race and the Incidence of Environmental Hazards: A Time for Discourse*. Boulder, CO: Westview Press.

Bullard, Robert D. 1983. "Solid Waste Sites and the Black Houston Community." *Sociological Inquiry* 53 (spring):273–88.

Bullard, Robert D., ed. 1993. *Confronting Environmental Racism: Voices from the Grassroots*. Boston: South End Press.

Bullard, Robert D. 1994a. *Dumping in Dixie: Race, Class, and Environmental Quality*, 2d ed. Boulder, CO: Westview Press.

Bullard, Robert D., ed. 1994b. *Unequal Protection: Environmental Justice and Communities of Color*. San Francisco: Sierra Club Books.

Church, Thomas W., and Robert T. Nakamura. 1993. *Cleaning Up the Mess: Implementation Strategies in Superfund*. Washington, D.C.: The Brookings Institution.

Clean Sites, Incorporated. 1990. *Hazardous Waste Sites and the Rural Poor: A Preliminary Assessment*. Alexandria, VA: Clean Sites, Incorporated.

Cohen, Steven. 1984. "Defusing the Toxic Time Bomb: Federal Hazardous Waste Programs." In *Environmental Policy in the 1980s: Reagan's New Agenda*, eds. Norman J. Vig and Michael E. Kraft, 273–91. Washington, D.C.: Congressional Quarterly Press.

Cohen, Steven, and Sheldon Kamieniecki. 1991. *Environmental Regulation Through Strategic Planning*. Boulder, CO: Westview Press.

Colglazier, E. W., T. Cox, and K. Davis. 1991. *Estimating Resource Requirements for NPL Sites*. Waste Management Research and Education Institute, University of Tennessee, Knoxville, Tennessee.

Congressional Budget Office. 1994. *The Total Costs of Cleaning Up Nonfederal Superfund Sites*. Washington, D.C.: U.S. Government Printing Office.

Cutter, Susan L. 1995. "Race, Class, and Environmental Justice." *Progress in Human Geography* 19 (1):111–22.

Feldman, David L., Jean H. Peretz, and Barbara D. Jendrucko. 1994. "Policy Gridlock in Waste Management: Balancing Federal and State Concerns." *Policy Studies Journal* 22 (4):589–603.

Fullerton, Don, and Seng-Su Tsang. 1993. "Environmental Costs Paid by the Polluter or the Beneficiary? The Case of CERCLA and Superfund." NBER Working Paper 4418. Cambridge, MA: National Bureau of Economic Research.

Glickman, Joan. 1994. "A Superfund Retrospective: Past, Present, and . . . . ." *National Journal*, January 29, pp. 4–9.

Greenberg, Michael R. 1994. "Separate and Not Equal: Health-Environmental Risk and Economic-Social Impacts in Remediating Hazardous Waste Sites." In *Environmental Contaminants and Health*, eds. Shyarnal Majumdar, F.J. Brenner, E.W. Miller, and L.M. Rosenfeld. Philadelphia: Pennsylvania Academy of Science.

Grunbaum, Werner F. 1988. "Judicial Enforcement of Hazardous Waste Liability Law." In *Dimensions of Hazardous Waste Politics and Policy*, eds. Charles E. Davis and James P. Lester, 163–75. Westport, CT: Greenwood Press.

Healy, Melissa. 1994a. "Environmental Justice for U.S. Minorities is Ordered." *Los Angeles Times*, February 12, p. A21.

Healy, Melissa. 1994b. "Superfund's Biggest Mess May Be in the Courthouse." *Los Angeles Times*, July 10, p. A3.

Hird, John A. 1994. *Superfund: The Political Economy of Environmental Risk*. Baltimore: The Johns Hopkins University Press.

Kraft, Michael E., and Denise Scheberle. 1995. "Environmental Justice and the Allocation of Risk: The Case of Lead and Public Health." *Policy Studies Journal* 23 (1):113–22.

Lavelle, Marianne, and Marcia Coyle. 1992. "Unequal Protection: The Racial Divide in Environmental Law." *The National Law Journal*, September 21, pp. S1–S12.

Lester, James P., David W. Allen, and David A. Lauer. 1994. "Race, Class, and Environmental Quality: An Examination of Environmental Racism in the American States." Paper presented at the Annual Meeting of the Western Political Science Association, Albuquerque, New Mexico, March 10–12.

Lindsey, Alfred, and Meg Kelly. 1994. "EPA's SITE Program: Sharing Innovation Risks with Industry." *EPA Journal* 20 (fall):24–26.

Mazmanian, Daniel, and David Morell. 1992. *Beyond Superfailure: America's Toxics Policy for the 1990s*. Boulder, CO: Westview Press.

National Commission on the Environment. 1993. *Choosing a Sustainable Future*. Washington, D.C.: Island Press.

Office of Technology Assessment, U.S. Congress. 1988. "Are We Cleaning Up? 10 Superfund Case Studies-Special Report." Washington, D.C.: U.S. Government Printing Office.

O'Leary, Rosemary. 1993. "The Progressive Ratcheting of Environmental Laws: Impact on Public Management." *Policy Studies Review* 12 (3/4):118–36.

Peretz, Jean H. 1992. "Equity under and State Responses to the Superfund Amendments and Reauthorization Act of 1986." *Policy Sciences* 25 (2):191–209.

Probst, Katherine N., and Paul R. Portney. 1992. *Assigning Liability for Superfund Cleanups: An Analysis of Policy Options*. Washington, D.C.: Resources for the Future.

Probst, Katherine N., Don Fullerton, Robert E. Litan, and Paul R. Portney. 1995. *Footing the Bill for Superfund Cleanups: Who Pays and How?* Washington, D.C.: The Brookings Institution and Resources for the Future.

Rabe, Barry G. 1994. *Beyond NIMBY: Hazardous Waste Siting in Canada and the United States*. Washington, D.C.: The Brookings Institution.

Ringquist, Evan J. 1995. "The Sources of Environmental Equities: Economic Happenstance or Product of the Political System?" Paper presented at the Annual Meeting of the Western Political Science Association, Portland, Oregon, March 16–18.

United Church of Christ, Commission for Racial Justice. 1987. *Toxic Wastes and Race in the United States*. New York: United Church of Christ.

United States Environmental Protection Agency. 1992. *Environmental Equity: Reducing Risk for All Communities*. Washington, D.C.: U.S. Government Printing Office.

United States General Accounting Office. 1994. *Superfund: EPA Has Opportunities to Increase Recoveries of Costs*. Washington, D.C.: U.S. Government Printing Office.

United States v. Chem-Dyne Corp., 572 F. Supp. 802. 1983.

United States v. Mirabile, 14 Env't. Law Rep. 20992. 1985.

United States v. Tyson, 25 Env't. Rep. Cas. 1899. 1986.

Zimmerman, Rae. 1993. "Social Equity and Environmental Risk." *Risk Analysis* 13 (6):649–66.

6 Environmental (In)Equity: Race, Class, and the Distribution of Environmental Bads

ANN O'M. BOWMAN

"N.Y. State Accused of Environmental Racism for Incinerator Site," read the headline in the *Christian Science Monitor* (1994, 11). The newspaper article featured residents of the downtown Albany area adjacent to the trash-burning incinerator complaining about the stench and cataloging the incidence of serious respiratory illnesses in the neighborhood. Those interviewed contended that officials had not responded to their concerns and their pleas to shut down the facility because "this area is 99 percent black. They [the officials] have never bothered." The residents believed that they were victims of "environmental racism," i.e., as members of a minority community, they were being forced to bear a disproportionate burden of pollution. New York State officials contended otherwise. They claimed that the racial characteristics of the neighborhood had nothing to do with the placement of the incinerator. The facility was a cogeneration or waste recovery operation—burning garbage and trash to provide heat for nearby government offices. The officials argued that, "the proximity to downtown government buildings was the key factor in the location of the incinerator." Yet when the incinerator malfunctioned and sent out a shower of unburned particles into the air and onto the ground (some landing at the governor's mansion), the incinerator was closed. The story quoted an environmentalist working with the New York Public Interest Research Group, an organization supportive of the residents' claims, who charged that "if it was in any other neighborhood in Albany, it [the incinerator] would have been shut down years ago."

The newspaper article captured the essence of contemporary disputes over environmental racism. In the words of a U.S. Environmental Protection Agency (EPA) administrator, "It's a fairness issue. It's unfair that these communities bear a disproportionate risk burden simply because of their race . . ." (*Christian Science Monitor* 1994, 11). The Albany incinerator example is but one case of a larger phenomenon. Two legal scholars put the issue this way:

> People of color throughout the United States are receiving more than their fair share of the poisonous fruits of industrial production. They live cheek by jowl with waste dumps, incinerators, landfills, smelters, factories, chemical plants, and oil refineries whose operations make them sick and kill them young. They are poisoned by the air they breathe, the water they drink, the fish they catch, the vegetables they grow, and in the case of children, the very ground they play on (Austin and Schill 1994, 53).

The language is undeniably powerful, but is it as accurate as it is forceful? As this chapter demonstrates, untangling the issue of environmental equity is neither simple nor straightforward. The concept itself is slippery; some of the research associated with it has been driven by ideology. That may, in part, be the reason for the inconsistent findings that characterize the literature. One group of researchers uncovers seemingly incontrovertible evidence of environmental racism; another finds it irrefutably absent. This chapter traces the evolution of the concept, seeking to expose its nuances. Following that, the emergence of environmental equity as a movement—both environmental and political—is explored. The penultimate section of the chapter tackles the question of extant research and its disparate findings. The last part addresses some of the unresolved issues.

ENVIRONMENTAL RACISM ⟶ ENVIRONMENTAL EQUITY ⟶ ENVIRONMENTAL JUSTICE

Although environmental racism as a concept first emerged after a well-publicized incident in North Carolina, it has origins in two literatures and movements with longer histories: grassroots environmentalism and civil rights. For environmentalists, the protests against the disposal of toxic soil in a rural southern community were emblematic of the "not in my backyard" or "NIMBY" phenomenon. Facilities such as hazardous waste landfills present a case of concentrated costs and diffuse benefits—the local community assumes a high proportion of the risk, the rest of the state, for example, enjoys the positive effects (use and revenues) of a nonproximate site. Decisions to site these facilities typically trigger a NIMBY reaction among residents of the unfortunate community. On the defensive, citizens formed local environmental organizations to oppose the facility. Although the organizational impetus is opposition to the facility, grassroots environmentalism is about empowerment, among other things (Gottlieb 1993).

The North Carolina case added another element to what might have been a standard NIMBY protest: the racial characteristics of the affected population. Warren County, the jurisdiction selected to host the new landfill, was majority African-American. Protests against the disposal facility attracted civil rights organizations and prominent African-American politicians to the fray. What might have otherwise been dismissed as a NIMBY event became a civil rights cause. Justifiably protectionist behavior by residents took on new meaning: it was a fight against environmental racism.

"Environmental racism" is descriptive of a condition that can be seen as part of a larger web of institutionalized racism. It is like racism in housing or employment, or racism in education policy. According to Collin, it is "race-based discrimination in environmental policymaking; race-based differential enforcement of environmental rules and regulations; the intentional targeting of minority communities for toxic waste disposal and transfer and for the siting of polluting industries; and the exclusion of people of color from public and private boards, commissions, regulatory bodies, and environmental nonprofit organizations" (1993, 41).

Although the dispute in North Carolina involved African-Americans, environmental racism has broadened beyond the black/white context. As Collin's definition in the preceding paragraph illustrates, phrasing such as "minority communities" and "people of color" characterizes the literature. To operationalize those terms, the United Church of Christ's Commission on Racial Justice (CRJ), in its landmark study, focused on four racial and ethnic groups: Blacks, Hispanics, Asian/Pacific Islanders, and American Indians. (CRJ used the U.S. Bureau of the Census' labels for those groups.) Increasingly, however, the term "minority groups" is being replaced by the phrase "people of color." The shift in terminology acknowledges the spread of the movement beyond U.S. borders into nations in which people of color constitute majority populations.

Despite the richness of the concept "environmental racism," a related term has gained in usage: environmental equity. It came to the fore for several reasons not in the least of which was the belief (in some instances, supported by evidence) that the victims of environmental "bads" frequently included low-income populations, regardless of race or ethnicity. The existence of class-based discrimination made environmental racism seem an incomplete description of the condition. Descriptive clarity aside, the term "environmental equity" was used in a 1992 report by the EPA in what the agency considered a neutral sense. Environmental equity could include environmental policymaking and the administration of environmental protection programs, as well as the more common understanding of it as the distribution and effects of environmental problems. Some of the leading researchers in the field such as Bullard opined that EPA's "environmental equity report reveals itself as a public relations ploy to diffuse the issue of environmental racism" (1993, 196). Thus employing the term "equity" rather than "racism" has substantive import.

More recently, the call for environmental equity has been supplanted by another rallying cry: environmental justice (Kraft and Scheberle 1995). The positive connotations of the word "justice" and its action orientation validate the term. Environmental justice is both a goal and a movement. As a conceptual construction or "frame," environmental justice contains specific claims related to the nature of environmental grievances. According to Capek, these claims include the right to:

(1) accurate information about the situation,

(2) prompt, respectful, and unbiased hearings when contamination claims are made,

(3) democratic participation in deciding the future of the contaminated community,

(4) compensation from parties who have inflicted injuries on the victims (1993, 8).

Although it is not posited as a right, Capek (1993) identifies another element in the environmental justice frame: the commitment to solidarity with victims of contamination in other communities.

Zimmerman offers this distinction between equity and justice. "Equity typically refers to the distribution of amenities and disadvantages across individuals and groups. Justice, however, focuses more on procedures to ensure fair distribution" (1994, 633). This sentiment is echoed by Torres, "if justice is to be achieved one must consider not only the distributional impacts that environmental remedies will have, but also the decisionmaking process by which such impacts are allocated" (1994, 451). Perhaps reflecting this broader meaning, the EPA changed the name of its Office of Environmental Equity to the Office of Environmental Justice.

The distinction both Zimmerman and Torres make between distributional equity and procedural equity, while noteworthy, may not get to the heart of environmental justice. To achieve environmental justice, Lake contends that full democratic participation is required "not only in decisions affecting distributive outcomes but also, and more importantly, in the gamut of prior decisions affecting the production of costs and benefits to be distributed" (1995, 7). Myriad layers of decisions must be peeled back. Consequently, he urges those committed to the goal of environmental justice to "mobilize a movement for self-determination" (Lake, 1995, 14). Only then will true environmental justice be attained. Others see the situation similarly. For example, Pulido (1994) argues that even with the democratization of the decisionmaking process, universal environmental quality will not be forthcoming. The failure to address social and spatial inequities, coupled with "the absence of public accountability in private production decisions" dooms the effort (Pulido, 1994, 921).

ENVIRONMENTAL RACISM: THE ISSUE ACHIEVES AGENDA STATUS

As noted, the cry "environmental racism!" was first heard in the early 1980s when protestors fought vigorously against the dumping of polychlorinated biphenyl (PCB)-contaminated soil in a rural, majority black North Carolina county.[1] Despite their lack of success in the short-term—the toxic soil was buried in Warren County—the protests sparked a movement that has become the subject of scholarly research and debate as well as government study and action.

Immediately after the Warren County protests, the U.S. General Accounting Office (GAO) was asked by Congress (more precisely, by the delegate to Congress from the District of Columbia, Walter E. Fauntroy) to study the demographic characteristics of four southern communities that contained commercial hazardous waste landfills. In 1983, the GAO released its report showing that although blacks comprised about twenty percent of the region (defined as EPA's Region IV), three of the four landfills were located in areas with majority black populations. The data also indicated that these areas contained a relatively high proportion of poor people, a substantial majority of whom were black. The GAO findings confirmed a pattern of locating disposal facilities that had been uncovered in Houston, a city in which blacks comprise slightly under thirty percent of the population. There, a study of the location of municipal solid waste disposal facilities found evidence of inequities in siting. Bullard's (1983) data showed that of the thirteen landfills or incinerators operated by the city, eleven were located in neighborhoods that had a majority black population.

Neither the GAO nor the Houston study generated the amount of attention as the 1987 report issued by the United Church of Christ's Commission on Racial Justice (CRJ). The CRJ study was a comprehensive, national investigation of the social and economic characteristics of areas containing specific environmental threats; namely, commercial hazardous waste facilities and uncontrolled toxic waste sites. The report concluded that although socioeconomic status played a role, "race proved to be the most significant among variables tested in association with the location of commercial hazardous waste facilities" (1987, xiii). This report served, in effect, to put the issue of environmental racism on the institutional agenda. In fact, it was the executive director of the CRJ, Benjamin Chavis, who popularized the term "environmental racism" at the press conference accompanying the release of the study.

Thus launched, several events conspired to keep the issue at the forefront. A host of grassroots organizations such as the Gulf Coast Tenants Organization, the Southwest Organizing Project, and the Commission for Racial Justice put traditional environmental groups on the spot by accusing them of elitism and racism (Bullard 1994a).[2] The courtroom provided another venue for charges of environmental racism. By the late 1980s, environmental justice groups were using civil rights statutes and constitutional guarantees such as the equal protection clause as the basis for their complaints.[3] In 1989, a Georgia case, East Bibb Twiggs Neighborhood Association v. Macon-Bibb County Planning and Zoning Commission, used the environmental discrimination argument to challenge the siting of a landfill. A similar complaint led to a Tennessee lawsuit, Bordeaux Action Committee v. Metro Government of Nashville. The following year, two environmental discrimination cases were heard: R.I.S.E., Inc. v. Kay and El Pueblo para El Aire y Agua Limpio v. Chemical Waste Management, Inc. None of the judicial rulings in these four cases found in favor of the plaintiffs. For example, in the R.I.S.E. (Residents Involved in Saving the Environment) lawsuit in Virginia, the federal court acknowledged the discriminatory racial impact in the pattern of landfill siting but concluded that "the intent to discriminate" had not been proven. The issue of intent has been the critical stumbling block in using civil rights statutes to challenge siting decisions. As Collin (1993) notes, successful litigation of violations of the equal protection clause requires that plaintiffs provide evidence of purposeful discrimination, an admittedly difficult task.[4]

Despite the judicial setbacks, environmental racism remained a salient political issue. In January 1990, the School of Natural Resources at the University of Michigan sponsored a conference called "Race and the Incidence of Environmental Hazards." This gathering of academics and activists adopted the term "environmental equity" as a means of broadening the focus beyond matters of race to issues of social class. Out of the conference came the Michigan Coalition, a group of activists and academics that pressed the EPA to take up the issue of environmental equity (Roque 1993). The EPA responded and in July 1990, the agency created an Environmental Equity Workgroup. One of the workgroup's tasks was to assemble and evaluate the evidence regarding the disproportionate risk burden borne by racial minority and low-income people.

In June 1992, the EPA's workgroup published its report, *Environmental Equity: Reducing Risk for All Communities* (1992). The report reviewed numerous studies and concluded that there appeared to be a link between the racial and socioeconomic characteristics of a community and its exposure to some types of pollutants. In a display of bureaucratic responsiveness, the agency established an Office of Environmental Equity in 1992 (eventually renamed the Office of Environmental Justice.)

The issue of environmental racism made its way to Congress during this period. An amendment in 1992 to the Resource Conservation and Recovery Act reauthorization bill sought to require "community information statements." These statements would identify the demographic composition of proposed waste site areas, assess the existing environmental burden in those communities, and estimate the cumulative impact of the proposed facilities (Bullard 1994b). That same year, Congressman John Lewis and Senator Al Gore introduced an environmental justice act that called for "a program to ensure nondiscriminatory compliance with environmental, health, and safety laws and to ensure equal protection of the public health" (Bullard 1994b, 16). Neither of these bills were passed.

The concept was further institutionalized when, in his Earth Day message in 1993, President Clinton directed EPA to work with the Department of Justice ". . . to begin an interagency review of federal, state and local regulations and enforcement that affect communities of color and low-income communities with the goal of formulating an aggressive investigation of the inequalities in exposure to environmental hazards" (U.S. EPA 1995, 3). That sentiment was extended in a 1994 executive order requiring federal agencies to insure that their programs did not unfairly inflict environmental harm on the poor and racial minorities (Cushman 1994). Executive Order 12898 instructed all federal agencies to develop a comprehensive environmental justice strategy that "identifies and addresses disproportionately high exposure and adverse human health or environmental effects of their programs, policies and activities on minority populations and low-income populations" (U.S. EPA 1995, 3).

ENVIRONMENTAL (IN)EQUITY: AN EXAMINATION OF THE EVIDENCE

Environmental equity does not suffer from a dearth of research. Myriad studies exist on the differential impact of environmental bads on various subgroups in the population. Careful examination of these studies suggests that a degree of caution, or perhaps a host of caveats, is advisable in assessing their explanatory value.[5] Some of the work has a prescriptive nature or advocacy orientation, such as the study of incinerators conducted by Greenpeace researchers Pat Costner and Joe Thornton (1990). In fact, much of the trend setting work, e.g., Bullard (1983) in Houston and Mohai and Bryant (1992) in Detroit, has been conducted by scholar/activists.

The review of the empirical literature that follows proceeds chronologically; representative studies from the 1970s, 1980s, and 1990s are presented. At issue, of course, is the fundamental question of distributional equity: are people of color and people in poverty experiencing a disproportionate pollution burden?

The 1970s: Race, Class, and Air Quality

In their chapter in the edited collection, *Race and the Incidence of Environmental Hazards*, Mohai and Bryant (1992) review the extant evidence on the distribution of environmental burdens. Their primary interest in the early studies was the findings, especially whether race or income was the more important influence. Searching the literature, they uncovered work that had been conducted long before the term environmental racism had even been coined. For example, research published in 1972 reported substantially higher exposure rates for low-income groups than upper-income groups to total suspended particulates and sulfates in the air. The findings for race were even more compelling. In the study, confined to three cities—Kansas City, St. Louis, and Washington, D.C., the exposure rate of racial minority groups was greater than that of the lowest income group. A critical question, however, is whether the findings were simply a function of the composition of the sample. That is, was there something unusual about the three communities that limited the generalizability of the results?

Other research of that era reported in the Mohai and Bryant study came to varying conclusions about the influence of income and race. An analysis of New Haven, Connecticut, published in 1976, found that census tracts with high concentrations of poor residents were associated with areas containing highly polluted air. There appeared to be no relationship, however, between polluted air and the concentration of African-American residents. In 1978, research on air pollution in Chicago, Cleveland, and Nashville revealed race to be more weakly correlated with pollutant level than was median family income. Extension of the research to cities in twenty-three states led to similar conclusions.

By the end of the 1970s, according to Mohai and Bryant, the study of air pollution had moved beyond subsets of cities. The results of a nationwide analysis of air pollution levels proved interesting, especially on the income issue. Rather than finding a negative relationship between income level and exposure to air pollution as the studies mentioned previously had, a positive one was found. Part of the explanation for the contrary findings has to do with the research design—the dependent variable was the estimated dollar damage suffered from exposure to air pollution rather than exposure levels themselves. Moreover, the analysis combined urban and rural areas. Regardless of income level, however, racial minorities suffered greater economic damage from air pollution than whites did.

Thus, long before the dispute in Warren County, North Carolina and even prior to the use of the term environmental racism, there was analytical evidence of the disproportionate impact of environmental bads, more precisely, air pollutants.[6] But that early work was narrow not only in scope, it was methodologically limited. Subsequent research has broadened the scope of the inquiry and sharpened its methodological edge.

The 1980s: Race, Class, and Toxins

As noted earlier, the 1982 GAO study of large commercial hazardous waste landfills in the South and Bullard's 1983 study of solid waste landfills and incinerators in Houston found evidence of environmental discrimination. Both of the studies arrive at their conclusions by strikingly similar logic. Because the proportion of African-Americans is higher in the areas near the facilities than it is in the region (GAO) or city (Bullard) as a whole, the conclusion is that environmental discrimination exists. Putting aside problems associated with sample selection (GAO) and definition of neighborhood (Bullard), the simple logic of proportionality is flawed. Comparing proportions of a sample to proportions of a larger entity begs for the use of, at a minimum, tests of statistical significance. Such tests would provide some assurance that the results occurred other than by chance. That resolved, there still may be other factors driving the purported relationship. Only by testing multivariate models can the relative influence of socioeconomic or racial characteristics be determined. In addition, measures of proportion reveal nothing about the distribution or clustering of the population (Been 1994). Density affects the impact of a facility even in areas with the same proportional characteristics. Further, if the contention is that a bias exists in siting facilities (and when the focus is on facilities, siting is a central concern), then the problem of timing and sequencing arises, that is, linking old siting decisions to current demographics.

Some of the limitations were addressed in two studies conducted during the 1980s, both involving toxic waste facilities and sites. The first study examined the location of abandoned hazardous waste sites in New Jersey—the state with the highest number of such Superfund sites on EPA's National Priority List (NPL). Most of the worst sites are clustered in the northeastern part of the state, a section that is highly urbanized and industrialized. Greenberg and Anderson (1984) offered five testable explanations for the location of these sites:

(1) Abandoned dump sites are located near hazardous waste producers, transporters and users, existing waste disposal sites, and major transportation routes in order to minimize the cost of disposal.

(2) Dump sites are not likely to be found in populous communities with strong, mayor-council forms of government, planning boards, and environmental commissions; with voters who are strongly supportive of environmental

issues; and in communities near important seats of political power. In other words, communities with little political power disproportionately bear the burden of such sites.

(3) Dump sites are likely to be located in communities with a large industrial, economic base and land uses compatible with industrial activities. Dump sites, then, are the negative side effect of an otherwise beneficial placement of industry in a community.

(4) Dump sites are not likely to be found in populous communities with high socioeconomic status, and in places with low numbers of young, elderly, and minorities, and where population growth is due to migration. Sites are located in low-status, high minority communities.

(5) Dump sites are located in places with the most favorable geological formations removed from population centers and water supplies. In other words, it is physical compatibility that determines location.

Statistical testing led Greenberg and Anderson (1984) to reject two of the hypotheses. The location of abandoned hazardous waste dump sites in New Jersey was not related to physical compatibility, and it is not a function of political powerlessness. The other hypotheses were supported by the data. Several factors differentiated the severely affected communities (those with major dump sites and those containing many dump sites) from the unaffected communities: an industrial economic base, proximity to potential sources of hazardous waste, and a population that has more poor residents and higher proportions of elderly, young, and African-Americans. More tellingly for the environmental equity thesis, when the analysis was confined to communities with one or two dump sites, the only factors that differentiated these communities from their "no dump" neighbors were the demographic characteristics of the residents.

The New Jersey findings lent credence to the class and race explanations found in the air pollution research of the 1970s and the waste site findings of the GAO (1983) and Bullard (1983). The CRJ study, with its national focus, added even more evidence. Two different types of hazardous waste sites were the foci: the operations known as transportation, storage, and disposal (TSD) facilities and the closed or abandoned sites that the EPA had listed in its "uncontrolled toxic waste site" data base. To determine whether class and race were associated with the location of TSDs, the nation was divided into areas by five-digit zip codes. Each area was placed into one of four mutually exclusive groups based on the number and size of TSD operations. Five independent variables were used in the analysis to capture race and ethnicity, socioeconomic status, and the extant hazardous waste profile of the area. Several statistical tests were performed, all of which pointed to the same conclusion: the minority population percentage was the "best" explanation for TSD location. It consistently outperformed the other variables. Areas with one commercial toxic waste facility had a minority population that was twice as high as neighborhoods without a facility. (In an appendix, state by state analysis was presented. Given the varying number of TSDs by state [Ohio and California have more than forty; Idaho, Iowa, Nevada, New Hampshire, and North Dakota have only one] and their different racial and ethnic make-ups, the minority population percentage variable is significant in approximately forty percent of the states.) CRJ's analysis of the uncontrolled toxic waste sites was less systematic but it, too, demonstrated the concentration of sites in high minority communities. Looked at from a different angle, approximately sixty percent of blacks and Hispanics lived in areas containing an uncontrolled hazardous waste site.

The 1990s: Race, Class, and Environmental Bads

The work that has been done in the 1990s has pushed the environmental justice issue in assorted directions, although the orientation remains one of distributional equity. The research continues to seek a definitive answer to the "is it race?," "is it class?," or "is it something else?" question.

Single-state studies such as those conducted in South Carolina have shed more light on the environmental equity at various levels of aggregation. Comparative county research in the state focused on three risk indicators: the number of acute airborne toxins, the amount of toxic releases, and the amount of hazardous waste generated. According to Cutter (1995), it was residents of racially-mixed, urbanized, average-income counties who bore the greatest exposure to these risks. Two other studies tested the relationships between socioeconomic characteristics and the location of hazardous waste facilities. Analysis of census tracts and block groups showed that TSDs were clustered in densely populated urbanized areas, not disproportionately located in minority or economically disadvantaged communities (Holm 1994). Crews-Meyer's (1994) research, set at both the county and block group levels, revealed little support for race and income as explanations for the location of hazardous waste sites. Instead, population size was the most powerful predictor of location. The South Carolina results, if generalizable beyond the confines of the state, raise questions about the universality of the environmental racism thesis.

Equity questions drove Hird's (1994) extension of Greenberg and Anderson's (1984) single-state work on Superfund sites to a national context. The multivariate model used in the analysis included measures of the hazardous waste milieu of the area, the potential political activism of the residents, and their socioeconomic and racial characteristics. The number of NPL sites in a county served as the dependent variable. Using tobit analysis, Hird found that counties with strong manufacturing bases contained more NPL sites. The political activism results were mixed; the findings regarding socioeconomic and racial characteristics were clear-cut. Contrary to expectations, poorer counties did not contain more NPL sites than their wealthier counterparts. In fact, it was the economically advantaged jurisdictions that had more of these sites. On the question of race, the findings were consistent with those of the CRJ study. When other factors were held constant, counties with higher percentages of nonwhites contained more Superfund sites. However, when Hird pursued the analysis, the link between race and the number of Superfund sites became problematic. Counties that exceeded the national average of nonwhite population percentage actually contained fewer than average NPL sites. When the focus shifted to counties with exceptionally high numbers of NPL sites (defined as ten or more), the nonwhite percentage was only slightly higher than average. (These unexpected relationships were not statistically significant.) Further extension of the research produced equally confounding results. The counties hosting the NPL sites scoring the highest on the EPA's Hazard Ranking System, ostensibly the most dangerous sites, had lower percentages of nonwhites (and lower rates of poverty and unemployment and higher median housing values).

Other studies have concentrated on commercial hazardous waste facilities currently in operation. However, the findings fail to provide definitive explanations for their location and number. Anderton et al. (1994) found little support for the argument of environmental racism in the location of TSDs. Looking beyond location to a TSD's plans for expansion (or reduction) of its waste processing capacity, Hamilton (1995) found mixed evidence of environmental racism. The Anderton et al. analysis, national in scope, was conducted at the census tract level. They conclude that "evidence of racial and ethnic inequity in location of hazardous waste facilities is almost nonexistent" (Anderton et al. 1994, 242). Instead, employment and occupation appear to have more to do with locational patterns.

The findings from the Hamilton (1995) study were not conclusive in either direction. In the analysis conducted at the county level, race was not associated with capacity expansion plans. Hamilton's data showed that in counties containing TSDs with expansion plans, the average nonwhite population was sixteen percent compared to fifteen percent in those counties with TSDs without net additions planned. Nevertheless, race was a statistically significant factor in plans to reduce processing capacity. That is, counties with higher nonwhite population percentages were less likely to contain a facility slated for a net reduction in capacity. At the zip code level, however, a higher percentage of nonwhites (25 percent) resided in neighborhoods with facilities targeted for expansion than in neighborhoods where facilities did not have expansions slated (18 percent).

Research on EPA enforcement and remediation actions offered a different take on the question of environmental inequities. According to Lavelle and Coyle (1992), agency behavior showed a pattern of racial and class disparities. The EPA levied more severe fines against polluters in white communities than in minority communities. As for cleaning up waste sites, the EPA took action more quickly at sites located in affluent neighborhoods than in poorer neighborhoods.

The research discussed thus far in this section shares one important characteristic: a reliance on a pre-existing unit of analysis, be it a county, a census tract, or a zip code area. Although these entities are useful for data collection, they do not offer uniform measures of space and distance—a particularly significant problem when the central question is patterns of distribution. A county may have a land area of twenty square miles; it also might be two hundred square miles. Census tracts and zip codes are derived from population characteristics; their boundaries are not uniform. Two recent studies have resolved the unit of analysis problem in rather creative fashions.

In a case study of the Devil's Swamp hazardous waste landfill near Baton Rouge, Louisiana, proximity was self-defined; that is, survey respondents were asked whether they lived near the facilities (Adeola, 1994). Race was a statistically significant predictor of residential proximity to hazardous waste dump sites and petrochemical plants. Forty-three percent of African-Americans and twenty-eight percent of whites indicated that they lived near the facilities, a statistically significant difference.

The proximity issue is being addressed with more precision in a study underway in Allegheny County, Pennsylvania (the Pittsburgh area) in 1994–95. Researchers for Resources for the Future have constructed imaginary circles centered at each industrial facility and drawn radii of one-half mile, one mile, and two miles (Glickman 1994). Facilities have been divided into two types: those that, because of their emissions, may pose chronic hazards and those that, because they store extremely hazardous substances, may pose acute hazards. By examining the areas formed by the circles and their overlapping portions, researchers could identify the "close-proximity" regions. Using geographical information systems (GIS), demographic characteristics could be calculated for inside and outside the close-proximity regions. In the close-proximity region for acute hazards, sixteen percent of the population was nonwhite; outside the region, the figure was eleven percent. Close-proximity regions also contained a higher proportion of poor residents than outside the region (sixteen percent to ten percent). The results for inside and outside the close-proximity region for chronic hazards were similar: higher proportions of nonwhites and the poor reside inside close-proximity regions than outside of them.

The Resources for the Future research adds an important dimension to the environmental discrimination issue when it focuses on risk-based equity measurements. The risk posed by the hazards was defined as "the expected annual number of persons exposed to accidental chemical releases" (Glickman 1994, 19). A risk indicator was created from the probability of an accidental chemical release, the size of the impact area, and the population density. The analysis showed that "nonwhites and poor people actually bear proportionately slightly less of the risk [of accidental chemical releases] than they would if equity existed" (Glickman 1994, 20).

CONCLUSION: UNRESOLVED ISSUES

Even as the most recent research has clarified some of the earlier work, significant issues remain as to the relationship of race and class to exposure to environmental hazards. One persistent question is which environmental bads ought to be studied? Two generally agreed upon categories of bads are natural resource depletion and pollution. These days, however, the environmental movement has moved beyond those categories. Most environmentalists would probably agree that exposure to chemicals in the workplace is an environmental bad. But where were environmentalists on issues such as migrant farm workers' exposure to pesticides? It has been the environmental justice activists who have extended the meaning of environmentalism. As Paehlke and

Rosenau note, "Until recently, the environmental movement has not emphasized the special political, economic, and personal interests of the disadvantaged segments of society" (1993, 674). As environmental justice becomes more central to environmentalism, will it take the movement in the direction of broader economic and social concerns? By the same token, as environmentalism means more, will it become an unwieldy umbrella term that is, ultimately, meaningless?

Beyond the question of "which environmental bads?" lies another question: What is the appropriate level of analysis? Hird contends that "the appropriate level of geographic resolution would be the one that includes the population affected by each site, but this varies dramatically from site to site" (1994, 131). He defends his use of counties in that they provide substantial variation nationally and offer sufficient size spatially to include most of the environmental and health effects. Moving to finer geographic resolution—such as the use of zip codes—has the advantage of greater specificity and precision in describing the characteristics of a neighborhood. Its disadvantage is that it misses site impacts that extend beyond those boundaries. A further complication is that governmental jurisdictions are not coterminous with environmental exposure areas.

It is frustrating to the activist to listen to quibbles of social scientists who appear to be nitpicking over seemingly technical matters such as sample size, operationalizations, and levels of statistical significance. The activist undoubtedly wants to shout words to the effect of "Just look at who lives in areas near incinerators and landfills. That's sufficient evidence of environmental discrimination!" And mutter something unpleasant about lies, damn lies, and statistics.

Two recent books take the activist perspective. The chapters in *Confronting Environmental Racism: Voices from the Grassroots* (Bullard 1993) and *Unequal Protection* (Bullard 1994b) make compelling reading. To suggest to low-income residents of Cancer Alley, Louisiana or to the African-Americans in the Carver Terrace section of Texarkana, Texas, or to Latino farm workers in Kettleman City, California that the statistical evidence of environmental inequities is mixed is to invite derision.[7] Yet the evidence, to this point, is mixed.

That conclusion produces another question: should policymakers wait until the evidence is incontrovertible? Legislatures in Arkansas and Louisiana, for example, enacted environmental equity bills in 1993. The Arkansas law discourages the siting of high-impact solid waste facilities within twelve miles of one another (Starkey 1994). Such a facility could be sited if specific economic benefits, e.g., fees and infrastructure improvements, are provided to the host community. Other states are considering legislation similar to that introduced in South Carolina which would limit the siting of hazardous waste generators and TSDs in parts of the state that have been identified as "environmental high risk areas." At the national level, bills have been introduced in Congress that would allow citizens to block the construction of waste facilities in communities that are environmentally disadvantaged.[8] Thus, despite continued uncertainty about the incidence of environmental inequity, policymakers are considering various actions. As Been (1994) suggests, however, until the relationship between the locally unwanted land uses and neighborhoods is sorted out, "proposed 'solutions' to the problem of disproportionate siting run a substantial risk of missing the mark." Extant research has done little to sort out that relationship. Perhaps a diachronic, multivariate design that is conducted at several levels of analysis is a fruitful way to proceed.

The final question involves sustainable development. Environmentalists have eagerly embraced the concept of sustainable development in its various formulations. The relationship between the economy and the environment is symbiotic: healthy economies need healthy environments. The merging of economic and environmental goals in the concept of sustainable development has implications for the environmental justice movement. Although environmental justice advocates seldom talk in terms of sustainability, their emphasis on local self-determination is similar to sustainable development's interest in scaled-down economies and communities. The sustainable development organization, Concern, Inc., describes a sustainable community as one that "seeks improved public health and a better quality of life for all its residents by limiting waste, preventing pollution, maximizing efficiency, and developing local resources to revitalize the local economy" (Geis and Kutzmark 1995, 5). Creating sustainable communities could generate environmental justice. However, if we were to achieve environmental justice, sustainability might result.

NOTES

1. Pulido (1994) cites two events as the catalysts for the environmental justice movement: the 1982 Warren County, North Carolina incident and, five years earlier, the mobilization of residents of the Love Canal area of New York. Others trace the roots of the movement to the actions of grassroots organizations such as the Mothers of East Los Angeles (MELA) (Boerner and Lambert, 1995). However, MELA's successful battles over the siting of a state prison and a hazardous waste incinerator in the area occurred in the mid- to late-1980s.

2. The charge of elitism has long been lodged at mainstream environmental groups. And even though environmental attitudes can be differentiated less by class now, it is middle- and upper-middle class individuals who are the most active in mainstream environmental organizations (Paehlke and Rosenau, 1993). As for race, the gap in support for environmental issues between whites and blacks has virtually disappeared. Part of this change is due to the redefinition of environmental issues to include urban health and workplace safety.

3. A 1979 lawsuit in Houston, Bean v. Southwestern Waste Management, was the first to use the Civil Rights Act as the basis for litigation in environmental protection. The plaintiffs contended that the siting of a municipal solid waste disposal facility violated the provisions of the Civil Rights Act (Bullard 1994a). Although the judicial ruling went against the plaintiffs, the legal strategy had important precedent-setting value, albeit somewhat deferred.

4. Because the "intent" requirement is a formidable obstacle, some legal strategists have argued for a different approach. Cole (1994) developed a four-tier litigation hierarchy for use in environmental justice cases, particularly those involving facility siting. He argues that challenges based on environmental laws themselves are the most likely to produce successful judicial outcomes. At the top of Cole's hierarchy is the use of environmental laws in a traditional manner such as a focus on procedural requirements. The second tier in the hierarchy is the creative use of environmental laws, e.g., putting a new spin on the public participation requirements. The next level in the hierarchy is civil rights statutes, especially Titles VI and VIII. Title VI, which covers recipients of federal funds, itself requires that litigants prove intentional discrimination but the regulations implementing Title VI across the federal government accept a discriminatory effect standard. The fourth—and least recommended—tier in the hierarchy is the use of a constitutional challenge based on the equal protection clause. As noted above, proving intentional discrimination is no small feat. The underlying logic of the hierarchy is the likelihood of success. As one moves from legal challenges based on environmental laws to those relying on constitutional claims, the number of judicial victories decreases dramatically.

5. There is no one best way to classify the work that has been done. It can be organized by the specific environmental bad studied, the unit of analysis used, the geographic scope of the research, the methodological and statistical techniques employed, and the findings reported.

6. One 1970's-era study looked at pollution problems other than air pollution. The research examined pesticide poisoning, noise pollution, solid waste, and risk of rat bites in addition to air pollution. Links between these environmental hazards and the income and racial characteristics of thirteen major urban areas were found. See the summary reported in Mohai and Bryant (1992).

7. Boerner and Lambert (1995) challenge the claims of environmental justice advocates in their article entitled "Environmental Injustice" that appeared in a journal with a decidedly conservative bent, *The Public Interest.*

8. One congressional proposal of 1994 faced the question of intentional discrimination head on. The provisions of the legislation introduced by Senator Paul Wellstone made it unnecessary to prove discriminatory intent. Instead, a judgment of disparate impact would be sufficient to prove unlawful discrimination. Congress has yet to pass this legislation.

REFERENCES

Adeola, Frances O. 1994. "Environmental Hazards, Health, and Racial Inequity in Hazardous Waste Distribution." *Environment and Behavior* 26: 99–126.

Anderton, Douglas L., Andy B. Anderson, John Michael Oakes, and Michael R. Fraser. 1994. "Environmental Equity: The Demographics of Dumping." *Demography* 31:229–248.

Austin, Regina, and Michael Schill. 1994. "Black, Brown, Red and Poisoned." In *Unequal Protection*, ed. Robert D. Bullard. San Francisco: Sierra Club Books.

Been, Vicki. 1994. "Locally Undesirable Land Uses in Minority Neighborhoods: Disproportionate Siting or Market Dynamics?" *Yale Law Journal* 103: 1383–1422.

Boerner, Christopher, and Thomas Lambert. 1995. "Environmental Injustice." *The Public Interest*, no. 118: 61–82.

Bullard, Robert D. 1983. "Solid Waste Sites and the Black Houston Community." *Sociological Inquiry* 53: 273–288.

Bullard, Robert D. 1993. "Conclusion: Environmentalism with Justice." In *Confronting Environmental Racism: Voices from the Grassroots*, ed. Robert D. Bullard. Boston: South End Press.

Bullard, Robert D. 1994a. *Dumping in Dixie*, 2nd ed. Boulder, CO: Westview Press.

Bullard, Robert D. 1994b. "Environmental Justice for All." In *Unequal Protection*, ed. Robert D. Bullard. San Francisco: Sierra Club Books.

Capek, Stella M. 1993. "The 'Environmental Justice' Frame: A Conceptual Discussion and an Application." *Social Problems* 40: 5–24.

Christian Science Monitor. 1994. "N.Y. State Accused of Environmental Racism for Incinerator Site." February 8, p. 11.

Cole, Luke W. 1994. "Environmental Justice Litigation: Another Stone in David's Sling." *Fordham Urban Law Journal* 21: 523– 545.

Collin, Robert W. 1993. "Environmental Equity and the Need for Government Intervention: Two Proposals." *Environment*. November 35: 41–43.

Costner, Pat, and Joe Thornton. 1990. *Playing with Fire*. Washington, D.C.: Greenpeace.

Crews-Meyer, Kelley A. 1994. "Hazardous Waste and Race in South Carolina." *The Forum* 5: 25–28.

Cushman, John H. Jr. 1994. "Clinton to Order Effort to Make Pollution Fairer." *New York Times*. February 10, pp. A1, C18.

Cutter, Susan L. 1995. "Race, Class, and Environmental Justice." *Progress in Human Geography* 19:111–22.

Geis, Dan, and Tammy Kutzmark. 1995. "Developing Sustainable Communities." *Public Management* 77: 4–13.

Glickman, Theodore S. 1994. "Measuring Environmental Equity with Geographical Information Systems." *Renewable Resources Journal* 12 (3): 17–21.

Gottlieb, Robert. 1993. *Forcing the Spring*. Washington, D.C.: Island Press.

Greenberg, Michael R., and Richard F. Anderson. 1984. *Hazardous Waste Sites: The Credibility Gap*. New Brunswick, N.J.: Center for Urban Policy Research.

Hamilton, James T. 1995. "Testing for Environmental Racism: Prejudice, Profits, Political Power." *Journal of Policy Analysis and Management* 14: 107–132.

Hird, John A. 1994. *Superfund: The Political Economy of Environmental Risk*. Baltimore: Johns Hopkins University Press.

Holm, Danika M. 1994. "Environmental Inequities in South Carolina: The Distribution of Hazardous Waste Facilities." Unpublished Master's Thesis. Department of Geography, University of South Carolina.

Kraft, Michael E., and Denise Scheberle. 1995. "Environmental Justice and the Allocation of Risk: The Case of Lead and Public Health." *Policy Studies Journal* 23:113–22.

Lake, Robert W. 1995. "Volunteers, NIMBYs, and Environmental Justice: Dilemmas of Democratic Practice." Presented at the Annual Meeting of the Association of American Geographers, Chicago, March 16–19.

Lavelle, Marianne, and Marcia Coyle. 1992. "Unequal Protection." *National Law Journal*. September 21, p. 52.

Mohai, Paul, and Bunyan Bryant. 1992. "Environmental Racism: Reviewing the Evidence." In *Race and the Incidence of Environmental Hazards*, ed. Bunyan Bryant and Paul Mohai. Boulder, CO: Westview.

Paehlke, Robert, and Pauline Vaillancourt Rosenau. 1993. "Environment/ Equity: Tensions in North American Politics." *Policy Studies Journal* 21: 672–686.

Pulido, Laura. 1994. "Restructuring and the Contraction and Expansion of Environmental Rights in the United States." *Environment and Planning A* 26: 915–936.

Roque, Julie A. 1993. "Environmental Equity: Reducing Risk for All Communities." *Environment* 35: 25–28.

Starkey, Deb. 1994. "Environmental Justice: Win, Lose, or Draw?" *State Legislatures* 20: 27–31.

Torres, Gerald. 1994. "Environmental Burdens and Democratic Justice." *Fordham Urban Law Journal* 21: 431–460.

United Church of Christ Commission on Racial Justice. 1987. *Toxic Waste and Race in the United States*. New York: United Church of Christ.

U.S. Environmental Protection Agency. 1992. *Environmental Equity: Reducing Risk for All Communities*. Washington, D.C.: EPA.

U.S. Environmental Protection Agency. 1995. "Draft Environmental Justice Strategy for Executive Order 12898." Washington, D.C.: EPA.

U.S. General Accounting Office. 1983. *Siting of Hazardous Waste Landfills and Their Correlation with Racial and Economic Status of Surrounding Communities*. Washington, D.C.: GAO.

Zimmerman, Rae. 1994. "Issues of Classification in Environmental Equity: How We Manage Is How We Measure." *Fordham Urban Law Journal* 21: 633–669.

SECTION FOUR

Public Versus Private Control Over Federal Lands

7 Bringing Private Management to the Public Lands: Environmental and Economic Advantages*

JOHN A. BADEN AND TIM O'BRIEN

With the Republicans winning majorities in both houses of Congress in 1994, some conservative observers hoped to curtail much of the environmental legislation passed in preceding years. Most environmentalists feared that important statutes would be eviscerated. The Wise Use movement had arisen as a cohesive and powerful political entity, committed to defending subsidies to mining, grazing, irrigation, and forestry. The principles of the "unholy trinity," environmentalists' label for protections from the regulatory takings of property, cost-benefit analysis of environmental regulations, and the diminution of unfunded mandates, were already important in congressional debates before the elections.

There was historical precedent for these hopes and fears. When James Watt became Reagan's Secretary of Interior, he exemplified the pro-business, anti-environmental position. Whether Republicans will allow hardheaded, principled reforms to win out over subsidies for the wealthy and well organized remains uncertain. What is certain is that a move toward private management could improve environmental quality, generate increased equity and economic efficiency, and enhance the welfare of future generations. Only by creating incentives for wise stewardship can we encourage sustainability over the long run.

This chapter begins with a review of the history of the federal government's land policies. The disappointing legacy of federal land

*Dean Lueck contributed to an earlier version of this paper.

ownership will then be examined from the perspective of the New Resource Economics, arguing in favor of relinquishing governmental management, if not ownership, of the federal lands. We will conclude with a brief examination of some mechanisms for managing land in an efficient, equitable, and politically palatable manner.

THE AMERICAN REVOLUTION AND FEDERAL LAND POLICY

The U.S. Constitution, and the ideology that supported it, had important implications for government land policy. A distinct feature of the new American government was its reliance on private property and free trade to advance the welfare of society.

Federal lands, or the "public domain," originally consisted of excess "western" lands that had been ceded by the original thirteen states. Simply put, the government's goal was to transfer these lands to private owners and to do so quickly. The policy of land disposal served two functions: it furthered the idea that resources were best managed by private individuals, and it provided the government with operating funds.

The disposal process began with the Ordinance of 1785, which allowed the federal government to sell its land to the highest bidder at a minimum of one dollar per acre, later increased to two dollars, with a 640-acre minimum purchase size. In 1841, Congress hastened the disposal process by passing the Preemption Act, which allowed settlers to "legally venture forth upon public surveyed land and stake a claim to the exclusion of all others" (Robbins 1942, 89). The Homestead Act of 1862 allowed individuals to acquire up to 160 acres of public land by simply living on it for a continuous period of five years and by paying a fee of less than fifty dollars. Three more homesteading acts were passed during the early 1900s. By 1934, well over one billion acres of the public domain had been disposed of, including grants to states and railroads, script purchase, preemption, and homesteading (see Table 7.1). The public domain was officially closed when President Roosevelt signed the Taylor Grazing Act in 1934.

In 1872, ten years after passage of the Homestead Act and accompanied by growing concern over the private abuse of public lands, Congress established Yellowstone National Park as a "public or pleasuring ground for the benefit and enjoyment of the people" (Petulla 1977, 230), marking the first major entry by the federal government into public land preservation. For conservationists, the establishment of the park was a milestone in their efforts to curb the exploitation of

Table 7.1. Important Public Land Laws

Year	Price per Acre	Size in Acres	Conditions
1785 (Ordinance of 1785)	$1 minimum	640 minimum	Cash sale; amended in 1785 to provide for payment of one-third in cash, the remainder in three months.
1820	$1.25 minimum	80 minimum	End of credit system; cash payment only.
1841 (Preemption Act)	$1.25 minimum	40 minimum; 160 limit on preemption	Cash only; established right of preemption, doing away with the necessity of renewing legislation.
1862 (Homestead Act)	$0.00	160 maximum	Payment of an entry fee and five years continuous residence; land could be preempted after six months residence for $1.25 per acre cash.
1873 (Timber Culture Act)	$0.00	160 maximum	Cultivation of trees on one-quarter of a 160 acre required.
1873 (Desert Land Act)	$1.25 minimum	640; reduced	Required irrigation within three years.
1909 (Enlarged Homestead Act)	$0.00	320 to 640	Five years residence with continuous cultivation.
1934 (Taylor Grazing Act)			Established grazing districts on one remaining federal lands and closed the lands to private settlement.
1960 (Multiple Use Sustained Yield Act)			Forest Service and BLM required to give equal attention and consideration to non-commodity uses of public range.

Table 7.1. Important Public Land Laws *(continued)*

Year	Price per Acre	Size in Acres	Conditions
1976 (Federal Land Policy and Management Act)			Reasserted the federal government's intent to retain ownership of federal lands.
1978 (Public Rangeland Improvement Act)			Provided funding for BLM management and improvement of public range.
1980 (Alaska National Interest Lands Conservation Act of 1980)			Designated 56.4 million acres of land as wilderness.

Source: Davis (1972, 104), Hess (1992, 106–07, 119–20), and Wilkinson (1992, 55).

natural resources. To understand how the shift in public policy from disposal to conservation came about, it is necessary to examine the history of conservation thought, especially during the Progressive era.

The History of Conservation Thought

American conservation ideology is rooted in the scientific utilitarian view of the eighteenth-century Enlightenment, the aesthetic-preservationist view of the Romantics, Jeffersonian agrarianism, and New England transcendentalism (see Huth 1957; Udall 1963; Petulla 1977). The ideas embodied in these four philosophies were nurtured and expanded during the 1800s, but it was not until the turn of the century that America produced a politically viable conservation movement—Progressive conservation.

Progressive conservation developed as people began to value nature other than for commodity production. Writers like Henry David Thoreau and Ralph Waldo Emerson and artists like George Catlin and Frederic Remington influenced those who could afford to value pristine environments. Scientists George Perkins Marsh, Carl Schurz, and John Wesley Powell had long condemned the institutions of private property and free enterprise and called for governmental intervention in protecting and managing natural resources (Nash 1976). As a result, by the 1860s, preservation had become a legitimate and valuable form of land allocation, and conservationists had begun to lobby for the federal protection of pristine lands. Over the next eighty years legislation, such as the Forest Reserve Act of 1891, which began the national forest system, the Civilian Conservation Corps, and the Tennessee Valley Authority, and federal water projects under the Bureau of Reclamation converted Progressive ideology into effective policy (Coggins and Wilkinson 1981, 118–20; Nash 1976, 46–52, 98; Petulla 1977, 309–28).

Even though the environmental movement has since shifted its emphasis to aesthetic values and ecology, it still embodies the Progressive view that a quality environment depends on governmental intervention. Legislation such as the National Wilderness Protection Act of 1964 and the National Environmental Policy Act of 1969, is a good example of how the environmental lobby has successfully promoted Progressive era thinking.

What Progressives did not notice was that private property rights were evolving on the commons as resources became more valuable (i.e., scarcer) and as technological improvements lowered the costs of defining and enforcing those rights (Anderson and Hill 1975). Nor did they recognize that certain land disposal policies, whose acreage restrictions largely ignored the character (primarily the aridity) of western land, contributed to fraud and waste. Progressives also confused the exploitation of natural resources with efficient resource use (Johnson and Libecap 1980). Some conservationists (e.g., Thoreau, Leopold, and Hardin) had criticisms of government control, but their views were often marginalized. With this brief history in mind, we now turn to an examination of public land management using an economic perspective.

THE NEW RESOURCE ECONOMICS: PERSPECTIVES ON THE COUNTERREVOLUTION

The paradigm provided by the New Resource Economics gives a consistent and logical framework for examining the record of public lands experiments. The approach has been termed "old ideas and new applications" and is a blend of neoclassical, property rights, public choice, and Austrian economics, specifically applied to the problems of natural resource management and allocation.

Neoclassical economics is the paradigm most often taught in American universities. Terry Anderson (1982) has identified its central elements as marginal analysis, information and uncertainty, and interest theory. Accordingly, the neoclassical microeconomic model analyzes and illustrates the efficiency of a competitive market. By recognizing that decisions are made at the margin in an uncertain world where information is scarce, the neoclassical model provides important insights into natural resource allocation. However, because the model emphasizes market equilibrium and underestimates the importance of institutions, it cannot fully explain how real-world decisions are made.

Property rights theory, a subset of neoclassical economics, developed rapidly during the 1960s following the publication of articles by Ronald Coase (1960) and Harold Demsetz (1967). Since then, a paradigm has developed, which assumes that each individual attempts to maximize his or her net welfare within the existing institutional setting. Property rights economics forces the analyst to examine the structure of property rights to resources in order to determine the incentives faced by decision-makers. Because transaction costs (the costs of getting parties together to agree to the terms of a contract) are nearly always positive, they must be considered when analyzing resource allocation. By linking ownership rights, incentives, and economic behavior, the property rights paradigm expands the scope of economics beyond market equilibrium.

Public choice theory, also a subset of neoclassical economics, is closely tied to the property rights paradigm (see Buchanan and Tullock 1962). Public choice economists recognize the importance of institutions and incentives in shaping economic behavior, but they focus on decisions made outside the market by voters, politicians, and bureaucrats. The growing public choice literature outlines why government's failure to allocate resources efficiently is the predictable consequence of information and incentives generated by institutional arrangements (see Niskanen 1971; Baden and Stroup 1979) and allows economists to examine critically the alternatives to market allocation.

Austrian economics, which also developed during the later 1800s, provided a different perspective, one that stresses the subjectivity of individually held values and emphasizes the market as a process that transmits knowledge of diverse and changing values through the price system (see Hayek 1945; Kirzner 1973). Austrian economists stress entrepreneurship; that is, the tendency of individuals motivated by profit to discover previously unrecognized ways to move resources to higher valued uses. The Austrian perspective also points to the inherent difficulties in centralized economic planning that are the result of the inability to obtain correct information (without prices) and the lack of socially efficient incentives. Like public choice theory, the Austrian paradigm generates skepticism of governmental success in efficiently allocating natural resources.

Using these four perspectives, the new resource economics offers a more general theory of natural resource allocation. It allows for an examination of the institutions through which resources are distributed, making it possible to arrive at realistic policy prescriptions. New resource economists recognize that since there is no perfect, costless economic system, sound policy must promote the least imperfect system.

Externalities and Market Failure

Externalities have been the overwhelming argument for governmental intervention in natural resource management. Positive or negative externalities occur when all of the effects of economic activity are not borne by the decision-maker (see Pigou 1932; Gwartney and Stroup 1983). When either kind of externality occurs, production will vary from the social optimum. Negative externalities, such as air pollution, tend to be overproduced (relative to the socially efficient level) because producers and consumers do not face the full cost of their activities. Positive externalities, such as scenic vistas and wildlife habitat, tend to be underproduced because producers receive less than the full benefit from their activities. Externalities may be more usefully viewed as a result of inadequate property rights management; that is, no one owns the air or the view, so there are insufficient incentives to use those resources efficiently (Coase 1960; Baden and Stroup 1979).

Public goods and common property are more extreme cases of the externality problem and provide the strongest argument for governmental intervention in the natural resource market. Public goods, such as national defense, are characterized by their nonexcludability and jointness of consumption; that is, the owner of the good cannot exclude nonpaying customers, and the consumption of the good by one individual does not alter consumption for the next individual (Samuelson 1954). Thus, public goods may be considered positive externalities. Many argue that parks and wilderness areas are public goods and, hence, must be provided by the state (Krutilla 1967).

Common property resources, resources that are accessible to everyone and are controlled by no one, provide an invitation for environmental degradation. Commonly owned air and water resources are overused and polluted by individuals seeking to maximize their own welfare by ignoring the costs imposed on others (Hardin and Baden 1977). Commonly held wildlife resources, such as the passenger pigeon and the American bison, have all been exploited under this arrangement. Like the public goods problem, the "tragedy of the commons" is a result of ill-defined property rights.

Market failure is the inability of real-world markets to match the social efficiency of the perfectly competitive equilibrium model (Bator 1958; Gwartney and Stroup 1983). From the perspective of the New Resource Economics, market failure can best be explained by the absence of well-defined, enforced and transferable private property rights. As Demsetz (1967) and others (Anderson and Hill 1975; Baden and Stroup 1981a) have noted, property rights to resources tend to evolve as the value of a resource becomes commensurate with the costs of defining and enforcing those rights.

Private Management of Public Lands

While the costs of establishing property rights to some resources are often prohibitively high and governmental action can be justified, governmental intervention into the management of resources such as land, water, and wildlife has effectively eroded or halted the evolution of property rights by regulating or establishing ownership and precluding private innovation. For example, it is difficult to contain and assign ownership to some aerial and waterborne pollutants, particularly nonpoint source pollution (e.g., automobile emissions). In these cases, regulations or market mechanisms, such as tradeable emissions permits, may be necessary to internalize external costs. But when government owns land or wildlife, which are more easily assigned ownership, it lowers the potential profit opportunities for entrepreneurs and thus hinders innovation. If there is little profit in owning an elk herd because it is publicly controlled, no one has a significant incentive to figure out how ownership could be established (perhaps by placing radio collars or brands on certain elk).

Governmental Failure

Just as market failure can be explained via the property rights paradigm, so can governmental failure. Because governmental decisionmakers do not hold property rights to the resources they allocate, they face no strong incentives to use the resources efficiently. Further, bureaucrats and politicians make decisions largely outside the market and, hence, do not receive information in the form of prices. Five phenomena explain why governmental agents tend to be largely ignorant of the marginal principle: (1) rational ignorance, (2) the special interest effect, (3) the bundle purchase effect, (4) the shortsightedness effect, and (5) little incentive for internal efficiency (Baden and Stroup 1979).

First, voters in a democratic society tend to be rationally ignorant of issues that do not immediately concern them (Downs 1957). Most Americans, for example, cannot name their own representative in Congress. Average members of interest groups, however, are acutely aware of how public policy directly influences their well being. Dairy farmers in Wisconsin usually know little about Montana wilderness policy, but they are keenly aware of the latest federal farm bill affecting dairy price supports. Likewise, Montana backpackers have little interest in midwestern farm policy, but they know a great deal about current policy on energy exploration in their favorite wilderness areas.

Second, when the vested interests of individuals are at stake and they believe they can affect the outcome, they make efforts to become informed and to influence public policy. When issues become sufficiently narrow and individual interests become sufficiently large, a narrowly focused, highly motivated special interest group is likely to wield enormous political influence (Olson 1971). When such a situation exists, as it often does in representative government, taxpayers contribute to the special interest kitty without their consent. From the perspective of the special interest, the treasury is a common resource pool (Baden and Stroup 1981a; Fort and Baden 1981).

Third, because individuals place only one vote in the political system for a representative who must speak for them on all issues, there is an inherent lack of precision in political decision making. Even well-informed voters have little hope of expressing all their preferences in a political setting. In direct contrast, in a market setting the "voter-buyer" can express his preference on a multitude of "issues," such as which, if any, skis to buy.

Fourth, since politicians and bureaucrats must satisfy current constituents, they suffer from shortsightedness. Future generations are rarely given genuine consideration in political-bureaucratic decisions. There is no a priori reason to expect that decisions made in the public sector will adequately consider the welfare of future generations.

Finally, there is little incentive for internal efficiency in the public sector. Decision-makers are not residual claimants; that is, they can rarely gain personal, material well being from making efficient choices. Similarly, they lose little by choosing inefficient alternatives. Authority and responsibility are separated under imperfect property rights arrangements. Recognizing the inherent imperfections in governmental decision making provides the new resource economist with a framework for examining the legacy left by the Progressives. This also explains why current public land policy does not help create a sustainable society.

THE LEGACY OF FEDERALLY OWNED NATURAL RESOURCES

The U.S. Forest Service

The U.S. Forest Service was established in 1897 to manage and conserve the forests for future generations. The agency now resides within the Department of Agriculture and is currently divided into nine regions with approximately 120 national forests. United States land ownership, including Forest Service holdings, is shown in Table 7.2.[1]

Forest Service management is strongly influenced by the Knutson-Vandenberg Act of 1930, the Brush Disposal Act of 1916, and the National Forest Management Act of 1976 (NFMA). In conjunction with bureaucracies' tendency to maximize budgets (Tullock 1965; Niskanen 1971, 1975; Drucker 1985; Johnson 1985), these acts have made timber sales the principle focus of the Forest Service. Budget maximizing

Table 7.2. Land Owned by the United States (in millions of acres)

Agency/Bureau	Public Domain	Acquisition	Total
Department of Agriculture			
Forest Service	163.5	28.6	192.1
Department of Energy			
Energy Research and Development	1.4	.7	2.1
Department of Interior			
Bureau of Land Management	340.0	2.3	342.3
Fish and Wildlife Service	80.0	4.7	84.7
National Park Service	65.3	7.0	72.3
Bureau of Reclamation	3.3	1.0	4.3
Tennessee Valley Authority	0.0	1.0	1.0
Department of Defense			
Air Force	6.9	1.1	8.0
Army	6.5	4.0	10.5
Navy	1.5	.8	2.3
Corps of Engineers	.7	7.7	8.4
All Other Agencies	3.4	.9	4.3
TOTAL	672.4	60.0	732.4

Source: General Services Administration (1983, 49-54).

actions have encouraged: (1) the use of management criteria without foundation in economic theory; (2) economic losses and; (3) damage to forest ecosystems (Dowdle 1981; O'Toole 1988, 1992).

As Niskanen (1971) noted, and Mitchell and Simmons (1994) updated, budget maximization consists of bureaucrats' efforts to increase their well being by expanding salaries, bureau output and power, and patronage. Forest Service employees pursue these goals in two ways. First, the agency biases its activities toward logging and road construction, and seeks to maximize the volume, not the net value, of timber sold. This increases the agency's overall budget because historically, Congress has appropriated 99% of the money requested for timber sales. Appropriations for recreation, research, wildlife, and watershed projects are less generous (O'Toole 1992).

Congress favors timber sales because they generate concentrated benefits in home districts, e.g., profits for companies and jobs for loggers, while imposing diffuse costs on the rest of society (Olson 1971). The Multiple Use Sustained Yield Act of 1960 strengthened the timber bias by requiring expenditures to promote recreation, wildlife, and watershed values, and thereby making sales preparation more expensive (Johnson 1985).

Second, Forest Service employees can use Knutson-Vandenberg (K-V), Brush Disposal, and NFMA receipts to pursue projects that are not funded by Congress. Under these laws, a portion of the revenues from timber sales are kept and are available for reforestation, prescribed burning, wildlife habitat enhancement, and other nontimber projects. In addition, about one-fourth to one-third of these funds go to administrative overhead (O'Toole 1988, 132; O'Toole 1992, 13). Few of the revenues collected from timber sales return to the U.S. Treasury. This means roading and administration costs are paid by taxpayers while the "profits" are retained by logging companies and the Forest Service.

Maximizing the volume of timber sold maximizes budgets because the Forest Service has no need to equate the marginal cost of a sale with the marginal benefit. The marginal costs are paid by the Treasury while the marginal benefits accrue, in part, to the Forest Service. Diminishing returns are not reached until an additional sale sparks opposition from environmentalists, recreationalists, or local communities, opposition that cuts into appropriations or control over forest "assets."

Laws such as the National Environmental Policy Act (NEPA) of 1969 have much smaller effects on agency behavior because they go against institutional interests. NEPA and certain court rulings require the Forest Service to determine the impact of road construction on wilderness areas. The agency resisted these mandates and continued to develop unroaded areas. Since wilderness preservation and primitive recreation offer the agency few budgetary benefits, this resistance is not surprising (O'Toole 1988, 160–166).

Because taxpayers subsidize the harvest of timber from national forests, private companies log even where total social costs exceed total social benefits. In particular, building roads into mountainous forests is very expensive. Subsidies make logging profitable even in the high, dry, and cold forests of the Rocky Mountain West—a region in which standing timber quality is usually quite low and environmental values are high.

Promoting and subsidizing timber sales on national forests has several consequences. First, although the Forest Service was given a high quality resource that has appreciated significantly in value, 75% of the national forests (90% in regions 2 and 4) lose money every year. In 1991, losses totaled more than $1 billion (Barlow et al. 1980; General Accounting Office 1984, 10; O'Toole 1992, 31). Second, although spreading timber sales across wide areas is necessary to secure broad-based congressional support and to facilitate spending discretionary funds in many areas, it can cause extensive environmental damage. For example, logging steep mountainsides and riparian areas increases erosion, damages water quality, and can harm fish populations (Grobey 1985; Jensen et al 1986, 6; O'Toole 1988, 74–79).

Third, efforts to maximize timber volume (e.g., biological yield) rather than timber value are inefficient. Thus, when the Forest Service is true to its claims of pursuing sustained yield management, it ignores interest rates and standing timber values. Although sustained yield is violated frequently in practice, it provides a useful lever for extracting congressional appropriations for more intensive timber management (Dowdle 1981; O'Toole 1988).

There are many specific examples of inefficient and anti-environmental policies. In one analysis of the San Juan National Forest, Hyde (1981) found that, despite high wilderness and recreational values, the Forest Service was expanding an already marginal timber program into 419,000 acres of roadless areas. In these areas, the costs to build roads alone exceeded the stumpage value of the timber.

The Forest Services sometimes justifies its actions by claiming they promote community stability, but evidence suggests these subsidies do little to help timber dependent communities. Dowdle and Hanke (1985) found federal timber management has actually encouraged the wood-products industry to move from the "Pacific Northwest, where 70% of the timber inventory is owned and managed by various" government agencies, to the Southeast, where most lands are private.

Thomas Power has found that nonlabor income (e.g., social security, dividend, and interest payments), local service sector employment, and recreation-associated income and employment now dominate the economies of areas formerly dependent on timber. He found logging and other commodity related employment was volatile; often, outsiders were employed rather than community residents (1987, 1989, 1991, 1992). Finally, O'Toole notes that the Forest Service has on many occasions failed to increase allowable cuts, even where ecologically feasible, to maintain community employment (1988; 1992). Neither theory nor practice support the notion that timber sales are important to community stability.

The management of the public forests has been inefficient and environmentally destructive. Despite the problems of bureaucratic management, private timber supplies remain strong and private forest owners are responding to increasing demands for wildlife and amenity production (see Dennis 1982; Reed 1993).

The Bureau of Land Management

The Bureau of Land Management (BLM) was established in the U.S. Department of the Interior in 1947. It administers more than 170 million acres of western rangeland that was withdrawn from the public domain by the 1934 Taylor Grazing Act. Today, the BLM controls a total of 269 million acres (Hess 1994a).

Prior to 1900, in places where stockmen's associations did not rule, the western range was an unregulated commons where overgrazing was widespread and costly (Libecap and Johnson 1981). Private property rights were evolving on the most productive rangeland, but there was little incentive to define and enforce rights on less productive land. The Unlawful Enclosures Act of 1885 made establishing property rights even more difficult. Acreage restrictions on homesteaders were set by easterners unfamiliar with the land's low productivity. While relatively few acres were officially claimed by settlers, ranchers established unofficial claims to much larger acreage in order to support economically viable operations.

To control the open access chaos it helped create, Congress passed the Forest Reserve Act of 1891, withdrawing forested public lands from private use. Still, large areas of public domain were not withdrawn and remained an unregulated commons. The passage of the Taylor Grazing Act of 1934 and the creation of the Grazing Service (later merged into the BLM) brought regulatory control to grazing on most public lands. Allocation of legal grazing permits went primarily to stockmen, a fact anticipated by stockmen when they lobbied for the Act.

The BLM bureaucracy, like the Forest Service, seeks to increase its institutional power and budget. The BLM was dissatisfied with the impermanent withdrawal of public lands and the discretion given to stockmen by the Taylor Grazing Act. By the 1970s the BLM sought change. To gain passage of the Federal Land Policy and Management Act of 1976 (FLPMA), the BLM manipulated data and argued that public range conditions were deteriorating. Public domain lands were permanently withdrawn and BLM regulatory powers were increased. In 1978, the Public Rangelands Improvement Act (PRIA) authorized greater funding for intensive management to improve range conditions. Large portions of this money were funneled to staff salaries instead (Hess 1992).

There are unintended consequences to this increase in bureaucratic resources and control. The BLM's desire for control, a desire consistent with Progressive ideology as well as bureaucratic incentives, led it to make permits insecure and untransferable. Under the Multiple Use Sustained Yield Act of 1960 and FLPMA, the BLM obtained the statutory authority to resist the political power of ranchers and thus to mold the permit system into its modern form. Gary Libecap (1981) and Karl Hess (1992) have shown that overstocking and underinvestment in range improvement are the result of changing and insecure property rights and direct pressures from the BLM bureaucracy.

Permits tend to exceed the biological carrying capacity of public range. But, since ranchers can lose the permits unless they fully utilize their grazing allotments, they have strong incentives to overgraze. There are few counter incentives. Ranchers incur minimal economic losses from degradation of public range because all they possess is the right to a certain quantity of grazing, not a stake in the quality of the land (see Foss 1960). Moreover, recreation, hunting, and fishing are precluded as alternatives to grazing (Hess 1994b).

Perhaps the most spectacular of all the inefficient programs promoted by the BLM is chaining (also practiced by the Forest Service): the removal of pinyon-juniper woodland to enhance the range for livestock grazing. Chaining does improve the range for cattle and sheep, but it also severely degrades the landscape, harms watersheds, destroys archaeological sites, and is economically unsound. Between 1950 and 1964, over three million acres of woodland were chained in the southwest and the Great Basin (Lanner 1981), much of it on BLM and Forest Service lands. Despite the ever-rising costs and reduced returns to ranching, chaining became an important part of agency budgets.

The BLM's record of inefficiency closely parallels that of the Forest Service and for essentially the same reasons. Management is by bureaucrats who lack residual claimancy and who are subjected to intense political pressures. Experience and economic theory indicate that federal resource management has severe shortcomings. Continued public ownership and management of land assets are likely to promote ongoing economic inefficiencies, environmental degradation, and social divisiveness (Stroup and Baden, 1973).

THE CASE FOR PRIVATE MANAGEMENT

Economic Efficiency

The best reason for private management of natural resources is to promote economic efficiency. Since economic efficiency can be defined as the allocation of scarce resources so that no one can be made better off without making someone else worse off, it is not difficult to see how increased efficiency is a worthy goal. When property rights are well defined, well enforced, transferable, and privately held, resources tend to be efficiently allocated via the market process. It is only with such arrangements that a sustainable society is possible.

The establishment of efficient property rights may be precluded for several reasons. The fugitive nature of migratory wildlife often makes it difficult to establish property rights. As resource and amenity values rise, however, the incentive to create property rights becomes stronger. At some cost one could brand blue whales and polar bears to define property rights. Further, governmental intervention may impede the evolution of property rights, as illustrated by the United States' failed public lands experiments. Perhaps government's most important role in natural resource management lies in fostering the definition and enforcement of property rights.

Recognizing governmental failure forces policy analysts to see that there are no perfect, costless solutions to natural resource problems. Prescribing effective policy becomes a choice between imperfect markets and imperfect governments, not an a priori condemnation of markets because they do not duplicate the competitive equilibrium of the neoclassical model. We have given just a few examples of the growing evidence, which suggests that governmental failures often exceed the failures of imperfect markets.

Economic Efficiency and Environmental Quality

Conservationists often argue that many environmental goods cannot be provided by the private sector, citing wilderness and wildlife as nearly perfect examples of public goods (Krutilla 1967). However compelling that logic may seem, private individuals and groups do provide environmental amenities for public and private consumption. Ranchers in Texas and Montana raise wildlife as well as cattle, and groups like the Nature Conservancy preserve natural areas (for other examples, see Dennis 1981, 1982; Smith 1981; Lucas

1994; White 1994). Bureaucratic management has done much to destroy systematically these kinds of environmental goods (see Baden and Stroup 1981a; Siffin 1981; Chase 1986; Reisner 1986; O'Toole 1988; Hess 1992, 1993). These private services might be more widespread if bureaucrats did not control a large portion of the nation's land.

Further, resources on the public lands are grossly underpriced, providing competition that is hard for private ventures to overcome. It is difficult to imagine how private timber companies in western Montana and northern Idaho could possibly compete with such zero priced amenity resources as the River of No Return and the Bob Marshall Wilderness area. The private producer must compete through higher quality. As demand for environmental goods increases and public lands suffer the "tragedy of the commons," however, we would expect private resource owners to divert more of their resources to the production of these goods. This is exactly what is occurring on some of the privately managed spring creeks in Montana, where owners charge fees for access to quality fishing streams.

If environmentalists are truly concerned with the wise use of natural resources, they should welcome private management. As Anderson and Hill (1980) have noted, increasing governmental control of resources greatly increases the likelihood that individuals will engage in transfer activity or negative-sum games, rather than productive activity or positive-sum games (see also Buchanan et al. 1980). When resource allocation is determined through the market, compromise is the rule and adversarial relationships are minimized. With political avenues blocked, conservationists could get on with the real business of conducting research on conservation, educating citizens, preserving natural areas, and advising resource developers. Information and incentives, not just ethical conversion, would encourage environmentally responsible activity.

The case for the private management of federal lands is persuasive. Wasteful lobbying efforts by environmentalists and resource developers would no longer be profitable, and resources would be channeled toward compromise and mutually beneficial activities. Natural resources would be extracted only when they could pay their way out of pristine environments, including the opportunity costs of foregone amenities. Individuals would have to pay for the goods and services they want, whether an alpine lake or so many acre-feet of irrigation water.

PRIVATE MANAGEMENT: CONFRONTING THE CRITICS

Several themes characterize the attacks on the establishment of private property rights in federal lands. Perhaps the most common is that federal lands are a citizen's birthright and must be provided free to the public. Another theme is that governmental managers will act in the public's long run interest and that private owners cannot be trusted to see beyond short run profits. It is assumed that public land sales, such as those advocated by Wise Use,[2] will yield a world in which large corporations own everything. Critics also contend that such programs may emerge as last ditch efforts to balance a runaway deficit in the federal budget. These criticisms are important and deserve serious attention. The first step is to separate ideology from economics.

Most environmentalists do not recognize the common-pool nature of the public lands. Just as the air is overused as a garbage dump because it is free, the public lands are overused because access is free or grossly underpriced. National parks are crowded and abused, prime hunting areas are overhunted, and popular wilderness areas are overrun by enthusiastic hikers. Ironically, conservationists who stress the finite nature of our world continue to insist that the public lands provide infinite opportunities for multiple use. While free access to the natural environment may be philosophically appealing, philosophy is far less effective than property rights in conserving resources (Demsetz 1967; Baden et al. 1981).

The fear that private management plans would place all land in the hands of development corporations is without foundation. Even corporations have limited resources, and they invest where the expected marginal payoff is highest. It is doubtful that they would squander resources on low-valued land. On land where the opportunity cost of development is high and the opportunity cost of preservation is low, conservation groups, ranchers, and farmers could reasonably compete with corporations and wealthy development interests.

There is also concern that the legitimate rights of long-term public land users would be ignored. A politically and economically sound program would recognize these rights and consider them either by compensation, preemption, or accommodation to existing rights. There is no reason to believe that corporations would force all western ranchers off the land (see Baden 1980) or that environmentalists would not be able to secure rights to ecologically significant areas via ownership, lease, or easement.

ESTABLISHING MARKETS: A PROGRAM FOR REFORM

The only sure way to foster economically and environmentally sound management of the federal lands is (1) to create private property rights in those lands and allow markets to be established, or (2) to devise innovative institutional arrangements that rely on private management. Economists familiar with the New Resource Economics offer various programs for creating private rights in public lands (see Baden and Stroup 1981b; Beckwith 1981; Dennis 1981; Smith 1981). We will examine some of these proposals and make some additional suggestions.

Baden and Stroup (1975) suggest that governmental ownership of land be retained but that private interests be given secure and transferable rights to commodity resources, such as timber or range. In such a system, the government would retain rights to such resources as wildlife and water. Marion Clawson (1982) has offered a variant of this approach, proposing a system of long-term leases with pullback modifications. The leases would have to satisfy all applicable laws, such as the National Environmental Policy Act. Clawson's proposal, however, does not allow for the transferability of rights, an essential ingredient for market efficiency. Such proposals make gains in efficiency, but they are still saddled with the bureaucratic oversight that limits efficiency.

Most other proposals concentrate on the rationale for divestiture rather than on specific implementation plans (Friedman 1962; Dolan 1971; Baden and Stroup 1981b; Beckwith 1981; Dennis 1981; Smith 1981). One of the first concrete proposals was offered by Baden and Stroup (1981b), who suggested that simple title to all wilderness areas be given to bona fide conservation groups, such as the Sierra Club or the Wilderness Society. Baden and Lueck (1982) have also proposed that wilderness areas be opened to "amenity homesteading" by nonprofit conservation groups.

Vernon Smith (1982) has offered a comprehensive privatization program, one that would include "all BLM, Forest Service, National Park, National Monument, National Recreation Area, continental shelf, deep sea bed, and military lands." Smith's plan would involve distributing equal shares of public land certificates to all adult citizens and then auctioning off the land over at least twenty years via a combinatorial sealed-bid auction. The certificates would be used to purchase land, and their value would be determined by the market. Smith's plan attempts to reconcile political and equity barriers and is perhaps the most promising proposal to date.

Since most people are skeptical of plans to sell the public lands, divestiture must begin with small parcels for which public ownership has no justification. In broad terms, land divestiture should be carried out with the following priorities: (l) small urban parcels, (2) small rural parcels, and (3) large rural parcels. The small parcels, perhaps anything less than twenty acres, could be simply sold to the highest bidder. Privatizing the remainder requires more sophisticated analysis.

There are eight criteria for a successful program, assuming that there is a reasonable degree of political sympathy toward privatization.

1. *Squatters' rights*. Before the general public is allowed to compete for any federal land, the legitimate rights of previous users must be recognized. Prior uses that should be recognized include grazing, mining, outfitting and guiding, and other special-use permits, such as ski resorts. All such preemption claims would have to be legitimized by an administrative court.

2. *Efficiency*. Transaction costs should be minimized by using different methods of disposal for different types of land. In some cases, auctions might be appropriate; in others, giveaways may be the least costly. The goal is not to maximize revenue, but to place management in the hands of responsible individuals.

3. *Public notice*. Any plan to privatize land should be open to public scrutiny. Reasonably well-informed individuals should not have to work hard to find out about land sales. While public comment may be negative, any evidence of backroom dealing would devastate the program.

4. *Time frame*. A definite time frame must be established. Twenty years might be long enough to avoid drastic shocks in the economic system but short enough to accommodate interests of those alive today.

5. *Parcel size*. Too often the government has incorrectly placed maximum acreage requirements on private claims. It is more desirable to dispose of parcels that are too large than too small. Secondary markets would be the ultimate determinant of efficient parcel size.

6. *Parcel selection*. Which parcels should be privatized first? The most equitable method is to divide the total number of

parcels (after size selection) by the number of years in the program and pick that number of parcels by lottery for sale each year.

7. *Administration.* Unfortunately, moving toward private management requires the establishment of an agency. The agency could be modeled after the extinct General Land Office, perhaps renamed the Land Resource Divestiture Agency (LRDA). LRDA would administer the program and would be designed along the lines of a predatory bureaucracy, so that it would have incentive to attack the budgets of existing federal land agencies (see Baden and Fort 1980). LRDA would expire after the last parcel was turned over to private managers.
8. *Covenants.* In some cases, it may be desirable to place restrictive covenants on developments that would affect irreplaceable biological, geological, historical, and archeological resources. Yellowstone National Park and the Grand Canyon would clearly be worthy of such covenants. Private enterprise would still yield efficient management of the resource without altering unique resources. Public access covenants may also be desired in some cases.

Using these criteria, a more specific private management or divestiture plan could be developed. In general, preemption claims should be honored first; where such claims have been validated by a court of law, rights to the land should be transferred to the claimants. Amenity lands could be given to bona fide environmental groups opened to homesteading. The remaining lands could be auctioned off in a manner similar to the plan devised by Smith (1982).

CONCLUDING THOUGHTS

The case for private management is strongest on lands that are valued primarily for commodity production, since the ease of establishing property rights limits external effects. Commercial timberland and rangeland fit this category, since there is no legitimate reason for them to be owned by the federal government. Amenity lands (e.g., parks, wilderness, and wildlife refuges) present some problems for efficient property rights solutions, but under the current system these lands are often overused. Innovative privatization programs that use compensation, preemption, and protective covenants could move these lands into private hands without dissipating social values.

As Thomas Sowell (1980, 123) has stated, "The social question then is—what is to be gained or lost by defining a property right, and on what basis should the right be assigned, and should it be transferable?" The evidence suggests that sustainability is best sought by making decision makers accountable for their actions, and giving them the information and incentives to make efficient and environmentally sensitive management decisions. Creating and enforcing private property rights encourages responsible, well-informed stewardship better than direct governmental management.

NOTES

1. Although the data in the table are from 1983, the amount of public land overseen by each agency and bureau has changed very little.

2. Wise Use is a diverse political movement partially committed to defending property rights against regulatory and legislative incursions and partially committed to maintaining subsidies for logging, grazing, irrigation, and mining.

REFERENCES

Anderson, Terry L. 1982. "The New Resource Economics: Old Ideas and New Applications." *American Journal of Agricultural Economics,* vol. 64:928–34.

Anderson, Terry L., and Peter J. Hill. 1975. "The Evolution of Property Rights: A Study of the American West." *Journal of Law and Economics* (April):163–79.

Anderson, Terry L., and Peter J. Hill. 1980. *The Birth of a Transfer Society*. Stanford, CA: Hoover Institution.

Baden, John. 1980. "Property Rights, Cowboys and Bureaucrats: A Modest Proposal." Pages 71–83 in *Earth Day Reconsidered,* ed. J. Baden. Washington, D.C.: Heritage Foundation.

Baden, John, and Rodney D. Fort. 1980. "Natural Resources and Bureaucratic Predators." *Policy Review* (winter):68–81.

Baden, John, and Dean Lueck. 1982. A Property Rights Approach to Wilderness Management. Paper presented at the Wilderness Society Conference on Federal Lands and the U.S. Economy.

Baden, John, and Richard Stroup. 1975. "Private Rights, Public Choices, and the Management of National Forests." *Western Wildlands* (autumn):5–13.

Baden, John, and Richard Stroup. 1979. "Property Rights and Natural Resource Management." *Literature of Liberty* 2:5–44.

Baden, John, and Richard Stroup, eds. 1981a. *Bureaucracy* vs. *Environment*. Ann Arbor: University of Michigan Press.

Baden, John, and Richard Stroup. 1981b. "Saving the Wilderness: A Radical Proposal." *Reason* (July):28–36.

Baden, John, Richard Stroup, and Walter Thurman. 1981. "Myths, Admonitions and Rationality: The American Indian as a Resource Manager." *Economic Inquiry* (January):132–43.

Barlow, Thomas J., Gloria E. Helf, Trent W. Orr, and Thomas B. Stoel. 1980. *Giving Away the National Forests*. Washington, D.C.: Natural Resources Defense Council.

Bator, Francis. 1958. "The Anatomy of Market Failure." *Quarterly Journal of Economics* (August):351–79.

Beckwith, James P., Jr. 1981. "Parks, Property Rights, and the Possibilities of the Private Law." *Cato Journal* 1:473–500.

Buchanan, James M., and Gordon Tullock. 1962. *The Calculus of Consent*. Ann Arbor: University of Michigan Press.

Buchanan, James M., Robert O. Tollison, and Gordon Tullock, eds. 1980. *Toward a Theory of the Rent-Seeking Society*. College Station: Texas A&M University Press.

Chase, Alston. 1986. *Playing God in Yellowstone: The Destruction of America's First National Park*. New York: Harcourt Brace and Company.

Clawson, Marion. 1982. *The Federal Lands Revisited*. Bozeman, MT: Center for Political Economy and Natural Resources, Montana State University.

Coase, Ronald. 1960. "The Problem of Social Cost." *Journal* of *Law and Economics* (October):1–44.

Coggins, George C., and Charles F. Wilkinson. 1981. *Federal Public Land and Resources Law*. Mineola, N.J.: The Foundation Press.

Davis, Lance E. 1972. *American Economic Growth: An Economist's History of the United States*. New York: Harper & Row.

Demsetz, Harold. 1967. "Toward a Theory of Property Rights." *American Economic Review* (May):347–59.

Dennis, William C. 1981. "The Public and Private Interest in Wilderness Protection." *Cato Journal* 1: 373–90.

Dennis, William C. 1982. *Private Land and Public Amenities.* Bozeman, MT: Center for Political Economy and Natural Resources, Montana State University.

Dolan, Edwin. 1971. "Why Not Sell the National Parks?" *National Review* (April 6): 362–65.

Dowdle, Barney. 1981. "An Institutional Dinosaur with an ACE." In *Bureaucracy vs. Environment,* ed. John Baden and Richard Stroup, 170–85. Ann Arbor: University of Michigan Press.

Dowdle, Barney, and Steve Hanke. 1985. "Public Timber Policy and the Wood Products Industry." Pages 77–102 in *Forestlands: Public and Private,* eds. R.T. Deacon and M.B. Johnson. San Francisco: Pacific Institute for Public Policy Research.

Downs, Anthony. 1957. *An Economic Theory of Democracy.* New York: Harper and Row.

Drucker, Peter. 1985. *Innovation and Entrepreneurship.* New York: Harper and Row.

Fort, Rodney D., and John Baden. 1981. "The Federal Treasury as a Common Pool Resource and the Development of a Predatory Bureaucracy." Pages 9–21 in *Bureaucracy vs. Environment,* eds. J. Baden and R. Stroup. Ann Arbor: University of Michigan Press.

Foss, Philip O. 1960. *Politics and Grass: The Administration of Grazing on the Public Domain.* Westport, CT: Greenwood Press.

Friedman, Milton. 1962. *Capitalism and Freedom.* Chicago: University of Chicago Press.

General Accounting Office. 1984. *Congress Needs Better Information on Forest Service's Below Cost Timber Sales.* Washington, D.C.: GAO.

General Services Administration. 1983. *Summary Report of the Real Property Owned by the United States throughout the World.* Washington, D.C.: Government Printing Office.

Grobey, John H. 1985. "Politics vs. Bioeconomics: Salmon Fishery and Forest Values in Conflict." Pages 169–200 in *Forestlands: Public and Private,* eds. R.T. Deacon and M.B. Johnson. San Francisco: Pacific Research Institute for Public Policy.

Gwartney, James, and Richard Stroup. 1983. *Economics: Private and Public Choice.* 3d ed. New York: Academic Press.

Hardin, Garrett, and John Baden, eds. 1977. *Managing the Commons.* San Francisco: Freeman.

Hayek, Friedrich A. 1945. "The Use of Knowledge in Society." *American Economic Review XXXV* (4): 519–30.

Hess, Karl Jr. 1992. *Visions Upon the Land: Man and Nature on the Western Range.* Washington D.C. and Covelo, CA: Island Press.

Hess, Karl Jr. 1993. *Rocky Times in Rocky Mountain National Park: An Unnatural History.* Niwot, CO: University Press of Colorado.

Hess, Karl Jr. 1994a. "The Western Public Range." *Different Drummer,* volume 1(2): 27–28.

Hess, Karl Jr. 1994b. "You Have to Overgraze." *Different Drummer,* volume 1(2): 43–44.

Huth, Hans. 1957. *Nature and the American.* Berkeley: University of California Press.

Hyde, William F. 1981. "National Forest Logs Red Ink for Treasury." *Wharton Magazine* (fall): 66–71.

Jensen, W.F., T.K. Fuller, and W.L. Robinson. 1986. Wolf Distribution on the Ontario-Michigan Border Near Sault-Ste. Marie. Unpublished report of the Minnesota Department of Natural Resources, Wildlife Populations and Research Group, Grand Rapids, MI. August.

Johnson, Ronald N. 1985. "U.S. Forest Service Policy and Its Budget." In *Forestlands Public and Private,* 103–133. San Francisco: Pacific Research Institute for Public Policy.

Johnson, Ronald N., and Gary L. Libecap. 1980. "Efficient Markets and Great Lakes Timber." *Explorations in Economic History* 17:372–85.

Kirzner, Israel. 1973. *Competition and Entrepreneurship.* Chicago: University of Chicago Press.

Krutilla, John V. 1967. "Conservation Reconsidered." *American Economic Review* (September):777–86.

Lanner, Ronald M. 1981. Chained to the Bottom. Pages 154–69 in *Bureaucracy vs. Environment,* eds. J. Baden and R. Stroup. Ann Arbor: University of Michigan Press.

Libecap, Gary D. 1981. *Locking up the Range.* San Francisco: Pacific Institute.

Libecap, Gary D., and Ronald N. Johnson. 1981. "The Navaho and Too Many Sheep: Overgrazing on the Reservation." Pages 87–107 in *Bureaucracy vs. Environment,* eds. J. Baden and R. Stroup. Ann Arbor: University of Michigan Press.

Lucas, E. 1994. "Successful by Nature." *Alaska Airlines Magazine* (August): 23–31.

Mitchell, William C., and Randy T. Simmons. 1994. *Beyond Politics: Markets, Welfare, and the Failure of Bureaucracy.* Boulder, CO: Westview Press.

Nash, Roderick, ed. 1976. *The American Environment*. Menlo Park, CA: Addison-Wesley.

Niskanen, William Jr. 1971. *Bureaucracy and Representative Government*. Chicago: Aldine-Atherton.

Niskanen, William Jr. 1975. "Bureaucrats and Politicians." *Journal of Law and Economics* 18 (December):617–44.

Olson, Mancur. 1971. *The Logic of Collective Action: Public Goods and the Theory of Groups*. Cambridge, MA: Harvard University Press.

Olson, Mancur. 1982. *The Rise and Decline of Nations*. New Haven: Yale University Press.

O'Toole, Randal. 1988. *Reforming the Forest Service*. Covelo, CA and Washington, D.C.: Island Press.

O'Toole, Randal. 1992. "A Citizen's Guide to the Forest Service Budget." *Forest Watch*, vol. 12(9).

Padover, Saul K. 1968. *The Living U.S. Constitution*. New York: New American Library.

Petulla, Joseph M. 1977. *American Environmental History*. San Francisco: Boyd and Fraser.

Pigou, Arthur C. 1932. *The Economics of Welfare*. 4th ed. London: MacMillan and Company, Ltd.

Power, Thomas. 1987. "To Be or Not To Be? The Economics of Development Along the Rocky Mountain Front." *Western Wildlands* 13 (3):20–25.

Power, Thomas. 1989. "Avoiding the Passive/Helpless Approach to Economic Development." *Forest Watch* 10 (4):16–18.

Power, Thomas. 1991. "Ecosystem Preservation and the Economy in the Greater Yellowstone Area." *Conservation Biology* 5(3):395–404.

Power, Thomas. 1992. The Employment Impact of the Northern Rockies Ecosystem Protection Act in Montana. Unpublished paper commissioned for the Alliance for the Wild Rockies. Missoula, MT.

Reed, Lawrence. 1993. "Privatization: Best Hope for a Vanishing Wilderness." Pages 153–163 in *Man and Nature*. Irving-on-Hudson: Foundation for Economic Education.

Reisner, Marc. 1986. *Cadillac Desert: The American West and Its Disappearing Water*. New York: Viking Penguin, Inc.

Robbins, Roy M. 1942. *Our Landed Heritage: The Public Domain*. Princeton, NJ: Princeton University Press.

Samuelson, Paul A. 1954. The Pure Theory of Public Expenditure. *Review of Economics and Statistics* (May):387–89.

Siffin, William J. 1981. "Bureaucracy, Entrepreneurship, and Natural Resources: Witless Policy and the Barrier Islands." *Cato Journal* 1:293–311.

Smith, Robert J. 1981. "Resolving the Tragedy of the Commons by Creating Private Property Rights in Wildlife." *Cato Journal* 1:439–68.

Smith, Vernon. 1982. "On Divestiture and the Creation of Property Rights in Public Lands." *Cato Journal* (winter): 663–86.

Sowell, Thomas. 1980. *Knowledge and Decisions.* New York: Basic Books.

Stroup, Richard, and John Baden. 1973. "Externality, Property Rights, and the Management of Our National Forests." *Journal of Law and Economics* 16(2):303–312.

Tullock, Gordon. 1965. *The Politics of Bureaucracy.* Washington, D.C.: Public Affairs Press.

Udall, Stewart. 1963. *The Quiet Crisis.* New York: Holt, Rinehart and Winston.

White, Daphne. 1994. "Taking a Walk on the Wild Side." *Hemispheres.* February.

Wilkinson, Charles F. 1992. *Crossing the Next Meridian: Land, Water, and the Future of the West.* Covelo, CA and Washington, D.C.: Island Press.

Wolf, Robert E. 1984. *State by State Estimates of Situations Where Timber Will Be Sold the Forest Service at a Loss or Profit.* Unpublished paper prepared for the Subcommittee on Interior Appropriation of the House Appropriations Committee, Washington, D.C., 7 March 1984, p. 1.

8 This Land is "Our" Land: The Case for Federal Retention of Public Lands

CHARLES DAVIS

A policy issue that often evokes a passionate response from people is the question of who controls federal lands. Should the U.S. government retain ownership of public lands currently managed by federal agencies such as the National Park Service, the Forest Service, the Bureau of Land Management, and the Fish and Wildlife Service? Or should these lands be sold to individuals or companies within the private sector? Advocates of retention often acknowledge ideological ties to Gifford Pinchot who argued that professional administrators within a federal agency were better able to determine the most appropriate mix of natural resource uses within the U.S. public lands in a manner that would provide "the greatest good for the greatest number over the longest time" (Hays 1959). They also emphasize the importance of collective or community goals and contend that amenity values, such as the preservation of natural areas within wilderness tracts or parks, are unlikely to be obtained under conditions of private ownership.

Others suggest that the protection of environmental values can be handled more effectively by marketplace operations than by governmental institutions. The attraction for supporters of public land disposition lies in the idea that private owners will make resource management decisions that are not only more efficient but environmentally responsible as well—particularly if legally enforceable property rights are established (Bish 1977; Stroup and Baden 1983). Moreover, free market environmentalists argue that public land managers have little incentive to adopt sound conservation practices, choosing instead to accomodate extractive users such as miners, ranchers, timber companies, and energy firms (Dennis and Simmons 1986).

This chapter offers an analysis of U.S. governmental policies pertaining to the public land disposition issue within the context of historical trends, economic analyses, and political perspectives. Either of the positions highlighted above can be shown to weigh selected policy values such as efficiency, representativeness, accessibility, and sustainable development differently.[1] I contend here that governmental ownership of public lands is preferable to market-based alternatives such as privatization since federal agencies are increasingly likely to make resource allocation decisions that combine public preferences with greater sensitivity to environmental concerns.

HISTORICAL VIEW OF PUBLIC LAND DISPOSITION

The U.S. government was actively involved in the acquisition and disposal of land between the late 1700s and the latter third of the nineteenth century. For Congress, the needs of a developing country understandably centered upon the relationship between the settlement of newly acquired territories and the provision of economic opportunity. Development was facilitated through land bounties for American soldiers serving in the Revolutionary War (in lieu of cash payments), a willingness to tolerate the presence of squatters seeking to eke out a living within undeveloped areas, and the enactment of homestead laws giving title for plots of land to would-be settlers in exchange for limited residency.

The allocation of land grants to railroads accelerated the construction of transportation links between eastern and midwestern population centers and western lands. Land was also given to territorial governments for the establishment of institutions of higher learning. The federal government sought elimination of competing land claims through military campaigns waged against indigenous peoples, and encouraged development by federal subsidization of water projects built by the U.S. Army Corps of Engineers (Clawson 1983; Dana and Fairfax 1980).

Thus, for most of this period developmental goals clearly overshadowed any notion that environmental conservation was a worthwhile policy goal. Within the context of a seemingly infinite resource base and an agrarian economy, the country lacked a conservationist ethos. Indeed, as Wallace Stegner noted in his description of early Americans' views toward undeveloped lands:

> Survival meant, in God's word, "subduing" the wild Earth . . . Civilization was a good; wilderness was what had to be subdued to create the human habitations that looked like progress and triumph even when they were only huts in a stump field (1990, p. 35).

While the desire to develop western territories clearly placed the need for an economic infrastructure to support irrigated agriculture at the head of the policy agenda, a combination of ideas and events emerged to increase public awareness of resource limits. The writings of John Wesley Powell and George Perkins Marsh in the 1860s and 1870s highlighted the ecological significance of forest and watershed preservation and warned about the long term negative consequences of a depleted resource base (Dana and Fairfax 1980). The temporal significance of these works from a public policy perspective was reinforced by increasing public concern about two aspects of industry logging practices (Clawson 1983).

The most obvious problem was the waste created by "rape and run" harvesting of mature timber. Encouraged by the availability of inexpensive forested lands and low capital requirements for getting into the lumber business, entrepreneurs took advantage of these opportunities by rapidly overharvesting forests and abandoning them for other tracts containing an abundance of trees. Left behind were scarred lands with diminished capacity for watershed protection or wildlife habitat, nor did these firms show any inclination to plant new seedlings or mitigate risks from fire or disease (Hays 1959). An unfortunate consequence was gradual deforestation spreading westward from New England through the Great Lakes states.

Public outrage was also aimed at rampant fraud and corruption found within land disposal actions. Trespass on public lands for the purpose of harvesting timber was common and efforts by General Land Office administrators to halt these activities were often met by fierce resistance by local sympathizers and, in some cases, public officials as well (Dana and Fairfax 1980). Numerous fraudulent schemes were devised to obtain timber under the guise of the Homestead Act of 1862. One of the more commonly used ploys by enterprising "settlers" revolved around a promise to reside and improve a parcel of forested land (the Act required a five year tenure commitment). The settler would then cut and sell the trees, put the property up for sale and move on. Sometimes individuals would use false names to buy up lands at the going rate of $1.25 per acre and sell these tracts for a substantial profit to firms or individuals for resource development purposes (Wilkinson 1992).

The congressional response to resource exploitation was the enactment of the Forest Reserve Act of 1891 which authorized the president to set aside or "reserve" national forests. Subsequent presidential proclamations resulted in the reservation of 17.5 million acres of public timberlands by 1897 and, in February of the same year, President Grover Cleveland issued an executive order calling for the withdrawal of an additional 21 million acres only ten days before the end of his term in office (Clarke and McCool 1985). The political backlash from this action was predictably negative and particularly intense among western legislators. The move reinforced their perception that Washington, D.C. based administrators were out of touch with regional needs. More importantly, the withdrawal of public forests marked a "turning point in changing the agenda for the public lands away from the promotion of settlement towards the conservation of natural resources" (Francis 1984).

Theodore Roosevelt's presidency provides a benchmark for the beginning of the Conservationist Era in 1901. His views toward natural resource stewardship were significantly affected by his association with Gifford Pinchot, a good friend and trusted advisor who was subsequently tapped to become the first Chief of the U.S. Forest Service. The philosophical orientation of these men has been referred to as "progressive conservationism" or the belief that wise use of public forest lands is best achieved by actively managing the resource under the principle of "sustained yield," taking into account a host of economic, social, aesthetic, and moral factors.

A key element of this new program was the belief that conservationist goals designed to produce the "greatest good for the greatest number for the longest time" could be more readily attained under conditions of federal ownership. To continue a process of selling or giving away large tracts of resource rich lands was a de facto invitation to waste, destruction, and the creation of monopolies (Dana and Fairfax 1980). Thus, public land retention in federal hands offered a useful means of demonstrating the benefits of scientific land management techniques as well as expressing progressive antipathy toward the growth of monopolizing business conglomerates.

Both public and congressional support for maintaining control over public lands have held steady or increased since that time (Francis 1984). Stronger congressional backing for this position could be attributed, in part, to policy decisions made by federal administrators which gave greater preference to resource conservation measures than efforts made by industries or private citizens to accelerate the development of natural resources. In 1906, President Theodore Roosevelt withdrew an additional six million acres of coal lands from homesteading, arguing that the need to develop the nation's renewable resources in an orderly fashion took precedence over the provision of speculative opportunities or quick riches to enterprising applicants. This produced a debate within Congress over conflicting policy objectives since a number of coal bearing deposits could be found beneath prime agricultural land. The issue was resolved through several laws passed between 1909 and 1916 which gave would be homesteaders the right to settle and acquire title to surface lands while subsurface coal or fossil fuel reserves were left in the hands of the federal government (Francis 1984).

A more dramatic shift in policy direction took place with the enactment of the Mineral Leasing Act of 1920. This statute amended the venerable Hardrock Mining Law of 1872 by establishing a new precedent—the idea of leasing fuel resources on the public domain instead of selling or giving away the land to prospective users (Dana and Fairfax 1980). Under this Act, the U.S. Interior Department was given a stronger role in land use decisions through its authority to deny or approve lease applications for resource extraction. Another provision of the law created royalty requirements for lessees (normally about 12.5% of the proceeds) and a form of revenue sharing which diverted a portion of the money to the states as well as the federal treasury (Arrandale 1983).

An additional boost to the goal of public land retention occurred in the mid-1930s through the efforts of President Franklin Roosevelt, Interior Secretary Harold Ickes and key legislators such as Congressman Ed Taylor of Colorado. In response to the deterioration of public rangelands because of severe drought and overgrazing by livestock operators, they sought a form of minimal regulation that would aid in the restoration of these lands and provide a modicum of economic stability for western ranchers. The result was congressional approval of the Taylor Grazing Act of 1934.

This Act authorized the Interior Department to set up grazing districts on public rangelands and established a federal Grazing Service to regulate use through the issuance of permits. Once again, it appeared that federal controls had been extended, albeit in a rather minimal fashion. Of greater significance was the subsequent decision by President Roosevelt to issue executive orders withdrawing all U.S. public lands from entry under the Homestead Act. This effectively closed the last major route to large scale disposition of federal lands (Culhane 1981).

After the end of World War II, attention was increasingly directed toward forms of public land use other than commodity production.

Forest Service and to a lesser extent U.S. Bureau of Land Management (BLM) officials found themselves squeezed by competing demands. On the one hand, the influx of returning soldiers resulted in growing demand for wood products used in residential home construction. An increase in timber harvests from national forests was viewed as a logical source to meet the demand and administrators, notably Forest Service Chief Richard McArdle, were willing to accelerate the process. As Wilkinson (1992) has indicated, "twice as much timber was cut during the sixteen years between 1950 and 1966 as had been cut during all of the previous forty-five years since the Transfer Act of 1905." Less timber was available from privately owned tracts because of intensive logging to meet military needs during the war as well as poor management on the part of lumber firms long accustomed to "cut and run" forestry practices (Clary 1986).

On the other hand, more Americans began to view western public lands as a recreational resource as the popularity of outdoor activities such as skiing, hunting, fishing, hiking, kayaking, rock climbing, and riding in off road vehicles (ORV) skyrocketed. This was reinforced by demographic trends such as the migration of people to urban centers located in the Pacific Coastal and Rocky Mountain states and by the tendency of newer residents to view nearby national forests in terms of their scenic or recreational qualities rather than commodity use (Hays 1991). At the same time, the growth of environmental organizations gave voice to those favoring public policies aimed at the conservation or preservation of natural resources as a political counterweight to politically influential commodity groups and their allies within the Interior Committees of Congress. Groups like the Sierra Club, the Wilderness Society, the Natural Resources Defense Council and Friends of the Earth worked particularly hard for ecologically sensitive land management policies in Washington and were able to score some legislative victories by the 1960s (Culhane 1981).

An assessment of public land statutes enacted during the 1960s and 1970s indicates that environmentalists, on balance were able to obtain a number of substantive policy gains linked directly or indirectly to retentionist goals. The inclusion of ecological and recreational as well as commodity production criteria within laws such as the Multiple and Sustained Yield Act of 1960 or the more far reaching National Environmental Policy Act of 1969 put land management agencies on notice that the doctrine of multiple use actually required explicit consideration of noncommodity values in use allocation decisions. A more dramatic departure from politics as usual resulted in a pair of key legislative triumphs for preservationist advocates—the Wilderness Act of 1964 and the Wild and Scenic Rivers Act of 1968. These laws are important because they demonstrate congressional receptivity to specialized land management goals based on amenity values with broad popular appeal as well as traditional commodity programs benefitting local or regional users.

A more direct expression of congressional intent on the question of who controls federal lands was contained within the Federal Land Management and Policy Act (FLPMA) enacted in 1976. This Act is best known as BLM's organic law, providing statutory authority for the agency's existence and a multiple use mandate for its program management activities. FLPMA also incorporated language detailing the need to consider environmental objectives along with natural resource production goals. But a key provision of the law formally did away with the notion that the federal estate was held in abeyance "pending disposition" by stating that the U.S. would retain and manage its public lands (Dana and Fairfax 1980).

However, this issue was not fully settled by congressional approval of FLPMA. A direct challenge was mounted by the Reagan Administration in the early 1980s through the so-called "privatization" initiative. The idea that selling off public lands made good sense financially as well as administratively was advanced by conservative economists such as William Niskanen and Steve Hanke, both of whom served on Reagan's Council of Economic Advisors. In general, they argued that public land managers had done a poor job of resource management because of an incentive structure that placed greater weight on political influence peddling than economic rationality (see also Baden and O'Brien in this volume). An obvious cure for this problem was the transfer of public lands to private ownership, thereby ensuring greater efficiency in resource allocation decisions (Nelson 1984; McCurdy 1984, 1986).

Support for the proposal in a pro-business administration was not difficult to come by. Trusted advisors such as presidential counselor Edwin Meese and OMB Director David Stockman were quick to "sign on" and on February 25, 1982, President Reagan signed an executive order creating a Property Review Board that would report directly to the White House. Key responsibilities of the new organization included the sale of surplus federal lands managed by BLM and the Forest Service. Shortly thereafter, the Property Review Board instructed the Interior Department and other federal agencies to develop plans for the sale of land and property based on a three part classification scheme that determined whether prospective lands should be retained or sold.

However, the political response to this issue was both immediate and negative, owing in part to political miscalculations made by administration officials. Stockman announced that one of the basic objectives of the program was to raise money for the government and indicated that as much as $17 billion could be obtained by selling federal property, including public lands, over a five year period (Nelson 1984). This created two major hurdles for program advocates. One was the basic incompatibility between efficiency and maximizing revenue to aid in deficit reduction. Small public land tracts surrounded by private property could conceivably be identified as prime candidates for the marketplace on efficiency grounds but might rank fairly low in comparison to larger parcels in terms of monetary gain (McCurdy 1984).

Second, Interior Secretary James Watt was put into a very uncomfortable position by this action. The political imperative to jump aboard the privatization bandwagon put him at odds with many public land user groups like miners, ranchers, loggers, and energy companies that formed his political support base. Traditional land management programs contain subsidies for users since operating costs often exceeded payments received. However, the clear implication of a move toward privatization was that natural resource payments from program beneficiaries would rise to more closely approximate "fair market value." Such actions were viewed as untenable and potentially catastrophic by smaller firms or individuals operating on the margins of profitability as well as most trade associations representing their interests and elected officials throughout the west (Culhane 1984).

The net result was the formation of a rather curious set of political bedfellows to oppose privatization. Ranchers and others associated with what Nelson (1984) referred to as the "subsidized Sagebrush" joined hands temporarily with environmentalists, private landowners, community leaders, and recreational users to express their displeasure, and they eventually succeeded. Secretary Watt announced in July 1983 that the Interior Department had reached an agreement with the Property Review Board to exclude public land tracts from government surplus property sales (Nelson 1984).

The importance of this particular controversy lies in the fact that it is one of the few cases involving the preferred role of government in determining the disposition of federal lands to be decided at the highest levels of government. It also demonstrates the gap between the economic and political marketplaces. The prospective gains to be realized from the privatization initiative were diluted considerably by the actions of both environmental and commodity groups who sought to minimize the impact of public land sales on their respective land use preferences.

Until recently, the question of federal retention of public lands had received little attention. However, the Republican successes in taking control over both the U.S. House of Representatives and the Senate in 1994 prompted Interior Secretary Babbitt and others to again discuss the possibility of selling off public land parcels to individual or corporate buyers. Other key players in these discussions include the new Chairs of the House Resources Committee, Representative Don Young (R-AK), and the Senate Energy and Natural Resources Committee, Senator Frank Murkowski (R-AK), who have exhibited a strong commodity production bias in past public land policy votes.

However, it is unclear whether the scope of these talks is likely to extend beyond the sale of smaller plots of federal land located in or near urban areas to include larger tracts of range or forested lands. Nor is it possible to determine whether Congress would approach this issue from a more ideological property rights perspective (such as privatization) or by pushing for development oriented changes within the context of existing land management policies.

ECONOMIC ANALYSES

Economic arguments for federal retention of public lands are closely linked to the concepts of "public goods" and "common property resources." Natural resources may be characterized as the former if they are indivisible, that is, resource use by one person does not significantly reduce the amount of the resource available for others, and if they are fully accessible to all prospective users (Tietenberg 1988). A commonly cited example is air quality since the benefits of providing it cannot be distributed in ways that allow firms to charge for the service. Thus, markets are unable to allocate resources efficiently and government shoulders the responsibility for providing clean air. Citizens, in turn, incur the costs of offering this good through taxes paid to one or more levels of government (Loomis 1993).

There are numerous examples of public lands resources with public good attributes. Some of the more publicized applications include the protection of habitat for rare and endangered species such as the northern spotted owl or the desert tortoise as well as unique physical resources such as the Grand Canyon, Carlsbad Caverns, or the geysers located within Yellowstone National Park. Each offers to prospective visitors the opportunity to observe objects or scenery that might not be accessible to them under private ownership. Or, as John Krutilla and his associates (1983, p. 551) indicate, "the market's rationing feature tends to reduce rather than increase benefits that potentially can be derived from public goods."

The management of common property resources such as rangelands or fisheries offers another rationale for federal control over resource decisions because of the tension between ecological limits and markets. Natural systems allow use within the "carrying capacity" of the resource; that is, the maximum sustained yield. If these limits are exceeded, the longer term survival of the resource is put in jeopardy (Hardin 1968).

Unfortunately, it is economically rational for individual users to make optimum use of common property resources in the short run since there are no guarantees that undertaking responsible conservation practices will result in similar actions by their competitors (Ingersoll and Brockbank 1986). This results in a downward spiral of ecologically destructive behavior which is shown in prior examples of deforestation within the northeastern and upper midwestern states (Clary 1986) as well as overgrazing on the open western rangelands prior to the enactment of the Taylor Grazing Act of 1934 (Box 1990).

Pressures to extract and develop natural resources are not restricted to the domestic marketplace. Another reason for an acceleration of developmental activities following the privatization of public lands is the lure of export markets for raw materials, an international trend that has grown dramatically over the past twenty years (Porter and Brown 1991). Within the U.S., a likely consequence of shifting from public to privately owned forests would be an increase in the sale of unprocessed softwood logs from forests in the Pacific Northwest, including Alaska, to Japan despite environmentalist concerns about the negative relationship between the rate of harvesting and the regenerative capabilities of forest ecosystems (Hoberg 1996).

There are clear incentives for transnational corporate officials (TNCs) to adopt a strategy of maximizing resource production activities in the short run over a longer term sustainable approach. The most important incentive is profit. Most TNCs rely on a cost benefit approach that focuses on the minimization of both labor and environmental regulatory compliance costs (Porter and Brown 1991). Efforts to bring about trade arrangements unfettered by sensitivity to environmental costs have been facilitated by agreements reached in the Uruguay Round of the General Agreement on Tariffs and Trade (GATT) to limit restrictions on trade—including export controls on forest products.

In addition, a lack of corporate accountability to communities affected by resource management decisions is reinforced by the growing geographical mobility of TNCs as well as changes in information technology and transportation. This increases the distance between producers and consumers and between employers and employees. According to Miller (1995), a consequence is that an "activity such as clear cut logging can register positively on a company's balance sheet and in a country's GNP without the community being compensated for the resulting damage, which can include flooding, drought, soil loss, and the cost of replanting."

Another justification for maintaining federal ownership of public lands lies in the need to deal with a commonly cited imperfection of the marketplace, i.e., negative externalities. This refers to the failure of buyers and sellers to absorb all the costs of a given transaction. If the remaining old growth forests in the Pacific Northwest are harvested because of their rather considerable commercial value to timber firms, a probable consequence is the continuing decline of endangered species such as the northern spotted owl. Since its survival is closely tied to the preservation of old growth habitat in national forests or BLM timberlands and industry officials are reluctant to forego potential income by leaving aside sizeable tracts of these trees, federal regulation to protect wildlife under the authority of the Endangered Species Act and the National Forest Management Act is the most viable means of addressing environmental impacts of this sort (Krutilla et al. 1983; Booth 1994).

The greatest single source of opposition to retaining lands is found within the writings of natural resource economists (Stroup and Baden 1983; Anderson and Leal 1991; Hess 1992). Those who advocate the privatization of federal lands argue that efficiency gains in resource allocation decisions provide an important rationale for policy change. But for this to occur, property rights must be "well-defined, well-enforced, transferable and privately held" (Baden and Lueck 1986). In practice, it is difficult to meet these conditions. As Loomis indicates, privatization policy proposals often take one of three forms—the sale of public land parcels to individuals, operating public lands on a "pay as you go" basis, or the management of federal lands as quasi-independent corporations. But all ignore an important characteristic of these lands, the lack of fit between natural resources and the market model of perfectly divisible resources with few or no impacts on innocent third parties (Loomis 1993).

Others argue that opposition to federal ownership on efficiency grounds is misplaced because of a failure to clarify what is meant by its use in differing contexts (Krutilla et al. 1983; Sagoff 1988). Bromley (1984) criticizes the use of economic efficiency by public lands policy analysts because they tend to neglect important conceptual distinctions such as technical efficiency (concern about the physical determinants of ideal outputs from the land), private economic efficiency (the ability of landowners to make land use allocation decisions in accordance with market signals) and social economic efficiency (the mix of federal land "products" is such that relevant social values from any two land uses are equal to the rate at which one must be sacrificed for the other after recognizing possible external effects). Put differently, natural resource administrators are often criticized for being "inefficient" in making resource allocation decisions. However, the force of this argument is lessened considerably if administrative decisions are evaluated from more than one conception of efficiency (Bromley 1984).

In addition, while efficiency-oriented or property-based concerns are at the root of many privatization or takings policy proposals advanced during the Reagan Administration and more recently by legislators within the new Republican controlled congress, not all analysts are inclined to accept the "gospel of efficiency" as the preeminent value within the public lands policy shrine. Competing values such as preserving wilderness, wildlife habitat and open public recreation, ensuring public accountability for resource allocation decisions, and maintaining a public legacy for future generations are already imbedded within numerous public land laws and enjoy widespread public support as well (Gregg 1991; Shindler, List and Steel 1993).

THE POLITICAL PERSPECTIVE

Political scientists writing about public lands policy have occasionally drawn attention to one of the more important reasons for preferring public control over public lands to private ownership, i.e., the utilization of a multiple-use framework by land management agencies such as BLM and the Forest Service that offers access to national forests and rangelands for a variety of groups with differing land use preferences. According to Miller (1987), this leads to a more pluralistic policymaking environment within an administrative setting, lessens agency dependence upon traditional commodity producers as a source of political support and increases political representativeness (see also Bradley and Ingram 1986).

It is unlikely that a private owner would incur the additional expense associated with the provision of public goods (although in some cases public access for recreational activities could be recaptured through user fees) since other land uses such as commodity production would offer a greater monetary return on his or her investment. But in most cases, public sector agencies are prepared to accommodate a more diverse array of interests, including those of U.S. residents living far away from affected areas (Clawson 1983).

There are several objections that have been raised about the ability or willingness of federal land managers to act as responsible stewards of the public lands. One of these, alluded to earlier, revolves around the assumption that federal retention of the public lands will inevitably lead to less efficient natural resource allocation choices since public administrators have not been subjected to the rigors of competition in the marketplace. Leaving aside the point that the meaning of efficiency is conceptually slippery and dependent upon decisional contexts, there are no empirical studies dealing with intersectoral differences in decision-making that demonstrate the superiority of industry officials over federal bureaucrats within this area of policy—or vice versa (Bromley 1984; Nelson 1984).

A second objection is aimed at the failure of professional land managers to make environmentally responsible land use allocation decisions because of their close ties to commodity groups. Much of the literature on the management of federal lands in the West from the latter part of the nineteenth century until the mid-1960s has depicted BLM and Forest Service administrators as key participants within a subsystem or "iron triangle" form of governance which benefitted user groups such as miners, loggers, ranchers, and energy firms (Foss 1960; Reich 1962).

Other members of the triangle included trade associations representing program beneficiaries, western legislators serving on the House and Senate Interior Committees, and administrators working for the U.S. Forest Service and the Interior Department. A consequence of subsystem dominance was the design of public programs such as the Knutson-Vandenburg Act (1930) and the Taylor Grazing Act (1934) which simultaneously created subsidies for commodity producers and organizational disincentives for public land managers to consider the environmental effects of their decisions (Culhane 1981; O'Toole 1988).

Studies do indicate that decisions made by BLM and Forest Service administrators exhibited a proindustry tilt from the 1930s through the 1950s, leading Wilkinson (1992) to characterize powerful user groups such as the National Cattlemens' Association or the American Mining Congress as the "Lords of Yesterday." In part, a strong emphasis on commodity development reflected a lack of ecological awareness since environmental organizations had not yet emerged as major policy players during this period of time. This orientation was reinforced by the regional makeup of the House and Senate Interior Committees. More than half of the committee members in each chamber represented western states, and they were fiercely protective of subsidized land use programs providing economic benefits to traditional constituencies (Graf 1990).

Beginning in the 1960s, the political climate improved dramatically for the enactment of ecologically friendly public land laws. This was partly attributable to the efforts of policy entrepreneurs in government such as Senators Gaylord Nelson, Ed Muskie, and Henry Jackson, who pushed for environmental legislation as well as Interior Secretary Stewart Udall who attempted to instill a stronger conservationist ethos within land management agencies during his eight year tenure.

Second, the interaction between events such as the Santa Barbara oil spill and Earth Day and extensive media coverage served to heighten public awareness of resource degradation, leading to a rise in public support for protective measures. Third, a corresponding increase occurred in the number and activity level of environmental organizations headquartered in Washington, D.C. (Vig and Kraft 1994).

In a collective sense, these trends influenced the direction and substance of public land laws. New policies with a decidedly preservationist bent were enacted that effectively reduced the availability of larger land tracts for extractive land uses.[2] Other statutes such as FLPMA and the National Forest Management Act of 1976 (NFMA) required that federal land management agencies utilize environmental criteria (e.g., protection of watersheds and wildlife habitat) in making use allocation decisions. But these policies, along with the landmark National Environmental Policy Act (NEPA), also incorporated major procedural changes, notably provisions requiring public participation and, in some cases, allowing citizen lawsuits as well. The net effect of these changes has been to expand the constituency base of BLM and the Forest Service to include recreationists and environmentalists in addition to commodity groups.

How have federal land management agencies responded to new policy mandates? While there are occasional studies of Forest Service administrators in timber rich Region 6 that suggest a pro-industry bias (Twight, Lyden and Tuchmann 1990) or behavior (Booth 1991), much of the research conducted over the past fifteen years suggests that public land managers are not captives of the commodity organizations but, in fact, tend to make decisions that take both amenity and production values into account (Culhane 1981; Fairfax 1984; Davis and Davis 1988; Sabatier, et al. 1995).

This research includes both case analyses as well as studies linking the attitudes of federal land managers with subsequent decisions or output indicators. Fairfax (1984) examined BLM's organizational evolution from the beginning of the Kennedy Administration through the early years of the Reagan Administration. She concludes that the agency began implementing a multiple-use management philosophy closely patterned after the Forest Service approach in the 1960s, a decade before it received permanent authorization to do so under FLPMA. BLM began work on several initiatiatives, including rangeland improvements and managing areas for recreation or wildlife, that would have been difficult to achieve politically in the pre-1960 era.

Other analysts have demonstrated the relationship between attitudes of BLM or Forest Service officials and subsequent decisions or output indicators for the production of commodity or recreational resources. Culhane's (1981) work based on field research carried out in the Rocky Mountain states in the early 1970s indicated that administrators were trying to accommodate diverse perspectives in making use allocation decisions. A later study of BLM administrators in Wyoming produced similar results (Davis and Davis 1988).

A more recent analysis of Forest Service decisions over a twenty year period concluded that national forest outputs reflected the interests of several stakeholders besides the timber industries. Other factors that were significantly related to resource management decisions included the land use preferences of national forest supervisors and the influence of environmental and wildlife preservation groups (Sabatier, Loomis and McCarthy 1995).

SUMMARY AND CONCLUSIONS

A strong case for the retention of public lands by the federal government can be made through an examination of historical, economic, and political factors. Policymakers in the early twentieth century became concerned about profligate resource use exemplified by the cut and run forestry practices that laid bare previously forested lands in the northeastern and upper midwestern states as well as the deterioration of western rangelands which was linked to overstocking by cattle barons. They recognized the need for the wise use and management of natural resources but the questions of how and by whom were left unsettled until the emergence of "progressive conservationism," a new philosophy of land use advanced by Gifford Pinchot during his service as Forest Service Chief under President Theodore Roosevelt.

Congress was persuaded that the best way to achieve a balance between resource use and conservation was through scientific management principles, such as multiple use and sustained yield, which would be implemented by public agencies staffed with experts. The idea of active intervention by government administrators to achieve land use objectives was strengthened by subsequent laws that placed virtually all public land uses such as energy development, livestock grazing, recreation, wildlife management, logging, and wilderness under the federal umbrella even though the era of disposition through homesteading did not formally end until the FLPMA statute was signed by President Ford in 1976. While there is general agreement that the sale of smaller land parcels that are surrounded by private property or located in or near urban areas warrants consideration, little support exists for the disposal of larger tracts of federal lands.

The case for governmental ownership is not significantly altered by arguments advanced by privatization advocates. Many national parks, forests and rangelands possess the attributes of "public goods" such as scenery, wildlife habitat, or archeological treasures that carry relatively little "book value" for private investors interested in lucrative land uses such as mining or logging. Nor is reliance on market-based decisions likely to provide a satisfactory answer for negative externalities created by user groups seeking to minimize the costs of extracting and processing natural resources. In addition, critiques of existing land management policies by free market environmentalists often rest on an overly narrow definition of "efficiency," which subordinates land uses ranking high on other political values such as accessibility or sustainability to those with greater short term economic benefits.

Ultimately, a policy of maintaining public lands under federal control provides our best chance for achieving a more sustainable land use policy which combines cultural, natural, economic and political factors (Wilkinson 1992, especially chapter 7) with a longer term resource management perspective (Ingersoll and Brockbank 1986). Federal land management agencies are more likely to emphasize the multiplicity of values that can be achieved in use allocation decisions through a multiple use management philosophy. Consequently, governmental agencies are well positioned to absorb or "internalize" the costs associated with the conservation of natural resources or the prevention of environmental damage elsewhere.

While the Forest Service and BLM have been criticized for prior neglect of conservationist practices, these agencies have increasingly made efforts to accommodate nontraditional constituencies under the environmental laws enacted over the past thirty years. Moreover, organizations committed to a conservationist land use philosophy will continue to hold the feet of agency officials to the fire thanks to procedural advantages contained within environmental statutes affording participation in administrative decisions, or, if necessary, litigation pursued through citizen lawsuit provisions of federal land and related environmental legislation.

NOTES

1. Sustainable development or sustainability are commonly used terms that are interpreted differently by scholars and natural resource professionals. In this chapter, I have adopted the definition offered by Robert Costanza and his associates. Sustainability refers to "a relationship between dynamic human economic systems and larger dynamic but, normally, slower-changing ecological systems in which a) human life can continue indefinitely; b) human individuals can flourish; c) human cultures can develop; but in which d) effects of human activities remain within bounds, so as not to destroy the diversity, complexity, and function of the ecological life support system" (Costanza 1995, pp. 332–33).

2. These include the original Wilderness Act of 1964 which continues to add land parcels to the National Wilderness Preservation System through the enactment of state sponsored wilderness bills and the Wild and Scenic Rivers Act of 1968.

REFERENCES

Anderson, Terry, and Donald Leal. 1991. *Free Market Environmentalism.* San Francisco: Pacific Institute for Public Policy.

Arrandale, Tom. 1983. *The Battle for Natural Resources.* Washington, DC: Congressional Quarterly, Inc.

Baden, John, and Dean Lueck. 1986. "Bringing Private Management to the Public Lands: Environmental and Economic Advantages." In *Controversies in Environmental Policy,* eds. Sheldon Kamieniecki, Robert O'Brien and Michael Clarke. Albany: State University of New York Press.

Bish, Robert L. 1977. "Environmental Resource Management: Public or Private?" In *Managing the Commons,* eds. Garrett Hardin and John Baden. San Francisco: W.H. Freeman.

Booth, Douglas. 1994. *Valuing Nature: The Decline and Preservation of Old Growth Forests.* Lanham, MD: Rowman & Littlefield.

———. 1991. "Timber Dependency and Wilderness Selection: The U.S. Forest Service, Congress, and the RARE II Decisions." *Natural Resources Journal* 31 (fall).

Box, Thadis W. 1990. "Rangelands." In *Natural Resources for the 21st Century,* eds. R. Neil Sampson and Dwight Hair. Washington, DC: Island Press.

Bradley, Dorothea, and Helen Ingram. 1986. "Science vs. the Grass Roots: Representation in the Bureau of Land Management." *Natural Resources Journal* 26 (summer).

Bromley, Daniel W. 1984. "Public and Private Interests in the Federal Lands: Toward Conciliation." In *Public Lands and the U.S. Economy,* eds. George M. Johnston and Peter M. Emerson. Boulder: Westview Press.

Clarke, Jeanne N., and Daniel McCool. 1985. *Staking Out the Terrain.* Albany: State University of New York Press.

Clary, David. 1986. *Timber and the Forest Service.* Lawrence: University of Kansas Press.

Clawson, Marion. 1983. *The Federal Lands Revisited.* Washington, DC: RFF.

Costanza, Robert. 1995. "Ecological Economics: Toward a New Transdisciplinary Science." In *A New Century for Natural Resources Management,* eds. Richard Knight and Sarah Bates. Washington, DC: Island Press.

Culhane, Paul. 1981. *Public Land Politics.* Baltimore: The Johns Hopkins University Press.

———. 1984. "Sagebrush Rebels in Office: Jim Watt's Land and Water Policies." In *Environmental Policy in the 1980s,* eds. Norman Vig and Michael Kraft. Washington, DC: CQ Press, 1984.

Dana, Samuel T., and Sally Fairfax. 1980. *Forest and Range Policy,* 2nd ed. New York: McGraw-Hill.

Davis, Charles, and Sandra Davis. 1988. "Analyzing Change in Public Land Politics: From Subsystems to Advocacy Coalitions." *Policy Studies Journal* 17 (fall).

Dennis, William C., and Randy T. Simmons. 1986. "From Illusion to Responsibity: Rethinking Regulation of Public Lands." In *Controversies in Environmental Policy,* eds. Sheldon Kamieniecki, Robert O'Brien, and Michael Clarke. Albany: State University of New York Press.

Fairfax, Sally. 1984. "Beyond the Sagebrush Rebellion: The BLM as Neighbor and Manager in the Western States." In *Western Public Lands,* eds. John G. Francis and Richard Ganzel. Totowa, NJ: Rowman & Allanheld.

Foss, Phillip O. 1960. *The Politics of Grass*. Seattle: University of Washington Press.

Francis, John G. 1984. "Realizing Public Purposes Without Public Ownership." In *Western Public Lands,* eds. John G. Francis and Richard Ganzel. Totowa, NJ: Rowman & Allanheld.

Graf, William L. 1990. *Wilderness Preservation and the Sagebrush Rebellions*. Savage, MD: Rowman & Littlefield.

Gregg, Frank. 1991. "Public Land Policy: Controversial Beginnings for the Third Century." In *Government and Environmental Politics: Essays on Historical Developments Since World War II*, ed. Michael J. Lacey. Baltimore: Johns Hopkins University Press.

Hardin, Garrett. 1968. "The Tragedy of the Commons." *Science* 162 (December).

Hays, Samuel P. 1959. *Conservation and the Gospel of Efficiency*. Cambridge, MA: Harvard University Press.

———. 1991. "The New Environmental West." *Journal of Policy History* 3 (3).

Hess, Karl. 1992. *Visions upon the Land: Man and Nature on the Western Range*. Washington, DC: Island Press.

Hoberg, George. 1996. "The Transformation of Federal Forest Policy." In *Western Public Lands and Environmental Politics*, ed. Charles Davis. Boulder, CO: Westview Press.

Ingersoll, Thomas G., and Bradley Brockbank. 1986. "The Role of Economic Incentives in Environmental Policy." In *Controversies in Environmental Policy*, eds. Sheldon Kamieniecki, Robert O'Brien and Michael Clarke. Albany: State University of New York Press.

Krutilla, John V., Anthony C. Fisher, William F. Hyde, and V. Kerry Smith. 1983. "Public versus Private Ownership: The Federal Lands Case." *Journal of Policy Analysis and Management* 2 (summer).

Leman, Christopher K. 1984. "How the Privatization Revolution Failed and Why Public Land Management Needs Reform Anyway." In *Western Public Lands*, eds. John G. Francis and Richard Ganzel. Totowa, NJ: Rowman & Allanheld, 1984.

Loomis, John B. 1993. *Integrated Public Lands Management*. New York: Columbia University Press.

McCurdy, Howard E. 1984. "Public Ownership of Land and the Sagebrush Rebellion." *Policy Studies Journal* 12 (March): 483–90.

———. 1986. "Environmental Protection and the New Federalism: The Sagebrush Rebellion and Beyond." In *Controversies in Environmental Policy*, eds. Sheldon Kamieniecki, Robert O'Brien and Michael Clarke. Albany: State University of New York Press.

Miller, Marian A.L. 1995. *The Third World in Global Environmental Politics.* Buckingham, United Kingdom: Open University Press.

Miller, Richard O. 1987. "Multiple Use in the Bureau of Land Management: The Biases of Pluralism Revisited." In *Federal Lands Policy,* ed. Phillip O. Foss. Westport, CT: Greenwood Press.

Nelson, Robert H. 1984. "The Subsidized Sagebrush: Why Privatization Failed." *Regulation* 8 (July/August).

O'Toole, Randal. 1988. *Reforming the Forest Service.* Covelo, CA: Island Press.

Porter, Gareth, and Janet Welsh Brown. 1991. *Global Environmental Politics.* Boulder, CO: Westview Press.

Reich, Charles. 1962. *Bureaucracy and the Forests.* Santa Barbara: Center for the Study of Democratic Institutions.

Sabatier, Paul, John Loomis, and Catherine McCarthy. 1995. "Hierarchical Controls, Professional Norms, Local Constituencies, and Budget Maximization: An Analysis of U.S. Forest Service Planning Decisions." *American Journal of Political Science* 39 (February).

Sagoff, Mark. 1988. *The Economy of the Earth.* New York: Cambridge University Press.

Shindler, Bruce, Peter List, and Brent Steel. 1993. "Managing National Forests: Public Attitudes in Oregon and Nationwide." *Journal of Forestry* 91 (July).

Stegner, Wallace. 1990. "It All Began with Conservation." *Smithsonian* 21 (April), p. 35.

Stroup, Richard, and John Baden. 1983. *Natural Resources: Bureaucratic Myths and Environmental Management.* San Francisco: Pacific Institute for Public Policy Research.

Tietenberg, Tom. 1988. *Environmental and Natural Resource Economics,* 2nd ed. Glenview, IL: Scott, Foresman & Company.

Twight, Ben, Fremont Lyden and E. Thomas Tuchmann. 1990. "Constituency Bias in a Federal Career System." *Administration and Society* 22 (May).

Vig, Norman, and Michael Kraft, eds. 1994. *Environmental Policies in the 1990s,* 2nd ed. Washington, DC: CQ Press.

Wilkinson, Charles. 1992. *Crossing the Next Meridian: Land, Water & the American West.* Washington, DC: Island Press.

SECTION FIVE

Trade and Sustainable Development

List of Abbreviations

AFTA	[Association of Southeast] Asian [Nations] Free Trade Area
APEC	Asia Pacific Economic Cooperation
CITES	Convention on International Trade in Endangered Species of Fauna and Flora
EAP	Environmental Action Plan
EU	European Union
FDI	foreign direct investment
GATT	General Agreement on Tariffs and Trade
IMF	International Monetary Fund
MMPA	Marine Mammals Protection Act [United States 1972]
NACE	North American Commission on the Environment
NAFTA	North American Free Trade Agreement
OECD	Organization for Economic Cooperation and Development
SEA	Single European Act
SEDESOL	Mexico's Social Development Secretariat
SEDUE	Mexico's Urban Development and Ecology Secretariat
TNCs	transnational corporations
UNCED	United Nations Conference on Environment and Development
UNCTAD-PTC	United Nations Conference on Trade and Development—Program on Transnational Corporations
WCED	World Commission on Environment and Development
WTO	World Trade Organization

9 Trade Liberalization and the Natural Environment: Conflict or Opportunity?

JULIANN ALLISON

The strident opposition of environmentalists to U.S. President Bush's February 1991 announcement that the United States, Canada, and Mexico would negotiate a North American Free Trade Agreement (NAFTA) made it clear that liberalization of trade in North America would depend on greater preservation of the natural environment. A former U.S. Deputy Trade Representative even remarked at the time, "I can think of no single issue in our international trade policy as important or as pressing as the environment."[1] Ultimately, widespread fear that freer trade would exacerbate environmental destruction in U.S.-Mexico border towns like Chilpancingo, a heavily polluted community located in a canyon below one of the largest industrial parks in Tijuana, compelled negotiators to promise that the NAFTA would set new, high standards of "environmental sensitivity and innovation," and "strengthen the relationship between economics and 'ecological stewardship'" (Aizeki 1993; Emerson 1993).

NAFTA's nominal support for sustainable development, and prohibitions against the lowering of U.S., Canadian, and Mexican environmental standards to attract new industry are, in fact, unprecedented in international trade agreements. NAFTA has even been called the "greenest-ever" such agreement (Reilly 1993). But is NAFTA's "green language" really so remarkable, considering the history of environmental regulation associated with European integration? And what are the implications of the European and North American efforts to balance economic integration and environmental protection for global trade liberalization? Is it true that economic growth is simply no longer synonymous with increased pollution, and that future international trade agreements will treat such important matters as the quality of water and air as a matter of course? Or are current international efforts to reconcile the effects of trade liberalization on the environment, and conversely, of environmental regulation on trade, really rooted in a transitory willingness to sacrifice profits for environmental quality?

This chapter provides answers to these questions as a means of evaluating the conflicts and potential opportunities inherent in the relationship between trade and the natural environment. It argues that European and North American efforts to incorporate environmental concerns into international trade agreements belie claims by economists that free trade necessarily improves the environmental quality of nations. Rather, whether or not environmental protection becomes a permanent and powerful feature of international trade agreements will depend on popular demands for, and national commitments to, sustainable economic growth. Drawing on a preliminary discussion of theories of economics, international politics, and the environment, the study compares environmental protection in the European Union (EU) and North America, under NAFTA, with that sanctioned by the General Agreement on Tariffs and Trade (GATT). This comparison suggests that regional integration and environmental activism have proven central to both European and North American efforts to protect the environment, which are held in check by the GATT's obligation to ensure the competitiveness of international trade.

APPROACHES TO THE TRADE-ENVIRONMENT RELATIONSHIP

Economic theory, international regimes, and environmental ethics provide three contrasting approaches to understanding the relationship between trade liberalization and the natural environment. According to the economic theory of externalities, the "greening" of international trade is a natural consequence of the efforts of national governments to establish markets for nature's goods and services.[2] Regime analysis of liberal trade theory, alternatively, suggests that domestic environmental policies are protectionist to the extent that they impede optimal specialization in the production of comparatively low-cost commodities, and therefore demand the standardization of procedures for weighing the costs and benefits of these national regulations and free international trade. Doubting the capacity of either markets or international institutions to provide sufficient protection for the natural environment, many environmentalists claim that the balanced trade and environmental policies necessary for sustainability will require a fundamental change in the value individuals and national governments accord the environment. Taken together, they suggest that the theoretical compatibility of freer trade and environmental quality depends on the institutionalization of a privileged role for domestic political concerns in the process of international economic integration.

TRADE AND ENVIRONMENTAL EXTERNALITIES

That trade may be instrumental as a source of domestic environmental regulations and international environmental cooperation lies in the definition of environmental degradation as an externality. Such an externality may be understood simply as a phenomenon—air or water pollution, for instance—whose costs are not adequately reflected in market prices.[3] Gasoline prices, for example, typically do not incorporate the full costs of polluting emissions on visibility and public health associated with the use of gasoline as an automotive fuel. An externality, such as air pollution caused by automobile exhaust, may be considered either "local," if it wholly impacts the domestic market, or "transboundary," meaning that it originates in one national market, but primarily affects foreign markets. Since the early 1970s, for instance, both U.S. and Canadian air quality regulations have effectively treated the nitrogen oxide found in automobile exhaust as a local pollution problem. Currently, emissions of nitrogen oxide are also being regulated as acid rain precursors under the 1991 Canada-United States Air Quality Agreement (U.S. Government and Government of Canada 1992).

If local, such market failures anticipate both potential of trade liberalization for damaging the environment, and the possibility that domestic environmental regulations will stymie international economic competition. Yet economic analyses suggest that international trade liberalization and domestic environmental regulation are actually complementary (Anderson 1992). Freer trade may, on the one hand, increase pollution in a nation, as a consequence of its citizens' higher incomes and expanded consumption, without concomitantly increasing that national government's investment in environmental protection. On the other hand, free trade's income and consumption effects may engender a stronger national "taste" for the environment, resulting in domestic pollution taxes and subsidies, environmental standards, and other regulations that need not inhibit competition. Whether or not the inherently interdependent processes of international trade liberalization and domestic environmental protection ultimately improve a nation's environmental quality and its general welfare is thus a function of the combined efficiency of its trade and environmental policies.[4]

Whereas economic analyses of local externalities suggest that gains from trade may yield greater environmental quality, or otherwise promote domestic environmental regulation, related analyses of transboundary externalities indicate that these gains provide an explicit incentive for international environmental cooperation. Transboundary externalities, or international "public bads" in the case of extreme or widespread pollution, arguably motivate the bargaining endemic to the joint efforts of national governments to improve the quality of the natural environment (Conybeare 1980; Allison 1993).

The upshot of these analyses is that the prospect of greater environmental quality provides an incentive for "victim" nations to compensate the responsible "polluter" for making regulatory changes needed for international cooperation. Although compensation may take the form of a direct side payment that just covers the costs of introducing "green" technologies or more stringent regulations, it frequently takes the form of linked gains in another issue area, such as trade. Such linkage primarily facilitates international environmental cooperation by enlarging the range of available side payments with the tradeoffs possible between gains from trade and protecting the natural environment. Environmental cooperation in Europe and North America, for example, has been largely contingent on the expectation of increasing gains from trade associated with regional integration (USTR 1992; Shea 1993). Alternatively, linked gains from trade may be used as leverage in international environmental negotiations. Negotiation of the Montreal Protocol (on Substances that Deplete the Ozone Layer), for instance, yielded trade sanctions to enforce compliance with international rules intended to protect the stratosphere (Benedick 1991).

In the case of international as well as local externalities, trade liberalization can be a mechanism for improving the quality of the natural environment along with the economic competitiveness of domestic economies. The extent to which this relationship holds depends on the relative domestic and international capacities of national governments to internalize the costs of environmental pollution. Given the common ability of industrialized nations to regulate trade-related increases in pollution efficiently (by subsidizing domestic adoption of cleaner production technologies or by instituting international regulations on the consumption of polluting products), most industrialized nations regard freer trade as unequivocally beneficial. Weak domestic systems of environmental regulation and limited influence over international regulatory schemes, however, render many developing nations far less sanguine. Mexican farmers, for example, have responded to their nation's lax enforcement of federal regulations on pesticide use and the United States' stringent inspection of agricultural imports at the border by spraying fast-decaying organophosphate compounds, which are lethal to field workers but leave little residue on produce. Gains from increased U.S.-Mexico trade in agricultural products during NAFTA's first year have, as a result, subjected Mexicans alone to the racing heartbeat, unconsciousness, headaches, fevers, nausea, and burning skin associated with overexposure to pesticides (Schrader 1995).

THE POSTWAR LIBERAL TRADE REGIME

International laws to balance domestic environmental policies, such as U.S. and Mexican pesticide regulations, against international free and fair trade objectives, have been institutionalized during the post-World War II era in what is known as the liberal trade regime. "Regime" refers to the principles, norms, rules and decision-making procedures that facilitate cooperation among nations in a given issue area, such as international trade (Krasner 1983). The postwar liberal trade regime, underpinned by the GATT, is acclaimed for establishing free trade prescriptions and prohibitions against unfair exchanges intended to protect nations and domestic groups from being unduly harmed by international economic competition. The GATT thus effectively recognizes the potential need to include such primarily domestic concerns as environmental preservation in international trade agreements. Generally, this inclusion is regarded as legitimate when it is evident that trade liberalization, which theoretically promotes the efficient use of natural resources, actually causes environmental harm as a result of its attendant economic distortions, combined with the sheer level of trading activities.

The explicit inclusion of environmental concerns in international trade agreements, however, reflects the differential responses of national governments to specific trade-related environmental threats. Consider, for example, the industrial contamination of waterways and air pollution from automobile and truck exhaust that have long been attributed to the increasing production and international movement of goods and services associated with European economic integration. The EU's characteristic reaction to members' unilateral efforts to assuage such threats to the environment and public health has been the regional harmonization of domestic water and air quality standards. Responding to environmentalists' fears that freer North American trade would only add to water and air pollution in the U.S.-Mexico Border Area, the U.S. government, in contrast, called for first an environmental impact statement, and then an environmental side agreement to the proposed NAFTA.

National and regional measures employed to mitigate the environmental effects of trade liberalization, though, often provoke claims that domestic environmental policies pose a threat to free trade. The GATT therefore includes tests to determine whether a domestic environmental policy is a justified burden on international trade, or simply "protectionist," on the basis of that policy's necessity, foremost intention, and proportionality to the environmental threat in question. In the case of the seminal 1991 "tuna test" discussed below, a GATT dispute resolution panel ruled that a U.S. ban on imports of tuna harvested with purse seine nets constituted an unnecessary quantitative import restriction.

The GATT thus serves as a global counterweight to national and regional efforts to balance trade and environmental policies. Through exceptions to the norms of nondiscrimination and unconditional reciprocity that undergird its principle of trade expansion through tariff reductions, the GATT encourages the more complete liberalization of international trade manifest in the formation and expansion of common markets and free trade areas. But it prohibits such special economic relationships as the EU and North America under NAFTA, to redefine free and fair trade by indiscriminately instituting environmental limitations on the liberalization of international trade. Indeed, any domestic or regional, environmental regulations judged to be unfair trade practices are vulnerable to reversal by the GATT's newly established enforcement body, the World Trade Organization (WTO) (Brownstein 1994; Sanger 1994).

INTERNATIONAL TRADE AND SUSTAINABILITY

The WTO threat provides some justification for environmentalists' concern that neither economic theory nor the liberal trade regime can ensure the sustainable patterns of resource use essential to the well-being of humans and national development. Rather, establishing a true balance between trade and the environment demands appreciation of humankind's intrinsic obligation to the rest of the natural world. Arguably, the development of such a shared morality "in respect of the [natural] environment" would engender an international commitment to control trade liberalization's impact on human health, endangered species and ecosystems (Stone 1993: 244). A moral imperative would thus replace economic gains as an incentive for national governments to include environmental concerns in their international trade agreements.

Constructing an environmental ethic pervasive enough to induce nations to sacrifice their individual gains from trade in the interest of the international "common good" represents a surmountable philosophical challenge (Daly and Cobb 1989; Stone 1993). A bona fide environmental ethic would, ideally, supersede the utilitarian truism—if we "foul our nest," humanity and nature both will suffer—that pervades the emergent relationship between trade and the environment with respect to both the process of economic integration in Europe and North America, and the progressive use of trade sanctions in international environmental agreements. Yet the potentially overriding human benefits of underdeveloped national assets, including tropical rainforests, fertile valleys, and teeming waterways, fundamentally limits the chances that any such anthropocentric collective decision-making mechanism will work to preserve wilderness and natural resources. What we need, according to many old-style conservationists, ecologists, contemporary environmental activists, and international legal scholars alike, is a principled definition of the proper balance between trade and the environment based on some moral vision of which "things" matter, and how people "ought" to live (Stone 1993).

Arguably, a vision replacing contemporary emphases on individual choice, technological advances, and economic growth with community welfare, sustainability, and appropriate technology would motivate national governments to negotiate international trade agreements that are responsive to national and nongovernmental environmental concerns. Such agreements would inevitably facilitate the establishment of global patterns of sustainable resource use so that economic growth would:

> . . . take place, and be maintained over time, within the limits set by ecology in the broadest sense—by the interrelations of human beings and their works, the biosphere and the physical and chemical laws that govern it (Ruckelshaus, 1990).

Broadly speaking, national governments have two means of developing the moral vision necessary to define and sustain a principled balance between trade and the environment. They might first establish some philosophical understanding of "fairness" with respect to trade liberalization's attendant redistribution of environmental quality as a component of each nation's share of the world's "wealth, opportunity and power" (Stone 1993). Strict egalitarianism, for example, would dictate the institutionalization of just compensation for those (less developed) nations that initially sacrifice their environmental quality for the sake of international gains from trade. A Rawlsian maxim in criteria would instead dictate that freer trade maximize the environmental quality and general welfare of the most disadvantaged nation or subnational group.[5]

Second, each national government might rely on the use of domestic political institutions and nongovernmental organizations by concerned citizens to develop a greater awareness of free trade's environmental implications. International trade liberalization will increase national environmental protection to the extent that people learn about the causal relationship between trade and the environment, and influence national trade policies through contributions to environmental organizations, green party membership, and lobbying on nature's behalf.

REGIONAL TRADE AGREEMENTS AND THE ENVIRONMENT

As the preceding discussion suggests, the relationship between freer trade and greater environmental quality is not automatic. Its existence and strength is instead determined by the international institutionalization of environmentally-conscious principles and decision-making procedures, combined with sustained environmental activism at the domestic level. It is therefore no wonder that differences in regional institutions and environmentalism, rather than economics, best explain variation in the EU's and North America's treatment of the natural environment in their respective agreements to liberalize trade. While Europeans have granted extensive environmental policy-making powers to a supranational regulatory body, the European Commission, U.S., Canadian, and Mexican citizens have just grudgingly permitted the North American Commission on the Environment (NACE), a trilateral oversight commission, to monitor their compliance with domestic environmental regulations.

Economic analyses, after all, anticipate only some movement of the polluting production of export goods from each continent's relatively wealthy nations to their poorer neighbors—i.e., from France and

Germany to Spain, Greece and Eastern Europe, and from Canada and the United States to Mexico. The ensuing competition to produce these goods yields an equilibrium that rests on the general convergence of the environmental standards of nations; while environmental regulation might improve in Poland with its EU admission, for instance, it would probably become weaker in Germany. The desire of national governments and individuals to correct for such trade-induced declines environmental quality, however, has been a driving force in the politics of both European and North American processes of economic integration. Moreover, the growth of the European Commission's environmental policy-making authority in the EU, and North America's establishing NACE to oversee and enforce U.S., Canadian, and Mexican environmental policies are indicative of wider-ranging regional efforts to incorporate domestic environmental concerns into preferential trade systems, as is allowed by standing exemptions to the GATT norms of nondiscrimination and reciprocity.

ENVIRONMENTAL PROTECTION IN THE EUROPEAN UNION

The EU's environmental policy-making process represents the oldest and most successful case of the regional institutionalization of environmental protection within a framework of economic integration. Although the 1957 Treaty of Rome that established the European Community did not include a regional environmental policy, the unilateral strengthening of production standards, such as limits on automobile emissions in response to green demands, almost immediately created a protectionist threat to free trade. Early directives were essentially frameworks for national policies that require domestic implementing legislation and governed the handling of dangerous substances as well as automobile emissions. They were followed in 1972 by the Council of Minister's commitment to initiate the first Environmental Action Plan (EAP). Its primary objectives were the development of community production standards to reduce pollution at the source, the institution of the "polluter pays principle", the improvement of the European quality of life through environmental protection, and the extension of community support for international cooperation whenever the magnitude of a regional environmental problem surpassed Europe's capacity to solve it. Subsequent plans have reiterated these aims, and additionally emphasized the importance of environmental research and impact assessments, sustainability, and the explicit harmonization of environmental standards.

The 1987 Single European Act (SEA), which amended the Treaty of Rome, increased the EU's jurisdictional authority with respect to the natural environment by mandating the European Commission to develop community standards conducive to the upward harmonization of domestic health, safety, and environmental standards. This first legal basis for European environmental policy-making extends successive EAP principles of source reduction, polluter pays and domestic policy harmonization by requiring the integration of relatively high minimum standards of environmental protection into other community policies. The SEA has furthermore facilitated the commission's legislation of such stringent standards—totaling more than 280 in 1991—by rendering a "qualified majority" in the Council of Ministers, rather than unanimity, sufficient for the passage of environmental directives germane to the process of European integration.[6] And a new "subsidiary principle" advocating the solution to environmental problems at the lowest capable level of government provides added support for national and subnational endeavors to adopt even stronger measures so long as they conform with relevant EU directives and regulations, and are not protectionist.[7]

The SEA, however, charged the European Court of Justice to determine on a case by case basis if a member's environmental policies are protectionist. In response to a justified individual, nongovernmental or national complaints that some domestic policy violates an EU environmental directive or regulation, the commission may take the transgressor to the European Court. Precedent suggests that the subsidiary principle will be balanced in such cases by the "doctrine of mutual recognition," which acknowledges the right of member governments to maintain different production standards within their own borders, but prohibits them from preventing the domestic sale of goods produced according to another member's standards (Alter and Meunier-Aitsahalia 1993). The court nevertheless upheld a Danish law requiring the sale of beer and soft drinks in returnable containers with mandated deposits. Ruling for the first time that greater environmental quality warranted a barrier to trade, it found the Danish law rightly proportional to Denmark's stated desire to reduce waste and amenable to easy compliance by international bottlers (Vogel 1993).

Though the court required less than two years to reach its decision in the Danish bottling case, the process of monitoring compliance with EU environmental directives and regulations often takes twice that long. By 1990, the growing backlog of noncompliance cases attributable to this lag had precipitated variation in domestic policies sufficient to undermine the community's drive to eliminate internal barriers to trade. Belgium, Greece, Italy, and West Germany, for instance, all failed to pass implementing legislation pursuant to twenty percent of the environmental directives entering into force that year (Shea, 1993). The European Council responded to this threat by adopting the "Declaration on the Environmental Imperative," which defines EU environmental legislation as "effective" only upon its full implementation and enforcement by member nations. And the European Parliament moved to create an independent Environment Agency to complement individual, organizational, and national attempts to monitor domestic compliance with specific EU environmental directives and regulations. Yet implementation of community standards remains incomplete (Wagerbaum 1990).

There are two forces, however, that suggest optimism with respect to the EU's exercise in the incorporation of environmental concerns into its progress toward full economic integration. The 1992 Maastricht Treaty's majority voting rules and "precautionary principle" together represent the first of these forces. As a result of an amendment to article 130r of the SEA, qualified majority is now the norm for environmental decision-making in the EU, which should further encourage the commission's legislation of community-wide environmental standards. Demanding policy action even in the absence of a clear causal, trade-related link between industrial processes and environmental damage, the precautionary principle should lead to a marked strengthening of existing as well as new EU environmental standards.[8]

Environmentalism is the second force. The surge of environmental sentiment and action that spurred the initial development of community environmental policy in the 1960s and 1970s has not waned. Such outspoken environmental groups as Friends of the Earth and Earth First, in fact, used environmental crises and educational campaigns to popularize the environmental and social costs of economic growth and integration through the following decade's recession-induced withdrawals of governmental support for environmental protection (Dalton 1993). Acid rain's toll on Scandinavia and Germany's Black Forest, for example, proved a cogent motivation for grassroots environmental activism in many European nations (Boehmer-Christiansen and Skea 1991). Moreover, alternative green parties that emerged during the same period, largely in response to mainstream parties ignoring environmental issues, have remained influential participants in EU politics. Green parties' electoral and legislative successes in member nations, such as Denmark and Germany respectively, continue to indicate widespread public support for the EU's emergent environmental and social agenda (Steele 1983; Kitschelt 1993).

EU SMALL CAR EMISSIONS STANDARDS

The combined influence of community institutions and the relative environmental activism of member nations is particularly clear in the negotiations that dominated the issue of small car emissions standards in the late 1980s. The issue itself originated nearly a decade earlier in the commission's recognition that variation in domestic automobile emissions standards posed not only a threat to public health, but also a significant barrier to economic integration. National differences with respect to permissible levels of lead in gasoline, for example, were already complicating efforts by automobile makers to design vehicles that would be marketable throughout the community (Corcelle and Johnson 1989; Vogel 1993). Reluctance on the part of some members, such as the former West Germany, to increase their lead content requirements, and on the part of others, such as Britain, to reduce theirs in the interest of intra-community trade delayed the Council of Environment Ministers support for the commission's attempts to harmonize these standards. The council did agree to establish maximum and minimum levels for the lead content of gasoline in 1978, however, following its adoption of directives that strengthened existing community standards for carbon and nitrogen emissions.

While the commission successfully strengthened these standards again in the early 1980s by phasing in the sale of unleaded gasoline and requiring at least twenty percent reductions in hydrocarbon and nitrogen emissions, the unwillingness of some manufacturers to update pollution abatement technologies complicated the institution of even more stringent measures. The problem was that further emissions reductions, modeled on the United States' exemplary 1983 air quality standards, would require the installation of catalytic converters. Though catalytic converters can reduce automobile emissions by up to ninety percent, they require unleaded gasoline, which would not be widely available before 1989, and must be replaced approximately every four years. Lean-burn engines, then capable of only fifty percent reductions, but more fuel efficient and less expensive to manufacture and install, represented the reigning alternative.[9]

It was the political capacities of members to adopt these competing abatement technologies that dominated debate over automobile emissions standards, which would affect industries and motorists throughout the community. The former West Germany, for instance, supported catalytic converters as the most convenient means for its large car exporters to meet the desired U.S. 1983 standards (Perrin-Pelletier 1989). Britain and France, respectively home to such major small automakers as Ford UK and Austin Rover and Renault and Peugeot, instead favored the less costly lean burn technologies (Kim 1992).

The 1987 "Luxembourg Compromise" sought to resolve these differences by requiring member governments to establish size-specific automobile emissions regulations and abatement schedules. Ideally, strict catalytic converter requirements for large and midsize vehicles would become effective beginning in 1989, while potentially less stringent small car emissions limits would not come into effect for another year or two. The harmonization of domestic automobile emissions standards essential to achieving greater environmental quality as well as a single car market thus remained optional. As a result, the ecologically vulnerable and environmentally conscious Netherlands, Denmark, and Greece, as well as the former West Germany, immediately considered the introduction of fiscal incentives for cleaner small cars in lieu of more stringent community regulation of emissions from these vehicles.

In response to the resultant division between this "ecological" coalition and the community's small car manufacturers, represented by Britain, France, Italy and Spain, the commission proposed the installation of either catalytic converters or lean-burn engines to reduce small car emissions by fifty-eight percent by 1992–93.[10] But due to a dispute over the legality of unilateral fiscal incentives, only Luxembourg, Ireland, and Belgium initially supported this 1988 proposal. By the time this dispute was resolved, the European Parliament had entered the fray. Duly impressed by the "greening" of European public opinion—increasing numbers of those polled desired stronger community regulation of the natural environment—the Parliament amended the council's position to reflect the United States' strict 1983 standards, including the installation of catalytic converters.[11]

This amendment immediately prompted the commission to revise its proposal. In 1989, the commission repeated its call for a choice of technologies to effect fifty-eight percent reductions in the small car emissions by 1991, but added the mandatory installation of catalytic converters to reduce these emissions by another thirty-six percent beginning in 1993.[12] The practical impossibility of amending the commission's proposal by unanimous vote forced the council to approve the directive at the risk of otherwise alienating both automobile makers and environmentalists only one week short of European elections. In fact, the council adopted a stricter directive intended to placate the former West Germany's demands for the immediate introduction of U.S. standards, and Danish, Dutch, and Greece concerns that their air pollution problems required even more restrictive measures. The 1989 directive on small car emissions standards mandated reductions in automobile emissions comparable to those in the United States by 1992, and furthermore sanctions the use of fiscal incentives by members to encourage clean car sales.[13]

NAFTA AND THE ENVIRONMENT

Of course, the most conspicuous regional attempt to protect the environment and liberalize trade simultaneously is manifest in NAFTA's prototypical "green" language and environmental side agreement. In marked contrast to the case of environmental policymaking by the EU, this recent North American cooperation to protect the environment actually preceded the formal process of economic integration in the region. As a result, regional institutions have been less accountable, relative to environmental activism, for fostering a positive relationship between trade and the environment in North America than in Europe. U.S. President George Bush and Mexican President Carlos Salinas de Gortari, in fact, immediately responded to fears among activists that the environmental costs of freer trade would far outweigh its commercial benefits by instructing the U.S. Environmental Protection Agency (EPA) and its Mexican counterpart, the Urban Development and Ecology Secretariat (SEDUE), respectively, to complete their Border Plan for cleaning up the U.S.-Mexico Border Area. Ultimately, widespread dissatisfaction with this plan induced the United States to insist that any NAFTA be conditional upon protection of the natural environment.[14]

Indeed, environmentalists were joined early on in their opposition to NAFTA by U.S. and Canadian industrialists concerned that weak environmental standards would give Mexico an unfair advantage in regional trade. Ensuing public debates therefore focused on the implications of North American free trade for Mexico's capacity to strengthen and enforce its environmental laws. Although research by economists and other specialists suggested that reduced barriers to trade would probably overwhelm Mexico's regulatory system in the short term, the general expectation was that economic growth associated with a NAFTA would eventually offset any damage to the natural environment (Grossman and Kruger 1991; Wallace 1991). The Bush Administration's Action Plan for the Border Area represents the United States' response to these findings. Introduced in conjunction with fast-track debates in Congress, the plan guaranteed U.S. financial aid in the amount of at least $384 million for Mexico's environmental monitoring and enforcement systems as well as binational sewage treatment and air pollution abatement programs.[15] It was this U.S. financial commitment to the Border Area environment that enabled the EPA and SEDUE to complete and distribute the Border Plan by February 1992 (Stammer and Pasternak 1992; Ryan 1993).

Initially, Mexico also responded to the evidence that the proposed NAFTA could cause significant degradation of its natural environment with increased appropriations for environmental protection. The centerpiece of Mexico's contribution to the Action Plan, for instance, was $460 million to be spent primarily on sewers, waste-water treatment, and road improvements ("Environmental Community Cites Flaws" 1992). Despite the comparability of consequent EPA and SEDUE regulatory activities in the Border Area, Mexican officials and the public at large increasingly feared that Mexico was slowly yielding its sovereign right to manage its natural environment to the United States. The Salinas administration therefore also adopted a "new approach" to environmental protection, which stresses the enforcement of Mexico's existing environmental regulations, rather than the formulation of new ones. This philosophical change motivated the May 1992 reorganization of SEDUE into the new Social Development Secretariat (SEDESOL), within which the "environmental attorney general's influence is at least as great as the environmental policymakers' (Colosio 1992).

This reorganization yielded significant improvements in Mexico's ability to enforce its environmental regulations, largely attributable to a twenty percent increase in the number of inspectors and inspections during SEDESOL's first year (Government of Mexico 1993a). Yet U.S. environmentalists insisted on not only "green language" in NAFTA, but also specific protections for the nation's high environmental standards, and additional funds to improve the quality of the Border Area environment (Lee 1993; Ryan 1993). U.S. President-elect Bill Clinton therefore formally conditioned the United States' passage of NAFTA on the conclusion of an environmental side agreement requiring the strict enforcement of environmental laws in North America. Given this U.S. condition, Canada and Mexico agreed in May 1992 to create NACE as an advisory body, even though neither of them felt that directly addressing domestic environmental policies in the context of international trade was appropriate. The United States, Canada, and Mexico extended NACE's power to advise on environmental matters to include the negotiation of a supplementary environmental agreement to NAFTA. These negotiations ended in August 1993, helping to break "the logjam" in parallel NAFTA negotiations (Shiver and Miller 1993).

Despite its enforcement mandate, the North American Agreement on Environmental Cooperation (i.e., NAFTA's environmental side agreement) does not authorize any supranational body to use fines or other penalties to exact compliance from industry with U.S., Canadian, and Mexican environmental laws. The agreement instead establishes new investigatory responsibilities for NACE, which include gathering and reviewing information in compliance with domestic environmental regulations in all three nations, and fostering trilateral efforts to raise and harmonize their environmental standards. NACE thus maintains its standing authority to advise on matters of enforcement, but only a two-thirds vote by its Ministerial Council may decide to fine or sanction NAFTA the national governments for violations of their own environmental standards. The potency of this final action, however, depends on a "quasi-legal" procedure's finding of some "persistent pattern of failure to effectively enforce" a given environmental regulation.[16]

The effectiveness of NAFTA's environmental side agreement therefore lies in the development of NACE's oversight authority and potential to influence funding for trilateral environmental activities. NACE, for example, is supposed to monitor the evolving relationship between U.S., Canadian, and Mexican environmental regulations and the liberalization of North American trade (Mumme 1993; Runge 1994). As such, NACE is authorized to take an active role in NAFTA's dispute resolution process by providing information about compliance with the agreement's public health and safety standards, publicizing any violations of them, and determining where to invest any revenue generated by the resultant legal action.

AIR QUALITY IN THE U.S.-MEXICO BORDER AREA

Of course, it is still to early to evaluate NACE. However, the relationship between North American free trade negotiations and the de facto harmonization of the U.S. and Mexican air quality standards suggests that NACE's efforts to maintain, and even strengthen, U.S., Canadian, and Mexican environmental standards will depend on sustained environmental activism as well as NAFTA's success. The impetus for the coordination of U.S. and Mexican air quality standards was, after all, the long-standing concern among environmentalists and border states that sulfur emissions from copper smelters across the border would significantly reduce the region's air quality. By the early 1980s, however, their demands for reduced emissions extended to smelters located within the United States as well as in Mexico. In response, the U.S. and Mexican governments quickly negotiated the framework for the *La Paz Agreement* in 1983; they resolved the smelter issue within this framework less than four years later.

By 1989, the United States and Mexico had also responded to the Border Area's more serious air pollution problems—the ozone, carbon monoxide, and nitrogen oxides found in smog, and air toxics—by agreeing to establish binational air quality monitoring programs intended to facilitate the development of harmonious abatement programs in selected pairs of border cities. Lack of a financial commitment on the part of the United States, however, compounded by Mexico's weak enforcement infrastructure, compromised full implementation of their agreements. Congress appropriated only $89,000 to help establish the Border Area's first international air quality monitoring network in El Paso/Ciudad Juarez, for instance, while SEDUE assigned too few additional personnel to assist the EPA in monitoring air quality at sites in Mexicali and Tijuana, Baja California, as well as in Ciudad Juarez (Reynoso 1993). The EPA and SEDUE, as a result, began early in 1990 to develop a plan to finance implementation of the U.S.-Mexico agreement on transboundary urban air pollution (and the previous four annexes to the *La Paz Agreement*). Its completion remained a distant prospect, however, Presidents Bush and Salinas effectively linked the Border Area environment to the NAFTA negotiations (Stammer and Pasternak 1992). The EPA and SEDUE completed their Border Plan within two years (Jones 1993).

The plan's air quality provisions, in particular, were drafted in accordance with Section 815 of the United States' 1990 Clean Air Act Amendments, which authorize the EPA to devise, in conjunction with the State Department and relevant border states, a bilateral air quality monitoring and abatement program for the Border Area. The emissions data and air pollution control strategies submitted by El Paso, Texas, and San Diego and Imperial County, California, thus generated the Border Plan's "wish list" of technical and administrative feats intended to yield cost-effective reductions in polluting emissions on both sides of the border by the end of the decade. This list includes inventorying polluting emissions in El Paso/Ciudad Juarez, estimating the distribution and transboundary fluxes of particulate concentrations in Imperial County/Mexicali, and improving public transportation in San Diego/Tijuana. Compliance of the Border Plan's air quality provisions will depend on continued U.S. and increased Mexican funding. Although congressional appropriations for air pollution abatement in the Border Area topped $179 million through FY 1994, whether or not U.S. financial assistance will continue apace remains uncertain. In light of the fall 1994 Peso Crisis, Mexico's matching support—some percentage of an estimated $9.5-$174 million in national environmental expenditures, exclusive of $1.5 of a $50 million World Bank loan—is likewise unknown.[17]

ENVIRONMENTAL PROTECTION AND THE GATT

Unlike either the case of European environmental policymaking or the "greening" of North American free trade, the GATT has failed in its related efforts to balance environmental protection and global trade liberalization. As a check on inclusion of domestic environmental concerns in regional and other multi-national trade agreements, the GATT has necessarily privileged the economic welfare of all members over the environmental commitments of any subgroup. Reflecting the post-war consensus that free trade enables economic specialization and attendant economic growth of nations, this oldest and largest trade agreement, in fact, makes no specific reference to the natural environment. Environmental protection, rather, has evolved as a potentially viable exception to the GATT's nondiscrimination and reciprocity norms. If universally implemented, national environmental standards that are established either to protect human, animal, or plant life or health, or to conserve natural resources, may be justifiable under GATT rules.

The GATT, however, has actually upheld a nation's domestic environmental standards only once between 1947 and 1990. A U.S.-Canadian dispute resolution panel, organized under the auspices of the GATT, ruled in 1990 that the United States' year-old prohibition on the transport of whole, live lobsters that had not reached sexual maturity into or out of the country represented a legitimate means of ensuring future lobster stocks (U.S. Congress, Office of Technology Assessment 1992). This ruling purportedly demonstrates that the GATT may be considered the global guarantor of the sovereign rights to protect natural resources from damage caused by either domestic production processes or imported products. So long as domestic environmental laws apply equally to domestic production and imports and are not disguised protectionism, the GATT should ensure the economic efficiency and growth necessary to finance environmental protection, and thereby foster the global harmonization of domestic environmental standards (Weiss 1992).

In theory, reduced barriers to trade should increase any pollution associated with the rising production of exportables in some nations, while the pollution experienced by the others decreases until all member governments adopt environmental regulations that are similarly conducive to free trade. However, there is no guarantee that this harmonization of environmental standards will adequately protect the natural environment. Environmentalists may, therefore, be justified in fearing that the GATT's new authority, lodged in the WTO, to enforce its rulings in disputes over member's environmental regulations will compel national governments to adopt increasingly weak standards of environmental protection. Precedent suggests that these rulings will continue to be based on the strict evaluation of disputed environmental laws in terms of four "GATT" tests.

"Necessity," the first of these tests, demands a finding that a nation's environmental objective would be unachievable by any means less burdensome to trade than the regulation in question.[18] Taken together, the second and third tests require that the disputed regulation be "primarily aimed at" environmental protection, rather than trade protection.[19] And the final test, "proportionality," calls for a balance between the national environmental benefits and international trade costs associated with that regulation.[20] In the future, however, automatic trade sanctions may follow domestic refusal to, say, repeal a federal conservation law or preempt a subnational chemical regulation that fails one or more of these tests. It follows that each member's right to withdraw notwithstanding, the authority of the WTO dispute resolution panel to impose sanctions and other trade penalties for violations of the GATT represents a potential threat to the natural environment (Healy 1994).

THE GATT "TUNA TEST"

The 1991 decision by a GATT dispute resolution panel that a U.S. ban on tuna imports from Mexico, imposed to protect dolphins from unintentional slaughter during tuna harvests, was incompatible with trade rules is central to the controversy surrounding its interpretation of environmental protection as a legitimate constraint on international trade. Not surprisingly, the panel's decision riled environmentalists, among them, former director of Friends of the Earth Jonathan Poritt, who later referred to the GATT as ". . . unaccountable, unreformable . . . and completely out of touch with the realities of today's world" ("Official Defends Environmental Policy" 1992; French 1992). That decision, moreover, sparked debate during the GATT's Uruguay Round agreement. At issue was the GATT's latent opposition to the inclusion of trade restrictions in such effective international environmental agreements as the Montreal Protocol. Also important was that organization's obtrusive failure to encourage members to take measures, unilaterally, to internalize environmental costs.

The U.S.-Mexico tuna dispute originated in Mexico's allegation that the U.S. tuna embargo discriminated against imported products, and thereby violated the GATT (Runge 1994). As a provision of the United States' Marine Mammals Protection Act (MMPA), the embargo was intended as an incentive to change the tuna industry's harvesting practices. By 1958, fishermen's age-old reliance on dolphins swimming on the ocean's surface to signal the presence of schools of tuna underneath had established the circling of dolphins with purse-seine nets as the most efficient way of harvesting tuna. U.S. tuna fleets, however, have been prohibited from using this method since the passage of the MMPA in 1972. Policymakers and environmentalists alike credit this Act for the reduction in the United States' incidental dolphin kills from 400,000 to less than 1,000 annually by the mid-1980s. Responding to this domestic success as well as evidence that some U.S. fleets were re-flagging and operating from foreign ports to circumvent the MMPA, environmental groups lobbied to extend the Act's prohibition against purse-seine nets to cover any vessel that harvests tuna destined for sale in the United States.

Acknowledging that such an extension would also improve the U.S. tuna industry's international competitiveness, Congress amended the MMPA in 1985 and again in 1988 to support bans on the import of yellowfin tuna from any nation whose average catch of dolphin, incidental to tuna harvested in the Eastern Tropical Pacific, was more than 1.25 times the United States' average incidental catch in that region. Yet requisite trade embargoes—against Equador, Panama, Mexico, Venezuela, and Vanuatu—were not initiated until 1991. The U.S. government's failure to enforce the Act against Mexico, in particular, is arguably attributable to the Reagan and Bush administration's reluctance to address environmental concerns explicitly in either the GATT or NAFTA negotiations (Mitchell and Adcock 1993). Thus once the controversial embargo was established, the United States urged Mexico to request GATT dispute resolution proceedings as opposed to raising the issue in the organization's general council meeting. Mexico's President Salinas not only complied, but also publicized his administration's financial support for the Cousteau Society's 10-point dolphin protection plan in the hopes of settling the dispute outside of the GATT. But the Salinas administration's ploy appeased neither U.S. lawmakers nor environmentalists.

A GATT dispute resolution panel ultimately upheld Mexico's challenge on the illegality of the U.S. regulation restricting tuna imports originating in nations with differing environmental laws. The panel ruled, more specifically, that because the U.S. government had sanctioned foreign tuna producers without comparably restricting their domestic competitors, its embargo not only violated the GATT's prohibition against quantitative import restrictions, but also discriminated against imported tuna. While the MMPA restricted tuna imports on the basis of an inherently unpredictable dolphin catch ratio, it regulates the tuna production process, referring to the use of purse-seine nets, in the United States. Moreover, the panel found the U.S. tuna embargo to be unnecessary with respect to the protection of animal life and health, or the conservation of natural resources. Yet, in an effort to ease NAFTA's passage, Mexico eventually did "take steps" to comply with the MMPA (Mitchell and Adcock 1993).

CONCLUSION: THE POLITICS OF TRADE AND THE ENVIRONMENT

Clearly, a comparison of environmental protection in the EU and in North America under NAFTA, with that allowable under GATT rules suggests that economic analyses provide only a limited explanation for the incorporation of domestic environmental concerns in their international trade agreements. In both Europe and North America, the efforts of national governments to offset the domestic impacts of regional integration have proven most significant in institutionalizing the current relationship between trade and the environment. For instance, the EU's response to European environmentalism is manifest in the SEA and Maastricht Treaty's expansion of the European Commission's authority to legislate community environmental policy. NACE's potential capacity to enforce U.S., Canadian, and Mexican environmental laws likewise reflects North America's response to citizen demands for a "greener" NAFTA.

Of course, at the core of such preferential trade systems as designated by the EU and NAFTA are exceptions to the liberal trade prescriptions codified in the GATT. These exceptions incipiently privilege environmental over economic prerogatives, but only when individuals and national governments honestly and actively seek to protect the natural environment. The postwar liberal trade regime so emphasizes economic competition that durable environmental activism is necessary to create and enforce environmental conditions on trade. Because this level of environmentalism is more easily generated at lower levels of aggregation, where individuals can most easily "see" the fruits of their efforts, the institutionalization of trade-related international environmental policy may continue to be limited geographically (Mowrey and Redmond 1993).

The pervasiveness of this political relationship between trade and the environment is also likely to be limited objectively, as is made clear in the GATT's continuing reluctance to address the issue explicitly. Despite the recognition among economists that the trade-environment link should grow stronger with the currently falling costs of environmental protection, even the most environmentally conscious Uruguay Round participants rejected the addition of "green" provisions to the agreement. Furthermore, there is still no reason to believe this position will change in response to claims made by activists that the WTO's statutory authority to overrule domestic environmental laws is indicative of the GATT's ignorance of reasonable bases for abridging free trade in the interest of greater environmental protection.

NOTES

1. Michael Smith, Deputy Trade Representative in the Reagan administration (Marshall 1992).

2. These absent markets are typically associated with "disputed, ambiguous or non-existent" property rights (Anderson and Blackhurst, 1992: 4).

3. See Baumol and Oates (1988) for a more complete discussion of various formal definitions of externalities.

4. Technically, this discussion applies to "small" nations whose policies do not affect world prices; for a more detailed account of free trade's welfare implications for these as well as large nations, see Anderson (1992) and Runge (1994).

5. The maximin behavior on which the Rawls (1971) criteria is based may be generally understood as minimizing the maximum loss that might be suffered. With respect to egalitarianism, the Stockholm Declaration of Principles' Recommendation 103 states that "where environmental concerns lead to restrictions on trade or to stricter environmental standards with negative effects on exports, particularly from developing countries, appropriate measures for compensation should be worked out within the framework of existing contractual and institutional arrangements . . ."

6. A qualified majority requires 54 or 76 votes; see Haigh (1992) on the environmental legislation tally for 1991.

7. Unlike directives, regulations become national law for all members of the community upon their passage.

8. Article 130r was introduced in the SEA's environmental chapter.

9. See Perrin-Pelletier (1989) and Kim (1992) on this technical debate, which here subsumes resolution of ancillary conflicts over the merits of the U.S. regulatory model, the true effectiveness of catalytic converters and the ultimate potential of lean-burn engines that remained in the research and development stage throughout the negotiation of the EU directive on small car emissions standards.

10. The ascendance of the Greens to the former West German Bundestag in 1982 signified that nation's increasing concern with the environmental effects of traffic and air pollution from automobile emissions, which only compounded its economic interest in strict EU air quality standards; then as now, air pollution was just as high on the Danish and Dutch political agendas, and of increasing important to Greece, where citizens demanded a government response to the public health threat posed by smog in and around Athens (Deming 1983; McCormick 1989: 124–125; "European Community" 1993). With respect to the small car manufacturers, see Kim (1992) on how small cars accounted for eighty-four percent of Italy's and sixty percent of France's total automobile production between 1987 and 1989.

11. Inglehart and Reif (1991: 1–26) corroborate oft-cited claims that, by the late 1980s, ninety-five percent of Europeans polled supported the community's increasing regulation of the natural environment.

12. Percent reductions calculated from figures provided in Kim (1992).

13. Directive 89/458/EEC (Kim 1992).

14. Canada responded to the start of U.S.-Mexican free trade negotiations in June 1990, and the stated intention of the United States to negotiate complementary free trade agreements with other American nations, by moving in late 1990 to support regional free trade; trilateral negotiations began in February 1991.

15. According to "Environmental Community Cites Flaws" (1992: 137), the United States immediately earmarked $143 million for the Border Area Clean-up (FY 1992) and budgeted an additional $241 million for FY 1993. The U.S. House of Representatives approved a two-year extension of Bush's fast track authority through June 1993 on May 23, 1991 (231–192), one day earlier than did the Senate (59–36) (the Omnibus Trade and Competitiveness Act of 1988 had already extended the president's extant fast-track authority to complete the Uruguay Round (GATT negotiations) and conduct bilateral negotiations (with Mexico) by June 1, 1991).

16. NAFTA's environmental side agreement provides for individuals and private groups as well as nations to petition the Secretariat to investigate U.S., Canadian, or Mexican failures to enforce their environmental laws; such investigations are intended as a basis for Ministerial decisions to establish a panel to arbitrate a given dispute (Winham 1993).

17. "Environmental Community Cites Flaws" (1992), Jehl and Abramson (1992) and Driscoll (1993) confirm and elaborate upon the United States financial commitment as outlined in the Border Plan. In addition to these sources, Government of Mexico (1993b) confirms Mexico's contribution. See Myerson (1995) and DePalma (1995) on the combined effect of NAFTA and the peso's devaluation on Mexico's capacity to sustain government spending.

18. GATT article XX(a) (public morality), XX(b) (for the protection of human, animal, or plant life or health) and XX(g) (relating to the conservation of natural resources); see also GATT article XI(2)(a) (legality of imposing trade restrictions to offset shortages, which may be interpreted to support the conservationist goal's of nations).

19. GATT article XX(g) arguably covers restrictions pursuant to natural resource conservation that appear in such international environmental agreements as CITES and the Montreal Protocol.

20. See the GATT's 1979 Standards Code, and note that national governments are expected to enforce proportionality in the formulation and implementation of environmental regulations at lower levels of government.

REFERENCES

Aizeki, Mizue. 1993. "Toxic Tijuana." *Shades of Green*, 2:3.

Allison, Juliann. 1993. "International Environmental Bargaining: A Game-theoretic Analysis of Air Quality Agreements in North America", prepared for delivery at the 1993 annual meeting of the American Political Science Association, Washington, D.C., 2–5 September.

Alter, Karen, and Sophie Meunier-Aitsahalia. 1993. "Judicial Politics in the European Community: European Integration and the Pathbreading Cassis de Dijon Decision." *Comparative Political Studies* 26: 535–561.

Anderson, Kym. 1992. "The standard welfare economics of policies affecting trade and the environment." In *The Greening of World Trade Issues*, eds. Kym Anderson and Richard Blackhurst, 25–48. Ann Arbor: The University of Michigan Press.

Anderson, Kym, and Richard Blackhurst, eds. 1992. *The Greening of World Trade Issues*. Ann Arbor: The University of Michigan Press.

Baumol, William J., and Wallace E. Oates. 1988. *The Theory of Environmental Policy*. Cambridge: Cambridge University Press.

Benedick, Richard Elliot. 1991. *Ozone Diplomacy: New Directions in Safeguarding the Planet*. Cambridge: Harvard University Press.

Boehmer-Christiansen, Sonja, and Jim Skea. 1991. *Acid Politics.* New York: Belhaven Press.

Brownstein, Ronald. 1994. "Critics See Foreign Ties as a Leash Around U.S. Neck." *Los Angeles Times,* 12 June.

Caldwell, Lynton Keith. 1990. *International Environmental Policy: Emergence and Dimensions,* second edition. Durham: Duke University Press.

Colosio, Luis Donaldo. 1992. Remarks to the U.S.-Mexico Border Environmental Assembly and Colloquy, Santa Fe, NM, 25 June.

Conybeare, John A. C. 1980. "International organization and the theory of property rights." *International Organization* 34: 307–334.

Corcelle, Guy, and Stanley P. Johnson. 1989. *The Environmental Policy of the European Community.* London: Graham and Trotman.

Dalton, Russell J. 1993. "The Environmental Movement in Western Europe." *Environmental Politics in the International Arena,* ed. Sheldon Kamieniecki, 41–68. Albany: State University of New York Press.

Daly, Herman E., and John B. Cobb, Jr. 1989. *For the Common Good: Redirecting the Economy Toward Community, the Environment and a Sustainable Future.* Boston: Beacon Press.

Deming, Angus (with Theodore Stanger). 1983. "The Greening of the Bundestag." *Newsweek* (11 April): 52.

DePalma, Anthony. 1995. "U.S. Aid Plan is Hardly a Cure-all." *The New York Times,* 22 February.

Driscoll, Jack. 1993. "NAFTA: An Opportunity for US" *The Boston Globe,* 1 June.

Emerson, Peter M. 1993. "NAFTA passage can help protect environment." *Austin American-Statesman,* 8 January.

"Environmental Community Cites Flaws in Border Plan, Environmental Review." 1992. *International Environment Reporter,* 11 March: 136–137.

"European Community." 1993. *International Environment Reporter,* 10 February: 81.

French, Hilary. 1992. "The Tuna Test: GATT and the Environment." *World Watch* (April): 9 and 34.

Government of Mexico. 1993a. "The Border Region". A Better Mexico* A Better Environment.

Government of Mexico. 1993b. "Environmental Budget Priorities". A Better Mexico*A Better Environment."

Grossman, Gene, and Alan B. Kruger. 1991. "Environmental Impacts of NAFTA." Discussion paper #158. Princeton: Woodrow Wilson School.

Haigh, Nigel. 1992. "The European Community and International Environmental Policy." *The International Politics of the Environment*, eds. Andrew Hurrell and Benedict Kingsbury, 228–249. New York: Oxford University Press.

Healy, Melissa. 1994. "Activists Say GATT May Hurt Environment." *Los Angeles Times,* 16 April.

Inglehart, Ronald, and Karlheinz Reif. 1991. "Analyzing Trends in West European Opinion: the Role of the Eurobarometer Surveys." *Eurobarometer: The Dynamics of European Public Opinion,* 1–26. New York: St. Martin's Press.

Jehl, Douglas, and Rudy Abramson. 1992. "Bush to Seek $100 Million Extra for Border Cleanup." *Los Angeles Times,* 23 January.

Jones, Bill, EPA Air and Toxics Division, Region 9. 1993. Interview with the author, 16 February.

Kim, Charlotte. 1992. "Cats and Mice: the Politics of Setting EC Car Emission Standards. Centre for European Policy Studies Working Document No. 64.

Kitschelt, Herbert. 1993. "The Green Phenomenon in Western Party Systems." *Environmental Politics in the International Arena*, ed. Sheldon Kamieniecki, 93–112. Albany: State University of New York Press.

Krasner, Stephen D. 1983. "Structural Causes and Regime Consequences: Regimes as Intervening Variables." *International Regimes* ed. Stephen D. Krasner. 1–22. Ithaca: Cornell University Press.

Lee, Thea. 1993. "Happily Never NAFTA." *Dollars and Sense.* (January/February): 12–15.

Macdonald, Doug. 1991. *The Politics of Pollution.* Toronto: McClelland and Stewart.

Marshall, Jonathan. 1992. "How Ecology is Tied to Mexico Trade Pact." *San Francisco Chronicle,* 25 February.

McCormick, John. 1989. *Acid Earth: the Global Threat of Acid Pollution.* London: Earthscan Publications, Ltd.

Mitchell, George H. Jr., and J. Patrick Adcock. 1993. "Between Compliance and Defiance: Executive Branch Disposition of 'Unwanted' Environmental legislation." Prepared for delivery at the annual meeting of the American Political Science Association, Washington, D.C., 2–5 September.

Mowrey, Marc, and Tim Redmond. 1993. *Not in Our Backyard: The People and Events That Shaped America's Modern Environmental Movement*. New York: William Morrow and Company, Inc.

Mumme, Stephen P. 1993. "Enforcing International Environmental Agreements: Lessons from the U.S.-Mexico Border." Presented at the Institute on Global Conflict and Cooperation's Conference on the Enforcement of International Environmental Agreements, La Jolla, CA, 30 September–2 October.

Myerson, Allen R. 1995. "Strategies on Mexico Cast Aside." *The New York Times*, 14 February.

"Official Defends Environmental Policy, Says GATT Rules Give Scope for Protection." 1992. *International Environment Reporter*, 23 September: 595–596.

Perrin-Pelletier, Francois. 1989. "The European Automobile Industry in the Context of 1992." *European Affairs* 2: 85–95.

Rawls, John. 1971. *A Theory of Justice*. Cambridge: Harvard University Press.

Reilly, William K. 1993. "The Greenest-Ever Treaty." *The New York Times*, 20 April.

Reynoso, Jesus. Air Quality Program Supervisor, El Paso City-County Health and Environmental District. 1993. Interview with author, 30 March.

Ruckelshaus, William D. 1990. "Toward a Sustainable World." *Managing Planet Earth: Readings from Scientific American*. New York: W.H. Freeman and Company.

Runge, C. Ford. 1994. *Freer Trade, Protected Environment: Balancing Trade Liberalization and Environmental Interests*. New York: Council on Foreign Relations Press.

Ryan, Richard W. 1993. "The North American Free Trade Agreement and Intergovernmental Managemcnt on the U.S.-Mexico Border: What is the Emerging Role for Local and State Governments?" Presented at the annual meeting of the Western Political Science Association Meeting, Pasadena, CA, 16–18 March.

Sanger, David E. 1994. "New Global Rules: GATT Body is Created to Oversee Commerce of 100 Countries." *The New York Times*, 2 December.

Schrader, Esther. 1995."A Giant Spraying Sound." *Mother Jones* (January/February): 33–36 and 72–73.

Shea, Cynthia Pollock. 1993. "European Environmental Policy: Effects of the Single Market." *International Environment Reporter*, 13 January: 30–34.

Shiver, Jube Jr., and Greg Miller. 1993. "New Pacts Break Logjam on Trade." *Los Angeles Times,* 14 August.

Stammer, Larry B., and Judy Pasternak. 1992. "Mexico's Pollution Clean-Up Tied to Trade Pact." *Los Angeles Times,* 27 February.

Steele, Ronald. 1983. "Germany's Romantic Radicals are becoming a Force to be Reckoned with—at Home and Abroad," *Vanity Fair* (September): 71–73.

Stone, Christopher D. 1993. *The Gnat is Older Than Man: Global Environment and Human Agenda.* Princeton: Princeton University Press.

U.S. Congress, Office of Technology Assessment. 1992. *Trade and the Environment: Conflicts and Opportunifies,* OTA-BP-ITE-94. Washington, D.C.: U.S. Government Printing Office.

U.S. Government and Government of Canada. 1992. *Canada-United States Air Quality Agreement, Progress Report.* Washington, D.C.: U.S. Government Printing Office.

U.S. Trade Representative (USTR). 1992. *Review of U.S.-Mexico Environmental Issues.* Washington, D.C.: U.S. Government Printing Office.

Vogel, David. 1993. "Environmental Policy in the European Community." *Environmental Politics in the International Arena,* ed. Sheldon Kamieniecki, 181–192. Albany: State University of New York Press.

Wagerbaum, Rolf. 1990. "The European Community's policies on implementation of environmental directives." *Fordham International Law Journal* 14: 455–477.

Wallace, Amy. 1991. "U.S.-Mexico Trade Pact Foes Assail Environmental Study." *Los Angeles Times,* 19 October.

Weiss, Edith Brown. 1992. "Agora: Trade and the Environment." *American Journal of International Law* 86: 700–735.

Winham, Gilbert R. 1993. "Enforcement of Environmental Measures: The North American Agreement on Environmental Cooperation." Presented at the Institute on Global Conflict and Cooperation's conference on the Enforcement of International Environmental Agreements, La Jolla, CA, 30 September–2 October.

10 International Trade and Sustainable Development

DAVID GOODMAN AND RICHARD B. HOWARTH

I. INTRODUCTION

The links between international trade, economic development, and environmental quality have come under increasing scrutiny in recent years. Though the ties between trade and development have been intensely studied, the role of trade liberalization in promoting human welfare is a point of long-standing controversy. Trade advocates argue that liberalization will promote economic growth, improving the prospects of producers and consumers in both industrialized and less developed nations. Critics worry that the benefits of trade are unevenly distributed, doing little to alleviate the fundamental inequities of the world economy. The ties between trade and the environment, in contrast, came to the attention of researchers and policy makers only in the 1990s, as disputes over the environmental impacts of the North American Free Trade Agreement (NAFTA) and the General Agreement on Tariffs and Trade (GATT) came to a head in international negotiations.

The political factors that support trade liberalization are relatively clear. The world economy reflects increasing degrees of regionalization and globalization in production and marketing by transnational corporations. Efforts to reduce trade barriers will generate substantial benefits for powerful political-economic actors. There are, however, important tensions between trade liberalization and other policy objectives. Policies to provide sustainable livelihoods for rural peasants in developing countries, for example, are sometimes characterized as distortionary measures that hinder economic progress. Although the GATT provides legal leverage for limiting the scope of environmental regulations, it does not at present offer a systematic approach for limiting the environmental harms that may result from increased trade. Based on these considerations, it is not obvious that simply extending existing institutions is the best way to advance the interests of the world's poor while maintaining the stability and resilience of ecological systems.

This chapter examines the concept of "sustainable development" as a unifying principle in the analysis of trade and environmental issues. The second section introduces the concept as it emerged in the international arena in the late 1980s and discusses the problems that have arisen in applying it to economic policy. The third section sketches recent trends in the world economy with an emphasis on the increasing roles of foreign direct investment, transnational corporations, and the regionalization of trade in shaping international economic institutions. The fourth section provides an overview of the trade/environment debate with a discussion of the circumstances under which trade liberalization yields favorable versus deleterious outcomes. The fifth section draws together the various strands of our analysis to establish some general conclusions.

THE WCED/UNCED PERSPECTIVE

The report of the World Commission on Environment and Development (WCED 1987), or the Brundtland Report as it is more widely known, argues that fundamental changes in the international trading system and global economic relations will be required to achieve sustainable development. The report notes that rising economic and geopolitical inequality has reinforced existing imbalances in international economic relations between developing nations and the advanced industrial countries. The report suggests that "Two conditions must be satisfied before international economic exchanges can become beneficial for all involved. The sustainability of ecosystems on which the global economy depends must be guaranteed. And the economic partners must be satisfied that the basis of exchange is equitable. For many developing countries, neither condition is met" (WCED 1987, p. 67).

Written at the height of the international debt crisis of the 1980s—the "lost decade" of development in Latin America and sub-Saharan Africa—the Brundtland Report identifies both long-term and conjunctural manifestations of asymmetrical international economic relations which militate against sustainability by intensifying "those forces that lead to environmental deterioration and resource depletion occurring at the expense of long-term development" (pp. 67–68). The asymmetries are reflected, it suggests, in unstable and adverse commodity terms of trade, rising debt service ratios, net resource transfers from poor to rich countries, reduced new capital flows, International Monetary Fund structural adjustment programs, and protectionist trade policies in Organization for Economic Cooperation and Development (OECD) economies (pp. 67–69). Brundtland is unequivocal in drawing direct causal links between the structure and operation of the global trade and financial system, on the one hand, and cumulative, mutually-reinforcing cycles of slower growth, falling living standards, poverty, hunger, and environmental degradation, on the other. "The critical situations in sub-Saharan Africa and the debt-strapped countries of Latin America demonstrate in an extreme way, the damaging impacts that unreformed international economic arrangements are having on both development and the environment" (p. 70).

With this forceful diagnosis, what reforms does Brundtland propose to untie the Gordian knot? Anticlimactically, it appeals in the short-term for more "effective and coordinated economic management among major industrial countries" (p. 75) to revitalize global economic growth, and observes that "In the longer-term, major changes are also required to make consumption and production patterns sustainable in a context of higher global growth" (p. 75). However, pragmatism prevails and the "reforms" comprise "the improvement of policies in areas where the scope for cooperation already is broadly defined: aid, trade, transnational corporations and technology transfer" (p. 76).

The Brundtland recommendations boil down to an anodyne blend of advice and exhortation that essentially adds only a gloss of sustainability to these policy areas. The Brundtland Commission concludes its discussion of international economic relations with the statement that "New dimensions of multilateralism are essential for human progress" and an expression of its confidence "that the mutual interests involved in environment and development issues can help generate the needed momentum and can secure the necessary international economic changes that will make it possible" (p. 90).

Discussions of the trade-environment nexus at the United Nations Conference on Environment and Development (UNCED) in June 1992 in Rio de Janeiro held closely to the agenda presented by its progenitor, the WCED. Its recommendations similarly involved tinkering with the existing system and institutional mechanisms combined with idealistic hopes for "a new and equitable global partnership"

(*The Rio Declaration*). The controversy aroused by Brundtland's emphasis on revitalizing global economic growth, via a "rather comfortable Keynesian reformism" (Adams 1990), was complemented by the UNCED commitment to a freer international trading system (Principle 12 of The Rio Declaration). According to the Agenda 21 Report, freer international trade contributes to environmental protection by enhancing competition and the efficiency of resource allocation. It is suggested that all nations, and particularly developing countries, would benefit from "an open, equitable, secure, nondiscriminatory, and predictable multilateral trading system" (Agenda 21, cited by Grubb et al. 1993, p. 103).

As in much of the subsequent conventional literature, issues are framed as if the environment, the environmental crisis, and what has to be sustained were located primarily, if not exclusively, south of the Equator, and the formulation of alternative paths of OECD development are ignored. The high resource-intensive patterns of consumption of the advanced industrial countries—so-called ecological over-population—were counterpoised in tit-for-tat fashion to population growth in developing countries during the Agenda 21 negotiations. Yet the more critical point is that "the UNCED agenda was incoherent unless development was broadened to include questions about the future development of industrialized countries" (Grubb et al. 1993, p. 32). This incoherence reveals a "fundamental paradox" at the heart of the UNCED agenda between development and environmental sustainability. "Development" is identified with the economic transformation of the South following in the mold adopted by the industrialized countries. Shades of modernization theory and the myth of convergence! However, environmental sustainability enjoins both advanced and developing countries to break this mold, so that the former abandon their present unsustainable growth trajectories and the latter do not replicate these previous patterns and yet attain higher income levels where basic needs can be met. Failure to address this contradiction by redefining and linking together "Northern sustainability" and "Southern development" provides "a poor basis on which to build 'a global partnership for sustainable development' in the 21st century" (Grubb et al. 1993, p. 33).

In effect, "development" remains synonymous with conventional economic growth, while sustainability is reduced to one possible constraint on economic efficiency, rather than an alternative vision of society. This displacement of the environment and sustainable development is perfectly illustrated by current debates on alternative models of development. Where "success" is unquestioningly equated with growth performance, these debates focus on the factors that explain the rapid economic growth of the East Asian "tigers," contrasting this with the alleged failure of other models of development, especially state-centered approaches (Wade 1990; Amsden 1994; Fishlow 1994). Yet one looks in vain for any evaluation of these models in terms of environmental sustainability. With growth defined as the sole end of "development," questions of institutional sustainability—designing and perpetuating policies, governance structures, and cultural values that foster economic growth—dominate the debate. The problem of ecological sustainability is, in this framework, relegated to secondary status if not altogether ignored.

Even when the issue of sustainable development, however defined, is raised, discussions are plagued with neat couplets that counterpoise the environment with the economy, job creation, population growth, etc. These binary oppositions presumably are a way of flagging the possibility of contradiction and the existence of tradeoffs. The theme of this paper, trade and the environment, has now joined this list of oppositional dichotomies (cf. the NAFTA debates). But this framing of the questions often sets the agenda. Such formulations funnel discussion into the reductionist world of the policy analyst and focus attention on making operational or technical adjustments rather than fundamental changes in the present system; for example, by "getting prices right." Thus Esty (1994) recently suggested that conflicts between trade liberalization, trade-generated economic growth and the environment can be "balanced" largely by environmental policy reform involving market-based environmental regulation to implement the polluter pays principle. The environment is subsumed by the market in such discourses, relegated to a place among the other normative dimensions potentially available to be "traded" against the abstract perfection of economic efficiency. In this construction, the primacy of the market and, as its corollary, governance by competitive forces, are unquestioned.

This emphasis on the microeconomic—individual markets, environmental "pricing," and choice—diverts attention from a wider set of legitimate questions raised by the notion of sustainable development. That is, questions of social organization and power in the constitution and operation of markets, initial endowments and property rights underlying distributions of income and wealth, and the sustainability of geopolitical relations. In this wider context, the dichotomies noted above are false since these phenomena are constitutive of the social process of environmental change under capitalism. As Michael Redclift (1987) observed about sustainable development, "It is central to the argument that 'development' be subjected to redefinition, since it is impossible for accumulation to take place within the global economic system we have inherited without unacceptable environmental costs." Running repairs to "business as usual" will not suffice. Furthermore, as we suggest below, the "business" of international trade has changed radically over the past twenty-five years, and not in the direction of greater openness and equity regarded as 'beneficial' by the UNCED Agenda 21 Report.

THE GLOBALIZING WORLD ECONOMY

Trade theorists envision a world of rational, self-governing agents who pursue mutual benefits through the exchange of goods and services. Conventional analysis abstracts from questions of power and distribution and the connections between economic and ecological systems. This section argues that trends towards the regionalization and globalization of economic institutions effectively concentrate power in the hands of a relatively small number of private-sector firms. In practice, trade liberalization reduces the ability of national and supranational agencies to pursue social and environmental objectives through economic policy.

It is misleading to define "trade" as if it involved mainly the international exchange of commodities between *discrete* national agents operating in markets determined by supply and demand. This world of sovereign, national economies, and separate national firms is rapidly being eroded. A high and rising proportion of international trade is not conducted at arm's length through world markets but is internalized by transnational corporations (TNCs) and involves intraindustry transactions between firms integrated into worldwide production systems and intrafirm hierarchies. As a reflection of this shift, the expansion and direction of world trade is led increasingly by foreign direct investment (FDI). These are but two characteristics of an emerging globalizing world economy that bears only fleeting resemblance to the models of trade theorists.

The need for new analytical and institutional frameworks to encompass these transformations is emphasized in two recent reports. The Group of Lisbon (1993) argues that "world economic development is no longer based on the exchange of flows amongst national economic entities interacting and competing with each other according to the old scheme of the international division of labor, based on each nation's comparative advantage" (p. 171). This change is echoed by the United Nations Conference on Trade and Development—Program on Transnational Corporations (UNCTAD-PTC 1993), which suggests that as international integration "moves from shallow trade-based linkages to deep international production-based linkages under the common governance of TNCs, the traditional division between integration at the corporate and country levels begins to break down. Because TNCs are internalizing activities spanning national boundaries, they encroach on areas over which sovereignty and responsibilities have traditionally been reserved for national governments. This raises issues of direct concern to the formation of national laws and regulations" (p. 161). The subsections below present some stylized facts and debates about the restructuring of the world economy in order to support this new perspective on international trade and to contextualize the discussion of mainstream views of trade and environment in the fourth section.

Spatial Concentration of Trade and Investment Flows

In the following paragraphs, we provide an overview of recent world-scale trends and corporate organizational change that are indicative of new directions in international economic integration. We focus on foreign direct investment as the leading integrative mechanism of the contemporary world economy, as well as one measure of corporate control over foreign productive assets. This control also can be achieved through nonequity arrangements of various kinds, of course.

The past decade has seen a remarkable acceleration in FDI and an accompanying rise in the number of companies opting to invest in foreign markets, rather than rely solely on trade linkages and exports (OECD 1992; UNCTAD-PTC 1993). "Since 1983 FDI flows expanded at an average rate of 34 percent compared with an annual rate of 9 percent for global merchandise trade" (OECD 1992, p. 12). International production and FDI-related trade have become key factors in the growth and integration of the world economy (UNCTAD-PTC 1993). By 1992, the global stock of FDI generated about $5.5 trillion in sales by foreign affiliates, surpassing world exports of goods and nonfactor services of $4 trillion, perhaps half of which represents intrafirm trade between TNC affiliates and parent firms. These linkages through the production and distribution networks of TNCs are designated as "deep integration" in contrast to "shallow integration" through open or arms length exchange. It is estimated that between one-quarter and one-third of private sector productive assets in the United States and Japan "are potentially under the common governance of TNCs pursuing integrated international production. For the world as a whole this percentage may be one-third" (p. 6).

FDI growth in the 1980s was marked by its strong and rising geographical concentration in the leading advanced industrial countries, as well as a sectoral shift from mining and manufacturing towards services, notably finance and trade-related services. Thus the share of the advanced industrial countries in total FDI inflows increased from 74 percent in 1981–85 to 83 percent in 1986–90 (UNCTAD-PTC 1993). FDI inflows to the developing countries rose almost twofold in absolute terms in the 1980s, averaging $16 billion annually in 1980–89, but their share of total worldwide FDI inflows only recovered in 1990 and 1991. FDI inflows to developing countries remained concentrated in Asia and Latin America, with the ten largest host countries accounting for 75 percent of these movements in the 1980s (OECD 1992).

The upsurge of FDI in the 1980s and its shifting geographical distribution is generally attributed to the interplay between short-run factors such as the strong growth of the world economy, the wave of acquisitions and mergers, and the pro-cyclical nature of FDI,[1] and longer-term factors which altered the underlying trend, principally policy changes and the structural effects of TNC operations (UNCTAD-PTC 1993). Policy changes include the liberalization of exchange and investment regimes, industrial privatization, and regional integration schemes, notably the single market of the European Union. These policy-related developments also are identified by the OECD (1992), which also observes that "The proliferation of quantitative restrictions, voluntary restraint agreements, orderly marketing arrangements, and anti-dumping rules since the late 1970s undoubtedly contributed to this rapid growth of FDI in the 1980s" (p. 12). In short, international companies resorted increasingly to FDI to circumvent these trade barriers and ensure participation in major markets. Both studies cited above identify the level of international production and the changing operational strategies of TNCs as important structural factors behind recent FDI trends.

From Shallow to Deep Integration in International Production

These strategies and associated organizational structures are discussed at length in UNCTAD-PTC (1993), which posits an evolutionary movement across a spectrum of cross-border integration mechanisms, beginning with "simple integration" and moving in recent years to "complex integration." The TNCs are seen as the formative element behind this temporally sequential movement, as they respond to competitive pressures, policy developments, and institutional change, with these decisions, in turn, shaping and deepening international economic integration. The simplest form of cross-border integration involves FDI in "stand-alone" or "multidomestic" affiliates to serve a host market or region, with a low degree of integration between the value-added chains of affiliates and parent firms. FDI to surmount trade barriers and other restrictive policies, such as those used to implement industrial import substitution programs favored by Latin American countries,[2] exemplifies such weak integration, where intrafirm linkages are limited mainly to ownership and technology transfer.

Movement to the next stage of "simple integration" between the value chains of parents and affiliates is associated by UNCTAD-PTC (1993) with freer trade policies, improved communications technologies and stronger international competition. Under this organizational form, parents integrate *specific* production activities performed by affiliates into their value-added chain, notably through outsourcing. In this case, affiliates become more dependent on parent firms for a variety of key activities, while parents now rely on their affiliates for some parts of their value-adding operations. According to the UNCTAD report, many TNCs are now evolving "complex integration" strategies, which potentially integrate all parts of the value-added chains of parents and affiliates. These "more recent" strategies involve both vertical and horizontal integration across national borders as foreign affiliates establish closer production and functional linkages not only with parent firms but also between themselves. In these emerging networks and new management approaches, affiliates tend to lose their earlier "profit center" status as their production activities become more specialized and are subordinated to the imperatives of firm-wide strategy. "Complex integration" at the intrafirm level also may be complemented by interfirm linkages created by strategic alliances to perform specific activities, which can redefine the boundaries of the firm.

These new deep or complex forms of integrated international production are emerging, under the pressures of competition, as propulsive mechanisms in the expansion of the world economy. UNCTAD-PTC (1993) estimates that roughly 25 percent of the productive assets in the United States and Japan "are potentially part of integrated international production," and "the share of world output potentially subject to integrated international production may well be around one-third" (p. 158). As noted earlier, this distinction between trade-based and international production-based linkages has significant implications for policy and governance, not least for proposals that seek to reconcile trade and environmental goals by adjusting market prices to reflect environmental externalities. Thus "With shallow integration, international trade results from the division of labor between independent producers in different countries" (p. 160). In this case, "The main interaction takes place in the international market, where buyers and sellers respond to market prices. The market is governed by a multilateral framework of rules and regulations, such as those of GATT, and/or, in some cases, by regional arrangements" (p. 160). However, regulatory frameworks for deep, integrated international production with significant intrafirm trade and resource flows "are as at yet partial—mostly regional" (p. 163). The UNCTAD-PTC concludes that "these qualitative and quantitative changes suggest that TNCs, with their functionally integrated production activities, are increasingly shaping the international economic system and relationships between national economies" (p. 164).

The UNCTAD-PTC (1993) report also draws attention to the spatial unevenness and polarities implicit in this new international system. As production-based integration rather than arm's length transactions increasingly becomes the formative influence on global economic growth and the international division of labor, "the growth potential of developing countries will depend to a large extent on their ability to participate in integrated international production and on the nature of their participation... TNCs have been focusing on the three regions of the Triad" and "Many developing countries have only been partially integrated into the evolving system" (p. 175). In addition, as location decisions focus increasingly on "national policies and institutions directly affecting the production process" (p. 225), trade liberalization will not ensure access to, nor full participation in, the emerging form of globalized world economy.

Regionalization and Continental Trade Blocs

The expansion of regional free trade areas and economic integration in the 1980s—the European Union, NAFTA, the Asia Pacific Economic Cooperation (APEC) forum and subregional groupings, such as Mercosur—is a major component of a broad conjuncture of world-scale processes and institutional developments that characterize the globalizing world economy. Discussion of regionalism proceeds on two main axes. The first examines the relationship of regional economic integration to globalization, a focal point of debates on future directions of change in the world economy. The second axis addresses the question of whether the preferential arrangements of regional trade blocs are more likely, on balance, to reduce or contribute to protectionist tendencies in the multilateral trading system.

Global regionalism as an institutionalized form of globalization is among several scenarios of the new "global world" presented in the recent report of the Group of Lisbon (1993). This scenario has two variants in which either centrifugal or centripetal forces are dominant. The respective outcome depends on whether the ethos of competition and free market governance prevails over mixed, cooperative forms of economy and governance in global geopolitical and economic relations. In the first variant, globalization occurs as "triadization" against a background of increasing techno-economic competition, integration, and regionalization between the industrial democracies of North America, Western Europe, and Japan. This form of globalization produces a stable, multi-polar, shared hegemony of *pax triadica*. "The *pax triadica* scenario implies a mixture of open competitiveness based (on) free market governance and nationally and regionally (continentally) 'protected' social market governance" (p. 118). Intensified competition, closer economic integration and "bloc to bloc" strategies between continentally-organized regions will accentuate centrifugal processes of fragmentation and accelerate the progressive *"de-linking"* of the triad from the rest of the world—a form of "truncated globalization."

In the second variant of the global regionalism scenario, globalization engenders "a double process of cooperative integration" (Group of Lisbon 1993, p. 120), first between regionally integrated entities and, second, at the global level. In this case, these regional entities underpin a new system of global cooperative governance, which is characterized by "(relatively) balanced relationships amongst comparable regional units, sharing inter-regional governing rules and institutions at the global level. Accordingly, the global system that would emerge from *regionalization* would no longer be a United 'Nations' but . . . would rather look like a United 'Federations' " (pp. 140–141, original emphasis).

The case for regionalism as a separate, alternative form of world economy, distinguishable from globalization, is forcefully presented by Hirst and Thompson (1992). In their view, "the globalization thesis" is unconvincing, which leaves open "the form of the global economy as the liberal multilateralism of the post-1945 period is forced on the defensive" (p. 369).[3] Liberal multilateralism, they suggest, will be replaced not by "globalization" but more likely by "the further development of a newly regionalized international economy, possibly dominated by a trilateralism of the US/NAFTA, the (expanded) European Union, and Japan (with or without possible Pacific Rim allies).

This itself will also involve an increase in bilateral negotiation between these major players and other lesser parties" (pp. 359–70).

Although Hirst and Thompson (1992) reject the notion of "a globalized economy," their prognosis appropriately returns to the broad concerns voiced by the Group of Lisbon (1993). That is, the forms of governance likely to develop in these blocs, which differ significantly in their internal formation and coordination, the nature of relations between these supra-national entities, and the future governance and management of the international system. These same concerns, though often formulated more narrowly, find resonance in the international trade literature on regionalism. A common formulation is to recognize the emergence of a regionalized world economy and then present regional free trade areas as possible obstacles to a freer multilateral trading system which, for most trade economists, is held to be synonymous with higher world welfare (see Allison in this volume). Such assessments of free trade areas frequently use a building block/stumbling block framework in which Viner's static trade creation and trade diversion effects[4] are distinguished from dynamic time-path questions (de Melo and Panagariya 1992). The static impact, which on balance may be positive or negative, refers to the immediate effects of regional integration on world welfare. Dynamic time-path questions, irrespective of the static impact, focus on the potential of regionalism as a stepping stone to multilateral free trade via the merging of regional blocs into a single world bloc (p. 6).

However, since "The theoretical literature on the economics of trading blocs is still in its infancy" (p. 7), and notably the exploration of dynamic time-path questions, analyses of regional integration have continued in the main to evaluate the static impacts. Policy discussions, more pragmatically, consider what type of multilateralism is likely to evolve in a regionalized international system with three dominant players, and the new international rules and organizations that will be needed to restrict the growth of protectionism.

One recent proposal recommends the notion of "open regionalism" as the guiding principle for the APEC forum and as a strategy to avoid inward-looking regionalism and further fragmentation of the global trading system (Bergsten 1994). Following this approach, APEC would negotiate regional agreements on issues unresolved or not yet tabled in the GATT and "then offer to open its accords to other countries, hopefully the entire GATT membership, that were willing to accept their obligations." APEC is, in essence, considering a whole new model of regional economic cooperation: a steady ratcheting up of trade liberalization between the regional and global levels that would confirm its dedication to "open regionalism" (p. 20). This proposal, if accepted, would distinguish APEC from subregional agreements in the Asia-Pacific area, such as the Association of Southeast Asian Nations free trade area (AFTA) and the NAFTA, whose benefits are restricted to member countries. Bergsten (1994) emphasizes that multilateralism also would gain further momentum if the expansion of the NAFTA into the Asia-Pacific region were to occur through negotiations covering all AFTA or APEC members rather than with individual countries.

These debates and the alternative scenarios of regionalism and the global trading system again reveal the vacuum of governance at the global level. Whether global integration occurs through global multilateralism or triadic competitive regionalism, these processes are likely to accentuate current trends towards spatial differentiation and fragmentation, effectively excluding four-fifths or more of the world's population. This reality stands in sharp contrast to the emphasis on international governance and cooperation that the concept of sustainable development seemingly entails.

TRADE AND THE ENVIRONMENT

Policy debates over trade and the environment have traditionally occurred in segregated domains involving distinct sets of stakeholders and decision-makers. Trade issues have been dominated by the clash of industry and labor interests over the relative importance of gaining access to foreign markets versus retaining high-wage jobs in domestic economies. Environmental issues, however, historically focused on conflicts over the respective roles of economic, health, and aesthetic values in promoting human welfare. Environmentalists typically view the conservation of natural resources and environmental quality as a moral priority that should not be compromised on purely pragmatic grounds. Critics of this approach argue that conservation effectively "locks up" the natural resources required to sustain economic growth and rising living standards.

The tension between these domains is clearly apparent in recent international negotiations on trade policy. Although both the WCED and UNCED concluded that trade, environment, and development are inseparable issues requiring careful policy integration, the latest round of GATT negotiations focused squarely on economic interests and constituencies with little input from environmentalists (Costanza et al. 1995). Those calling for consideration of the environment were, at times, criticized as closet protectionists using conservationist rhetoric to advance underlying parochial interests.

Although NAFTA contains explicit language calling for the coordination of trade and environmental policies, its main environmental provisions are contained in a side agreement that was negotiated only after it became apparent that addressing the environment was critical to ratification in the U.S. Senate. Esty (1993) notes that NAFTA creates explicit institutions for resolving international environmental disputes, taking an important step towards harmonizing trade and environmental policies. Critics, however, worry that the side agreement contains few enforceable provisions; the extent to which it will ameliorate NAFTA's perceived environmental impacts remains uncertain (Costanza et al. 1995).

The Welfare Implications of Trade Liberalization

The theoretical argument for trade liberalization stems from a central assumption of economic analysis: Individuals, firms, and nation-states engage in trade because of the logic of comparative advantage and the gains associated with specialization. Consider, for example, the case of an advanced industrial society that holds the technologies and skilled workers needed to manufacture automobiles but lacks the oil resources required to produce gasoline. A less developed nation, in contrast, lacks expertise in manufacturing but enjoys rich crude oil reserves. In the absence of trade between these two nations, neither would be able to make use of automotive transport since neither would have access to both vehicles and the fuel required to operate them. The exchange of goods between the two nations, however, would allow each society to make more effective use of its resources, creating clear gains from trade that would leave both sides better off.

Although this hypothetical example is simplistic, it captures the essential reasoning that supports free trade as a policy priority. Unfettered markets, proponents suggest, are a desirable form of economic organization because, under idealized conditions, they result in a Pareto efficient resource allocation. At such an outcome, potential gains from trade are fully exploited so that it is impossible to make one person or group better off without making another worse off. Since there is no obvious reason to oppose policies that improve the welfare of all individuals, the logic for free trade is seemingly compelling. Trade barriers, in this view, impair economic efficiency and thus reduce social welfare.

A deeper analysis, however, points to complexities in gauging the welfare effects of trade liberalization. One question concerns alleged departures from the idealized conditions under which competitive markets are Pareto efficient (Ekins et al. 1994; Runge 1995). It is well known, for example, that markets will yield efficient outcomes only if decision-makers (individuals and firms) bear the full social cost of their actions and are unable to impose externalities on others. Externalities, however, are pervasive in the environmental arena, where resources such as clean air, clean water, a stable ozone layer, and the preservation of biodiversity are public goods that are not owned and controlled by private economic actors. In the absence of explicit policies to protect environmental quality, it is likely that these resources will be overutilized.

A key concern of environmentalists focuses on the role trade liberalization might play in exacerbating environmental degradation. Developing countries, for example, commonly lack the institutions and policies required to protect environmental quality. Policies, where they do exist, are often poorly enforced and/or ineffective. Trade agreements that stimulate investment and production in developing countries, especially in resource-intensive heavy industries, might exacerbate existing environmental problems. According to this view, trade liberalization should not proceed without explicit attention to the environment (Costanza et al. 1995).

The evidence that trade liberalization is harmful to the environment is not clearcut. One widely cited example focuses on the *maquiladoras* of the U.S.-Mexico border region (Runge 1994, ch. 3). *Maquiladoras* are foreign-owned establishments that import raw materials duty-free and pay export duties only on the value added in production activities taking place in Mexico. Dating to trade policies established in the 1960s, the *maquiladora* sector has generated serious air pollution, water quality, and hazardous waste problems that affect both Mexicans and adjacent residents of the United States. These problems have been caused in large measure by Mexico's comparatively lax environmental standards.

The agricultural sector of the European Union, in contrast, provides an example where trade liberalization and environmental objectives can work hand in hand (Runge 1994, ch. 3). European farmers enjoy hefty subsidies and significant protection from international competition. Relaxing these trade barriers would result in reduced agricultural production in the region and increased imports from the U.S. and other nations. Since European farmers use proportionately more fertilizer and pesticides than their U.S. counterparts, trade liberalization might, in this instance, reduce the net environmental impacts of agriculture.

Proponents of free trade argue that the environmental impacts of trade liberalization can be ameliorated or even reversed through targeted environmental policies. Esty (1994), for example, holds that trade liberalization will yield net economic benefits provided that environmental externalities are internalized using pollution taxes, transferable permits, and related measures (see Allison in this volume). In practice, however, trade liberalization is unlikely to await the promulgation and enforcement of comprehensive environmental policies. Moreover, theoretical research suggests that the net benefits of trade liberalization need not be positive if the removal of trade barriers exacerbates existing externalities (Runge 1995). It is therefore inappropriate to draw sweeping generalizations about the supposed benefits of trade reforms without examining the particulars of each case.

A closely related question concerns the distribution of the benefits from trade (Ekins et al. 1994). If, for example, the principal beneficiaries of trade are transnational corporations and urban elites in developing countries, while pollution adversely affects populations of the working poor, any inference that the promotion of free trade is socially warranted is contentious to say the least, deviating from the emphasis on meeting basic needs in defining sustainable development. In this scenario, workers are asked to accept jobs (a benefit) in exchange for impaired environmental conditions (a cost). Balancing these costs and benefits raises difficult economic and ethical dilemmas. It is hardly safe to assume that workers, as a group, would be left better off through the change.

Environmental impacts notwithstanding, the question of distribution raises fundamental issues for trade liberalization. Liberalization, for example, generally favors the replacement of labor-intensive peasant agriculture with modern industrial agriculture. Substantial benefits accrue to large operators with access to capital and markets, as well as to subsidized producers in the developed countries with the considerable fiscal advantage of export enhancement programs. Falling commodity prices, however, undercut the position of peasant agriculturalists, driving them to accept wage employment in industrial centers as a means of supporting their families. In aggregate terms and using conventional welfare measures, this process produces net benefits since average incomes rise. But the process may be accompanied by an uneven distribution of benefits and increased levels of inequality, as well as the loss of national food security as import dependence becomes structurally entrenched.

In Mexico, for example, NAFTA and earlier unilateral trade liberalization policies are provoking a substantial shift from the production of maize using traditional methods to the importation of low-price maize grown in the United States (Foley 1995). This shift will erode the terms of trade for traditional farmers, effectively reducing their standard of living. It also threatens to reduce the genetic diversity of maize resources since Mexico, the original source of maize, is rich with varieties that are maintained only through small-scale agriculture.

Here again, advocates of trade liberalization are quick to point out standard remedies based on first-best approaches to economic policy. In the absence of externalities, the net monetary benefits of trade liberalization are generally positive. From this it follows that the winners from such policies could, in principle, compensate the losers so that all members of society were made better off. In practice, however, liberalization measures are often implemented without compensatory policies that ease the hardships of the disenfranchised. As Samuelson (1962) points out, "Practical men and economic theorists have always known that trade may help some people and hurt others" (p. 823). If liberalization policies lead to redistributions of wealth from the poor to the rich, they can hardly be reconciled with the concept of sustainable development, which promotes economic justice as an essential social priority.

CONCLUSION

The concept of sustainable development—ensuring that economic policies in both developing and advanced industrial societies meet present needs "without compromising the ability of future generations to meet their own needs" (WCED 1987, p. 43)—constitutes an important shift away from the market-oriented approach that equates welfare with higher monetary income and favors trade liberalization as an engine of growth. While free traders point to economic efficiency as their overriding objective, the sustainability criterion, if taken at face value, points to trade as socially desirable only under certain conditions. First, the fruits of economic activity must be equitably distributed, with a focus on meeting the basic needs of the world's poor. Second, economic activities should respect the interests of future generations, preserving the integrity of ecological processes and natural systems so that the life opportunities of future people are undiminished relative to the present (Page 1983; Daly and Cobb 1989).

It is not surprising that this ethically-grounded approach suggests different policy conclusions than traditional approaches that focus solely on economic efficiency. Sustainable development, for example, is sharply inconsistent with trade policies that promote urbanization and industrialization while at the same time undercutting the livelihoods of rural peoples. Similarly, sustainability imposes a concern for environmental and resource conservation as a central priority that should be incorporated in all levels of decision-making. Trade policies, in this view, should be evaluated based on their consistency with environmental objectives.

Such a perspective is generally consistent, however, with the view that trade liberalization can be used as an effective means of promoting human welfare. But while trade advocates sometimes favor liberalization almost as an end in itself, the arguments presented above suggest that the removal of trade barriers can, in practice, yield either positive or negative social and environmental consequences. Under sustainable development, liberalization becomes a potential tool for promoting independently defined concepts of the good society. Discriminating between beneficial and deleterious policies requires careful attention to the details and cannot be established by a priori arguments.

Our review of trends in the international political economy is not encouraging in this regard. The rise of transnational corporations may be understood through a variety of theoretical lenses. One interpretation, however, is that TNCs succeed because of economies of scale in production, distribution, and coordination. Without a doubt, trade liberalization stands to benefit TNCs in rather obvious ways. In one sense, liberalization improves access to global markets, facilitating the internationalization of production and marketing activities. In a similar vein, the GATT and related trade policies restrict the ability of nation-states to regulate the environmental and social impacts of commercial activities, making it easier for TNCs to pass on uncompensated costs to third parties.

Proponents argue that trade liberalization will promote economic development and improved living standards in both industrialized and developing nations. Krugman (1981, 1987), however, points out that this conventional wisdom is premised on a model of perfectly competitive markets that abstracts from the dimensions of real-world economic organization that we describe in the previous section. If, for example, production possibilities are described by external economies of scale, liberalization may, in fact, exacerbate existing inequalities between industrialized and less developed societies. Under this model, the gains from trade might be captured in large measure by industrialized societies and TNCs that enjoy substantial head starts in technology and worldwide marketing.

Krugman's analysis is unsettling for proponents of sustainable development in at least two respects. First, the argument that international economic institutions are insufficient to alleviate North-South inequities is broadly consistent with the stylized facts that led to the Brundtland Report and UNCED discussions. Second, the analysis suggests that fundamental changes in these institutions will be required to achieve the aims of sustainable development. The required reforms would entail effective international cooperation to protect the environment and to redirect the global economy towards meeting the basic needs of the world's poor. As we have seen, however, the authority and competence of international governance is tenuous at best; the world community is currently far from achieving the unity envisioned by the WCED.

Indeed, very much to the contrary, since global economic trends point to a growing privatization of power that is likely to obstruct rather than promote desired changes in income distribution and environmental quality. Viewed from this perspective, policies to promote the further liberalization of trade may in fact hinder rather than advance the aims of sustainable development.

NOTES

1. By which trends and shifts in FDI are positively correlated with cyclical movements in economic activity in the major industrial economies.

2. These programs sought to promote industrialization by providing incentives to national firms and multinational corporations, notably in the form of trade protection, to stimulate domestic production of manufactured goods previously imported.

3. Briefly, this rejection of globalization is based on the highly contingent, and often reversible, nature of many recent trends; the continued salience of the nation-state; trends towards reregulation; the dominance of multinational over truly transnational forms of corporate organization, and the assertion that "Perhaps the most significant post-1970s development, and the most enduring, is the formation of supra-national trading and economic blocs" (Hirst and Thompson 1992, p. 369).

4. These effects refer to the once-and-for-all or static impacts on the direction of trade following the formation of a customs union or a preferential regional trade agreement. Trade creation may arise from increased specialization between the new partners, but this may be offset, partially or completely, by the diversion of trade from former trading partners excluded from the customs union.

REFERENCES

Adams, W.M. 1990. *Green Development: Environment and Sustainability in the Third World*. London: Routledge.

Amsden, A.H. 1994. "Why Isn't the Whole World Experimenting with the East Asian Model to Develop? Review of the *East Asian Miracle*." *World Development*, vol. 22, pp. 627–633.

Bergsten, C.F. 1994. "APEC and World Trade: A Force for Worldwide Liberalization." *Foreign Affairs*, May/June, pp. 20–26.

Costanza, R., J. Audley, R. Borden, P. Ekins, C. Folke, S.O. Funtowicz, and J. Harris. 1995. "Sustainable Trade: A New Paradigm for World Welfare." *Environment*, vol. 35(5), pp. 16–44.

de Melo, J., and A. Panagariya. 1992. *The New Regionalism in Trade Policy*. Washington, D.C.: The World Bank.

Daly, H.E., and J. Cobb. 1989. *For the Common Good*. Boston: Beacon Press.

Ekins, P., C. Folke, and R. Costanza. 1994. "Trade, Environment and Development: The Issues in Perspective." *Ecological Economics*, vol. 9, pp. 1–12.

Esty, D.C. 1993. "Integrating Trade and Environment Policy Making: First Steps in the North American Free Trade Agreement." In *Trade and the Environment: Law, Economics, and Policy*, eds. D. Zaelke, P. Orbuch, and R.F. Housman. Washington, D.C.: Island Press.

Esty, D.C. 1994. *Greening the GATT: Trade, Environment, and the Future*. Washington, D.C.: Institute for International Economics.

Fishlow, A. 1994. "Economic Development in the 1990s." *World Development*, vol. 22, pp. 1825–1832.

Foley, M.W. 1995. "Privatizing the Countryside: The Mexican Peasant Movement and Neoliberal Reform." *Latin American Perspectives*, vol. 22, pp. 59–76.

The Group of Lisbon. 1993. *Limits to Competition*. Lisbon: Gulbenkian Foundation.

Grubb, M., M. Koch, A. Munson, F. Sullivan, and K. Thomson. 1993. *The "Earth Summit" Agreements: A Guide and Assessment*. London: Earthscan.

Hirst, P., and G. Thompson. 1992. "The Problem of 'Globalization': International Economic Relations, National Economic Management, and the Formation of Trade Blocks." *Economy and Society*, vol. 21, pp. 357–396.

Krugman, P.R. 1981. "Trade, Accumulation, and Uneven Development." *Journal of Development Economics*, vol. 8, pp. 149–161.

Krugman, P.R. 1987. "Is Free Trade Passé?" *Journal of Economic Perspectives*, vol. 1(2), pp. 131–144.

Organization of Economic Cooperation and Development (OECD). 1992. *International Direct Investment: Policies and Trends in the 1980s*. Paris: OECD.

Page, T. 1983. "Intergenerational Justice as Opportunity." In *Energy and the Future*, eds. D. Maclean and P.G. Brown. Totowa, New Jersey: Rowman and Littlefield.

Redclift, M.R. 1987. *Sustainable Development: Exploring the Contradictions*. London: Methuen.

Runge, C.F. 1994. *Freer Trade, Protected Environment: Balancing Trade Liberalization and Environmental Interests*. New York: Council on Foreign Relations Press.

Runge, C.F. 1995. "Trade, Pollution, and Environmental Protection." In *Handbook of Environmental Economics*, ed. D.W. Bromley. Oxford: Blackwell Publishers.

Samuelson, P.A. 1962. "The Gains from International Trade Once Again." *Economic Journal*, vol. 72, pp. 820–829.

United Nations Conference on Trade and Development—Program on Transnational Corporations (UNCTAD-PTC). 1993. *The World Investment Report 1993—Transnational Corporations and Integrated International Production*. New York: United Nations.

Wade, R. 1990. *Governing the Market: Economic Theory and the Role of Government in East Asian Industrialization*. Princeton: Princeton University Press.

World Commission on Environment and Development (WCED). 1987. *Our Common Future*. Oxford: Oxford University Press.

SECTION SIX

Environment and National Security

11 The Limits of Environmental Security

DANIEL DEUDNEY

INTRODUCTION

Like all biological organisms, humans are vitally dependent upon their physical environment. Since the beginning of recorded history, groups have competed—often violently, over environmental factors, particularly fertile soil, fresh water, and various earth minerals.[1] Over the last two centuries the explosive progress in science and technology and the emergence of societies of unprecedented wealth seemed to have loosened the iron grip of natural scarcity upon human life. But over the last several decades environmentally abusive practices, compounded by the sheer weight of human numbers and the power of industrial technology, have led to the degradation of environmental factors, such as clean air, biological diversity, and shielding from ultraviolet radiation that humans had been able to take for granted throughout history.

Because the institutions and ideologies of nation-state and interstate conflict are so hegemonic in both world politics and international relations theory, and because violence has historically occurred over competition for environmental scarcities, there is a natural tendency for people to think about environmental problems in terms of national security. Initial moves to connect security and national security with environmental issues were made by Lester Brown of the Worldwatch Institute (1977). More broadly, Richard Ullman proposed "redefining security" to encompass a wide array of threats, ranging from earthquakes to environmental degradation (1983). Arthur Westing pointed to the destruction of the environment caused by war, and hypothesized that interstate war and other forms of violence would result from resource scarcity and environmental degradation (1986). Patricia Mische proposed to "reconceptualize sovereignty" in order to focus on "ecological security" (1989). Most of the pioneering conceptual work on environmental security was done by advocates of greater environmental awareness. Such concepts were advanced to prevent an excessive focus on military threats during the renewed cold war tensions and heightened "national security" concerns of the late 1970s and early 1980s. They also were extrapolations from the fears of resource wars that had been widely discussed in the wake of the oil crises of 1973 and 1979, the formation of commodity cartels, and rapid price rises of oil and other earth minerals during the 1970s.

By the late 1980s and early 1990s "environmental security" became a broad movement, had generated an empirical research agenda, and had begun to shape policy. Numerous environmental advocates, including (but not limited to) Hal Harvey, Jessica Tuchman Mathews, Michael Renner, Norman Myers, Gwyn Prins, and Peter Gleick wrote extensively in favor of "redefining national security" to encompass resource and environmental threats (Harvey 1988; Renner 1989; Mathews 1989; Myers 1989; Gleick 1991). Due to the interest and support of several major foundations in the United States, numerous conferences were held, and large numbers of researchers began addressing issues of "environmental security." A major research effort, headed by Thomas Homer-Dixon of the University of Toronto and partially sponsored by the American Academy of the Arts and Sciences, has explored more systematically the links between environmental degradation, renewable resource scarcity, and violent conflict.

As the cold war began to wind down during the late 1980s, "environmental security" began to attract the interest and support of many associated with military organizations who saw environmental missions as a means to maintain financial support and organizational significance. Others saw environmental deterioration, particularly in Third World countries, as part of an ominous new threat to Western interest and world order. This new security fear was catalyzed in Robert Kaplan's horrific travel report, "The Coming Anarchy," and his widely cited conclusion that "the environment is *the* national security issue of the 21st century" (1994). With apocalyptic speculations of "chaos" in the Third World, "environmental security" became a contender in the United States's effort to formulate a new post-cold war foreign policy.[2]

In the late 1980s and early 1990s "environmental security" also began to register in the world of policy. Senator Albert Gore has spoken extensively in favor of thinking of the environment as a "national security issue" (Shabecoff 1990). Senator Sam Nunn's initiative for the

U.S. Department of Defense to spend $200 million for efforts in environmental monitoring and research brought this new agenda to the traditional American national security organizations. An effort in the United Nations General Assembly was mounted to declare environmental degradation to be a security issue.

This environmental security paradigm and agenda initially seemed straightforward and noncontroversial. But in the early 1990s as this movement was growing rapidly, a range of objections and doubts were raised by me (Deudney 1990, 1991) and a few others (Finger 1991; Dalby 1992; Conca 1994)—some sympathetic to environmental concerns and others not. Since these debates were first joined, extensive research has been undertaken, and heated debates about environmental security have occurred in many policy and academic fora. In this chapter I revisit and refine my arguments against the environmental security paradigm and program, modifying and augmenting them where appropriate.

Overall, skepticism is not only still warranted, but confirmed and strengthened. Specifically, I make three claims. First, it is analytically misleading to think of environmental degradation as a national security threat because the traditional focus of national security—interstate violence—has little in common with either environmental problems or solutions. Second, the effort to harness the emotive power of nationalism to help mobilize environmental awareness and action may prove counterproductive by undermining globalist political sensibility. And third, environmental degradation is not very likely to cause interstate wars.

ASSESSING THE SIMILARITIES BETWEEN ENVIRONMENTAL DEGRADATION AND NATION-STATE SECURITY

One major strand of "environmental security" thinking has sought to redefine "national security" or more broadly "security" to encompass threats to well-being that have traditionally been outside their domain. Historically, conceptual shifts of this sort have often accompanied important changes in politics, as new phrases are coined and old terms are appropriated for new purposes.[3] Epochal developments like the emergence of capitalism, the growth of democracy and the end of slavery were accompanied by shifting, borrowing, and expanding political language. The wide-ranging contemporary conceptual ferment in the language used to understand and act upon environmental problems is therefore both a natural and an encouraging development.

But not all neologisms and linkages are equally plausible or useful. Until this recent flurry of reconceptualizing, the concept of "national security" (as opposed to national interest or well-being) has been centered upon *organized violence*.[4] As is obvious to common sense and as Hobbes argued with such force, security from violence is a primal human need because loss of life prevents the enjoyment of all other goods. Although various resource factors, such as access to fuels and ores, were understood as contributing to state capacities to wage war and achieve security from violence, they were security issues because of their links to state and war-making capability rather than intrinsically seen as "security" threats in their own right.

Before either "expanding" the concept of "national security" to encompass both environmental and violence threats, or "redefining" "national security" or "security" to refer mainly to environmental threats, it is worth examining just how much the national pursuit of security from violence has in common with environmental problems and their solutions.

Military violence and environmental degradation are linked directly in at least three major ways. First, the pursuit of national security from violence through military means consumes resources (fiscal, organizational, and leadership) that could be spent on environmental restoration. Because approximately one trillion dollars is spent worldwide on military activities, substantial resources are involved. However, this relationship is not unique to environmental concerns, and there is no guarantee that money saved from military expenditures would be spent on environmental restoration. And the world can afford environmental restoration without cutting military expenditures.

Second, war is directly destructive of the environment. Some of this destruction is an unintentional effect of war, while some of it is the intentional destruction of the natural environment, or "environmental warfare." In ancient times, the military destruction of olive groves in Mediterranean lands contributed to the longlasting destruction of the land's carrying capacities (Ponting 1992) (although military destruction was probably far less significant than mundane agricultural and grazing practices). More recently, the United States' bombardment and use of defoliants in Indochina caused significant environmental damage. During the Gulf War of 1991, Saddam Hussein's retreating forces set the oil fields of Kuwait on fire, causing massive ecological damage and resource wastage (Greenpeace 1991). Most ominously, extensive use of nuclear weapons would have significant impacts on the global environment, including altered weather patterns (i.e., "nuclear winter") and further depletion of the ozone layer

(Ehrlich et al. 1984). Awareness of the environmental effects of nuclear weapons played an important role in mobilizing popular resistance to the arms race and in generally de-legitimizing the use of nuclear explosives as weapons, first in the concern over atmospheric testing during the late 1950s and early 1960s and then over nuclear winter in the mid-1980s.

Third, preparation for war poses a significant environmental burden. Preparation for war is a resource intensive activity. Preparation for war has also generated large quantities of toxic and radioactive materials. Over the last half-century, the nuclear weapons states, particularly the United States and the Soviet Union, generated enormous quantities of radioactive waste as a by-product of the nuclear weapons development and production (Renner 1991). Safely handling these materials is expensive, requires highly competent organizations, and as with other large and complex technical systems, accidents, catastrophic on a local and sometimes regional scale, are inevitable. Perhaps most disastrously, a waste dump at a Soviet nuclear weapons facility exploded and burned in 1957, spreading radioactive materials over a large area near the Urals (Medvedev 1990).

In summary, war and the preparation for war are clearly environmental threats and consume resources that could be used to ameliorate environmental degradation. These environmental impacts mean that the war system has costs beyond the intentional loss of life and destruction. But most environmental degradation is not caused by war and preparation for war. Even if the direct environmental effects of preparing for and waging war were completely eliminated, most environmental degradation would remain. Environmental degradation's main sources and solutions are found outside the domain of the traditional national security system related to violence.

The war system is a definite but limited threat to the environment, but in what ways is environmental degradation a threat to "national security"? One answer to this question, advanced by many analysts of environmental security, is to broaden the definition of national security to encompass environmental harms. Making such an identification can be useful conceptually and analytically if the two phenomena—security from violence and from environmental threats—are similar. How similar are these two phenomena regarding: (1) type of threat, (2) source of threat, (3) degree of intentionality, and (4) the types of organizations involved ? (summarized in Figure 10.1).

First, environmental degradation and interstate violence both entail threats, but they are very different in character. Both violence and environmental degradation may kill people and may reduce human

Figure 10.1. Conceptual and Organizational Mismatches

	conventional national security	*global habitability*
type of threat	— violent death, — destruction of property — loss of independence	wide range of harms: aesthetics, disease, natural integrity
source of threat	— mainly outside — other states armed with weapons	— both inside and outside — wide range of sources: individuals, corporations, governments
degree of intentionality	— direct and high — vs accidental war	— largely unintentional side-effects of routine activities — vs accidental spill
types of organizations involved	— specialized, — secretive, — removed from civil society	— all sizes — in situ change of many mundane activities: land use, waste treatment, farming, factory design.

well-being. But not all threats to life and property are threats to security. Disease, aging, crime, and accidents routinely destroy life and property, but we do not think of them as "national security" threats or even threats to "security." (Crime is a partial exception, but crime is a "security" threat at the individual level because crime involves violence.) And when an earthquake or hurricane strikes with great force, we speak about "natural disasters," or designate "national disaster areas," but we do not speak about such events threatening "national security." If everything that causes a decline in human well-being is labelled a "security" threat, the term loses any analytical usefulness and becomes a loose synonym of "bad."

Second, the scope and source of threats to environmental well-being and national-security-from-violence are very different. There is nothing about the problem of environmental degradation that is particularly "national" in character. Few environmental threats afflict just one nation-state, and they often spill across the borders of the nation-states, or affect the global commons beyond their jurisdiction. At the same time, most environmental problems are not "international," because many perpetrators and victims are within the borders of one nation-state. Individuals, families, communities, other species, and future generations are harmed. A complete collapse of the biosphere would surely destroy nation-states as well as everything else, but there is nothing distinctively national about either the causes, the harms, or the solutions that warrants us giving such privileged billing to the "national" grouping.

A third misfit between environmental well-being and national-security-from-violence stems from the differing degrees of *intention* involved. Interstate violence threats typically involve a high degree of intentional behavior. Organizations are mobilized, weapons procured, and wars waged with relatively definite aims in mind. In contrast, environmental degradation is largely unintentional, a side-effect of many other activities. With the exception of "environmental warfare" no one really sets out with the aim of harming the environment.

Fourth, organizations that provide protection from violence differ greatly from those in environmental protection. National-security-from-violence is conventionally pursued by organizations with three distinctive features. Clearly military organizations are secretive, extremely hierarchical and centralized, and typically deploy vastly expensive, highly specialized, and advanced technologies. Also, citizens typically delegate the goal of achieving national security to remote and highly specialized organizations that are far removed from the experience of civil society. Lastly, the specialized, professional group staffing these national security organizations are trained in the arts of killing and destroying.

In contrast, responding to the environmental problem requires very different approaches and organizations. Change is required in certain aspects of virtually all mundane activities from house construction, farming techniques, sewage treatment, factory design, and land use. The routine behavior of virtually everyone must be altered. This requires behavior modification *in situ*. And the professional ethos of environmental restoration is husbandmanship—more respectful cultivation and protection of plants, animals and the land.

In summary, national-security-from-violence and environmental habitability are far more dissimilar than similar. Given these differences, linking them via re-definition risks creating a conceptual muddle rather than a paradigm or worldview shift. If all the forces and events that threaten life, property and well-being (on a large scale) are understood as threats to national security, the term will come to be drained of useful meaning. This is even more of a problem for "comprehensive security" paradigms that add all threats to all subjects together. If all large-scale evils become threats to national security, the result will be a *de-definition* rather than a *re-definition* of security. To speak meaningfully about actual distinct and different problems it will be necessary to invent new or redefine old words to serve the role performed by the old spoiled ones.

ENVIRONMENTAL SECURITY AS A MOTIVATIONAL STRATEGY

Despite the great differences between threats to traditional national security and to the environment, some environmentalists want to conflate or link them as part of a motivational strategy. People take national security threats seriously. As a result, they are willing to bear heavy costs, in financial and material resources, in organizational commitment and attention, and in compromised liberties and lost lives. Advocates of environmental security reason that if people reacted as urgently and effectively to environmental problems as to the national-security-from-violence problem, then much more effort and resources would be directed to environmental problems. Thus, one aim of redefined national security or environmental security is not to describe or understand the world more accurately, but rather to stimulate, motivate, and even inspire action. Environmental security is thus part of a rhetorical and psychological strategy to redirect social forces now expended upon war and interstate violence toward environmental amelioration. In keeping with this purpose, much of the "environmental security" literature aims to persuade and inspire as much as to analyze and inform.

This motivational strategy is neither original nor unique to the environmental cause. The effort to establish what William James called a "moral equivalent to war" has long been the dream of social reformers. But channelling the energies behind war into constructive directions by this kind of rhetorical linkage has not been particularly successful. In the United States this kind of strategy has been widely tried, as political leaders and their speech writers have launched a "War on Poverty," a "War on Crime" and a "War on Drugs." But these social problems—like the environment—have little in common with the pursuit of national security from violence, and they have proven deeply intractable. As Ken Conca has pointed out, the discourse of "national security" has a set of powerful associations that cannot simply be re-directed (Deudney 1990; Conca 1994).

History and logic suggest that rhetorical motivation strategies are not likely to be very effective. But an even more serious problem is that they may be counterproductive to achieving environmental sustainability because of what might also be brought into the environmental politics along with enhanced concern and motivation. "National security" claims are politically potent because they have been connected to state institutions, national identities, and international war. Is it feasible to redirect the social energies and symbolic change of national security without also bringing assumptions, norms, practices, and institutions of national security? Or, to the extent that redirection is accomplished by re-definition and rhetorical re-deployment, will other aspects of traditional security approaches be brought into environmental politics? In short, will this strategy generate, as Jyrki Kakonen puts it, "green security or a militarized environment"? (1994)

To assess the unintentional side effects of this motivational strategy, it is necessary to examine the cluster of interrelated assumptions, norms, ideologies, identities, and institutional practices that most characterize the definition and pursuit of national security. The model for national security in world politics is the early modern European political order and its globalization. State institutions, national identities, and interstate war have such persistence in world politics because they powerfully reinforce one another. As the historian Michael Howard has observed: "Self-consciousness as a Nation implies, by definition, a sense of differentiation from other communities, and the most memorable incidents in the group memory usually are of conflict with, and triumph over, other communities. It is in fact very difficult to create national self-consciousness *without* a war" (1979). States enter the equation by making war, which in turn strengthens states. As Charles Tilly, summarizing the dominant view of political scientists and historians, puts it, "states make war and war makes states" (1985). States build and sustain national political identities congruent with their borders and their purposes through educational systems, public ceremonies, and direct indoctrination that make central use of memories of war. This powerful triumvirate of states, nations, and war has defined "national security." To assess the potential risks of the environmental security motivational strategy, it is necessary to consider several major and interrelated assumptions. Norms, identities, practices and organizations of national security, and how they might shape environmental politics, must be compared to the central dentities, practices, and organizations most intimately related to environmental sustainability. (see Figure 10.2)

At first glance, the most attractive feature of linking fears about environmental threats with national security mentalities is the sense of urgency created, and the corresponding willingness to accept great personal sacrifice. If the basic habitability of the planet is being undermined, then some crisis mentality is warranted. But it is difficult to

Figure 10.2

	Conventional National Security	*Consequence for Environmental Politics*	*Global Sustainability Paradigm*
Institution	Strong state	war against society totalitarianism	local and global
Identity	nationality	reinforce "us" vs "them"	bioregional, global, planetary
Authority	state sovereignty	impede interstate agreements	diffuse & divided; future generations & other species

engender a sense of urgency and a willingness to sacrifice for extended periods of time. Crises call for resolution, and the patience of a mobilized populace is rarely long. For most people exertion in a crisis is motivated by a desire to return to normalcy, for the problem to be resolved once and for all. Such a cycle of passivity and arousal is not likely to make much of a contribution to establishing sustainable patterns of environmentally sound behavior. Furthermore, "crash" solutions are often bad ones—more expensive, centralized, and poorly designed than typical government programs.

Framing the environmental problem as a national security threat is also likely to entail the expansion of state involvement in regulating and managing the environment, and the growth of state capabilities. In many developing countries, states are weak and oppressive, and political identities are not national. In this context, framing environmental problems as national security threats could provide a mandate for coercion. In Africa where the political identities do not correspond to the borders of the state system, states tend to be both weak and highly oppressive. Already many developing countries are practicing what Nancy Peluso has termed "coercive conservation," the use of state power to dispossess locals of their traditional natural resources in order to benefit state elites and multinational corporations (1993). As the anthropologist Jason Clay has pointed out, in many parts of the developing world, and particularly its tropical rain forests, states are dispossessing and destroying indigenous peoples whose claim to distinct national identity is high, but whose potential or statehood is very low or nonexistent (1994).

Expanding the security state also puts individual freedom at risk. As James Der Derian has pointed out, "security" also means "to tie down" or "prevent from moving" (1995). A "security jacket" protects by confining. To ask the state to act to secure against a threat often involves erosion of individual liberty and greater restraint and oppression. Strong states have been the greatest source of security threats in the twentieth century: authoritarian and totalitarian states have murdered more of their citizens than died in all interstate wars, and most deaths in war occurred in conflicts started by aggressive authoritarian and totalitarian states. Given this record, an agenda of "comprehensive security," or "ultimate security" advocated by some well-meaning environmentalists has a sinister potential (Myers 1993). Because almost all human activities affect the environment in some way or another, assigning states the task of environmental security could provide the foundation for a comprehensive despotism. Is it possible for the state to provide comprehensive security without imposing total control?

National security is also closely connected to the institution of state sovereignty. In the society of states, sovereignty has come to mean the existence in a polity of a final and undivided authority over a particular territory, which only states can possess, and the reciprocal recognition of this authority which states extend to each other. The hegemony of this system of legitimate authority has marginalized the claims to sovereignty, autonomy, and authority of other actors both within states and outside them. When issues of national security are at stake, states tend to be highly jealous of their sovereign prerogatives, fearing that its loss or compromise will leave them subordinate and therefore vulnerable. Responding to international and global environmental problems often requires arrangements that divide and pool authority, and thus run against the normal practices of state sovereignty. Therefore, an enhanced state concern for its sovereign prerogatives could greatly impede international environmental cooperation.

Several of these patterns can be seen in the "energy security crisis" in the United States during the 1970s. Aiming for the "moral equivalent of war," President Carter's effort to mobilize public awareness and forge a public consensus about energy conservation produced a flurry of activity that subsided once the immediate symptoms of the problem receded. The initiatives advanced by both parties in Congress and the White House emphasized nuclear energy and expanded fossil fuel production, and largely neglected less-centralized, less-capital intensive, and less-environmentally destructive technologies. In order to insure that the massively subsidized macroenergy projects would not be impeded by citizen participation and environmental reviews, Carter proposed an "energy mobilization board" with broad powers. And a Byzantine system of price controls was imposed instead of market mechanisms.

A second apparently valuable similarity between the national security mentality and the environmental problem is the tendency to use worse case scenarios as the basis for planning. However, military organizations are not unique in this regard. The insurance industry routinely prepares for the worst possibilities, and many fields of engineering, such as aeronautical design and nuclear power plant regulation, also employ extremely conservative planning assumptions. Therefore, it is not necessary for environmental policy to be modelled after national security and military organizations to achieve risk-averse planning.

Third, the conventional national security mentality and its organizations are deeply committed to zero-sum thinking. "Our" gain is "their" loss. Trust between national security organizations is extremely low. The prevailing assumption is that everyone is a potential enemy and that agreements mean little unless congruent with immediate interests. If the Pentagon had been put in charge of negotiating an ozone protocol, we might still be stockpiling chloroflourocarbons as a bargaining chip. Conventional national security organizations have short-time horizons. The pervasive tendency for national security organizations to discount the future and pursue very near-term objectives is a poor model for achieving environmental sustainability.

Finally, and perhaps most importantly, privileging national identity and security collides directly with worldviews and identities supportive of sustainable environmental practices. The "nation" is not an empty vessel or blank-slate waiting to be filled or scripted, but is instead profoundly linked to "us versus them" thinking. The tendency for people to identify themselves with various tribal and kin groupings is as old as humanity. However, in the last century and a half the sentiment of nationalism, amplified and manipulated by mass media propaganda techniques, has been an integral part of totalitarianism and militarism. Nationalism means a sense of "us versus them" of the insider versus the outsider, of the compatriot versus the alien. The stronger the nationalism, the stronger this cleavage, and the weaker transnational bonds. Nationalism reinforces militarism, fosters prejudice and discrimination, and feeds the quest for "sovereign" autonomy.

In contrast, in the environmental sphere "we have met the enemy and they are us," as the comic strip figure Pogo aptly put it. As noted earlier, existing "us" versus "them" groupings in world politics match very poorly the causal lines of environmental degradation. At its most basic level, the environmental problem asks us to redefine who "us" encompasses. Coping with global problems and new forms of interdependence requires replacing or supplementing national with other forms of group identity. Privileging the nation also directly conflicts with the globalism that has been one of the most important aspects of environmental awareness. The resolution of many global environmental problems requires great, even unprecedented, types of international cooperation. Fueling the fires of nationalist sentiment and identification creates a barrier to be overcome. Framing environmental problems as threats to national security risks undercutting the globalist and common fate understanding of the situation and the sense of world community that may be necessary to solve the problem. In short, if environmental concerns are wrapped in national flags, the "whole earth" sensibility at the core of environmental awareness will be undermined.

If environmental degradation were to be widely understood as a "national security" problem, there is also a danger that the citizens of one country will feel much more threatened by the pollution from other countries than by the pollution created by their fellow citizens. This could increase international tensions and make international accords more difficult to achieve, while diverting attention from internal clean-up. For example, Americans could become much more concerned about deforestation in Brazil than in reversing the centuries of North American deforestation. Taken to an absurd extreme—as national security threats sometimes are—seeing environmental degradation in a neighboring country as a national security threat could evoke interventions and armed conflicts.

Americans have been leaders in defining and advancing the environmental paradigm and program, and the particular experiences of the United States heavily shape it. The role of state and nation in the United States has been anomalous, and account for the relative blindness of American "environmental security" analysts to the risks of the environmental security motivational strategy. The American Constitutional order is an elaborate system of constraints on the accumulation of centralized state power, and even in the twentieth century has served as a powerful impediment to responding to the needs of industrialism and international involvement. External military threats to national security have been catalysts to state-building in the United States in the twentieth century. Given this, Americans seeking to build stronger governmental institutions often have found it expedient to frame their social welfare agendas in the terms of national security (Leuchtenberg 1964). But in much of the rest of the world, too much rather than too little state power has threatened public security and liberty. Similarly, nationalism in the United States has centered upon liberal and civic rather than ethnic identities, and these distinctive identity claims have been countered rather than embodied fractious ethnicities and moderated conflicts.[5] Context makes connotation, and evoking national security in the United States has far different and more innocent implications than it does in much of the rest of the world.

Fortunately, environmental awareness need not depend upon coopted "national security" thinking. Integrally woven into ecological awareness are a powerful set of values and symbols—ranging from human health and property values to beauty and concern for future generations. These norms and symbols draw upon basic human desires and aspirations and are powerful motivators of human action. Far from needing to be bolstered by "national security" mindsets, a "green" sensibility can make strong claim to being the master metaphor for an emerging post-industrial civilization. Instead of attempting to gain leverage by appropriating "national security" thinking, environmentalists should continue developing and disseminating this rich emergent worldview.

Recasting the Nation

Transposing existing "national security" thinking and approaches to environmental politics is likely to be both ineffective, and to the extent effective, counterproductive. But the story should not end with this negative finding. Fully grasping the ramifications of the emerging environmental politics requires a radical rethinking and reconstitution of many of the major institutions of industrial modernity, including the nation. The nation and the national, as scholars on the topic emphasize, are complex phenomena because so many different components of identity have become conflated with or incorporated into national identities. Most important in the Western construction of national identity have been ethnic, religious, language, and state components. There is, however, one dimension of the national—loyalty to place—that has been underappreciated, but which opens important avenues for thinking about identity as ecology becomes politically contested. Identification with a particular physical place, what Wright labels "geopiety" and Tuan labels "topophilia" has been an important if underappreciated building block of national identity (Tuan 1976, 1994). As Edmund Burke, the great philosopher of nationalism, observed, the sentimental attachment to place is among the most elemental widespread and powerful of forces, both in humans and in animals. Over the last several centuries the nation-state has both sought to shape and exploit this sentimental attachment.

With the rise of greater ecological awareness, this sense of place and threat to place takes on a new character. In positing the "bioregion" as the appropriate unit for political identity, environmentalists are recovering and redefining topophilia/geopiety in ways that subvert the state-constructed and state-supporting nation. Whether the bioregion is understood as a particular locality defined by ecological parameters, or the entire planet as the only naturally autonomous bioregion, environmentalists are in effect asserting what can appropriately be called "earth nationalism" (Deudney 1995). This construction of the nation has radical implications for existing state and "international" political communities. This emergent earth nationalism is radical both in the sense of returning to fundamental roots, and in posing a fundamental challenge to the state sponsored and defined concept of "nation" now hegemonic in world politics. It also entails a powerful and fresh way to conceptualize environmental protection as the practice of "national security."

ENVIRONMENTAL DEGRADATION AS A CAUSE OF VIOLENT CONFLICT AND INTERSTATE WAR

Many are attracted to conceptualizing environmental concerns as a national security threat because they expect environmental scarcities and change to stimulate conflict, violence, and interstate war. States often fight over what they value, particularly if related to "security." If states begin to be much more concerned with resources and environmental degradation, particularly if they think environmental decay is a threat to their "national security," then states may wage wars over resources and pollution. Much of the recent literature on the impacts of climate change upon world politics posits conflictual and violent outcomes (Gleick 1989a, 1989b). As Arthur Westing puts it: "Global deficiencies and degradation of natural resources, both renewable and nonrenewable, coupled with the uneven distribution of these raw materials, can lead to unlikely—and thus unstable—alliances, to national rivalries, and, of course, to war" (1986). In emphasizing such outcomes, environmental security analysts join Realist international relations theorists in characterizing international political life as particualarly prone to conflict and violence.

To analyze fully the prospects for violent outcomes is a vast and uncertain undertaking.[6] Because there are nearly 200 independent states, and because resource and environmental problems are diverse and not fully understood, generalizations are hazardous and are sure to have important exceptions. To assess the prospects for resource and pollution wars, I will first make several general points about the methodological weaknesses of recent studies on environmental conflict, consider several overall features of contemporary world politics that make such conflict unlikely, and then examine more closely the six major scenarios for environmental conflict most discussed by environmental security analysts. In general I argue that studies on environmental conflict are deeply flawed in their methodology, that important features of world politics—most notably the world trade system and the widely diffused violence capabilities—make interstate violence and war much less likely than environmental security analysts would have us believe, and that these doubts are vindicated by a more balanced consideration of the most frequently discussed scenarios.

Most of the recent work on environmental conflict and violent change suffers from important methodological problems which cast serious doubt on many of their disturbing conclusions. First, many studies on environmental conflict purport to have found trends in the frequency with which environmental scarcities produce conflict. However, it is only possible to find a trend after comparing the historical frequency of conflict against the possible cases of environmental scarcities, make a similar calculation for the present, and then compare past with present frequency. Unfortunately, most studies on environmental conflict and change do not make historical assessments, and even more alarmingly, fail to consider or even profile the entire set of contemporary cases of environmental scarcity and change to ascertain how many of them have resulted in violent conflict. A second methodological problem is that analysts of environmental conflict do not systematically consider the ways in which environmental scarcity or change can stimulate cooperation. This lacuna is particularly glaring because analysts typically advocate more cooperation as a response to the scarcities and changes they identify or foresee. In short, the early studies did not control for other sources of conflict.

Another major limitation of most studies on environmental conflict is that they rarely consider the character of the overall international system in assessing the prospects for conflict and violence. Of course, it is impossible to analyze everything at once, but conclusions about conflictual outcomes are premature until the main features of the world political system are factored in. The frequency with which environmental scarcity and conflict will produce violent conflict, particularly interstate wars, is profoundly shaped by three features of world politics: (1) the extent of international trade, (2) the security practices and institutions of international society such as international organizations, alliances, and balancing; and (3) the existence of nuclear weapons that make interstate war prohibitively costly, and (4) the diffusion of conventional arms, which make conquest and occupation of territory extremely difficult. These deeply rooted material and institutional features of the contemporary world order greatly reduce the likelihood that environmental scarcities and change will lead to interstate violence.

Resource Wars

Few scenarios seem more intuitively sound than that states will begin fighting each other as the world runs out of usable natural resources. The popular metaphor of a lifeboat adrift at sea with declining supplies of clean water and rations suggests there will be fewer and fewer opportunities for positive-sum gains between actors. Many ideas about resource war are derived from the cataclysmic world wars of the first half of the twentieth century. Influenced by geopolitical theories that emphasized the importance of land and resources for Great Power status, Hitler in significant measure fashioned Nazi war aims to achieve resource autonomy.[7] The aggression of Japan was directly related to resource goals: lacking indigenous fuel and minerals, and faced with a slowing tightening embargo by the Western colonial powers in Asia, the Japanese invaded Southeast Asia for oil, tin, and rubber (Crowley 1966). Although the United States had a richer resource endowment than the Axis powers, fears of shortages and industrial strangulation played a central role in the strategic thinking of American elites about world strategy (Spykman 1942). And during the cold war, the presence of natural resources in the Third World helped turn this vast area into an arena for East-West conflict (Eckes 1979). Given this record, the scenario of conflicts over resources playing a powerful role in shaping international order should be taken seriously.

However, there are three strong reasons for concluding that the familiar scenarios of resource war are of diminishing plausibility for the foreseeable future. First, the robust character of the world trade system means that states no longer experience resource dependency as a major threat to their military security and political autonomy. During the 1930s the world trading system had collapsed, driving states to pursue autarkic economies. In contrast, the resource needs of contemporary states are routinely met without territorial control of the resource source. As Ronnie Lipschutz has argued, this means that resource constraints are much less likely to generate interstate violence than in the past (Lipschutz 1989).

Second, the prospects for resource wars are diminished by the growing difficulty that states face in exploiting foreign resources through territorial conquest. Although the invention of nuclear explosives has made it easy and cheap to annihilate humans and infrastructure in extensive areas, the spread of conventional weaponry and national consciousness has made it very costly for an invader, even one equipped with advanced technology, to subdue a resisting population—as France discovered in Indochina and Algeria, the United States in Vietnam, and the Soviet Union in Afghanistan.[8] The lower levels of violence capability matter most for conquering and subduing territory, and here the Great Powers have lost effective military superiority and are unlikely soon to regain it.

Third, the world is entering what H.E. Goeller and Alvin M. Weinberg have called the "age of substitutability," in which industrial technology is increasingly capable of taking earth materials such as iron, aluminum, silicon, and hydrocarbons that are ubiquitous and plentiful and fashioning them into virtually everything needed by modern societies (Goeller and Weinberg 1967; Larson, Ross and Williams 1986). The most striking manifestation of this trend is that prices for virtually every raw material has been stagnant or falling for the last several decades despite the continued growth in world economic output. In contrast to the expectations widely held during the 1970s that resource scarcity would drive up commodity prices to the benefit of Third World raw material suppliers, prices have fallen, with disastrous consequences for Third World development.

Water and Oil

The general features of contemporary world politics overlooked by most environmental security analysts suggest that resource war scenarios are not very plausible, but two difficult cases—water and oil—warrant more specific attention.

Fresh water is a vital resource that is scarce and becoming scarcer in many parts of the world. In desert and semi-arid regions that make up over a third of the earth's land area, water scarcities exert an overwhelming influence because without fresh water these lands are unable to support much life, human or otherwise. In water-deficient regions, violent conflicts over access to supplies of fresh water have occurred since the beginning of recorded history. The potential for conflict is further exacerbated by the fact that many important rivers flow across the lands of many countries, and interstate borders divide underground aquifers.

Given these realities, it is not surprising that "water wars" have been one of the most frequently hypothesized form of resource wars, particularly in the Middle East, a water scarce region with particularly volatile and violent political relations (Bulloch and Darwish 1993). Here researchers can point to ample anecdotal evidence that conflicts over water will cause wars, such as former Egyptian President Anwar Sadat's prediction that Egypt's next war will be over water, or the threats that Turkey has made to cut off the flow of water in the Euphrates at Iraq's expense. The hydrologist Peter Gleick, one of the most prolific environmental security analysts studying water, claims to have found a "trend toward more conflict" and a "disturbing trend toward the use of force in resource-related disputes" (Gleick 1992). This conclusion is, however, not really supported by evidence, and is flawed by the methodological problems mentioned earlier. Asserting a trend is unwarranted because Gleick does not examine the past incidence of water conflict, which necessitates a comparison between the number of actual cases of violent conflict and the possible universe of such cases. The analysis of the present and future is also anecdotal, and the assertion of a trend is not backed by a comparison of the actual violent water conflicts against the possible ones. Indeed, much of Gleick's evidence consists of the large number of jointly shared water resources. However, importance riparian states have attached to water resources, and the almost complete absence of violent conflict in these cases suggests that violent conflict over scarce water is a very rare, nearly nonexistent, phenomenon in contemporary world politics.

Furthermore, those who hypothesize increased violent conflict over water do not consider the ways in which water scarcity has stimulated cooperation and provided disincentives to violent conflict. Precisely because so many rivers are international, their development requires interstate cooperation. To the extent that states wish to gain the benefits of these jointly owned resources they are forced to cooperate in their development. There are many important examples of such cooperation that have already occurred, perhaps most notably the Parana River in South America, which Brazil, Paraguay, and Argentina have cooperatively developed. Furthermore, once dams and other extensive infrastructure have been built, interstate violence becomes an increasingly costly option to pursue. The plausibility of using the "water weapon" of closing off the flow of water to the detriment of downstream users must be weighed against the vulnerability of dams to military attack. Some analysts have pointed to the vulnerability of the Aswan High Dam on the Nile to possible Israeli attack as a factor in inducing Egypt to make peace with Israel. Also, because the political relations of the Middle East are so volatile and violent, it is unwise to extrapolate a global trend from largely hypothetical developments in this one region.

Oil is the second "hard case" for the skeptic of resource wars. The stakes in the recent Gulf War were of concern to the general world community not just because of the particularly bald character of the Iraqi aggression and its implications for the security of small states, but also because of Kuwait's extensive oil reserves. Because the Persian Gulf region contains two-thirds of the world's proven oil reserves, and because many of the states in this region are so militarily weak relative to their neighbors, war over oil remains a distinct possibility. This region is both unique and exceptional, and the ways in which the international community responded to Iraqi aggression is likely to serve as a further deterrent to others. With the possible exception of the tiny country of Brunei in Southeast Asia, it is hard to find other examples of states that are as oil rich, population poor, and militarily weak in such proximity to militarily powerful states as the Persian Gulf emirates vis-a-vis Iraq and Iran. Furthermore, the swift and decisive way in which nearly the entire international community responded to Iraqi aggression is likely to further raise the threshold for other states contemplating similar aggressions.

Power Imbalances

Second, environmental degradation may affect interstate relations in such a way as to cause war by altering the relative power capacities of states. Alterations in relative power position can contribute to wars either by tempting the newly stronger states to aggress upon the newly weaker ones, or by leading the newly weakened ones to attack and lock in their power position relative to their neighbors before their power ebbs any further. Abundant support for such scenarios can be drawn from history, and international relations scholars have extensively studied such phenomenon (Gilpin 1981).

However, such alterations in the relative international power potential of states might not lead to war as readily as the lessons of history suggest because economic power and military power are perhaps not as tightly coupled as in the past. The relative economic power positions of major states such as Germany and Japan have altered greatly since the end of World War II. But these changes, while requiring many complex adjustments in interstate relations, have not been accompanied by war or threat of war. In the contemporary world, whole industries rise, fall, and relocate, often causing quite substantial fluctuations in the economic well-being of regions and peoples, without producing wars. There is no reason to believe that changes in relative wealth and power positions caused by the uneven impact of environmental degradation would be different in their effects.

Part of the reason for this loosening of the economic-military link has been the nuclear revolution, which has made it relatively cheap for the leading states to sustain a mutual kill capacity. Given that the superpowers field massively oversufficient nuclear forces at the cost of a few percent of their GNP, environmentally-induced economic decline would have to be extreme before their ability to field a minimum nuclear deterrent would be jeopardized.

Pollution Spillover Wars

A third possible route from environmental degradation to interstate conflict and violence is pollution across interstate borders. It is easy to envision situations in which country A upstream and upwind dumps an intolerable amount of pollution on a neighboring country B, causing country B to attempt to pressure and coerce country A into eliminating its offending pollution. Some envision such conflict of interest leading to armed conflict.

Fortunately for interstate peace, strongly asymmetrical and significant environmental degradation between neighboring countries are relatively rare. Probably more typical is the situation in which activities in country A harm parts of country A and country B, and in which activities in country B harms parts of both countries, too. This creates complex sets of winners and losers, and thus a complex array of potential intrastate and interstate coalitions. In general, the more such interactions are occurring, the less likely it is that a persistent, significant, and highly asymmetrical pollution "exchange" will occur. The very multitude of interdependency in the contemporary world, particularly among the industrialized countries, makes it unlikely that intense cleavages of environmental harm will match interstate borders, and at the same time not be compensated and complicated by other military, economic or cultural interactions. Resolving such conflicts will be a complex and messy affair, but they are unlikely to lead to war.

Struggles over the Global Commons

Fourth, there are conflict potentials related to the global commons. Many countries contribute to environmental degradation, and many countries are harmed, but because the impacts are widely distributed, no one country has an incentive to act alone to solve the problem. Solutions require collective action, and with collective action comes the possibility of the "free rider." In the case of a global agreement to reduce carbon dioxide emissions to reduce the threat of global warming, if one significant polluter were to resist joining the agreement, with the expectation that the other states would act to reduce the harms to a tolerable level, the possibility thus arises that those states making the sacrifices to clean up the problem would attempt to coerce the "free rider" into making a more significant contribution to the effort.

It is difficult to judge this scenario because we lack examples of this phenomenon on a large scale. "Free-rider" problems may generate severe conflict, but it is doubtful that states would find military instruments useful for coercion and compliance. If, for example, China or Russia decided not to join a carbon dioxide agreement, it seems unlikely that the other major countries would really go to war with such powerful states. Overall, any state sufficiently industrialized to be a major contributor to the carbon dioxide problem is likely to present a very poor target for military coercion.

Impoverishment, Authoritarianism, and War

In the fifth environmental conflict scenario, increased interstate violence results from internal turmoil caused by declining living standards. Many commentators on the environmental crisis emphasize that the basic source of environmental distress is the modern success in producing wealth. Some maintain that new technology, institutional reform, new attitudes, and more efficient capital investment can largely solve the environmental problem without sacrificing high standards of living. Others, however, are more pessimistic, asserting that the great wealth produced (if unevenly distributed) since the industrial revolution cannot be sustained. In this view, the only way to prevent ecological collapse (and the resulting economic collapse) is through radically lower standards of living.

Ramifications of economic stagnation upon politics and society could well be major and largely undesirable. Although the peoples of the world could perhaps live peacefully at lower standards of living, reductions of expectations to conform to these new realities will not come easily. Faced with declining living standards, groups at all levels of affluence can be expected to resist reductions in their standard of living by pushing the deprivation upon other groups. Class relations would be increasingly "zero sum games" producing class war and revolutionary upheavals. Faced with these pressures, liberal democratic and free market systems would increasingly be replaced by authoritarian systems capable of maintaining minimum order.[9]

The international system consequences of these domestic changes may be increased conflict and war. If authoritarian regimes are more war-prone because of their lack of democratic control, and if revolutionary regimes are war-prone because of their ideological fervor and lack of socialization into international norms and processes, then a world political system containing more such states is likely to be increasingly violent. The historical record from previous economic depressions supports the general proposition that widespread economic stagnation and unmet economic expectations contributes to international conflict.

Although initially compelling, this scenario has flaws as well. First, the pessimistic interpretation of the relationship between environmental sustainability and economic growth is arguably based on unsound economic theory. Wealth formation is not so much a product of cheap natural resource availability as of capital formation via savings and more efficient ways of producing. The fact that so many resource-poor countries, like Japan, are very wealthy, while many countries with more extensive resource endowments are poor, demonstrates that there is no clear and direct relationship between abundant resource availability. Environmental constraints require an end to economic growth based on growing raw material through-puts, rather than an end to growth in the output of goods and services.

Second, even if economic decline does occur, interstate conflict may be dampened, not stoked. In the pessimistic scenario, domestic political life is an intervening variable connecting environmentally induced economic stagnation with interstate conflict. How societies respond to economic decline may in large measure depend upon the rate at which such declines occur. An off-setting factor here the possibility that as people get poorer, they will be less willing to spend increasingly scarce resources for military capabilities. In this regard, the experience of economic depressions over the last two centuries may not be relevant, because such depressions were characterized by under-utilized production capacity and falling resource prices. In the 1930s increased military spending had a stimulative effect, but in a world in which economic growth had been retarded by environmental constraints military spending would exacerbate the problem.

State Collapse

The sixth, and perhaps most plausible, scenario for environmental conflict centers upon internal political conflict arising from environmental scarcities and change. This scenario has been emphasized by Thomas Homer-Dixon and the other members of his research team (Homer-Dixon 1991, 1994). This research suffers from the methodological problems discussed earlier, both absence of historical comparison and a failure to examine cases of environmental change that either did not lead to violent conflict or that stimulated cooperative arrangements. As such it demonstrates neither trends nor verifies propositions on causal relationships. Nevertheless, the work of this research project marks a considerable advance on what came before and makes three important contributions. First, it advances the field's conceptualization of the processes and pathways in which environmental scarcities, particularly in degraded or depleted renewable resources of forests, fisheries, and soils, can cause or exacerbate social conflicts to the point of violence. Although such process tracing falls short of the verification of causal propositions, it sheds important light on the ways in which social and natural systems can interact. Second, its careful case studies of ecological and social developments has moved the field beyond the reliance upon anecdotal evidence, and thus helped lay the ground work for further analysis. Third, it should be noted that Homer-Dixon and his colleagues have not found much merit in the scenarios for interstate conflict, and thus have largely corroborated the doubts raised by critics of the first wave of environmental security work.

Assuming that environmental degradation can lead to internal turmoil and state collapse, what are the international ramifications? Should some areas of the world suffer this fate, the impact of this outcome on international order may not, however, be very great. If a particular country, even a large one like Brazil, were to disintegrate tragically, among the first casualties would be the capacity of the industrial and governmental structure to wage and sustain interstate conventional war. As Bernard Brodie observed about the modern era, "the predisposing factors to military aggression are full bellies, not empty ones" (Brodie 1972, p.14) The poor and wretched of the earth may be able to deny an outside aggressor an easy conquest, but they are themselves a minimal threat to outside states. Offensive war today requires complex organizational skills, specialized industrial products, and surplus wealth.

In today's world everything is connected, but not everything is tightly coupled. Regional disasters of great severity may occur, with scarcely a ripple in the rest of the world. Idi Amin drew Uganda back into savage darkness, the Khmer Rouge murdered an estimated two million Cambodians, and the Sahara has advanced across the Sahel without the economies and political systems of the rest of the world being much perturbed. Indeed, many of the world's citizens did not even notice.

In summary, the case for thinking environmental degradation will cause interstate violence is much weaker than commonly thought. In part this is because of features of the international system—particularly the hypertrophy of violence capability available to states—that have little to do directly with environmental matters. Although many analogies for such conflict draw from historical experience, they fail to take into account the ways in which the current interstate system differs from earlier ones. Military capability sufficient to make aggression prohibitively costly has become widely distributed, making even large shifts in the relative power potential of states less likely to cause war. Interstate violence seems to be poorly matched as a means to resolve many of the conflicts that might arise from environmental degradation. The vitality of the international trading system and the more general phenomenon of complex interdependency also militate against violent interstate outcomes. The result is a world system with considerable resiliency and enough "rattle room" to weather significant environmental disruption without large-scale violent interstate conflict.

CONCLUSION

The degradation of the natural environment upon which human well-being depends is a challenge of far-reaching significance for human societies everywhere. But this challenge has little to do with the national-security-from-violence problem that continues to plague human political life. Not only is there little in common between the causes and solutions to these two problems, but the nationalist and militarist mind-sets closely associated with "national security" thinking directly conflict with the core of the environmentalist worldview. Harnessing these sentiments for a "war on pollution" is a dangerous and probably self-defeating enterprise. And fortunately, the prospects for resource and pollution wars are not as great as often conjured by environmentalists.

The pervasive recourse to "national security" paradigms to conceptualize the environmental problem represents a profound and disturbing failure of imagination and political awareness. If the nation-state enjoys a more prominent status in world politics than its competence and accomplishments warrant, then it makes little sense to emphasize the links between it and the emerging problem of the global habitability.[10] Nationalist sentiment and the war system have a long established logic and staying power that are likely to defy any rhetorically conjured "re-direction" toward benign ends. The movement to preserve the habitability of the planet for future generations must directly challenge the power of state-centric nationalism and the chronic militarization of public discourse. Environmental degradation is not a threat to "national security." Rather, environmentalism is a threat to the conceptual hegemony of state-centered "national security" discourses and institutions. For environmentalists to dress their programs in the blood-soaked garments of the war system betrays their core values and creates confusion about the real tasks at hand.

NOTES

1. For an overview of the role of environmental factors in early theories of politics, see Deudney 1989.

2. For accounts of the influence of "environmental security" in the Clinton administration, see: Rosner 1994a, 1994b.

3. For a discussion of the interplay between conceptual, terminological, and political change, see Skinner 1989; Farr 1989.

4. A particularly lucid and well-rounded discussion of security, the state, and violence is found in Buzan 1983.

5. Here I follow the classic picture drawn by Kohn 1957.

6. For a useful survey of theories relevant for such analysis, see Homer-Dixon 1990.

7. For discussions of resource autarky during the 1930s, see Emeny 1934; Rich 1973; Carr 1972.

8. Among the most recent versions of the argument that war is of declining viability are: Luard 1989 and Mueller 1989.

9. For discussion of authoritarian and conflictual consequences of environmental constrained economies, see Ophuls 1976; Leeson 1979; Gurr 1985; and Heilbroner 1974.

10. For a particularly lucid argument that the nation-state system is overdeveloped relative to its actual problem-solving capacities, see Modelski 1972.

REFERENCES

Brodie, Bernard. 1972. "The Impact of Technological Change on the International System," in *Change and the Future of the International System*, eds. David Sullivan and Martin Sattler. New York: Columbia University Press.

Brown, Lester. 1977. "Redefining National Security," Worldwatch Paper # 14.

Bulloch, John, and Darwish, Adel. 1993. *Water Wars: Coming Conflicts in the Middle East*. London: Victor Collancx.

Buzan, Barry. 1983. *People, States, and Fear: The National Security Problem in International Relations*. Chapel Hill, N.C.: The University of North Carolina Press.

Carr, William. 1972. *Arms, Autarchy, and Aggression: A Study in German Foreign Policy, 1933–1939*. London: Edward Arnold.

Clay, Jason. 1994. "Resource Wars: Nation and State Conflicts of the Twentieth Century," in *Who Pays the Price ? The Sociocultural Context of Environmental Crisis*, ed. Barbara Rose Johnston. Washington D.C.: Island Press.

Conca, Ken. 1994. "In the Name of Sustainability: Peace Studies and Environmental Discourse," in *Green Security or Militarized Environment*, ed. Jyrki Kakonen. Aldershot: Dartmouth.

Crowley, James. 1966. *Japan's Quest for Autonomy: National Security and Foreign Policy, 1930–1938*. Princeton: Princeton University Press.

Dalby, Simon. 1992. "Ecopolitical Discourse: 'Environmental security' and Political Geography." *Progress in Human Geography*, 16:503–522.

Der Derian, James. 1995. "Security," in *On Security*, eds. Beverly Crawford and Ronnie Lipschutz. New York: Columbia University Press.

Deudney, Daniel. 1989. "Early Theories of the Influence of Geography and the Environment Upon Politics," chapter III of *Global Geopolitics: Materialist World Order Theories of the Late 19th and Early 20th Centuries*. Unpublished PhD dissertation, Politics Department, Princeton University.

Deudney, Daniel. 1990. "The Case Against Linking Environmental Degradation and National Security." *Millennium* 19:461–476.

Deudney, Daniel. 1991. "Environmental Security: Muddled Thinking." *Bulletin of the Atomic Scientists* 47:3.

Deudney, Daniel. 1995. "Ground Identity: Nature, Place, and Space in the National," in *The Return of Culture and Identity to International Relations Theory*, eds. Yosef Lapid and Friedrich Kratochwil. Boulder, Colorado: Lynne Reinner.

Eckes, Alfred E., Jr. 1979. *The United States and the Global Struggle for Minerals.* Austin, Texas: University of Texas Press.

Ehrlich, Paul R., Carl Sagan, Donald Kennedy, and Walter Orr Roberts. *The Cold and the Dark: The World After Nuclear War.* New York: W.W. Norton.

Emeny, Brooks. 1934. *The Strategy of Raw Materials.* New York: Macmillan.

Farr, James. 1989. "Understanding Political Change Conceptually," in *Political Innovation and Conceptual Change,* eds. Terence Ball et al. Cambridge: Cambridge University Press.

Finger, Mathias. 1991. "The Military, the Nation State, and the Environment." *The Ecologist* 21:5.

Gilpin, Robert. 1981. *War and Change in World Politics.* Cambridge: Cambridge University Press.

Gleick, Peter. 1989a. "The Implications of Global Climatic Changes for International Security." *Climatic Change* 15:309–325.

Gleick, Peter. 1989b. "Global Climatic Changes and Geopolitics: Pressures on Developed and Developing Countries," in *Climate and Geo-Sciences,* eds. A. Berger et al. Amsterdam: Kluwar Academic Publishers.

Gleick, Peter H. 1991. "Environment and Security: The Clear Connections." *Bulletin of the Atomic Scientists* 47:3.

Gleick, Peter. 1992. "Water and Conflict," occasional paper series of the Project on Environmental Change and Acute Conflict, number 1.

Goeller, H.E., and Weinberg, Alvin. 1967. "The Age of Substitutability." *Science* 201.

Greenpeace, 1991. *On Impact: Modern Warfare and the Environment: A Case Study of the Gulf War.* Washington D.C.: Greenpeace.

Gurr, Ted. 1985. "On the Political Consequences of Scarcity and Economic Decline." *International Studies Quarterly* 29:51–75.

Harvey, Hal. 1988. "Natural Security." *Nuclear Times,* March/April, 24–26.

Heilbroner, Robert. 1974. *An Inquiry Into the Human Prospect.* New York: W.W. Norton.

Homer-Dixon, Thomas. 1990. "Environmental Change and Human Conflict," working Paper, Cambridge, MA.: American Academy of the Arts and Sciences.

Homer-Dixon, Thomas. 1991. "On the Threshold: Environmental Change as a Cause of Acute Conflict." *International Security* 16:2.

Homer-Dixon, Thomas. 1994. "Across the Threshold:Environmental Scarcities and Violent Conflict: Evidence from Cases." *International Security* 19:1.

Howard, Michael. 1979. "War and the Nation-State." *Daedalus*, fall.

Kakonen, Jyrki, ed. 1994. *Green Security or Militarized Environment*. Aldershot, U.K.: Dartmouth.

Kaplan, Robert. 1994. "The Coming Anarchy." *The Atlantic Monthly*, February.

Kohn, Hans. *American Nationalism: An Interpretative Essay*. New York: Macmillan.

Larson, Eric D., Marc H. Ross, Robert H. Williams. 1986. "Beyond the Era of Materials." *Scientific American* 254:34–41.

Leeson, Susan M. 1979. "Philosophical Implications of the Ecological Crisis: The Authoritarian Challenge to Liberalism." *Polity* 11.

Leuchtenburg, William E. 1964. "The New Deal and the Analog of War," in *Change and Continuity in Twentieth Century America*, ed. John Braeman. Columbus, Ohio: Ohio University Press.

Lipschutz, Ronnie D. 1989. *When Nations Clash: Raw Materials, Ideology and Foreign Policy*. Cambridge, MA: Ballinger.

Luard, Evan. 1989. *The Blunted Sword: The Erosion of Military Power in Modern World Politics*. New York: New Amsterdam Books.

Mathews, Jessica Tuchman. 1989. "Redefining Security." *Foreign Affairs* 68:162–177.

Medvedev, Zhores A. 1990. *The Nuclear Disaster in the Urals*. New York: W.W. Norton.

Mische, Patricia M. 1989. "Ecological Security and the Need to Reconceptualize Security." *Alternatives* 14:389–427.

Modelski, George. 1972. *Principles of World Politics*. New York: The Free Press.

Mueller, John. 1989. *Retreat from Doomsday: The Obsolescence of Major War*. New York: Basic Books.

Myers, Norman. 1989. "Environmental Security." *Foreign Policy* 74:23–41.

Myers, Norman. 1993. *Ultimate Security: The Environmental Basis of Political Stability*. New York: Norton.

Ophuls, William. 1976. *Ecology and the Politics of Scarcity*. San Francisco: Freeman.

Peluso, Nancy. 1993. *Rich Forests, Poor People*. Berkeley: University of California Press.

Ponting, Clive. 1992. *A Green History of the World: The Environment and the Collapse of Great Civilizations*. New York: St. Martin's.

Renner, Michael. 1989. "National Security: The Economic and Environmental Dimensions." Worldwatch Paper Number 89.

Renner, Michael. 1991. "Assessing the Military's War on the Environment," in *State of the World 1991*, ed. Lester Brown. New York: Norton.

Rich, Norman. 1973. *Hitler's War Aims: Ideology, The Nazi State, and the Course of Expansion*. New York: W.W. Norton & Co.

Rosner, Jeremy D. 1994a. "Is Chaos America's Real Enemy? The Foreign Policy Splitting Clinton's Team." *Washington Post Outlook*, September 14.1.

Rosner, Jeremy D. 1994b. "The Sources of Chaos." *The New Democrat*, November 20–22.

Shabecoff, Philip. 1990. "Senator Urges Military Resources Be Turned to Environmental Battle." *New York Times*, June 29, 1A.

Skinner, Quentin. 1989. "Language and Political Change," in *Political Innovation and Conceptual Change*, eds. Terence Ball et al. Cambridge: Cambridge University Press.

Spykman, Nicholas John. 1942. *America's Strategy in World Politics: The United States and the Balance of Power*. New York: Harcourt, Brace and Co.

Tilly, Charles. 1985. "War Making and State Making as Organized Crime," in *Bringing the State Back In*, eds. Peter Evans, Dietrich Rueschemeyer, and Theda Skocpol. Cambridge: Cambridge University Press.

Tuan, Yi-Fu. 1976. "Geopiety: A Theme of Man's Attachment to Nature and Place," in *Geographies of the Mind*, eds. David Lowenthal and Nartyn J. Bowden. New York: Oxford University Press.

Tuan, Yi-Fu. 1994. *Topophilia: A Study of Environmental Perception, Attitudes, and Values*. Bloomington: University of Indiana Press.

Ullman, Richard. 1983. "Redefining Security." *International Security*, summer.

Westing, Arthur H. 1986. "Global Resources and International Conflict: An Overview," in *Global Resources and Environmental Conflict: Environmental Factors in Strategic Policy and Action*, ed. Westing. New York: Oxford University Press.

12 Linking Environment, Culture, and Security*

MARGARET SCULLY GRANZEIER

> What sets worlds in motion is the interplay of differences, their attractions and repulsions. Life is plurality, death is uniformity, by suppressing differences and peculiarities, by eliminating different civilizations and cultures, progress weakens life and favors death, impoverishes and mutilates us. Every view of the world that becomes extinct, every culture that disappears, diminishes a possibility of life.
>
> Octavio Paz (1967; quoted in Davidson, 1993)

Ethnic conflicts, escalating tensions over the distribution and ownership of scarce resources, the complexities of global economic interdependence, and the effects of severe ecological degradation challenge the usefulness of conventional notions of security (Lynn-Jones and Miller 1995; Tickner 1995). Although the meaning of security has been examined in many disciplines, including peace and conflict studies, geopolitics, international human rights and environmental law, applied anthropology, feminist studies, and traditional security studies,[1] there is no consensus regarding the fundamental assumptions, characteristics, or priorities of international security, much less a consensus about the theoretical salience and practical applicability of the term "environmental security" (Buzan 1991; Romm 1993).

---

* The author gratefully acknowledges the careful review and helpful suggestions offered by Timothy Breen Granzeier, George A. Gonzalez, Sheldon Kamieniecki, Michael Kraft, Alison Dundes Renteln, Marilyne Scully, J. Ann Tickner and Robert O. Vos.

The concept of "eco-cultural security" introduced in this chapter addresses a theoretical and normative weakness in the international relations and security studies literatures. This perspective challenges the conventional, state-centric, zero-sum notions of security that focus on military threats to stability and order, and questions the neglected confluence of environmental and cultural preservation issues. The eco-cultural security paradigm combines a reconsideration of security with the goals of protecting and sustaining the environment, guaranteeing the protection of human and environmental rights, and maintaining cultural integrity. This approach attempts to provide a new, ideally more comprehensive, conceptual and normative tool for analyzing security issues.[2] A more thorough understanding of the political, social, and cultural intricacies implicit in many security dilemmas will facilitate theory building, the development of empirically testable hypotheses (Haftendorn 1991), and the creation of culturally sensitive policies and institutions to eliminate the sources of insecurity. The so-called environmental refugee, or "environmentally displaced," will illustrate the practical intersection of environmental, cultural, and security issues.[3]

This chapter begins with a review of the literature in the field of international security scholarship as it pertains to human rights, cultural rights, and environmental protection. The research in this newly emerging field is rich in contextual detail and theoretical diversity, but it has not produced a comprehensive, yet analytically useful model of the relationship of environmental and human rights to cultural security. In response, this chapter is designed as a speculative study to explore the most notable advocates and critics of the "environmental security debate," and to assess the prospects of the eco-cultural perspective for future empirical research.

CRITICS OF ENVIRONMENTAL SECURITY

In a recent survey of the field of security studies, the existence of nonmilitary threats to states and individuals is acknowledged; however, these phenomena, including environmental "hazards," are summarily dismissed as irrelevant to the study of security (Walt 1991). Including environmental issues in security scholarship is viewed as an excessive attempt to broaden the scope of security that would ultimately "water-down" its "intellectual coherence" and complicate the search for solutions to problems such as transnational environmental pollution (Walt 1991). Moreover, the inclusion of environmental degradation in security would not eliminate the inevitability of war and conflict (Walt 1991).

The criticism sketched above rests upon a narrow definition and understanding of security as "the study of the threat, use and control of military force" (Walt 1991, p. 212). This "realist" preoccupation with interstate conflict and military-strategic themes precludes the inclusion of nonmilitary threats to ecosystem survival. Accordingly, security, as it is generally understood from the standpoint of realism, is equated with the maintenance of stability, order, and a balance of power between states in the international system. Walt's criticism of environmental security reveals a reliance on the ability of researchers to disaggregate explicit military threats to security from the entire spectrum of possible threats to security. The justification for dismissing nonmilitary threats to security on the basis that they may fall outside the realm of traditionally defined security and strategic studies, however, is not compelling. This position may actually stem from the perceived need to preserve the discipline rather than allow it the flexibility to provide an explanation for contemporary social, political, and environmental developments.

A more sympathetic critic of environmental security has investigated the possible causal, instrumental, definitional, and normative linkages between the environment and war and peace. Lothar Brock's (1991) contribution to the debate provides several critical caveats to the assumption that transboundary environmental pollution and the degradation of global environmental resources constitute a nonmilitary threat to the security of humanity and the natural world. This criticism suggests that emphasizing the security component of environmental disruption will divert attention and resources away from research and policymaking efforts which address other important nonmilitary threats to societal security, such as coerced cultural assimilation, involuntary migration, and economic exploitation. Brock (1991) contends that discussions of environmental security should not imply that military threats are diminishing in importance or likelihood. He affirms that, historically, environmental degradation has precipitated military conflict, military activity may degrade the environment, and deliberate manipulation or degradation of the environment during wartime has been used as a strategy to broaden the options of traditional warfare (Brock 1991; Kakonen 1992, 1994; Plant 1994; Westing 1986, 1994).

Although his critique is particularly sympathetic to the necessity of enlarging the scope and definition of security to include nonmilitary threats, Brock (1991) nonetheless cautions against the temptation to give environmental issues preeminence over other economic or societal components of security and to argue simultaneously that environmental security occurs within the context of a "comprehensive" understanding of security. This is a valid position, and the eco-cultural paradigm (outlined later in this chapter) avoids this problem by considering environmental threats as both ultimate and proximate causes of insecurity.[4] Solutions must entail an appreciation of the concrete social, economic, and cultural contexts in which threats to security develop (Johnston 1994; Davidson 1994; Sponsel 1995).

Daniel Deudney (1990, 1991, 1994) presents a particularly critical analysis of the weaknesses inherent in efforts to portray environmental problems as potential security issues. He is especially concerned about the social, political, and military implications of conceptualizing environmental issues and conflict within this framework. Deudney (1990) argues that it is misleading to link concepts which share few of the same definitional, normative, or analytical components. He also asserts that it is confusing to equate instances of environmental degradation to security because the two issues differ with regard to the type and source of threat involved, the degree of intentionality, and the types of organizations involved (Deudney 1990).

Moreover, Deudney (1990) believes that the "associated mindsets" of conventional security and discussions regarding environmental quality are fundamentally different as well, which serves to further complicate attempts to link coherently the two phenomena. He contends that, although thinking about environmental problems globally is important, advocates of environmental security often commit what he refers to as the "error of aggreglobalism," which Deudney defines as "the exaggeration of global interdependencies that result from piling semirelated problems into a single syndrome" (Deudney 1994, p. 81). Another aspect of his critique is that environmental degradation is not likely to be the primary source of conflict and instability in the future (Deudney 1990). Finally, he asserts that advocates of an environmental security paradigm do not clearly articulate its relationship to other paradigms such as that of sustainable development or conceptions about intergenerational equity (Deudney 1994).

On the surface, this appears to be a compelling indictment of environmental security. Indeed, Deudney's analysis implicitly questions the utility of systematic, analytical investigation to explore the relationships between environmental damage and social, economic, political, and cultural devastation. At its core, however, Deudney's perspective relies on a narrow and limited interpretation of security.

Deudney tacitly acknowledges that the world is different today, and that the global community is presented with numerous, unprecedented challenges to ecosystem health and sustainability. An uncomfortable tension exists, however, in that Deudney acknowledges these changes in the state of the world, and simultaneously utilizes a traditional, realist paradigmatic framework of analysis that is presented as immutable and static. Moreover, he assumes that security mechanisms are a wholly inappropriate response to environmental threats, and may, in fact, weaken the cause of environmentalism.

Contrary to Deudney's implication, to define certain instances of severe environmental degradation and resultant social and cultural destruction as security threats does not necessitate an exclusively military-strategic response. He refers to the attempts to link environmental protection and conflict as the "blood soaked garments" of environmentalism (Deudney 1991). This phrase, while dramatic and critical, reveals a firm reliance on a traditional, time worn understanding of the scope and definition of security studies. By contrast, security, as it is understood in the alternative model of eco-cultural security, is not restricted to the realm of state-centric political subjects of violence, stability, overt conflict, and the defense of territorial and domestic sovereignty.

ADVOCATES OF ENVIRONMENTAL SECURITY

As Table 12.1 indicates, theoretical approaches to environmental and security issues may pertain to one or more of four categories: (1) the normative, definitional, and analytical "mismatch" between environmental protection and national security; (2) the relationship between war (and war preparations) and environmental degradation; conflicts over scarce resources, i.e., water conflicts (Lipschutz 1992; Gleick 1993, 1994; Lowi 1993); or environmental change that indirectly causes or exacerbates conflict when it occurs in tandem with other factors such as population growth or involuntary migration (Homer-Dixon 1993 a,b, 1994 a,b; Myers 1993; Westing 1986, 1994); (3) the existence of human and environmental rights[5] to environmental security, and by extension, an "environmental security ethic"; and (4) the various effects of environmental change (natural, human-induced or a combination thereof) that jeopardize cultural integrity and environmental sustainability (Miller and Gomez 1993; Johnston 1994; Sponsel 1995).

The first key perspective, a critical approach to subsuming environmental protection issues within the rubric of security, has been

Table 12.1. Approaches to Environment and Security

Theoretical Approach	*Key Perspectives*
Environmental issues are not subsumed within national security rubric	Environment and security share few normative, conceptual, definitional linkages; efforts to link them are misguided and may weaken the cause of environmentalism; military mechanisms poorly suited to respond to ecological problems
"Environmental Scarcities"/ Ecological Degradation and Conflict, War, and War Preparations	Deliberate wartime damage; Severe resource scarcity or degradation may precipate acute conflict, or result in socio-political or economic breakdown.
Human Rights / Environmental Rights	Environmental rights are a prerequisite to fulfillment of other basic human rights.
Eco-Cultural Security	Effects of sever environmental disruption violate cultural rights and customary law, dismantle cultural cohesion, and may eradicate cultures by damaging elements of the natural environment central to cultural identity and practices; impetus for forced migration ("environmental refugees"). Includes a moral obligation to protect nature and humanity; conservationist ethic; and premised on notion of 'intergenerational equity.'

outlined in the previous section of this chapter. In addition to briefly reviewing research in the next two categories of environment and security scholarship, this chapter suggests that the fourth category, that of eco-cultural security, may provide more promise for theory building and policy making, the creation of legal human rights instruments, and efforts to achieve "sustainable development."

In the late 1970s, and in the wake of the pessimistic report *Global 2000*, many pioneers in the areas of environmental law, international human rights, public policy and security studies had already foreseen the need to reconsider the concept of security in light of global environmental developments which threatened to undermine the earth's ability to sustain life (Brown 1977, 1986; Stephenson 1988; Milbrath 1989; Timoshenko 1992; Mische 1992). *Global 2000* warned that due to increased pressures on the earth's resources as a result of rapid population growth, the widening gap between rich and poor, and the severe deterioration of ecosystems resulting in increased vulnerability to natural and human disasters, states must cooperate and make difficult political choices to avoid future ecological and societal instability (Kegley and Witkopff 1988). More recently, scientific reports and policy recommendations regarding the depletion of the ozone layer, the potential effects of global climate change, rapacious deforestation, soil erosion, desertification, and water and air pollution (IPCC 1990; Schwartz 1994) have created additional impetus to respond properly to environmental changes that threaten human survival and may engender conflict. Many advocates of environmental security recognize the need to draw upon a broad range of disciplines to solve these new challenges to global environmental and cultural security (Kolodzieg 1992).

The quest for human security today requires more than merely reconstructing the notion of security while simultaneously relying on exclusively realist[6] or neorealist assumptions about the state and the international system (Buzan 1991; Tickner 1995). Some international relations scholars contend that security, historically framed in its "masculine" terminology and subject matter, has had a leveling effect in terms of underlying, gendered sources of inequality and vulnerability (Tickner 1995). Furthermore, security, when viewed through the statist, "neutral" and "objective" lens of the realist paradigm, only serves to perpetuate a mythical, "partial" view of reality (Tickner 1995). Other scholars argue that the post-cold war world presents unprecedented challenges to state sovereignty, identity, stability, maintenance of peace, and preservation of cultural integrity that are not satisfactorily explained or understood vis-à-vis the traditional security model (Buzan 1991; Miller and Gomez 1993; Lynn-Jones and Miller 1995). An emerging trend in recent environment and security research is to define the dimensions of the security framework as inclusively as is necessary to incorporate the complexities and interconnectedness of global environmental issues and their social context.

Environmental Degradation and Acute Conflict

The most common references to (and criticisms of) the environmental security literature pertain to the contributions of researchers in the second general category of environment and security: the relationships between severe environmental degradation and conflict. In general, these scholars contend that the concept of security must be reevaluated or enlarged to include both indirect and direct effects of conflict on the environment, as well as the possibility that instances of severe environmental scarcities will indirectly cause or exacerbate preexisting conflict (Westing 1986; Buzan 1991; Homer-Dixon 1993a,b; Tuchman Matthews 1994; Romm 1993). This category also includes analyses of resource scarcity conflicts, such as those over water resources in the Middle East and North Africa (Lipschutz 1992; Lowi 1993; Gleick 1993, 1994). In this way, environmental degradation is viewed as either the instrument through which war or conflict is waged, the subject of contention and hostility (scarce resources), or the catalyst for social, political, cultural, and economic breakdown. Accordingly, the advocates of situating analyses of environmental issues within the framework of conflict concentrate primarily on three issues: (1) the global nature of environmental threats to ecosystem health and well-being; (2) the universal qualities of security and its relationship to conflict over natural resources and (3) the need to mobilize international efforts and resources to mitigate the effects of vast environmental degradation.

Leading empirical research in this area[7] indicates that environmental degradation, increased resource demand from population growth, and unequal distribution of resources, are three critical aspects of "environmental scarcity," whose combined interactions affect millions of people.[8] There is preliminary evidence to suggest that the state is increasingly vulnerable to the social and political effects of "environmental scarcities," and that the capacity of states and their societies to adapt to environmental change may be further complicated and undermined by these environmental scarcities (Homer-Dixon 1994). Although many scholars in this category of environment and security relationships argue that severe environmental degradation and scarcities are likely to result in interstate wars, Homer-Dixon (1994) and his colleagues contend that environmental scarcity is likely to result in "diffuse, persistent and subnational" conflicts. Furthermore, as environmental scarcity passes a "threshold" of severity or irreversibility, it becomes an *exogenous* influence on society, and cannot be subordinated to the realm of institutional or policy mechanisms (Homer-Dixon 1994). Although not without its critics (Deudney 1994; Levy 1994, 1994), this scholarship represents a significant advancement in the information available regarding the interrelationships between environmental and social change.

Human Rights, Environmental Protection, and Ecological Security

Another theoretical approach to examining the intricate connection between humans and the natural environment situates environmental and security issues within the framework of international human rights. This "third generation" of human rights includes *inter alia* the rights to a sound environment (Timoshenko 1992). Principle I of the Stockholm Declaration states, for example, that "Man has the fundamental rights to freedom, equality and adequate conditions of life, in an environment of a quality that permits a life of dignity and well-being . . . " (United Nations Conference on the Human Environment 1972). The United Nations International Covenant on Social, Economic, and Cultural Rights has specified, in Article 25 of the Universal Declaration of Human Rights, that a standard of living adequate for the health and well-being of individuals and communities exists in the goal of "the improvement of all aspects of environmental and industrial hygiene" (Uibupuu 1977). In addition, many indigenous leaders, through the Working Group on Indigenous Populations, which is affiliated with the United Nations Comission on Human Rights, have written a "Draft Declaration on the Rights of Indigenous Peoples." This draft declaration contains many references to the importance of linking the protection of environmental sustainability and cultural rights (Draft Declaration on the Rights of Indigenous Peoples 1993). Moreover, the United Nations Conference on Environment and Development (UNCED) Agenda 21, in chapter 26, "Recognizing and Strengthening the Role of Indigenous People and Their Communities" affirms that "In view of the interrelationship between the natural environment and its sustainable development and the cultural, social, economic and physical well-being of indigenous people, national and international efforts to implement environmentally sound and sustainable development should recognize, accommodate, promote and strengthen the role of indigenous peoples and their communities" (UNCED, Agenda 21, 1992). These international declarations illustrate the proposition that the protection of the health, stability and safety of the ecosystem is an essential prerequisite to the attainment of other basic human rights (United Nations Economic and Social Council 1994).

The principle of a "right to environment" maintains that all human beings have an intrinsic, inalienable right to live in an environment adequate for their continued health and well-being, but in addition, have a moral and ethical responsibility to ensure the protection and preservation of the global environment for the benefit of present and future generations (Brown Weiss 1992; Timoshenko 1992;

Nickel and Viola 1994). The full recognition and legal protection of the environment may imply the protection of cultural heritage and intellectual property (Herz 1993; UN Chronicle 1993a,b). The notion of responsibility for future generations is referred to as "intergenerational equity," and by definition, requires equal access to and enjoyment of a clean, healthy environment among generations and between members of a generation regardless of nationality (Brown Weiss 1992). According to this perspective, natural resource exploitation, depletion, and environmental degradation violate the principles of "intergenerational equity" and unfairly interfere with the rights of future generations to enjoy the benefits of the world's resources (Brown Weiss 1992).

Advocates of the "right to environment" approach to environmental security contend that a clean, stable, healthy environment (environmental protection and conservation) is a fundamental right because it is a necessary precondition to the fulfillment of other basic human rights. Some scholars assert that existing international human rights procedures can (and should) be used to promote and protect rights to environmental security (Clay 1993; Timoshenko 1992). They do acknowledge, however, that such procedures are largely remedial in nature and would not necessarily serve to prevent harm. Moreover, human rights doctrine, by definition, applies to human interests and may not be conceptually appropriate in an environmental context.

The promotion of a substantive environmental right to security offers a comprehensive approach to meaningful and effective environmental protection. Nevertheless, several unresolved conceptual challenges to the "human rights to environmental security" perspective limit its theoretical coherence. These challenges include: (1) the *definition* of a healthy, balanced, and secure environment; (2) the relationship between environmental security and "sustainable development;" (3) the position of environmental security within the concept of *comprehensive* security; (4) the implementation and enforcement of environmental rights to security; and (5) the scope of the practical applicability of rights to environmental security (e.g., all humankind, the protection of outer space). The implicit danger is that the notion of human and environmental rights to security will be little more than a rhetorical expression since these key conceptual difficulties have yet to be adequately resolved, especially in view of post-cold war realities.

There are several normative and practical problems underlying the concept of a right to environmental security. In the first place, although a right to a secure and healthy environment may be intuitively appealing, to a deep ecologist, for example, it may be deemed offensive. This human rights perspective demonstrates an anthropocentric tendency to consider environmental protection through a utilitarian framework which, while resting on a series of arguments concerned with the preservation of ecosystem sustainability, ultimately reduces the goal of ecosystem preservation to serve human interests. Generally speaking, this type of preservationist appeal moves from a narrow concern for the specific utilization of nature, to the indirect importance of nature as integral to the stability of the ecosystem to support and enhance the quality and productivity of human life. Accordingly, efforts to achieve environmental and cultural security may be implicitly undermined. Activities that necessarily involve resource over-exploitation and environmental degradation, for example, are implicitly condoned because all nonhuman components of the earth are considered in terms of their practical and instrumental values to human well-being. The inclusion of environmental security under the rubric of an international human rights doctrine is justified on the grounds that these policies would benefit human society.

Another weakness inherent in this discussion of international human rights to environmental security pertains to the non-justiciability of a human right to a healthy environment. An environmental right (to security) per se does not exist as either a recognized or an enforceable international law (Sands 1993). In addition, the current structure of the international system, as defined in terms of state sovereignty, further complicates efforts to identify and hold accountable the party responsible for degrading the environment or destroying a group's ability to sustain itself and its culture (Schwartz 1994; Sponsel 1995). To a certain degree, all states have been responsible for committing some sort of transboundary pollution or environmental damage, thus little incentive exists to make such claims against another state.

Eco-cultural Security

The fourth category of environment and security relationships is eco-cultural security. The eco-cultural approach to international security encompasses the concept of human rights to a clean and healthy environment and situates it within a broader analytical framework that acknowledges the importance of preventing future environmental harm and its effects on cultural security. If severe environmental harm compromises a group's fundamental cohesion, traditional practices, customs, language, and homeland, then a security threat exists. Moreover, this situation may lead to conflict with other groups over scarce resources, or intragroup conflicts, often due to rapid population growth and increased pressures on already marginalized lands (Westing 1986; Homer-Dixon 1993a,b, 1994a,b). At issue is a conflict between individual and communal rights, and also between diverse, often misunderstood cultural practices and contemporary development schema that harm natural systems (Kesmanee 1994; Prill-Brett 1994).[9] The eco-cultural security model focuses on a dilemma of environmental justice, namely, the distribution of common resources. What is the "proper" ordering of needs and values given competition over limited resources, claims of cultural preservation, and the rights of individuals and communities to cultural survival with dignity?

Conventional conceptions of security narrowly focus on conflict, strategic-military issues, international and domestic stability, and freedom-from-violence. This theoretical framework cannot adequately address ecological and cultural security concerns. Environmental abuses which rob the soil, air, and water of their balance, health, and vitality, simultaneously rob human societies of the same key elements of survival. The problem involves a series of social, political, and cultural issues: a failure to acknowledge or accept the confluence of morality and international politics; the failure to recognize the underlying environmental problems forcing many people away from their traditional homelands; the failure to consider the survival of cultural diversity and rights to self-determination and sovereignty as important as ecosystem biodiversity; and the failure of international law and institutions to redress the grievances of those who by virtue of their unequal power and status vis-à-vis the international system are marginalized. These groups are excluded, not only from the debate, but also from the right to security and protection. The structural composition of the international system (and the traditional concept of nation-state sovereignty), and the manner in which power is distributed throughout the international system impedes the ability of indigenous communities to prevent or respond to much of the environmental harm that threatens their existence. These principles of state sovereignty and economic self-reliance thwart the efforts of human rights activists and environmentalists, as many states continue to exploit their own people and their natural resource base simultaneously.

A global pattern has emerged in which a variety of practices are systematically destroying indigenous language, culture, and the natural resource base. These activities include massive mining[10] and logging operations,[11] industrial pollution, development activities (e.g., the construction of dams and reservoirs, and hydroelectric power) and the activities related to war[12] and war preparations (such as nuclear testing and the storage and disposal of radioactive waste). These activities, alone or occurring in tandem with natural disasters, such as floods, earthquakes or famines, serve to unravel the cultural fabric of many communities dependent upon the environment to survive.

Systematic investigation of endangered peoples worldwide illustrates a widespread pattern of human-induced cultural and environmental destruction (Miller and Gomez 1993; Wilmer 1993; Davidson 1994). This research indicates that the confluence of ecosystemic and cultural damage may stem from a variety of factors: (1) the perceived incompatibility between the process of state-building and development and the continued survival of indigenous peoples; (2) the utilization of economic prosperity (usually through resource and energy exploitation) as the primary yardstick of "progress;" and (3) the belief that many intrastate conflicts result from indigenous insubordination rather than from violations of land, language, and religious rights (Clay 1993; Sponsel 1995). For many political elites, the preservation of environmental and cultural rights to self-determination and security of indigenous peoples are not compatible with, or easily reconciled with, perceived national security or economic interests (Clay 1993). This tension can become greater in situations involving the rights to and distribution of valuable or strategic natural resources. The efforts to preserve cultures and protect communities from eradication, therefore, must be premised on: (1) the rights of self-determination, control, and ownership of traditional homelands; (2) the rights to religious, linguistic, and cultural expression; and (3) the acceptance by the international community of indigenous participation in the development of laws and policies (Curtis 1992; Sponsel 1995).

The eco-cultural paradigm of environmental security provides a theoretical framework in which the results of human-induced environmentally destructive practices and projects may be identified and analyzed. The eco-cultural approach assumes that a combination of factors undermine the ability of indigenous communities to fend off threats to their homelands, resources, and security. These factors range from the structural or systemic attributes of the international system and the relative bargaining power and influence of indigenous people vis-à-vis the rest of the world, to the level of state elites and non-indigenous people who profit from the status-quo or are struggling to survive in the face of competition over limited resources, to the individual characteristics of the indigenous people themselves (Clay 1993; Homer-Dixon 1993; Sponsel 1995; Davidson 1994).

Some scholars claim that indicators which assess physical characteristics, governing property laws, extent of cultural freedom, conflicts and alliances, and migratory trends of indigenous communities can constitute a basis for analysis of the communities (e.g., Clay 1993). In turn, this evaluation can identify the cultures whose survival and quality of life is most severely threatened. Moreover, it may help to identify under which circumstances these threats are made manifest and how to predict and prevent future threats. Sadly, however, such instances of ecological and cultural security abound.[13]

At the Intersection of Cultural and Environmental Insecurity: Environmental Refugees

In many less developed countries, government policies that permit over-exploitation and degradation of the natural resource base have led to the forced migration of many already poor, subsistence farmers and tribal communities to even more fragile, marginal lands (El-Hinnawi 1989; Jacobson 1988). One of the most visible symptoms of the intersection of environmental and cultural destruction is the existence of the so-called environmental refugee or environmentally displaced (Jacobson 1988; Westing 1992; Trolldalen 1992; Schwartz 1993; Fornos 1993).

Environmental refugees are forced to flee from their traditional homeland because of a serious change, or "environmental disruption," in the nature of their environment due to natural disasters exacerbated by human activities, the construction of dams or irrigation systems, toxic contamination, rampant deforestation and resultant erosion. These conditions have endangered or adversely affected the quality of their life and their ability to survive.[14] Although the "environmental refugee" is a somewhat controversial issue (Deudney 1991; McGregor 1994; Suhrke 1994), empirical evidence reveals that millions of people may be displaced primarily as a result of desertification and deforestation (Jacobson 1988; Trolldalen 1992; Westing 1992, 1994). International assistance and protection will probably "miss the mark" in the case of these environmentally displaced people because they do not fall within the traditional international legal definition of "refugee" and because there is not a clearly defined environmental right, per se (Timoshenko 1992; Loescher 1995; Weiner 1995). Existing laws must be altered and the traditional, narrow understanding of the scope of security issues must be reevaluated to incorporate and protect the needs of these new types of refugees (Helton 1994).

There are many examples of environmental refugees. The construction of dams in India, for example, has displaced some 1.2 million people and has destroyed hundreds of villages, traditional homelands, and land presumed to be sacred by the inhabitants (Maloney 1991). In the Chittagong Hills of Bangladesh, the construction of the Kaptai Dam uprooted more than 100,000 indigenous peoples and flooded forty percent of the arable farmable land in the region without much warning. The government in Bangladesh has promoted discriminatory policies which have resulted in the virtual extinction of the Hill peoples' culture and more than 50,000 have fled to India (Davidson 1994). In Canada, the construction of hydroelectric power plants have forcibly relocated many indigenous Inuit communities and deprived them of their rights to traditional homelands and access to natural resources and areas deemed sacred for religious and cultural purposes. Since the 1970s, the Cree in Quebec have also witnessed the destruction of traditional hunting and fishing sites, the contamination of land, water, and fish stocks with mercury, the destruction of spawning grounds and disruption of migration patterns of various animals, and the forced relocation of several villages because of the dams constructed by Hydro-Quebec (Clay 1993; Davidson 1994).

The fate of another indigenous community, the Penan people in Malaysia, is also uncertain. Enormous logging operations and forestry ventures in Malaysia, responsible for the highest rate of deforestation in the world, have completely deforested one-third of the forested land in the state of Sarawak in just two decades. The logging operations remove the forest canopy and expose the soil to rain, dramatically increasing the rate of erosion. The local streams and rivers have become polluted, killing fish and other aquatic life. Although the government has acknowledged that soil erosion and siltation are paramount concerns, the lucrative logging concessions, owned by a few political families in Malaysia, continue to destroy the environment and have threatened the security and existence of the Penan people (Clay 1993).

The Penan have a spiritual and physical dependence on nature due to their subsistence practices and religious tenets. The logging activities and associated development, however, have a destructive impact on the sustainability of the traditional Penan territory and culture. Penan are forcibly evicted from their homelands and have been imprisoned for expressing opposition against the activities of logging concessions (Hitchcock 1994). Not only will the Penan lose many species of plants used for medicinal and religious purposes, they will lose control over their natural resources, in general, forcing them to abandon their traditional relationship with the environment. The intrusion of massive logging ventures, such as those in Penan territory, accelerate the assimilation and acculturation of indigenous tribes like the Penan, and destroy familial cohesion by luring away family members in search of more lucrative migratory wage labor.

CONCLUSION

The international community is faced with an unprecedented challenge to respond to new threats to cultural and environmental security and to develop strategies for predicting and preventing future harm. Creative policy solutions may include the establishment of cooperatives, sharing environmentally appropriate technology, mapping ancestral indigenous territories to facilitate and protect land claims, and the creation of protected reserves where appropriate, to mention a few.

The preservation of the natural environment and cultural identities depends, to a certain degree, on the international acceptance of a theory of environmental ethics, such as an holistic, eco-cultural security approach. Eco-cultural security includes nonhuman natural values, traditional human-centered obligations and security issues, as well as moral obligations to protect the environment. The preservation of sacred forests, for example, would be mandated out of a fundamental sense of moral responsibility to preserve nature directly and to ensure the continued security and well-being of its inhabitants. According to this eco-cultural security perspective, the issues are no longer framed in terms of simple economic development and military security concerns, on the one hand, and the protection of cultural and environmental diversity, on the other.

Instead, the conception of a moral sense of obligation to nature necessarily complicates the environmental security equation. A less anthropocentric system of ethics focused on eco-cultural security simultaneously justifies human rights, environmentalist, and security positions. In this manner, the eco-cultural model constitutes a potential starting point for international dialogue concerning development policy and security issues, tradeoffs between competing groups over resources, and issues of global equity. The price ought to be shared internationally for the overwhelming cost incurred to the environment as a result of unfettered development and exploitative practices. Legal and normative conflicts will continue to occur over the "proper" hierarchical ordering of needs and values in the face of competition over limited resources and claims of cultural self-preservation. It is likely the incidence of environmental/culture security conflicts will only continue to escalate as the quality and quantity of natural resources continue to diminish.

NOTES

1. For a variety of disciplinary approaches to the topic of environment and security: Boulding (1992); Brock (1991); Brown Weiss (1992); Buzan (1991); Clarke (1993); Demko and Wood (1994); Der Derian (1995); Fornos (1993); Gleick (1991); Kakonen (1994); Kesmanee (1994); Kraft (1994); McGregor (1994); Miller (1993); Sands (1993); Stephenson (1988); Suhrke (1994); Tickner (1995); Westing (1986).

2. Several international relations scholars have argued against the classical state-centered definitions of security and favor instead a more comprehensive, "world order" approach to security, or one based on the individual instead of the state (Booth and Smith 1991; Klare and Thomas 1991; Walker 1988; Falk 1992)

3. An "environmental refugee" has been defined by Essam El-Hinnawi as refugees "who have been forced to leave their traditional habitat, temporarily or permanently, because of a marked environmental disruption (natural and/or triggered by people) that jeopardized their existence and/or seriously affected the quality of their life." See also Fornos 1992.

4. For an explanation of ultimate and proximate factors related to environmental degradation, see Shaw (1989).

5. An extensive literature has developed concerning the confluence between environmental and human rights. See, especially, Edith Brown Weiss 1992; Nickel and Viola 1994.

6. For an excellent, critical overview of the multiplicity of "realisms" see Der Derian 1995. Although Der Derian (1995) cautions against the tendency to consider "realism" as a "coherent school" of thought, "realism" is generally considered to be state-centric, with an emphasis on power politics, the balance of power, conflict and diplomatic relations between states (Alker and Biersteker 1995). "Neorealism," considered by many to be an attempt to "advance" realism and make it more "scientific," is also centered on the state as the primary unit of analysis, and focuses on the creation and analysis of theories of war and strife (Alker and Biersteker 1995).

7. This section summarizes some of the key findings identified by the researchers in the "Environmental Change and Acute Conflict" project led by Thomas Homer-Dixon at the University of Toronto.

8. A major finding by Homer-Dixon and his colleagues has been the identification of *multiple* types of "environmental scarcities," rather than focusing entirely on environmental degradation (Homer-Dixon 1994).

9. For an interesting analysis of the cultural perception of risk with regard to environmental hazards and culturally sensitive international conservation strategies, see Kottak and Costa (1993).

10. The Roxby/Downs Mine/Olympic Dam, a rich source of uranium, has destroyed a sacred area of "mound spring" which is of profound significance to local aborigines in Arabana, Oceania. The Olympic Dam operates under the cloak of secrecy, and prohibits the Kokatha people access to sacred sites crucial to their cultural and religious identity (Clay 1993; Davidson 1994).

11. In West Papua, logging operations have destroyed all but a small area of the Moi rain forest, and consequently, have disrupted the Moi's livelihood, cultural cohesion, and continuity, and has ruined many sacred sites in the forest (Clay 1993; Davidson 1994).

12. For example, in Vietnam and Cambodia, the lingering effects of the war, napalm bombing, and chemical defoliation of the land continue to threaten the survival of tribal peoples. The full extent of the ecological damage caused by the burning of the oil fields in Kuwait during the Persian Gulf War is unclear.

13. See, for example, Catanese 1991; Clarke 1993; Maloney 1991; Sanders 1991; UN Chronicle 1993 a,b.

14. The Natural Heritage Institute and Universities Field Staff International have published numerous excellent case studies and empirical reports concerning the complex interrelationship between issues such as involuntary migration (environmental refugees) in Haiti, Africa, Brazil, and India due to environmentally harmful development projects. See, for example, Catanese (1991); Tamondong-Helin and Helin (1990); Sanders (1990); and Maloney (1990).

REFERENCES

Alker, Hayward, and Theodore Bierseker. 1995. "The Dialectics of World Order: Notes for a Future Archaeologist of International Savior Faire." In *International Theory: Critical Investigations.* James Der Derian, ed. New York: New York University Press.

Booth, Ken, and Steve Smith, eds. 1995. *International Relations Theory Today.* University Park: The Pennsylvania State University Press.

Boulding, Elise. 1992. *New Agendas for Peace Research: Conflict and Security Reexamined.* Boulder and London: Lynne Rienner Publishers.

Brock, Lothar. 1991. "Peace Through Parks: The Environment on the Peace Research Agenda." *Journal of Peace Research* 28, 407–423.

Brown, Lester R. et al., eds. 1986. *State of the World 1986.* New York: Norton.

Brown, Lester R. 1977. Redefining National Security. Worldwatch Paper #14, October, 1977.

Brown Weiss, Edith. 1992. *Environmental Change and International Law: New Challenges and Dimensions.* Tokyo: UN University Press.

Buzan, Barry. 1991. *People, States, and Fear: An Agenda for International Security Studies in the Post-Cold War Era,* second edition. Boulder: Lynne Rienner Publishers.

Catanese, Anthony V. 1991. Field Staff Report No. 17. Haiti's Refugees: Political, Economic, Environmental. Universities Field Staff International and Heritage Institute.

Clarke, Michael. 1993. *New Perspectives on Security.* London and New York: Brassey's.

Clay, Jason W. 1993. "Looking back to Go Forward: Predicting and Preventing Human Rights Violations." In *State of the Peoples: A Global Human Rights Report on Societies in Danger.* Marc S. Miller, ed. Boston: Beacon Press.

Curtis, Sue Ann. 1992. "Cultural Relativism and Risk Assessment Strategies for Federal Projects." *Human Organization* 51, 1.

Davidson, Art. 1993. *Endangered Peoples.* San Francisco: Sierra Club Books.

Demko, George S., and William B. Wood, eds. 1994. "Introduction: International Relations Through the Prism of Geography." In *Reordering the World: Geopolitical Perspectives of the 21st Century.* Boulder: Westview.

Der Derian, James, ed. 1995. *International Theory: Critical Investigations.* Washington Square, New York: New York University Press.

Deudney, Daniel. 1994. "Ultimate Security: The Environmental Basis of Political Stability." (Review) Issues in *Science and Technology* 11, 81–84.

Deudney, Daniel. 1991. "Environment and Security: Muddled Thinking." *The Bulletin of Atomic Scientists* 47, 3, 22–29.

Deudney, Daniel. 1990. "The Case Against Linking Environmental Degradation and National Security." *Millennium* 19, 3, 461–476.

Draft Declaration on the Rights of Indigenous Peoples. 1993. Miller et al. 1993. *State of the Peoples: A Global Human Rights Report on Societies in Danger.* Boston: Beacon Press.

Durailappah, Anathn K. 1993. *Global Warming and Economic Development: A Holistic Approach to International Policy, Cooperation and Coordination.* Boston: Kluwer Academic Publishers.

El-Hinnawi, Essam. 1989. *Environmental Refugees.* Nairobi: United Nations Environment Programme.

Falk, Richard. 1992. *The Western State System.* Princeton, N.J.: Princeton University Center of International Studies.

Fornos, Werner. 1993. "Desperate Departures: The Flight of Environmental Refugees: Vulnerable Yet Unrecognized." Paper presented at the U.N. Expert Group Meeting on Population, Distribution, and Migration, 18–22 January, Santa Cruz, Bolivia.

Gleick, Peter H. 1991. "Environment and Security: The Clear Connection." *The Bulletin of Atomic Scientists* 47, 3, 17–21.

Gleick, Peter H. 1993. "Water and Conflict: Fresh Water Resources and International Security." *International Security* 18, 79–112.

Gleick, Peter H. 1994. "Reducing the Risks of Conflict Over Fresh Water Resources in the Middle East," 41–54. Issac and Shuval. eds. *Water and Peace in the Middle East.* Elsevier Science B.V.

Haftendorn, Helga. 1991. "The Security Puzzle: Theory-Building and Discipline-Building in International Security." *International Studies Quarterly* 35, 3–17.

Helton, Arthur C. 1994. "Displacement and Human Rights: Current Dilemmas in Refugee Protection." *Journal of International Affairs* 47, 379–398.

Herz, Richard. 1993. "Legal Protection for Indigenous Cultures: Sacred Sites and Communal Rights." *Virginia Law Review* 79, 3, p. 691-716.

Homer-Dixon, Thomas F. 1994a. "Environmental Scarcities and Violent Conflict: Evidence from Cases." *International Security* 19, 5–40.

Homer-Dixon, Thomas F. 1994b. "Environmental Scarcity and Intergroup Conflict." In Michael T. Klare and Daniel C. Thomas, eds. *World Security.* New York: St. Martin's Press.

Homer-Dixon, Thomas F. 1993a. "Environmental Scarcity and Global Security." Headline Series. Foreign Policy Association, No. 300, fall 1993.

Homer-Dixon, Thomas F., Jeffrey H. Boutwell, and George W. Rathjens. 1993b. "Environmental Change and Violent Conflict." *Scientific American*, 38–45, February 1993.

Hurrell, Andrew. 1994. "A Crisis of Ecological Viability? Global Environmental Change and the Nation State." *Political Studies*, 42: 146–65.

Intergovernmental Panel on Climate Change (IPCC). 1990. Climate Change: The IPCC Scientific Assessment: Final Report of the Working Group I. New York: Cambridge University Press.

International Covenant on the Rights of Indigenous Nations. Authorized Version Initialized July 28, 1994. Geneva, Switzerland. The Fourth World Documentation Project: Olympia, Washington.

Jacobson, Jodi L. 1988. Environmental Refuges: A Yardstick of Habitability. WorldWatch paper 86. Washington, D.C.: WorldWatch Institute.

Johnston, Beverly Rose. 1994. *Who Pays the Price? The Socio-cultural Context of the Environmental Crisis.* Washington, D.C.: Island Press.

Kakonen, Jyrki, ed. 1994. *Green Security or Militarized Environment?* Brookfield: Dartmouth Publishing Company Limited.

Kakonen, Jyrki, ed. 1992. *Perspectives on Environmental Conflict and International Politics.* London and New York: Pinter Publishers.

Kegley, Charles, and Eugene R. Witkopff. 1988. *The Global Agenda: Issues and Perspectives.* Second Edition. New York: Random House.

Kesmanee, Chupinit. 1994. "Dubious Development Concepts in the Thai Highlands: Chao Khao in Transition." *Law and Society Review* 28, 3.

Klare, Michael T., and Daniel C. Thomas, eds. 1991. *World Security: Challenges for a New Century.* New York: St. Martin's Press.

Kolodzieg, Edward A. 1992. "Renaissance in Security Studies? Caveat Lector!" *International Studies Quarterly* 36, n. 4, 421–439.

Kottak, C. P. and Costa, A. C. G. 1993. "Ecological Awareness, Environmental Action, and International Conservation Strategy." *Human Organization,* 52, 4, 335–343.

Kraft, Michael T., ed. 1994. Peace and World Security Studies: A Curriculum Guide. Sixth Edition.

Leibler, Anthony. 1992. "Deliberate Wartime Environmental Damage: New Challenges for International Law." *California Western Law Journal* 23, 67–137.

Levy, Marc. 1994. Global Environmental Degradation, National Security and U.S. Foreign Policy, Working Paper No. 9. Project on the Changing Security Environment and American National Interests, John M. Olin Institute for Strategic Studies, Harvard University.

Levy, Marc. 1995. "Time for a Third Wave of Environment and Security Scholarship?" Environmental Change and Security Project: Report, Issue 1 (spring 1995), Woodrow Wilson Center, pp. 44–46.

Lipschutz, Ronnie D. 1992. What Resources Will Matter? Environmental Degradation As A Security Issue. Paper prepared for a symposium on "Environmental Dimensions of Security." Annual meeting of the American Association for the Advancement of Science, Chicago.

Loescher, Gil. 1993. *Beyond Charity: International Cooperation and the Global Refugee Crisis.* New York: Oxford University Press.

Lowi, Miriam R. 1993. "Bridging the Divide: Transboundary Resource Disputes and the Case of the West Bank Water." *International Security* 18, 113–138.

Lynn-Jones, Sean, and Steven E. Miller, eds. 1995. *Global Dangers: Changing Dimensions of International Security.* London: MIT Press.

Maloney, Clarence. 1991. Field Staff Reports No. 14. Environmental and Project Displacement of Population in India. Part I: Development and Deracination. and Part II: Land and Water. University Field Staff International and Natural Heritage Institute.

McGregor, JoAnn. 1994. "Climate Change and Involuntary Migration: Implication for Food Security." *Food Policy* 19, 120-132.

Milbrath, Lester. 1989. *Envisioning a Sustainable Society.* Albany: State University of New York Press.

Miller, Marc S., and Gale Goodwin Gomez, eds. 1993. *State of the Peoples: A Global Human Rights Report on Societies in Danger.* Boston: Beacon Press.

Mische, Patricia. 1992. "Security through Defending the Environment: Citizens Say Yes!" In *New Agendas for Peace Research,* ed. Elise Boulding. Boulder: Lynne Rienner.

Myers, Norman. 1993a. *Ultimate Security: The Environmental Basis of Political Stability.* New York: W.W. Horton.

Myers, Norman. 1993b. "Environmental Refugees in a Globally Warmed World." *Bioscience* 43, 752–762.

Nickel, James W., and Eduardo Viola. 1994. "Integrating Environmentalism and Human Rights." *Environmental Ethics* 16, 3, 265–275.

Plant, Glen. 1994. *Environmental Protection and the Law of War: A Fifth Geneva Convention of the Protection of the Environment in Time of Armed Conflict.* London and New York: Belhaven Press.

Prill-Brett, June. 1994. "Indigenous Land Rights and Legal Pluralism Among Philippine Highlanders." *Law and Society Review* 28, 3.

Romm, Joseph J. 1993. *Defending National Security: The Nonmilitary Aspects.* New York: Council on Foreign Relations Press.

Sanders, Thomas G. 1991. Field Staff Report No. 20 Northeast Brazilian Environmental Refugees: Part I: Why They Leave and Part II: Northeast Brazilian Environmental Refugees: Part II: Where They Go. University Field Staff International and the Natural Heritage Institute.

Sands, Philippe. 1993. "Enforcing Environmental Security." *Journal of International Affairs* 46, 367–390.

Schwartz, Michelle L. 1994. Report on Desertification and Migration: Mexico and the United States. Prepared for United States Commission on Immigration and Reform. Washington, D.C.: Natural Heritage Institute.

Shaw, R. Paul. 1989. "Rapid Population Growth and Environmental Degradation: Ultimate versus Proximate Factors." *Environmental Conservation* 16, 199–208.

Sponsel, Leslie. 1995. "The Killing Fields of the Brazilian and Venezuelan Amazon: The Continuing Destruction of the Yanomami and their Ecosystems by Illegal Gold Miners: Future Scenarios and Actions." In *The Knowledge to Act: Coming to Terms with Environmental and Human Rights,* ed. Pamela J. Puntenney. Paper presented at the American Anthropological Association Annual Conference, Atlanta, Georgia.

Stephenson, Carolyn M. 1988. "The Need For Alternative Forms of Security: Crises and Opportunities." *Alternatives* 8, 55–76.

Suhrke, Astri. 1994. "Environmental Degradation and Population Flows." *Journal of International Affairs* 47, 473–496.

Tamondong-Helin, Susan, and William Helin. 1991. Field Staff Report No. 22, Migration and the Environment: Interrelationships in Sub-Saharan Africa. Universities Field Staff International and Natural Heritage Institute.

Tickner, J. Ann. 1995. "Re-visiting Security." In *International Relations Theory Today,* eds. Ken Booth and Steve Smith. University Park, PA: Pennsylvania State University Press.

Tickner, J. Ann. 1995. "Has Morgenthau's Principles of Political Realism: A Feminist Reformulation" (1988). In *International Theory: Critical Investigations,* ed. James Der Derian. Washington Square, New York: New York University Press.

Timoshenko, Alexandre. 1992. "Ecological Security: Response to Global Challenges." In *Environmental Change and International Law: New Challenges and Dimensions,* ed. Edith Weiss Brown. UN University Press.

Trolldalen, Jon Martin. 1992. Environmental Refugees: A Discussion Paper. Working Paper in Resource and Environmental Geography, Series B. World Foundation for Environment and Development in cooperation with the Norwegian Refugee Council. Solo: Bergersens Tykkeri & Forlag.

Tuchman Matthews, Jessica. 1994. "The Environment and International Security." In World Security: Challenges for a New Century, eds. Michael T. Klare and Daniel C. Thomas. New York: St. Martin's Press.

Uibupuu, Henn-Juri. 1977. "Redefining Security." *International Security* 8, 129–153.

UN Chronicle. 1993a. "The Development Dilemma: Sustaining Resources, Improving Livelihoods." *UN Chronicle* 30, 45–48. United Nations Publications.

UN Chronicle. 1993b. "Conserving Heritage: Cultural and Intellectual Property Rights." *UN Chronicle* 30, 50–52.

United Nations Conference on the Human Environment. 1972. Stockholm, Sweden.

United Nations Economic and Social Council. 1994. Commission on Human Rights, Sub-Commission on Prevention of Discrimination of Minorities. Forty-sixth Session. "Review of Further Developments in Fields With Which the Sub-Commission Has Been Concerned: Human Rights and the Environment: Final Report prepared by Mrs. Fatma Zohra Ksentini, Special Rapporteur."

Walt, Steven M. 1991. "The Renaissance of Security Studies." *International Studies Quarterly* 35, 211–241.

Weiner, Myron. 1995. "Security, Stability, and International Migration." In *Global Dangers: Changing Dimensions of International Security*, eds. Sean M. Lynn-Jones and Steven E. Miller. Cambridge, Mass.: MIT Press.

Westing, Arthur H., ed. 1986. Global Resources and International Conflict. Stockholm International Peace Research Institute. Oxford and New York: Oxford University Press.

Westing, Arthur H. 1992. "Environmental Refugees: A Growing Category of Displaced Persons." *Environmental Conservation* 19, 201–207.

Westing, Arthur H. 1994. "Perspectives on Environmental Conflict and International Politics" (review). *Environment* 36, 30–32.

Wilmer, Franke. 1993. *The Indigenous Voice in World Politics: Since Time Immemorial.* Newbury Park and London: Sage Publications.

Conclusion: Obstacles to Achieving Sustainability*

GEORGE A. GONZALEZ

As Robert O. Vos points out in his introductory chapter, there are three dominant approaches to the issue of sustainability in the environmental literature and contemporary politics. The free-market approach to sustainability suggests that a sustainable society can be achieved by relying on the price signals provided by the market. These price signals alert us that a particular resource is becoming relatively scarce. In response to these price signals, societal actors take appropriate husbandry measures. Additionally, increasing prices associated with resource depletion will provide incentives to develop technologies that either create substitutes for the depleted resource, or induce a more efficient and sustainable utilization of the resource in question. Therefore, the key to achieving sustainability for free-market advocates is to establish property rights, and, subsequently, markets for natural resources. Through this creation and maintenance of markets we can harness the energy and ingenuity derived from the pursuit of self-interest, and channel this energy and ingenuity into the development of a sustainable society.

While the free-market advocates tout the infinite possibilities when humankind's intellect and initiative are tapped by market forces, ecological-science advocates, according to Vos, focus on the finite nature of the natural environment. Ecological-science advocates argue that regardless of the limitless potential of humanity, natural resources are

*I would like to thank Jezabel Montero, Sheldon Kamieniecki, Robert O. Vos, and Frank Janeczek for their insightful comments on previous drafts.

finite and that this human potential will invariably run up against the limitations of the environment. In light of these limitations, ecological-science advocates believe that there needs to be some type of intervention to ensure that economic and population growth do not overrun the capabilities of the earth to support life. Additionally, ecological-science proponents seriously question the ability of technology to overcome the constraints placed on humanity by nature. As such, they strongly caution against placing all of our faith in the creation of new technologies to rescue humankind from potential environmental disasters created by excessive exploitation and disregard for the limited capacities of environmental sinks to regenerate natural resources. Ecological-science advocates point to the difficulty of establishing property rights over several important resources, and they also point out the negative environmental effects of privatizing certain resources.

In sharp contrast to the free-market proponents and the ecological-science advocates who view nature and the environment as an instrument to be used for the benefit of humankind, deep ecologists, as Vos explains, contend that nature and the environment have subjectivity. In other words, nature and humankind have equal moral standing and should have equal legal standing. Therefore, for deep ecologists the exploitation and destruction of the natural world is unjust and immoral. Given their view of nature, sustainability from the deep ecologist perspective is about sustaining nature. It is not about sustainable human societies, and how to exploit nature for an infinite period of time. Deduced from their conception of sustainability is the deep ecologist's notion that humanity's existence should be congenial to sustaining nature and should cease to be exploitative of it. Hence, they propose that humankind develop an eco-centric ethos, and reconfigure human existence to co-exist harmoniously with the natural world.

This debate over sustainability exposes important obstacles that exist to our attaining a sustainable society. This chapter explores two major obstacles to establishing a sustainable society, namely the ideology of Liberalism and the political power of industry. First, however, the chapter reviews the major obstacles to sustainability as outlined in the book, as well as the reasons for optimism shared by the various contributors in the volume.

REVIEWING FLASHPOINTS OF CONTROVERSY

Within the debate over sustainability we have identified several key flashpoints of controversy. The controversy of risk assessment, for instance, is over whether risk-based methodologies can offer an effective and fair tool to measure environmental risk to humans and ecosystems, and therefore further sustainability. The flashpoint of alternative regulatory approaches is comprised of debates over the most effective means to internalize the costs of negative environmental externalities. These externalities pose serious and long-term threats to our environment and thus to sustainability. The controversy invoked by the environmental justice issue can potentially impugn the legitimacy, and hence undermine the effectiveness, of environmental public policy—a key vehicle to achieving sustainability (assuming, of course, some degree of government action is necessary). The dispute over public versus private control of the federal lands focuses upon how to manage most effectively, and make sustainable, those lands presently under the management of the federal government. The flashpoint of international trade and sustainable development grapples with the question of how and under what circumstances is free trade conducive to the development of environmentally sustainable societies. Finally, there is a serious question as to whether environmental issues should be incorporated into national security objectives and whether doing so would augment the development of sustainable societies.

The authors who explore these controversies uncover several potential obstacles to achieving a sustainable global society. Linder, for example, is skeptical of the ability of risk assessment methodologies to serve the ends of sustainability. He argues that the scientific concept of risk has historically been used to mask the influence and biases created by political interests and values. Interests and values which, according to Linder, are antithetical to any meaningful concept of environmental sustainability. Bryner points out that political opposition by industry prevents emission taxes—arguably the most effective regulatory means of forcing the internalization of the costs of negative environmental externalities—from being enacted. Bowman shows that previous research yields mixed findings with respect to whether there is any relationship between race, class, and the siting of waste dumps. These muddled results mean that issues of justice and equity will continue to fester. Hence, on the one hand, the legitimacy of environmental policy will continue to be questioned by those who suspect that racial and class biases are involved in the making of important environmental decisions. On the other hand, the inconclusive findings do not provoke decision makers to address the concerns and issues raised by environmental justice advocates since they remain unconvinced that these concerns and issues are reflected in the long-term pattern of, for example, waste dump sitings. Baden and O'Brien are convinced that, as long as the public lands remain under federal control, inefficient environmental decision-making processes will continue to reign over these extensive holdings.

The book's focus on obstacles to developing sustainable societies is not solely confined to American politics and policy. At the international level, Goodman and Howarth argue that sustainability and environmental concerns must be more prominently and effectively codified into free-trade issues, if such trade is going to be consistently congenial to the environment and sustainability. Deudney contends that environmental and sustainability goals are conceptually and institutionally incompatible with national security goals. Scully Granzeier disagrees. Still, she remains doubtful that the issue of cultural security will ever be adequately incorporated into notions of national security, primarily because the groups which are culturally threatened by environmental degradation do not have the political power to have their issues brought to the international forefront. Moreover, Scully Granzeier contends that our dominant notions of national security have so far appeared impervious to including wider concerns beyond those of maintaining the state.

The contributors, however, do make arguments that offer promise and hope that sustainability is within reach. Rosenbaum, for instance, argues that risk based methodologies can serve as a scientific rationale and an effective means through which to measure environmental risks, and thereby achieve sustainability. Cohen offers an effective regulatory approach through which to induce industrial compliance with environmental regulations. Bryner points out that if emissions trading programs are employed under certain circumstances and are highly specified, they can serve as an effective tool through which to internalize the costs of pollution. Kamieniecki and Steckenrider point to data which strongly suggest that racial and class biases are not present in the Superfund decision making process, and that issues concerning "who pays" for the clean-up of abandoned toxic waste sites can be resolved. Davis argues for the continued management of the public lands by the national government because federal officials are already incorporating elements of sustainability into their decisions concerning the management of these lands. Allison is hopeful that through increased environmental awareness, and a growing environmental ethos, environmental and sustainability initiatives will increasingly be incorporated into international free-trade decisions.

The contributors in this book have taken readers several steps forward in understanding the obstacles to developing sustainable societies and the many ways they might be overcome. The next step is to consider what additional research must be conducted in order to achieve environmental sustainability. Given the incredible challenge that faces society in developing sustainable systems, future researchers must, among other things, address the force of capitalism. Capitalism has developed increasingly new and powerful means to exploit nature, and it has become the dominant global economic system. This does not mean that capitalism must be rejected outright, but it may require substantial reform in order to develop and maintain sustainable societies.

A SUSTAINABLE CAPITALISM

With the realization that most key policy debates are taking place wholly within the Liberal paradigm or free-market approach, as well as the reality that present policies are implemented within this paradigm, an important question is whether the global ecosystem is sustainable under the capitalist system. In other words, does the free-market notion of sustainability actually offer us a sustainable society, or is this Liberal conceptualization of sustainability simply an attempt on the part of free-market advocates to co-opt an idea that has gained a measure of popularity? There is no immediate answer to this question. However, in light of the very real possibility that the environment is not sustainable within the present, largely unregulated free-market framework, we must ask ourselves whether capitalism and the present configuration of political power are amenable to significant societal change that could more effectively promote and proximate sustainability.

According to the ecological science approach, the present form of capitalism would require substantial reform before it could approach environmental sustainability. As O'Connor (1994) points out, there are several substantial reforms that can be implemented under capitalism to extend the life of the environment and natural resources without changing the fundamental nature of capitalism and abandoning the free market. According to O'Connor:

> One necessary step, practically speaking, toward ensuring a sustainable capitalism—defined in some sense of 'ecologically rational or sound'—would be national budgets that put high taxes on raw material inputs (e.g., coal, oil, nitrogen) and certain outputs (e.g., gasoline, chemical building blocks), meanwhile slapping value-added taxes on a wide range of environmentally unfriendly consumer products (cars, plastic products, throwaway cans)—complete with an enforce-

> able 'green label' policy that would exempt genuinely green products, with 'green' defined strictly in terms of ecological impacts at every stage of the production, distribution, and consumption process. Other steps would include national expenditure policies that heavily subsidize solar energy and benign alternative energy sources; technological research that leads to eliminating toxic chemicals and other substances at their source; innovations in mass transit; improvements in occupational health and safety conditions coupled with national, regional, and community enforcement procedures; and a redefinition and reorientation of scientific and technological priorities generally (1994, 156).

However, as O'Connor immediately points out, "In few political entities is this kind of green budget—with appropriate changes in methods of national income accounting—being developed, except on paper by a marginalized group of green economists and activists" (1994, 156). Furthermore, few advanced capitalist countries promote such "green" policies in their foreign policies, nor are the implementation and enforcement of "green" policies pursued in most international environmental and trade regimes.[1]

Additionally, O'Connor's proposals highlight the fact that while the U.S. and other advanced capitalist countries may have impressive and extensive legal structures designed to regulate air pollution, water pollution, hazardous waste, and pesticides, most existing environmental, industrial, and taxation policies are not comprehensively designed to promote sustainability. In other words, most existing environmental policies are primarily concerned with the immediate protection of humans from the harmful effects of pollution, and they are not constructed or implemented to help humankind establish sustainable societies.[2]

As pointed out by O'Connor, the problem of developing a capitalist system that is more congenial to sustainability than it presently is does not lie with the inability of policymakers to conceptualize and formulate environmentally friendly reforms that are compatible with the free market allocation of resources. Instead, the difficulty lies in getting such reforms enacted by legislatures and effectively implemented by government agencies. Two sources of this difficulty are the normative system of thought that underlies capitalism (i.e., Liberalism) and the ability of business and industry to resist unwanted environmental reforms. Future research on sustainable societies must take these factors into account.

LIBERALISM AND SUSTAINABILITY

Cahn (1995) examines the relationship between Liberal thought and the environment. He argues that the dominant system of thought in the United States is not compatible with wide-ranging and aggressive environmental policies. The reasons are twofold. First, the U.S. lacks a normative tradition that emphasizes community and community well-being above individual self-aggrandizement. Cahn points out that a discourse of civic republicanism was prominent during the prerevolutionary period. This discourse did emphasize the community and the greater good, but it was marginalized after the American Revolution when political and economic elites became convinced that "common" people could not set aside their immediate self-interest to promote the greater good. According to Cahn, this belief was crystallized by Shay's Rebellion in the 1780s, which was a revolt by western Massachusetts farmers against the foreclosure of their farms (1995, 4).

With no competing discourse, Liberalism became the dominant form of political and social thought in the United States (Hartz 1955). Liberalism contends that society and the greatest good is most effectively served by allowing individuals to pursue unremittingly their self-interest. Therefore, goals and means which are designed on a communal basis, as opposed to harnessing the energy of self-interest, are doomed to be inefficient, ultimately ineffectual, and potentially oppressive. An important addendum to Liberal thought is that the state, the only community-wide institution, takes on a limited role within society. This role is one of providing the legal and physical infrastructure necessary to allow individuals to pursue their self-interest. Beyond this limited role state behavior from the Liberal perspective is viewed suspiciously (Cahn 1995, chapter 1).

According to Cahn, the lack of a salient normative discourse emphasizing community, and the dominance of the Liberal discourse which emphasizes the individual and the pursuit of self-interest, bodes badly for environmental policy in the U.S. for two reasons. First, the environment is an issue that for the most part can only be pursued through community or state action, and not through the pursuit of individual self-interest. Therefore, the environment is a goal that calls for a form of political and social action that is foreign to Liberal notions of societal action. Cahn aptly describes this dilemma for an American society steeped in Liberalism which has increasingly become concerned with the health of the environment:

> In the absence of an explicit language of communal rights, there is little prospect of limiting concrete property rights for an abstract public good. The narrow Liberal definition of communal good has consistently allowed individual and corporate claims of property rights to outweigh the need for serious environmental regulation . . . As a consequence of the parameters imposed by the problematic Liberal definition of communal good, the American policy process is fundamentally limited in its ability to confront environmental issues adequately (1995, 7).

However, not only does environmental policymaking require a form of political behavior which is alien to Liberal thought—perhaps even hostile to it—but environmental policymaking calls for the curving of that social behavior which Liberalism venerates (i.e., the pursuit of self-interest through property relations). Cahn argues that:

> Locke's concern with property was a function of survival, not greed. One's property would ensure self-preservation, and ultimately liberty. The role of the state, therefore, is to protect private property. If property rights were ensured, individuals would be able to take care of themselves. Sustenance, liberty, and security are all a function of material wealth. As a result, Liberal policy decisions have traditionally been subservient to economic concerns (1995, 8).

With this primacy accorded self-interest and the right to property, the development and enforcement of environmental policy, with its emphasis on regulated property use, is problematic within a Liberal ideological framework. Again, Cahn accurately explains this tension between Liberal values and environmental goals:

> The tension between public rights and private rights is nowhere felt more strongly than in environmental policy. Environmental policy is predicated on regulating the use and development of private property. Without redefining traditional Lockean property rights, environmental policy proposes to legislate what property owners can and cannot do with their property. Traditional concepts of Liberal civic virtue say nothing to this dilemma (1995, 8).

In light of the absence of a community based discourse, and the dominance of Liberalism with its emphasis on individual self-interest, Cahn proceeds to dedicate the bulk of his book to exposing the major weaknesses of environmental policy in the U.S. He argues that if existing U.S. policy is not weak with respect to its laws, then it is in the case of its application (1995, chapters 4–7). Ultimately, he believes that

U.S. environmental laws and policies are more designed as symbolic responses to public concerns than as sincere attempts to resolve environmental hazards (1995, chapter 2). Or alternatively, that is what they become in the face of a Liberal court system, legal structure, and political culture which privileges individual self-interest and property rights over that of the abstract public good. Therefore, while the United States may have some of the most stringent environmental laws in the world, applied within Liberalism they become relatively ineffective over the long run.

INDUSTRY AS AN OBSTACLE TO ACHIEVING A SUSTAINABLE SOCIETY

Another obstacle to the reconfiguration of society and the economy to serve potentially better the goals of sustainability is the economic and political power of industry. One does not have to draw on the Power Elite theory of a Domhoff (1983; 1978; 1990) or the Structural Marxism of a Poulantzas (1973) (also see Offe [1984; 1985] and O'Connor [1973; 1984]) to explain how businesses possess disproportionate political power within a capitalist political system. For this conclusion, one need only look at the neopluralist writings of McConnell (1966), Lowi (1979), and the later writings of Dahl and Lindblom (1976) (also see Olson [1971]; Edelman [1964; 1971; 1977; 1988]; Stigler [1971]; Lindblom [1977; 1983]; Wilson [1980]; and Mcfarland [1987; 1991; 1992]).

In a significant modification to their pluralist model, for example, Dahl and Lindblom conclude that business and industry leaders wield significantly greater political power than other groups because businesspeople are charged with the responsibility of organizing and deploying a capitalist society's productive forces:

> . . . [B]usinessmen are not ordered by law to perform the many organizational and leadership tasks that are delegated to them. All these societies operate by rules that require that businessmen be induced rather than commanded. It is therefore clear that these societies must provide sufficient benefits or indulgences to businessmen to constitute an inducement for them to perform their assigned tasks.
>
> The consequence of these arrangements—peculiar as they would appear to a man from Mars—is that it becomes a major task of government to design and maintain an inducement system for businessmen, to be solicitous of business interests, and to grant to them, for its value as an incentive, an intimacy of participation in government

> itself. In all these respects the relation between government and business is unlike the relation between government and any other group in the society (Dahl and Lindblom 1976, xxxvii).

Hence, this control over the economy that capitalist societies afford the businessperson results in the "privileged participation of business" in government.

The power of industry, however, is not only derived from their control of a capitalist society's means of production. In addition, industry controls disproportionate amounts of many political resources, such as campaign funds, legal expertise, and technical knowledge. As Lindblom points out:

> No other group of citizens can compare with businessmen, even roughly, in effectiveness in the polyarchal [i.e. pluralist] process. How so? Because, unlike any other group of citizens, they can draw on the resources they command as public 'officials' [leaders of corporations] to support their activities in polyarchal politics (1977, 194).

The superiority of industrial resources can be seen in the case of the 1990 Clean Air Act. During the year leading up to the passage of the Act, industry PACs, with an interest in environmental legislation, donated nearly $612,000 to members of the House Committee charged with marking-up the legislation. In contrast, environmental groups gave little or no money to these same key House members (Alston 1990).

The deployment of these resources, as well as industry control over the productive forces of society, can help explain why congresspeople who were sympathetic to industry preferences dominated the congressional policy-making process with respect to the 1990 Clean Air Act. In contrast, environmentalists, and their congressional allies, with the exception of one relatively minor issue, failed in their attempts to shape directly the content of the Act (Gonzalez 1995).[3] As a consequence, the 1990 Clean Air Act, while relatively tough in controlling some pollutants and setting some deadlines, was significantly weaker than it would have been had environmentalists had more influence over the process.[4]

However, this is not to suggest that industry, as a special interest, never loses. It is to say that industry opposition to any reconfiguration of the economy would serve as a significant barrier to achieving change, and, in particular, to achieving sustainability. Thus, when environmentalists grapple with policy issues, they must not only attempt to ensure that their discussions and proposals are congenial to Liberal philosophical precepts, but they must also contend with the power of industry. The more congenial an environmental policy proposal is to industry preferences, the more likely it is to become law. In this respect, environmental discussions and proposals must be just as mindful of the power of industry as they are of the Liberal principles that guide government officials and the public. Future researchers should pay more attention to this factor in their analyses of environmental politics and policy.

With respect to the environment, the factors of Liberal normative principles and the power of industry are mutually reinforcing. Liberalism helps to inform the political behavior of industry leaders, and the political power of industry helps to enforce Liberal principles. Given this symbiotic relationship, both Liberalism and the political behavior of industry must change if capitalism and the free market is to become more consistent with efforts to establish a sustainable society. Hence, future research must be committed to understanding how Liberalism and the political behavior of industry must change in order to establish a sustainable society.

The global spread of capitalism and free market relations, particularly over the last decade, could potentially pose a serious challenge to efforts to develop sustainable societies. Whether this challenge can be successfully met as we enter the twenty-first century is uncertain. Much of this uncertainty is rooted in doubts about the ability of the free market to serve as an effective mechanism to build a sustainable society. In light of these doubts, deep ecologists, such as Milbrath (1989), argue that the only way for humanity to develop a sustainable society is to abandon capitalism, as well as the normative system and distribution of political power which are based upon capitalism. Hence, concerns abound about the possible incapacity of our normative thought and our political institutions to respond adequately to our society's environmental problems, and to act effectively to establish an environmentally sustainable society.

NOTES

1. Examples of the few international environmental agreements that have had effective and substantial impacts on the environment are the Montreal Protocol, the International Convention for the Regulation of Whaling (ICRW), and the Convention on International Trade in Endangered Species (CITES). With respect to international trade agreements, the North American Free Trade

Agreement (NAFTA) is one of the few trade agreements that incorporates important environmental rules, however, a question remains on how effective they will be.

2. Nearly all environmental policies deal with a single medium, are short-sighted, and are not comprehensive.

3. Business's defeat, and in turn environmentalists' single victory in the House Committee, concerned a provision in President Bush's bill that would have allowed automobile manufacturers to meet emission standards through the averaging of fleet emissions, as opposed to imposing regulations on each individual automobile. Therefore, environmentalists' sole House victory, and their major congressional victory, prevented the final legislation from approving a change in administrative rules concerning the regulation of automobiles (Hager 1989, 2452; Gonzalez 1995).

4. While a domestic issue is utilized here to illustrate the political power of industry, Allison's and Goodman and Howarth's chapters also point to the strong influence of industry over the development of international environmental and trade regimes.

REFERENCES

Alston, Chuck. 1990 (March 17). "As Clean-Air Bill Took Off, so did PAC Donations." *Congressional Quarterly Weekly Report*: 811–7.

Cahn, Matthew A. 1995. *Environmental Deceptions: The Tensions Between Liberalism and Environmental Policymaking in the United States*. Albany: State University of New York Press.

Dahl, Robert A., and Charles E. Lindblom. 1976. "Preface" in *Politics, Economics, and Welfare*. New Haven, CT: Yale University Press.

Domhoff, G. William. 1978. *The Powers that Be*. New York: Random House.

———. 1983. *Who Rules America Now?* Englewood Cliffs, NJ: Prentice-Hall.

———. 1990. *The Power Elite and the State*. New York: Aldine de Gruyter.

Edelman, Murray. 1964. *The Symbolic Uses of Politics*. Urbana, IL: University of Illinois Press.

———. 1971. *Politics as Symbolic Action*. Chicago: Markham Publishing Company.

———. 1977. *Political Language: Words That Succeed and Policies that Fail*. NY: Academic Press of Harcourt Brace Jovanovich.

———. 1988. *Constructing the Political Spectacle*. Chicago: The University of Chicago Press.

Gonzalez, George A. 1995 (March 16–18). "The Power Elite and State Autonomy Models of Public Policy-Making: A Case Study of the 1990 Clean Air Act." Portland, OR: The Western Political Science Association Conference.

Hager, George. 1989 (Sept. 23). "Bush Scores Early Victory in Clean Air Markup." *Congressional Quarterly Weekly Report*, pp. 2451–2.

Hartz, Louis. 1955. *The Liberal Tradition in America*. New York: Harcourt Brace Jovanovich.

Lindblom, Charles E. 1977. *Politics and Markets: The World's Political-Economic Systems*. New York: Basic Books.

———. 1983 (June). "Comment on Manley." *The American Political Science Review* 77: 384–6.

Lowi, Theodore J. 1979. *The End of Liberalism: The Second Republic of the United States*. New York: W.W. Norton. Original published in 1969.

McFarland, Andrew S. 1987 (April). "Interest Groups and Theories of Power in America." *British Journal of Political Science* 17: 129–147.

———. 1991 (July). "Interest Groups and Political Time: Cycles in America." *British Journal of Political Science* 21: 257–86.

———. 1992. "Interest Groups and the Policymaking Process: Sources of Countervailing Power in America." In *The Politics of Interests: Interest Groups Transformed*, edited by Mark P. Petracca. Boulder, CO: Westview Press.

McConnell, Grant. 1966. *Private Power and American Democracy*. New York: Knopf.

Milbrath, Lester W. 1989. *Envisioning a Sustainable Society: Learning Our Way Out*. Albany: State University of New York Press.

Poulantzas, Nicos. 1973. *Political Power and Social Classes*. London: New Left Books.

O'Connor, James. 1973. *The Fiscal Crisis of the State*. New York: St. Martin's Press.

———. 1984. *Accumulation Crisis*. New York: Basil Blackwell.

———. 1994. "Is Sustainable Capitalism Possible?" in *Is Capitalism Sustainable?*, edited by Martin O'Connor. New York: Guilford Press.

Offe, Claus. 1984. *Contradictions of the Welfare State*. Cambridge, MA: M.I.T. Press.

———. 1985. *Disorganized Capitalism*. Cambridge, MA: M.I.T. Press.

Olson, Mancur. 1971. *The Logic of Collective Action: Public Goods and the Theory of Groups*. Cambridge: Harvard University Press. Original published in 1965.

Stigler, George J. 1971 (spring). "The Theory of Economic Regulation." *Bell Journal of Economics and Management Science* 2: 3–21.

Wilson, James Q. 1980. "The Politics of Regulation" in *The Politics of Regulation*, edited by James Q. Wilson. New York: Basic Books.

CONTRIBUTORS

Juliann Allison is assistant professor in the Department of Political Science at the State University of New York at Binghamton, where she teaches international environmental politics, international political economy, women in politics, and research methods. In addition to international economic and environmental cooperation, her research interests include bargaining theory and negotiation analysis, evolutionary processes and models, and the role of domestic politics in international relations. Her most recent publications appear in the *Journal of Conflict Resolution* and *Shades of Green*.

John A. Baden is founder and chairman of the Foundation for Research on Economics and the Environment (FREE). FREE is a market-oriented research and education foundation with offices in Seattle, Washington and Bozeman, Montana. Dr. Baden is a leader in developing the New Resource Economics, an incentive-based approach to environmental and natural resource management that stresses private property rights and the market process as policy instruments. Dr. Baden received his Ph.D. from Indiana University in 1969 and then was awarded a National Science Foundation Postdoctoral Fellowship in environmental policy. He has held endowed professorships, received teaching awards, and is the author or editor of seven books, numerous journal articles on energy and natural resources, and has a syndicated column in *The Seattle Times*. He is currently an affiliate professor in the School of Business at the University of Washington. For the past four years he has organized a series of week-long seminars in environmental economics and policy for federal judges.

Ann O'M. Bowman is professor of government and international studies at the University of South Carolina. She has published extensively on state politics, hazardous waste management, and environmental policy. *Cityscapes and Capital* is her most recent book. In 1995–96 she held the Odense Chair of American Studies as a Fulbright scholar in Denmark.

Gary Bryner is professor in the Department of Political Science at Brigham Young University, where he directs the Public Policy Program. He is the author of *Blue Skies, Green Politics: The Clean Air Act of 1990*, second edition, 1995. He has written extensively on clean air and other environmental policy issues.

Steven Cohen is the director of the Graduate Program in Public Policy and Administration and the associate dean of the School of International and Public Affairs at Columbia University. He has served as a policy analyst in the U.S. Environmental Protection Agency. He is the coauthor of *The New Effective Public Manager* and has published numerous articles on public management innovation and environmental management.

Charles Davis is professor in the Department of Political Science at Colorado State University. His teaching and research interests lie in the areas of environmental policy and public administration. He is the editor of a forthcoming book entitled *Western Public Lands and Environmental Politics* and the author of *The Politics of Hazardous Wastes*. He has written numerous book chapters and journal articles on various topics related to environmental and public lands policy.

Daniel Deudney is the Janice and Julian Bers Assistant Professor in the Department of Political Science at the University of Pennsylvania. His research interests lie mainly in international relations theory, political theory, and environmental politics. He has published extensively on topics related to environment and energy, nuclear and space issues, and international relations theory.

George A. Gonzalez is a Ph.D. candidate in the Department of Political Science at the University of Southern California. His main research interests lie in state theory and environmental policy. He is writing his dissertation on the development of environmental policy. He is presently a lecturer at San Jose State University.

David Goodman is professor of Environmental Studies at the University of California, Santa Cruz. He previously was associated with the Department of Economics, University College London and the Institute of Latin American Studies, University of London. His most recent publication, co-authored with Michael Redclift, is *Refashioning Nature: Food, Ecology, and Culture* (Routledge 1991). His current research interests focus on the international agro-food system, the environment, and the globalizing world economy.

Margaret Scully Granzeier received her M.A. in political science from the University of Toronto, and she is currently a Ph.D. candidate in the Department of Political Science at the University of Southern California. Her major research interests include international environmental politics, political theory, international relations, and human rights. She is presently involved in research projects on sovereignty and environmental protection and on environmental and cultural rights.

Richard B. Howarth is assistant professor of Environmental Studies at the University of California, Santa Cruz. After receiving his doctorate from the Energy and Resources Program at the University of California, Berkeley, he worked at the Lawrence Berkeley National Laboratory on questions of energy economics and policy. His current research interests focus on the economics of sustainable development, global environmental change, and natural resource economics. His publications include contributions to the *American Economic Review* and the *Handbook of Environmental Economics* (Blackwell 1995).

Sheldon Kamieniecki is professor and chair of the Department of Political Science and director of the Environmental Studies Program at the University of Southern California. His journal articles, book chapters, and books have focused on various environmental policy issues, including air and water pollution control and hazardous and toxic waste management. His most recent book, *Environmental Politics in the International Arena: Movements, Parties, Organizations, and Policy,* explores the dynamic forces shaping national and international environmental policies.

Stephen H. Linder is associate professor in Management and Policy Sciences in the School of Public Health at the University of Texas. His recent work on risk has appeared in the *Journal of Health*

Politics, Policy, and Law and *Policy Sciences*. He has held faculty positions at Tulane and the University of California, Los Angeles. His other research areas of interest include policy and institutional design.

Tim O'Brien is a policy analyst for Foundation for Research on Economics and the Environment (FREE). As a student of political economy and environmental policy, he writes and edits a number of publications, including columns for *The Seattle Times* and *The Wall Street Journal*. He also coordinates FREE's summer conferences for federal judges, writers, academics, and business people. He majored in economics and political science at Kenyon College and graduated with honors.

Walter A. Rosenbaum is professor in the Department of Political Science at the University of Florida and adjunct research professor, Department of Environmental Medicine, Tulane University Medical College. He has published numerous books and articles related to environmental and energy policy. He has also been a senior analyst and special assistant to the assistant administrator of the U.S. Environmental Protection Agency. He is currently a consultant to the U.S. Department of Energy on projects related to the environmental cleanup of the nation's nuclear weapons production sites.

Janie Steckenrider is assistant professor in the Department of Political Science at Loyola Marymount University. She has published journal articles and book chapters on aging policy and is co-editor of *New Directions in Old Age Policies*. She has received grants from the National Institute on Aging to support her research, and she has served on the boards of hospitals, nursing homes, and senior citizens commissions.

Robert O. Vos is a Ph.D. candidate in the Department of Political Science at the University of Southern California. His major research interests include environmental politics, policy, and theory as well as social movements and political geography. He has published a book chapter on radical environmental movements and an article on environmental justice issues in *Urban Geography*. He is also an accomplished cellist and regularly performs professionally in the U.S. and abroad.

Index